Flow-Based Programming,
2ND EDITION

[Page intentionally left blank]

Flow-Based Programming, 2ND EDITION:

A New Approach To Application Development

J. Paul Morrison, 2011

Copyright Page & Trademarks

Copyrights

Copyright © 2010, 2011 by J.P. Morrison Enterprises, Ltd.
Author: J. Paul Morrison

ISBN: 1451542321

EAN-13: 9781451542325

Printed by CreateSpace, DBA of On-Demand Publishing LLC, part of the Amazon group of companies.

All rights reserved.

Information about 1st Edition (1994):

Copyright © 1994 by van Nostrand Reinhold
Author: J. Paul Morrison

Library of Congress Catalog Card Number: 94-1822
ISBN: 0-442-1771-5

Copyright Page & Trademarks

Trademarks

The following are trademarks or registered trademarks of International Business Machines, Inc.:

BMS	MFS
CICS, CICS/ESA	MQSeries
CMS	MVS, MVS/ESA
CMS Pipelines	PDF
CP/CMS	PGF
DB2	PL/I
DFDM	REXX
DL/I	RPG
GDDM	System/370
GPSS	VM/XA
IBM	VS/COBOL II
IMS, IMS/ESA, IMS TM	VTAM
ISPF	

The following are products of their respective suppliers:

C, C++	Objective-C
C#	Smalltalk V/PM
Java	UNIX
Linda	Phenom
Microsoft Works	Pentium

If any of the other products mentioned below are trademarked, hopefully it will be understood that there is no intent to infringe on the trademark.

Preface to 1st Edition (1994)

This book describes a highly productive approach to application development, based on a new and significantly different programming paradigm, referred to as "Flow-Based Programming" (FBP). Although at least one very large application built using software based on these concepts has been in continuous use for about 20 years [as of 1994 – over 35 now, in 2010], it is not well known to the programming community, so it will be novel to most of the readers of this book. During the time it has been under development and in use, it has been found to significantly enhance both the productivity of the programmers who use it and the reliability and maintainability of applications built with it.

The material described here has practical application to many of the problems that beset today's information technology industry. At the same time it has solid theoretical underpinnings and also strong affinities with a lot of other theoretical work going forward in universities and research institutions worldwide. A number of articles on this concept have appeared over the years in different publications, but they have been widely scattered and I feel that no single article has been able to do justice to the whole set of concepts. Therefore, it seems timely to assemble this material into a single book, thus allowing it to be presented as a coherent whole.

Flow-Based Programming provides a view of data processing that is consistent from the largest scale (e.g. organizations talking to other organizations) all the way down to the programming level, without the sudden changes of viewpoint characteristic of conventional programming. It can be used from early in the design stage all the way through to implementation, in a seamless manner. It is a good match with design techniques such as Structured Analysis, and with a number of implementation approaches, such as prototyping and incremental development. It is a natural reuse tool and strongly supports good programming disciplines. It has many non-procedural aspects, which give it many of the advantages of this type of code. It should not be surprising, therefore, that it has caught the interest of some of the most experienced people in our business. I feel strongly, and hope to prove in this book, that these concepts have the potential to save computer-using organizations significant amounts of money and, perhaps more importantly, to lay the foundations of a true software marketplace and programming discipline in the broadest sense.

This book is aimed at systems architects, software and hardware engineers, application developers and analysts, researchers – in fact, everyone who is involved in computing or even just interested in the field. Educators should find that this book places a number of the advanced

Preface to 1st Edition (1994)

concepts of computing science into context in a natural way and perhaps will find this book of assistance in passing them on to their students.

This book is not intended to be a manual for any one piece of software, but as a fairly general introduction to a new and powerful set of concepts. Like object-oriented programming, FBP does involve a new programming paradigm, which profoundly changes the way programmers look at the process of constructing applications. Although a number of its concepts seem very different from conventional programming, there are many real-world analogies that help the reader make the transition to this new way of thinking about building systems. Also, once the basics have been mastered, most of the remaining material will follow naturally. It is interesting to note that, in the long run, FBP appears to be on a convergent path with the more advanced work in object-oriented programming. I also hope that this book might contribute somewhat towards bridging the present divide in the area of computer programming between business and academia.

Markham, ON, Canada, 1994

Preface to 2nd Edition (2010)

Since it has been about 15 years since the publication of the 1994 edition, and the industry is very different from where it was in those days, it seems timely to produce a new edition, which will try to capture some of the effects of the drastically changed computing environment on our thinking about Flow-Based Programming. Of course, there is much that has not changed, and FBP is still far ahead of the pack! One major difference, however, is that people all over the world are discovering its advantages, and in fact there are now a number of companies that have been explicitly set up to capitalize on these concepts.

This edition keeps most of the original chapters, but I have dropped quite a bit of material that I judge to be of little interest to 21st-century readers. In particular, there will be less emphasis on mainframe systems and software, as this does not seem to be an area where the new concepts are taking root. However, as I feel that "number-crunchers" will be around for quite a while longer, some of that material will be retained. There has been such an explosion of new material in the last few years that I hope my readers will forgive me if a certain patchiness results! Of course, the 1994 edition still remains available second-hand, and a PDF version of that edition is available at *http://www.jpaulmorrison.com/fbp/book.pdf*. As we have moved into an Internet world since my book was published, there is now a web site describing the concepts behind FBP at *http://www.jpaulmorrison.com/fbp/*, and a wiki with a lot of interesting comments and feedback at *http://www.jpaulmorrison.com/cgi-bin/wiki.pl*.

An article on FBP has been on Wikipedia for several years: *http://en.wikipedia.org/w/index.php?title=Flow-based_programming&oldid=363964067*. The latest version now reflects the chapter numbers in the current edition of this book.

All references to OOP have been changed to OO, which seems to have become the current usage.

In the previous edition there was an Appendix describing THREADS, an early C implementation. I have now expanded it to add high-level descriptions of two more recent ones, namely a Java implementation (JavaFBP) (*http://www.jpaulmorrison.com/fbp/#JavaFBP*) and a C# implementation (C#FBP) (*http://www.jpaulmorrison.com/fbp/#CsharpFBP*), and have reduced the amount of information on THREADS (*http://www.jpaulmorrison.com/fbp/#THREADS*), as this can still be found on the web site. THREADS is in process of being upgraded to use Windows "fibres" (Windows spells it "fiber", but I am going to stay with the Canadian spelling in what follows), and there are some other minor changes to take advantage of the Microsoft C++ compiler.

Preface to 2nd Edition (2010)

In addition to the above, I am including some information about DrawFBP (*http://www.jpaulmorrison.com/fbp/#DrawFBP*), an FBP diagramming tool written in Java.

There is also an additional chapter attempting to sketch out what I call the "FBP explosion" that has taken place over the intervening 15 years (starting on page 281). It is really impossible to do it justice as the number of references grows even as I write this, but hopefully this will give you some flavour of what has been happening! In particular, I would like to direct your attention to two sections, contributed by David Johnson and Dr. Ernesto Compatangelo, respectively, at the end of this chapter, both very thought-provoking – in different ways.

Where web URLs are included in the text, I will be approximately following the AMA Guidelines, as described in *http://en.wikipedia.org/wiki/Citing_Wikipedia#AMA_style* (retrieved 2009-12-06).

Note that, due to the changing nature of information media, this edition places much more emphasis on electronic resources, rather than on paper resources as in the first edition. Where I have links in the text, I will not repeat them in the bibliography. When quoting from Wikipedia, I will usually remove any hyperlinks. A number of the quotes in this new edition are taken from blogs, including the FBP wiki. As this book is intended for Print On Demand, any comments where this is not the case, or the original authors have changed their views, can be corrected along the way, so please let me know!

In the 1994 edition I used the term "process" for the basic unit of concurrency – however, it has been pointed out that this term is somewhat ambiguous, as it has different usages in different environments. The term "unit of concurrency" seemed a bit cumbersome, so I tried Googling "unit of concurrency", and found the following synonyms:

process (Erlang)	vat (E language)
actor (actor theory)	island (Tweak)
agent	task (Ada)
transaction	resource (Minuet)
thread	stage (John Hartmann's CMS Pipelines)
operator (MIT, Expressor, et al.)	

We might add to that list:

- coroutine (Conway)

All of the terms listed above have connotations which could cause confusion for various groups of readers, so I have decided to stay with the (in my opinion) most general term "process" (it *is* used by Erlang), and take my chances!

Unionville, ON, Canada, 2011

Acknowledgments

To my wife, for her loving support, encouragement, and sound common sense, and for having helped to make the time available that I needed to finish this process. I have always thought that a programmer's wife has to be a bit of a saint – and now I'm convinced of it!

To the late Wayne Stevens, my friend and mentor, who died too young, for his creativity and sense of fun, his openness to new ideas, his wide-ranging knowledge and experience, and his perennial optimism and enthusiasm. This book is intended to be in a small way a tribute to his memory.

To my son – who, thanks to his education in computer science at the University of Waterloo and at MIT, is at ease in esoteric areas that I can hardly guess at – for his useful and always constructive input and comments. Also to my daughter and the rest of my family, including my highly intelligent grandson, for their support and encouragement!

To Nate Edwards, Skip Folden, Harrison Tellier, Bob Kendall, Perry Crawford, Bob Ballow, and many of the "old guard", who understood intuitively the ideas I talk about in this book, but retired before they could get anyone to listen. I always enjoy your anecdotes, your optimism, and your down-to-earth attitudes. There are also others who have encouraged me over the years who are too many to mention – you know who you are! Thank you all!

To the various teams I have worked with over the years at IBM, several of whose personnel are mentioned in this book. In particular, the last team I worked with at IBM – one of the best I have ever worked with, and a number of whom have become personal friends. It was a pleasure and an essential part of my education working with you all! Also to Robbie Kemeny, who very early on helped me to develop some of the key ideas during after-work bus rides up the side of Mount Royal in Montréal, and to our director, Doug Croth, who was excited about the concept and promoted it strongly within our organization.

Also to the team in Japan who succeeded in putting out the only official IBM FBP product that has made it into the marketplace so far. Although it was definitely a team effort, I would like to make special mention of my friend Kenji Terao, who saw the potential years before most other people and was key to getting the concept accepted by IBM Japan.

I must also mention the people at the company that decided to use an untried technology to help build one of the biggest business systems every built in Canada, and the people from IBM Canada, particularly John Jensen, and from the IBM Federal Systems Division, particularly Kim

Acknowledgments

Seward and Paul Weiler, who helped me to first sell and then implement it.

Next I would like to thank IBM Canada for supporting this work over some 20 years until my retirement in 1992, and for their kind permission for me to talk about my experiences during this time. Of course, it should be made clear to the reader that the views expressed in this book are purely my own, not those of the company. As I look back over my years with IBM in three different countries, I realize that I have been more fortunate than most to have been able to work on so many exciting things for a very large part of that time.

I would very much like to thank my editors – in particular Risa Cohen – at van Nostrand Reinhold (sadly, no longer extant) and Northeastern Graphic Services (the same, apparently – at least I can't find them on the Internet), who together helped to turn my book from a dream into a reality. It was largely Risa's vision and enthusiasm that ensured that my book saw the light of day – sadly, the company was not around long enough after the book's publication to assist in its promotion, or to benefit from its later success. However, I feel that they did a fantastic job, and deserve much credit for having supported me during the first few difficult years.

Now, in a new century, I would like to thank the many people who have supported me in my attempts to spread the word about Flow-Based Programming – in particular, the brilliant systems designer and architect, Denis Garneau, who was always willing to boost my morale when I needed it! And also the distinguished pioneer in software engineering methodology, Ed Yourdon, for supporting me, and for including my book in his list of "Cool Books" (*http://www.yourdon.com/personal/books/gentech/index.html*). There are also a vast number of people who have suggested changes and improvements to this book – you are really too many to list in one place, but where I have quoted your suggestions, your names appear in the text. I should however mention Michael Beckerle (Mike) and Sebastian Ertel, as their projects constitute a major extension to the fundamental FBP concepts. Mike Beckerle is a computer scientist who has been advocating and using FBP concepts across his career at Torrent Systems, Ascential Software, and IBM. He is currently (April 2010) CTO at Oco, Inc. A recent project, called "Ohua", is open source, and is available on SourceForge. I would also like to thank belatedly, with 20-20 hindsight (!), two of my managers at IBM Canada: Wayne Giroux, who was one of the first to see the potential of FBP (back in 1969), and John Devereux, who "persuaded" me to transfer to Toronto, Ontario – which turned out to be a far better move than I could have expected, and without which my life would have followed a radically different course.

Disclaimers

1. I may at times inadvertently use the pronoun "he" to refer to individuals in general. If I do, I wish to state that this is not to be taken as implying any particular gender. Unfortunately, English lacks a good pronoun meaning "he" or "she".

2. Added for the 2nd edition: All website links were correct and active at the time of publishing, but the author cannot claim any responsibility for the validity or content of these websites at a later date. However, Wikipedia references contain version information, as that is recommended practice when citing Wikipedia.

3. Anywhere I use the term "Wikipedia", I am referring to "Wikipedia, The Free Encyclopedia". While I understand that Wikipedia is a collaborative project, and that therefore Wikipedia descriptions should not be taken as gospel truth, most of the definitions and descriptions I cite are so generic that there can be little doubt as to their accuracy. Where there is any doubt, I have attempted to independently verify them. As Wikipedia articles change over time, all Wikipedia URLs specify the exact version of the article referenced. All Wikipedia text cited in this book is released under CC-BY-SA – please refer to *http://creativecommons.org/licenses/by-sa/3.0/legalcode*.

4. Unless otherwise specified, the term "ports" will refer to Flow-Based Programming *ports*: the point of attachment of a process and a connection.

5. The page numbers that often follow chapter references usually refer to the first page of that chapter, except where explicitly stated.

6. After having lived in the UK, the US, and Canada, I am afraid my spelling is now a mixture of all the different usages – what Wikipedia user boxes refer to as "mixed English". Apologies to anyone who may be bothered by this!

7. Occasionally in the literature, one finds the word "data" being treated as a plural, presumably that of the slightly archaic word "datum". It is high time to put this affectation to rest. For most of the time I have worked in the computer industry, "data" has been a collective noun, taking singular verbs and adjectives, just like "information", which means approximately the same thing. I remember protesting against this particular piece of pedantry in the early '80s, but apparently the rulebook was never updated! This is also allowed to be specified in Wikipedia user boxes: *"This user recognizes that 'data', 'media', and 'agenda', have become incorporated into English as singular nouns."*

Prologue

Some of my colleagues have suggested that I fill in some background to what you are going to read about in this book. So let me introduce myself.... I was born in London, England, just before the start of World War II, received what is sometimes referred to as a classical education, learned to speak several languages, including the usual dead ones, and studied Anthropology at King's College, Cambridge. I have since discovered that Alan Turing had attended my college, but while I was there I was learning to recognize Neanderthal skulls, and hearing Edmund Leach lecture about the Kachin, so I regret that I cannot claim to have programmed EDSAC, the machine being developed at Cambridge, although I later took an aptitude test for another marvelous machine, J. Lyons and Co.'s LEO (Lyons Electronic Office), whose design was based on EDSAC's. But maybe computing was in the air at King's!

In 1959 I joined IBM (UK) as an Electronic Data Processing Machines Representative. I had come into computers by a circuitous route: around the age of 12, I got bitten by the symbolic logic bug. This so intrigued me that all during my school and university years I read up on it, played with the concepts for myself, and looked forward to the time when all the world's problems would be solved by the judicious rearrangement of little mathematical symbols. Having also been fascinated by the diversity of human languages since childhood, the idea of really getting to the root of what things *meant* was very exciting. It wasn't until later in life that I realized that many great minds had tried this route without much success, and that, while it is certainly a beguiling concept and there have been many such attempts in earlier centuries, the universe of human experience is too complex and dynamic, with too many interacting factors, to be encoded in such a simple way. This does not mean that attempts to convey knowledge to a computer will not work – it is just that there seem to be certain built-in limitations. The human functions which we tend to think of as being simple, almost trivial, such as vision, speech comprehension or the ability to make one's way along a busy street, are often the hardest to explain to a computer. What we call common sense turns out to be quite uncommon....

While symbolic logic has not delivered on its original promise of making the world's important decisions simpler, it is perfectly adapted to the design of computers, and I became fascinated by the idea of machines which could perform logical operations. This fascination stayed with me during my 33 years with the IBM Corporation in three different countries (by the way, this is why most of the systems I will be mentioning will be IBM systems – I apologize for this, but that's my background!), but I've always been struck by the apparent mismatch between the power of these machines and the difficulty of getting them to do what we wanted. I gradually came to

Prologue

concentrate on one basic problem: why should the process of developing applications on computers be so difficult, when they can obviously do anything we can figure out the rules for?

There is definitely an advantage to having cut my proverbial teeth in this field at a time when very few people had even heard of computers: over the intervening years I have had time to digest new concepts and see which of them succeeded and which failed. Since the '60s, many concepts, techniques and fads have sprung up with great attendant fanfare, and have either faded out or just become part of the regular curriculum. Ideas which took a decade or two to evolve are now familiar to kids fresh out of university. I got advance notice of many of these concepts, and often had time to understand them before they became widespread! A list of these wonders would be too long to include here, and perhaps only of interest to historians. Some of them fell by the wayside, but many of them are still around – some good and some not so good! We who were working in the field also certainly contributed our fair share of techniques and fads, also some good and some not so good!

I think my first enthusiasm was compiler compilers. I first worked with a fascinating system called BABEL – appropriate name – which was going to make it far easier to write compilers. I still use some of its ideas today, almost 50 years later. A high-level description can be found on the *FBP Wiki*. We shall see later in this book that there are interesting parallels between compiler theory and the subject matter of this book, and there seems to be an important role for what are sometimes called "mini-languages" (I will be talking some more about them in Chapter 17 – page 172). Certainly compiler compilers comprise a piece of the answer, but they did not result in the productivity improvement that we were looking for.

I have also always been taken with interpreters – I believe my first exposure to these was BLIS (which stood for the Bell Laboratories Interpretive System), which made the IBM 650 look like a sequential machine. Probably the characteristic of interpreters which really appeals to people is the ability to debug without having to change languages. Of course, some of the recent debugging tools are starting to bring this capability to the world of Higher Level Languages (HLLs), but the ability to just slot in a TYPE or "say" command and rerun a test is so impressive that the majority of languages which became really popular have been interpreters, no matter how awkward the syntax! In a survey of machine cycle usage done some years ago at IBM's Research Center at Yorktown Heights, they found that the vast majority of cycles were being used by CMS EXEC statements – strings of commands for the CMS operating system glued together, using a really simple syntax, to do specific jobs of work.

Another important concept for productivity improvement is that of a reusable subroutine library. I also believe strongly that reuse is another key piece of the solution, but not exactly in the form in which we visualized it in those days. In company after company, I have seen people start up shared subroutine libraries with a fine flurry of enthusiasm, only to find the action slowing to a standstill after some 30 or 40 subroutines have been developed and made available. Some companies are claiming much higher numbers, but I suspect these are shops which measure

Prologue

progress, and reward their people, based on how many subroutines are created and added to the library, rather than on whether they are actually used. Although organizational and economic changes are also required to really capitalize on any form of reuse, I believe there is a more fundamental reason why these libraries never really take off, and that is the philosophy of the von Neumann machine. I will be going into this in more detail in Chapter 1 (page 1), but I found I was able to predict which subroutines would land up in these libraries, and it was always "one moment in time" functions, e.g. binary search, date routines, various kinds of conversions. I tried to build an easy-to-use, general purpose batch update (yes, I really tried), and I just couldn't do it (except for supporting a tiny subset of all the possible variations)! This experience is what got me thinking about a radically different approach to producing reusable code. I hope that, as you read this book, you will agree that there *is* another approach, and that it is completely complementary to the old one.

Rapid prototyping and the related idea of iterative development were (and are still) another enthusiasm of mine. I view rapid prototyping as a process of reducing the uncertainties in the development process by trying things out. I believe that *anything* you are uncertain about should be prototyped: complex algorithms, unfamiliar hardware, database structures, human interfaces (especially!), and so on. I believe this technique will become even more important in the next few decades as we move into ever more complex environments. Here again, we will have to modify or even abandon the old methodologies. Dave Olson's 1993 book, "*Exploiting Chaos: Cashing in on the Realities of Software Development*", describes a number of approaches to combining iterative development with milestones (well-defined stages in the development of a project) to get the best of both worlds, plus some fascinating digressions into the new concepts of chaos and "strange attractors". There are some very strange attractors in our business!

I have also believed for some time that most prototypes should not just be thrown away once they have served their purpose. A prototype should be able to be "grown", step by step, into a full-fledged system. Since the importance of prototypes is that they reduce uncertainty, rewriting applications in a different language is liable to bring a lot of it back!

The pattern of all these innovations is always the same – from the subroutine to object-oriented programming: someone finds a piece of the answer and we get a small increment in productivity, but not the big break-through we have been looking for, and eventually this technique makes its way into the general bag of tricks that every experienced programmer carries in his or her back pocket.

By the way, I should state at the outset that my focus is not on mathematical applications, but on business applications – the former is a different ball-game, and one happily played by academics all over the world. Business applications are different, and much of my work has been to try to determine exactly why they should be so different, and what we can do to solve the problem of building and maintaining them. These kinds of applications often have a direct effect on the competitiveness of the companies that use them, and being able to build and maintain this type of

Prologue

application more effectively will be a win-win situation for those of us in the industry and for those who use our services.

Before I start to talk about a set of concepts which I think really does provide a quantum jump in improving application development productivity, I would like to mention something which arises directly out of my own personal background. Coming from an artistic background (my mother was an artist), I find I tend to think about things in visual terms. One of the influences in the work described in this book was a feeling that one should be able to express applications in a graphical notation which would take advantage of people's visualization abilities. This feeling may have been helped along by exposure to a system called GPSS (General Purpose Simulation System). This system can be highly graphical, and it (along with other simulation systems) has another very interesting characteristic, namely that its constructs tend to match objects in the real world. It is not surprising that Simula (another language originally designed for simulation) is viewed as one of the forerunners of many of today's advanced programming languages. I believe that GPSS was one of the triggers that started me thinking about application development from a very different direction – of course it also helped that that my introduction to data processing was through Unit Record, not computer logic, as would have been the case if I had any computer science training in university (it didn't exist in those days!).

Another effect of my personal orientation is a desire, almost a preoccupation, with beauty in programming. While I will stress many times that programming should not be the production of unique pieces of cabinetry, this does not mean that programs cannot exhibit beauty. There are places and times in the world's history where people have invested great creativity in useful objects such as spoons or drinking cups. Conversely, the needs of primitive mass-production, supported by a naïve view of value, resulted in factories turning out vast numbers of identical, artistically crude objects (although obviously there were some exceptions), which in turn are thought to have led to a deadening of the sensibilities of a whole culture. I believe that modern technology therefore can do more than just make our lives more comfortable – I believe it can actually help to bring the aesthetic back into its proper place in our life experience.

One more comment about my personal biases (of which I have many, so I'm told): it has always seemed to me that application design and building is predominantly a creative activity, and creativity is a uniquely human ability – one that (I believe) computers and robots will never exhibit. On the other hand, any activity which bores people should be done by computers, and will probably be done better by them. So the trick is to split work appropriately between humans and machines – it is the partnership between the two that can lead to the most satisfying and productive era the world has ever known (I also read a lot of science fiction!). One of the points often missed by the purveyors of methodologies is that each stage of refinement of a design is not simply an expansion of information already in existence, but a creative act. We should absolutely avoid reentering the same information over and over again – that's boring! – but, on the other hand, we should never imagine that any stage of refinement of a design can somehow be

Prologue

magically done without human input. Robots are great at remembering and following rules – only humans create.

Corollary I: Do not use humans for jobs computers can do better – this is a waste of human energy and creativity, the only real resource on this planet, and demeans the human spirit.

Corollary II: Do not expect computers to provide that creative spark that only humans can provide. If computers ever do become creative, they won't be computers any more – they will be people! And I do not consider creativity the same as random number generation....

The other personal slant I brought to this quest was the result of a unique educational system which inculcated in its victims (sorry, students) the idea that there is really no area of human endeavour which one should be afraid to tackle, and that indeed we all could realistically expect to contribute to any field of knowledge we addressed. This perhaps outdated view may have led me to rush in where angels fear to tread.... However, this pursuit has at the least kept me entertained and given my professional life a certain direction for several decades.

In past centuries, the dilettante or amateur has contributed a great deal to the world's store of knowledge and beauty. Remember, most of the really big paradigm shifts were instigated by outsiders! The word "amateur" comes from the idea of loving. One should be proud to be called an computing amateur! "Dilettante" is another fine word with a similar flavour – it comes from an Italian word meaning "to delight in". I therefore propose another theorem: if an activity isn't fun, humans probably shouldn't be doing it. I feel people should use the feeling of fun as a touchstone to see if they are on the right track. Here is a quote from my colleague, P.R. Ewing, which also agrees with my own experience: "The guys who turn out the most code are the ones who are having fun!" Too many experts are deadly serious. Play is not something we have to put away when we reach the state of adulthood – it is a very important way for humans to expand their understanding of the universe and all the interesting and delightful beings and things that occupy it. This feeling that the subject matter of this book is *fun* is one of the most common reactions we have encountered, and is one of the main things which makes my collaborators and myself believe that we have stumbled on something important. In what follows I hope to convey some of this feeling. Please forgive me if some whimsy sneaks in now and then!

Table of Contents

Copyright Page & Trademarks...iv
Preface to 1st Edition (1994)..vi
Preface to 2nd Edition (2010)..viii
Acknowledgments..x
Disclaimers..xii
Prologue..xiii
Chap. I: Introduction..1
Chap. II: Higher-Level Languages, 4GLs and Source Code Reuse...15
Chap. III: Basic Concepts...20
Chap. IV: Reuse of Components..41
Chap. V: Parametrization of Reusable Components..54
Chap. VI: First Applications using Precoded Components..58
Chap. VII: Composite Components..71
Chap. VIII: Building Components & Some More Simple Applications.....................................77
Chap. IX: Substreams and Control IPs..90
Chap. X: Some More Components and Simple Applications..97
Chap. XI: Data Descriptions and Descriptors..110
Chap. XII: Tree Structures..120
Chap. XIII: Scheduling Rules..126
Chap. XIV: Loop-Type Networks..135
Chap. XV: Implementation, Network Splitting and Client-Server...140
Chap. XVI: Deadlocks: Their Causes and Prevention...156
Chap. XVII: Problem-Oriented Mini-Languages...172
Chap. XVIII: A Business-Oriented Very High Level Language..178
Chap. XIX: Synchronization and Checkpoints...185
Chap. XX: General Framework for Interactive Applications..195
Chap. XXI: Performance Considerations...210
Chap. XXII: Defining Networks...227
Chap. XXIII: Related Compiler Theory Concepts..235
Chap. XXIV: Streams and Recursive Function Definitions..240
Chap. XXV: Comparison between FBP and Object-Oriented Programming........................248
Chap. XXVI: Related Concepts and Forerunners..268
Chap. XXVII: The FBP Explosion...281
Chap. XXVIII: Endings and Beginnings..326
Appendix: FBP Implementations and Diagramming Tool..336
Glossary of Terms...343
Bibliography..345
Index...351

Chap. I: Introduction

Imagine that you have a large and complex application running in your shop, and you discover that you need what looks like fairly complex changes made to it in a hurry. You consult your programmers and they tell you that the changes will probably take several months, but they will take a look. A meeting is called of all the people involved – not just programmers and analysts, but users and operations personnel as well. The essential logic of the program is put up on the wall, and the program designers walk through the program structure with the group. During the ensuing discussion, they realize that two new modules have to be written and some other ones have to change places. Total time to make the changes – a week!

Quite a few parts of this scenario sound unlikely, don't they? Users, operations people and programmers all talking the same language – unthinkable! But it actually did happen just the way I described. The factor that made this experience so different from most programmers' everyday experience is the truly revolutionary technology I will be describing in this book.

While this technology has been in use for productive work for almost 40 years, it has also been waiting in the wings, so to speak, for its right time to come on stage. Perhaps because there is a "paradigm shift" involved, to use Kuhn's phrase (Kuhn 1970), it has not been widely known up to now, but I believe now is the time to open it up to a wider public.

As the late Wayne Stevens, the noted writer on the subject of application design methodologies, pointed out in several of his books, this technology provides a consistent application view from high level design all the way down to implementation. It allows applications to be built using reusable "black boxes" and encourages developers to construct such black boxes, which can then improve the productivity of other developers. It forces developers to focus on data and its transformations, rather than starting with procedural code. It encourages rapid prototyping and results in more reliable, more maintainable systems. It is compatible with distributed systems,

Chap. I: Introduction

and appears to be on a convergent path with object-oriented programming. In this book, I will describe the concepts underlying this technology and give examples of experience gained using it. Does it sound too good to be true? You be the judge! In the following pages, we will be describing what I believe is a genuine revolution in the process of creating application programs to support the data processing requirements of companies around the world.

Today, in the early years of a new millennium, the bulk of all business programming is done using techniques which have not changed much in 50 years. Most of it is done using what are often called Higher-Level Languages (HLLs), by far the most popular of which is COBOL, the Common Business-Oriented Language, originally developed in 1959 (coincidentally the year I joined IBM!). A distant second is probably PL/I, not as widespread in terms of number of customers, but in use at some of the biggest organizations in North America. C, now C++, appears to be gaining steadily in popularity, especially as it is often the first programming language students encounter at university. It appears to be especially convenient for writing system software, due to its powerful and concise pointer manipulation facilities, but by the same token, it may be less well adapted for writing business applications. Some languages are used by particular sectors of the programming community or for certain specialized purposes. There are also the "4th generation languages", which are higher level than the HLLs but usually more specialized.

There are plenty of design methodologies and front-end tools to do them with, but most of these do not really affect the mechanics of creating programs. After the design has been done, the programmer still has the job of converting his or her elegant design into strings of commands in the chosen programming language. Although generators have had some success, by and large most of today's programmers painstakingly create their programs by hand, like skilled artisans hand-crafting individual pieces of cabinetry. One of the "grand old men" of the computing fraternity, Nat Rochester, said a number of years ago that programming probably absorbs more creativity than any other professional pursuit, and most of it is invisible to the outside world. Things really haven't changed all that much since those days. There are also what might be called procedural or organizational approaches to improving the application development process, e.g. "structured walk-throughs", the "buddy" system, "chief programmer teams", third-party testing. My experience is that the approaches of this type which have been successful will still be valid whatever tool we eventually use for producing applications. However, if all you do is take the existing hand-crafting technology and add a massive bureaucracy to cross-check every chisel stroke and hammer blow, I believe you will only get minor improvements in your process, and in fact at a considerable cost in productivity and morale. What is needed instead is a fundamental change in the way we do things, after which we will be able to see which procedures and organizations fit naturally into the new world.

It is a truism that most businesses in the Western world would stop functioning if it were not for the efforts of tens of thousands, if not hundreds of thousands, of application programmers. These

Chap. I: Introduction

people are practising a craft which most of the population does not understand, and would not be willing to do if it did. The archetypal programmer is viewed as a brilliant but impractical individual who has a better rapport with computers than with people, slaving long hours at a terminal which is at the very least damaging to his or her eyesight. In fact, of course, the programmer is the key interface between his clients, who speak the language of business, and the computer and its systems, which speak the language of electrons. The more effectively and reliably the programmer can bridge between these worlds, the better will be the applications which he or she builds, but this requires an unusual combination of talents. If you have any of these paragons in your organization, guard them like the treasures they are! In what follows, one of the recurring themes will be that the problems with today's programming technology arise almost entirely from the continuing mismatch between the problem area the programmer works in and the tools he or she has to work with. Only if we can narrow the gap between the world of users and that of application developers, can we produce applications which fit the needs of users and do it in a timely and cost-effective manner.

The significant fact I have come to realize is that application programming in its present form really *is* hard and in fact has not progressed all that much since the days of the first computers. This lack of progress is certainly not due to any shortage of advocates of this or that shiny new tool, but very few of these wonder products have delivered what was promised. When I started in the business in 1959, we already had higher-level languages, interpreters and subroutine calls – these are still the basic tools of today's programming professionals. The kind of programming most of us do has its roots in the procedural programming that arose during the '40s and '50s: this new invention called a computer filled a growing need for repetitive, mainly mathematical calculations, such as tide tables, ballistics and census calculations. In these areas, computers were wildly successful. However, even then, some of the experts in this new world of computing were starting to question whether procedural application programming was really appropriate for building business applications. The combination of more and more complex systems, the sheer difficulty of the medium programmers work in and the need for businesses to reduce overhead is resulting in more and more pressure on today's programming professionals.

Adding to the pressure on our programmers is the introduction of multicore computers – it is generally accepted that, to properly take advantage of the power of these new machines, programmers have to write multithreaded code. Unfortunately, this is extremely difficult to get right, and most such programs don't scale up very well. Thus it was a very pleasant surprise to find out that FBP allows programmers to write multithreaded code, easily and safely – and in fact they don't even have to think of it as multithreaded code! Yes, it does involve a paradigm change, but as I will try to show, it is a change that brings programming more in line with other types of industrial design.

In addition, as programmers build new systems, these add to the amount of resources being expended on maintaining them, to the point where the ability of many companies to develop new

Chap. I: Introduction

applications is being seriously impacted by the burden of maintaining old systems. This in turn adversely affects their ability to compete in the highly competitive global market-place. Many writers have talked about the programming backlog – the backlog of programming work that DP departments are planning to do but can't get to because of lack of resources. I have also heard people use the phrase "hidden backlog" – this is programming work that users would like to get done but know there's no point in even talking to their DP department about, so it tends not to show up in the statistics!

At one time, it was predicted that more telephone switchboard operators would be needed than the total number of available young ladies. Of course, this problem was solved by the development of automatic telephone switching systems. Similarly, many people believe the present situation in computing can only be solved by a quantum jump in technology, and of course each new software technology claims to be the long-awaited solution. I and a number of other people believe that the concepts described in what follows really do have the potential to solve this problem, and I hope that, as you read this book, you will come to agree with us. However, they represent a true paradigm change which fundamentally changes the way we look at the programming process. Like many important discoveries, this new paradigm is basically quite simple, but far-reaching in its implications.

Mention of a new paradigm makes one immediately think of another new paradigm which is growing steadily in popularity, namely object-oriented programming (usually abbreviated to OO). What I am about to describe is not OO, but bears certain similarities to it, and especially to the more advanced OO concepts, specifically the concept of "active objects". In the long run, these two paradigms appear to be on a converging path, and, as I will be describing in Chapter 25 (page 248), I believe that the combination of these two sets of concepts will achieve the best of both worlds. In most of this book, however, I will be presenting our concepts and experience as they evolved historically, using our own terminology, although I will be using examples built using one such OO-based implementation, JavaFBP (described in more detail in one of the appendices).

After a few years in the computer business, I found myself puzzling over why application programming should be so hard. Its complexity is certainly not the complexity of complex algorithms or logic. From an arithmetic point of view, one seldom encounters a multiplication or division in business programming, let alone anything as arcane as a square root. The vast majority of business applications do such things as transforming data from one format to another, accumulating totals or looking up information in one file and incorporating it into another file or a report. Given what seems like a fairly simple problem space, I wondered why application development should be so arduous and why, once built, a program should be so hard to maintain. Over the last few years, I and a number of other workers in the field have come to believe that the main cause of the problem is in fact the same thing that powered the computer revolution itself, namely the von Neumann computer model.

Chap. I: Introduction

This model is the traditional one that has been so productive over the last five decades, designed around a single instruction counter which walks sequentially through strings of codes that tell it what to do at each step. These codes can be treated both as data (e.g. by compilers) and as commands. This design is usually, but not necessarily, combined with a uniform array of memory cells from which the instructions take data, and into which they return it. As described in a 1990 article by L. G. Valiant, the power of this model derives from the fact that it has acted as a bridge between the twin "diverse and chaotic" worlds (in his words) of hardware and software, while allowing them to evolve separately. But, by the same token, its very success convinced its practitioners that the problems we are facing cannot possibly be due to any fundamental problems with this set of concepts. Programmers are not bright enough, they don't have good enough tools, they don't have enough mathematical education or they don't work hard enough – I'm sure you've run into all of these explanations. I don't believe any of these are valid – I believe there is a far more fundamental problem – namely that, at a basic level, the medium is simply inappropriate for the task at hand. In fact, when you look at them objectively, the symptoms our business is experiencing now are quite characteristic of what one would expect when people try to do a complicated job using the wrong tools. Take a second and really try to imagine building a functioning automobile out of clay! It's highly malleable when wet, so you should be able to make anything, but after it has been fired it is very hard but very brittle! In fact that's quite a good analogy for the "feel" of most of our applications today!

The time is now ripe for a new paradigm to replace the von Neumann model as the bridging model between hardware and software. The one we will be describing is similar to the one Valiant proposes (I'll talk about this in more detail in Chapter 26 – page 268) and in fact seems to be one of a family of related concepts which have appeared over the last few years in the literature. The common concept underlying much of this work is basically that, to solve these problems, we have to relax the tight sequential programming style characteristic of the von Neumann machine, and structure programs as collections of communicating, asynchronous processes. If you look at applications larger than a single program or go down inside the machine, you will find many processes going on in parallel. It is only within a single program (job step or transaction) that you still find strict traditional, sequential logic. We have tended to believe that the tight control of execution sequence imposed by this approach is the only way to get predictable code, and that therefore it was necessary for reliable systems. It turns out that machines (and people) work more efficiently if you only retain the constraints that matter and relax the ones that don't, and you can do this without any loss of reliability. The intent of this book is to try to describe a body of experience which has been built up using a particular set of implementations of this concept over the years, so I will not go into more detail at this point. In this chapter, we will be talking more about the history of this concept than about specific implementations or experience gained using them.

Another factor which makes me think it is timely for this technology to be made public is that we are facing a growing crisis in application development. At the same time as new requirements are

Chap. I: Introduction

appearing, the underlying technology is changing faster and faster. The set of concepts I will be describing seems to fit well with current directions for both software and hardware. Not only can it support in a natural manner the requirements of distributed, heterogeneous applications, but it also seems an appropriate programming technology for the new multiprocessor machines being worked on by universities and leading-edge computer manufacturers all over the world. As the Wayne Stevens has pointed out in several of his articles (e.g. Stevens 1985), the paradigm we will be describing provides a consistent, natural way to view systems, from the workings of whole companies all the way down to the smallest computer component. Since you can describe manual applications with data-flow diagrams, even the connection between manual and system procedures can be shown seamlessly.

In what follows, I will be using the term "Flow-Based Programming" (or FBP for short), suggested by Eric Lawton of IBM, to describe this new set of concepts and the software needed to support it. We have in the past used the term "Data Flow" as it conveys a number of the more important aspects of this technology, but there is a sizable body of published work on what is called "dataflow architectures" in computer design and their associated software (for instance the very exciting work coming out of MIT), so the term dataflow may cause confusion in some academic circles. It was also pointed out to me several years ago that, when control flow is needed explicitly, FBP can provide it by the use of such mechanisms as triggers, so the term Flow-Based Programming avoids the connotation that we cannot do control flow. This is not to say that the two types of data flow do not have many concepts in common – dataflow computer architectures arise also from the perception that the von Neumann machine design that has been so successful in the past must be generalized if we are to move forward, whether we are trying to perform truly huge amounts of computation such as weather calculations or simply produce applications which are easier to build and maintain.

One significant difference between the two schools, at least at this time, is that most of the other data flow work has been mathematically oriented, so it tends to work with numbers and arrays of numbers. Although my early data flow work during the late 60s also involved simple numeric values travelling through a network of function blocks, my experience with simulation systems led me to the realization that it would be more productive in business applications to have the things which flow be structured objects, which I called "entities". This name reflected the idea that these structured objects tended to represent entities in the outside world. (In our later work, we realized that the name "entity" might cause confusion with the idea of entities in data modelling, although there are points of resemblance, so we decided to use a different word). Such a system is also, not coincidentally, a natural design for *simulating* applications, so the distinction between applications and their simulations becomes much less significant than in conventional programming. You can think of an entity as being like a record in storage, but active (in that it triggers events), rather than passive (just being read or written). Entities flow through a network of processes, like cars in a city, or boats in a river system. They differ from the mathematical tokens of dataflow computers or my early work chiefly in that they have *structure*: each entity

Chap. I: Introduction

represents an object with attributes, for example an employee will have attributes such as salary, date of hire, manager, etc. As you read this book, it should become clear why there has to be at least one layer of the application where the entities move as individual units, although it may very well be possible to integrate the various dataflow approaches at lower levels.

At this point I am going to have to describe FBP briefly, to give the reader something to visualize, but first a caveat: the brief description that follows will probably not be enough to let you picture what FBP is and how it does it. If we don't do this at this point, however, experience shows that readers find it hard to relate what I am describing to their own knowledge. The reverse risk is that they may jump to conclusions which may prevent them from seeing what is truly new about the concepts I will be describing later. I call this the "It's just a..." syndrome.

In conventional programming, when you sit down to write a program, you write code down the page – a linear string of statements describing the series of actions you want the computer to execute. Since we are of course all writing structured code now, we start with a main line containing mostly subroutine calls, which can then be given "meaning" later by coding up the named subroutines. A number of people have speculated about the possibility of instead building a program by just plugging prewritten pieces of logic together. This has sometimes been called 'Legoland' programming. Even though that is essentially what we do when we use utilities, there has always been some doubt whether this approach has the power to construct large scale applications, and, if it has, whether such applications would perform. I now have the pleasure to announce that the answer is "Yes" to both these questions!

The "glue" that FBP uses to connect the pieces together is an example of what Yale's Gelernter and Carriero (1992) have called a "coordination language". I feel the distinction between coordination languages and procedural languages is a useful one, and helps to clarify what is different about FBP. Conventional programming languages instruct the machine what logic to execute; coordination languages tell the machine how to coordinate multiple modules written in one or several programming languages. There is quite a bit of published material on various approaches to coordination, but much of that work involves the use of special-purpose languages, which reduces the applicability of these concepts to traditional languages and environments. Along with Gelernter and Carriero, I feel a better approach is to have a language-independent coordination notation, which can coordinate modules written in a variety of different procedural languages. The individual modules have to have a common Application Programming Interface (API) to let them talk to the coordination software, but this can be relatively simple.

Coordination and modularity are two sides of the same coin, and several years ago Raoul de Campo of IBM Research in Yorktown Heights coined the term "configurable modularity" to denote an ability to reuse independent components just by changing their interconnections. Nate Edwards of the same organization expanded on this idea (Edwards 1977), and stated that in his view this characteristic is fundamental to *all* successful reuse systems, and indeed to all systems which can be described as "engineered". While Nate Edwards' work is fairly non-technical and

Chap. I: Introduction

pragmatic, his background is mainly in hardware, rather than software, which may be why his work has not received the attention it deserves in the software domain. One of the important characteristics of a system exhibiting configurable modularity, such as most modern hardware or Flow-Based Programming, is that you can build systems out of "black box" reusable modules, much like the chips which are used to build logic in hardware. You also, of course, have to have something to connect them together with, but they do not have to be modified in any way to make this happen. Of course, this is characteristic of almost all the things we attach to each other in real life – in fact, almost everywhere except in conventional programming. In FBP, these black boxes are the basic building blocks that a developer uses to build an application. New black boxes can be written as needed, but a developer tries to use what is available first, before creating new components. In FBP, the emphasis shifts from building everything new to connecting preexisting pieces and only building new when building a new component is cost-justified. Nate Edwards played a key role in getting the hardware people to follow this same principle – and now of course, like all great discoveries, it seems that we have always known this! We have to help software developers to move through the same paradigm shift. If you look at the literature of programming from this standpoint, you will be amazed at how few writers write from the basis of reuse – in fact the very term seems to suggest an element of surprise, as if reuse were a fortuitous occurrence that happens seldom and usually by accident! In real life, we *use* a knife or a fork – we don't *re*use it!

We will be describing similarities between FBP and other similar pieces of software in later chapters, but perhaps it would be useful at this point to use Microsoft DOS or UNIX™ pipes to draw a simple analogy. If you have used either of these systems you will know that you can take separate programs and combine them using a vertical bar (|), e.g.

$$A \mid B$$

This is a very simple form of what I have been calling coordination of separate programs. It tells the system that you want to feed the output of A into the input of B, but neither A nor B have to be modified to make this happen. A and B have to have connection points ("plugs" and "sockets") which the system can use, and of course there has to be some software which understands the vertical bar notation and knows what to do with it. Based on this simple mechanism, you can take components and combine them to do all sorts of useful tasks as needed. This is described in more detail in Chapter 26 (page 268).

FBP broadens this concept in a number of directions which vastly increase its power. It turns out that this generalization results in an approach to building applications which is very different from the conventional approach, and which results in systems which are both more reliable and more maintainable.

Applications using FBP systems therefore basically all have the following components:
- a number of precoded, pretested functions, provided in object code form, not source code

Chap. I: Introduction

- form ("black boxes") – this set is open-ended and (hopefully) constantly growing
- a "scheduler" – a piece of software which coordinates the different independent modules, and implements the API (Application Programming Interface) which is used by the components to communicate with each other and with the scheduler
- a notation for specifying how the components are connected together into one or more networks (an FBP application designer typically starts with pictures, and then converts them into specifications to be executed by the scheduler)
- this notation can be put into a file for execution by the scheduler software. In the only implementation of FBP ever actually marketed by IBM (DFDM – described in the next section of this chapter), the network could either be compiled and link-edited to produce an executable program, or it could be interpreted directly (with of course greater initialization overhead). In the interpreted mode, the components are loaded in dynamically, so you can make changes and see the results many times in a few minutes. As we said before, people found this mode extremely productive. Later, when debugging was finished, you could convert the interpretable form to the compilable form to provide better performance for your production version.
- procedures to enable you to convert, compile and package individual modules and partial networks
- documentation (reference and tutorial) for all of the above

In the above list I have not included education, but of course this is probably the most important item of all. To get the user started, there is a need for formal education – this may only take a few days or weeks, and I hope that this book will get the reader started on understanding many of the basic concepts. However, education also includes the practical experience that comes from working with many different applications, over a number of months or years. In this area especially, we have found that FBP feels very different from conventional programming. Unlike most other professions, in programming we tend to underestimate the value of experience, which may in fact be due to the nature of the present-day programming medium. In other professions we do not recommend giving a new practitioner a pile of books, and then telling him or her to go out and do brain surgery, build a bridge, mine gold or sail across the Atlantic. Instead it is expected that there will be a series of progressive steps from student or apprentice to master. Application development using FBP feels much more like an engineering-style discipline: we are mostly assembling structures out of preexisting components with well-defined specifications, rather than building things from scratch using basic raw materials. In such a medium, experience is key: it takes time to learn what components are available, how they fit together and what trade-offs can be made. However, unlike bridge-builders, application developers using FBP can also get simple applications working very fast, so they can have the satisfaction of seeing quite simple programs do non-trivial things very early. Education in FBP is a hands-on affair, and it is really a pleasure seeing people's reactions when they get something working without having to write a

Chap. I: Introduction

line of code!

Now that graphics hardware and software have become available at reasonable cost and performance, we can build powerful graphical front-ends for our FBP systems. Since FBP is a highly visual notation, we believe that a graphical front-end is one of the keys to its wider acceptance. In Chapter 27 (page 281), you will see that graphical front-ends and visual languages have started popping up like mushrooms in the grass! In 2008 and 2009 we developed a graphical tool called DrawFBP, written using Java AWT, Java Swing and the Java 2D API – this tool captures connectivity information, as well as the spatial positions of the blocks and arrows, so that it can actually generate a running JavaFBP program. It also supports what is sometimes called "stepwise decomposition", allowing the system to be built up a layer at a time. The majority of the diagrams in this book were built using this tool.

Now I feel it would be useful to give you a bit of historical background on FBP: the first implementation of this concept was built by myself in 1969 and 1970 in Montréal, Québec. Its first incarnation was called (somewhat tongue-in-cheek) Data-Oriented Organization Running Multiple Asynchronous Tasks (DOORMAT). I still think this is a wonderful acronym, but it was felt (probably correctly!) that it would not command sufficient respect, so we renamed it the Advanced Modular Processing System (AMPS), and it was used for a number of customer applications at the IBM Montréal Data Centre. This technology proved very productive – so much so that it was taken into a major Canadian bank, where it was used for all the batch programming of a major on-line system. This system and the experience gained from it are described in a fair amount of detail in an article I wrote a few years later for the IBM Systems Journal (Morrison 1978).

Although the concepts are not well known, they have actually been in the public domain for many years. The way this happened is as follows: in late 1970 or early '71 I approached IBM Canada's Intellectual Property department to see if we could take out a patent on the basic idea. Their recommendation, which I feel was prescient, was that this concept seemed to them more like a law of nature, which is not patentable. They did recommend, however, that I write up a Technical Disclosure Bulletin (TDB), which was duly published and distributed to patent offices world-wide (Morrison 1971). A TDB is a sort of inverse patent – while a patent protects the owner but requires him or her to try to predict all possible variations on a concept, a TDB puts a concept into the public domain, and thereby protects the registering body from being restricted or impeded in the future in any use they may wish to make of the concept. In the case of a TDB, it places the onus on someone else who might be trying to patent something based on your concept to prove that their variation was not obvious to someone "skilled in the art".

Towards the end of the '80s, Wayne Stevens and I jointly developed a new version of this software, called the Data Flow Development Manager (DFDM). It is described in Appendix A of what I think was Wayne's last book (Stevens 1991) (which, by the way, contains a lot of good material on application design techniques in general). What I usually refer to in what follows as

Chap. I: Introduction

"processes" were called "coroutines" in DFDM, after Conway (1963), who described an early form of this concept in a paper back in the '60s, and foresaw even then some of its potential. "Coroutine" is formed from the word "routine" together with the Latin prefix meaning "with", as compared with "subroutine", which is formed with the prefix meaning "under". (Think of "*co*operative" vs. "*sub*ordinate").

DFDM was used for a number of projects (between 40 and 50) of various sizes within IBM Canada. A few years later, Kenji Terao got a project started within IBM Japan to support us in developing an improved version for the Japanese market. This version, marketed under the name

"Data Flow Programming Manager" (データ・フロー・プログラミング 管理), is, at the time of writing, the only official IBM FBP product which has been made available in the marketplace, and I believe enormous credit is due to Kenji and all the dedicated and forward-looking people in IBM Japan who helped to make this happen. While this version of DFDM was in many ways more robust or "industrial strength" than the one which we had been using within IBM Canada, much of the experience which I will be describing in the following pages is based on what we learned using the IBM Canada internal version of DFDM (roughly 1983 – 1990), or on the still earlier AMPS system (1969 – 1976). Perhaps someone will write a sequel to this book describing the Japanese experience with DFDM...

After I retired from IBM, I wrote a C implementation, which attempted to embody many of the best ideas of its ancestors, called THREADS – THREads-based Application Development System (I love self-referential names!). Like DFDM, it also has interpreted and compiled versions, so applications can be developed iteratively, and then compiled to produce a single EXE file, which eliminates the network decoding phase. The first version of THREADS used C functions `longjmp` and `setjmp`, plus some hardware-level code, to switch between a number of separate stacks. However, the code was somewhat hardware- and operating system-specific, so in 2009 I started converting THREADS to use the new Windows "fibres" facility. Although the revised code has survived some of its early tests, it needs a lot more testing. The latest information can be found on the FBP web site (*http://www.jpaulmorrison.com/fbp/threads.htm*).

A few years later, Java and C# versions were implemented, called (unimaginatively) JavaFBP and C#FBP. They can both be found on the author's FBP web site, and on SourceForge (*https://sourceforge.net/projects/flow-based-pgmg/*).

The terminology used in this book is not exactly the same as that used by AMPS and DFDM, as a number of these terms turned out to cause confusion. For instance, the data chunks that travel between the asynchronous processes were called "entities" in those systems, but, as I said above, this caused confusion for people experienced in data modelling. They do seem to correspond with the "entities" of data modelling, but "entities" have other connotations which could be misleading. "Objects" would present other problems, and we were not comfortable with the idea of creating totally new words (although some writers have used them effectively). The "tuples" of Carriero and Gelernter's Linda (1989) are very close, but this name also presents a slightly different image from the FBP concept. We therefore decided to use the rather neutral term "information packet" (or "IP" for short) for this concept. This term was coined by Herman van Goolen of IBM Netherlands as part of work that we did after DFDM, in which we tied FBP concepts in with other work appearing in the literature or being developed in other parts of IBM. Some of the extensions to the basic AMPS and DFDM substructure that I will be talking about later were also articulated during this period. When I need to refer to ideas drawn from this work I will use the name FPE (for Flow-Based Programming Environment), although that is not the acronym used for that project. THREADS and its successor implementations follow this revised terminology, and include a number of ideas from FPE.

As I stated in the prologue, for most of my 50 years (I can't believe it!) in the computer business I have been almost exclusively involved with business applications. Although business applications are often more complex than scientific applications, the academic community generally has not shown much interest in this area up until now. This is a "catch 22" situation, as business would benefit from the work done in academia, yet academia (with some noteworthy exceptions) tends not to regard business programming as an interesting area to work in. My hope is that FBP can act as a bridge between these two worlds, and in later chapters I will be attempting to tie FBP to other related theoretical work which working programmers probably wouldn't normally encounter. My reading in the field suggests that FBP has sound theoretical foundations, and yet it can perform well enough that you can run a company on it, and it is accessible to trainee programmers (sometimes more easily than for experienced ones!). AMPS has now been in production use for over 35 years, supporting one of the biggest companies in North America. Business systems have to evolve over time as the market requirements change, so clearly their system has been able to grow and adapt over the years as the need arose – this is a living system, not some outdated curiosity which has become obsolete with the advance of technology.

And now I would like to conclude this chapter with an unsolicited testimonial from a DFDM user, which we found particularly satisfying:

> "I have a requirement to merge 23 ... reports into one .... As all reports are of different length and block size this is more difficult in a conventional PLI environment. It would have required 1 day of work to write the program and 1 day to test it. Such a program would use repetitive code. While drinking coffee 1 morning I wrote a DFDM network to do this. It was complete *before the coffee went cold* [my italics]. Due to the length of time from training to programming it took 1 day to compile the code. Had it not been for the learning curve it could have been done in 5 minutes. During testing a small error was found which took 10 minutes to correct. As 3 off-the-shelf coroutines [components] were used, PLI was not required. 2 co-routines were used once, and 1 was used 23 times. Had it not been for DFDM, I would have

told the user that his requirement was not cost justified. It took more time to write this note than the DFDM network."

Notice that in his note, Rej (short for Réjean), who, by the way, is a visually impaired application developer with many years of experience in business applications, mentioned all the points that were significant to him as a developer – he zeroed right in on the amount of reuse he was getting, because functions he could get right off the shelf were ones he didn't have to write, test and eventually maintain! In DFDM, "coroutines" are the basic building blocks, which programmers can hook together to build applications. They are either already available ("on the shelf"), or the programmer can write new ones, in which case he or she will naturally try to reuse them as often as possible – to get the most bang for the proverbial buck. Although it is not very hard to write new PL/I components, the majority of application developers don't want to write new code – they just want to get their applications working for the client, preferably using as little programming effort as will suffice to get a quality job done. Of course there are always programmers who love the process of programming and, as we shall see in the following pages, there is an important role for them also in this new world which is evolving.

Rej's note was especially satisfying to us because he uses special equipment which converts whatever is on his screen into spoken words. Since FBP has always seemed to me a highly visual technique, I had worried about whether visually impaired programmers would have any trouble using it, and it was very reassuring to find that Rej was able to make such productive use of this technology. In later discussions with him, he has stressed the need to keep application structures simple. In FBP, you can use hierarchic decomposition to create multiple layers, each containing a simple structure, rather than being required to create a single, flat, highly complex structure. In fact, structures which are so complex that he would have trouble with them are difficult for everyone.

Rej's point about the advantages of keeping the structures simple is also borne out by the fact that another application of DFDM resulted in a structure of about 200 processes, but the programmer involved (another very bright individual) never drew a single picture! He built it up gradually using hierarchical decomposition, and it had one of the lowest error rates of any application in our shop.

In what follows, I will be describing the main features of FBP and what we have learned from developing and using its various implementations. Information on some of these has appeared in a number of places and I feel it is time to try to pull together some of the results of our experience with these concepts into a single place, so that the ideas can be seen in context. A vast number of papers have appeared over the years, written by different writers in different fields of computing, which I believe are all various facets of a single diamond, but I hope that, by pulling a lot of connected ideas together in one place, the reader will start to get a glimpse of the total picture. Perhaps there is someone out there who is waiting for these ideas, and will be inspired to

Chap. I: Introduction

carry them further, either in research or in the marketplace!

Chap. II: Higher-Level Languages, 4GLs and Source Code Reuse

In the Prologue, I alluded to the concept of compiler compilers. At the time I was most interested in them (the mid-'60s), the accepted wisdom was that more sophisticated compilers were the answer to the productivity problem, and tools that would make it easy to produce compilers or even families of compilers would give us the much-needed productivity improvement. During the late '50s many of the popular Higher-Level Languages (HLLs) got their start: obvious examples are COBOL, FORTRAN, PL/I, plus more esoteric languages, such as SNOBOL for pattern matching, and IPL/V and LISP for list processing. So this was not an unreasonable expectation. It was clear to everyone that an expression like:

```
W = (X + Y) / (Z + 3)
```

Figure 2.1

was infinitely superior to the machine language equivalent, which might look something like the following:

```
LOAD Z
ADD 3
STORE TEMP
LOAD X
ADD Y
DIV TEMP
STORE W
```

Figure 2.2

Chap. II: Higher-Level Languages, 4GLs and Source Code Reuse

This is an imaginary machine with a single working register, but you get the general idea. One of the reasons the syntax shown on the first line could so effectively act as a bridge between humans and computers was that it was syntactically clean, and based on a solid, well-understood, mathematical foundation – namely arithmetic... with the exception of a rather strange use of the equals sign!

During this period it was expected that this expressive power could be extended to other functions that machines needed to perform. COBOL was going to be the language that enabled the person in the street, or at least managers of programmers, to program computers! Algol became a program-level documentation standard for algorithms. IBM developed PL/I (I worked on one rather short-lived version of that); people developed compilers in their basements; graduate students wrote compilers for their theses at universities (they still do). There was always the feeling that one of these languages was going to be the key to unlocking the productivity that we all felt was innate in programmers. While it is true that the science of compiler writing advanced by leaps and bounds, by and large programmer productivity (at least in business application development) did not go up, or if it did, it soon plateaued at a new level.

One language which I feel deserves special mention is APL – APL (named after the book A Programming Language by Ken Iverson) is an extremely powerful language, and it also opened up arcane areas of mathematics like matrix handling for those of us who had never quite understood it in school. Being able to do a matrix multiply in 5 key-strokes **(A+.×B)** is still a level of expressiveness that I think few programming languages will ever be able to match! Its combination of sheer power in the mathematical area allowed one to get interesting programs up and running extremely fast. I once read a comment in a mathematical paper that the author didn't think the work would have been possible *without* APL – and I believe him. Although it was used a certain amount in business for calculation-oriented programming, especially in banking and insurance, and also as a base for some of the early query-type languages, APL did little for most commercial programming, which was still plodding along using COBOL, and more recently PL/I, PASCAL, BASIC, C...

APL to me also illustrates in a different way the importance of minimizing the "gap" between idea and its expression – along with many of the most popular programming languages, it is an interpreter, which means that you can enter the program, and then immediately run it, without having to go through a compile step. Personally, I feel this is more perception than actual fact (as one can build compilers which are so fast that the user doesn't perceive them as a barrier), but the fact remains that some very awkward languages have become immensely popular because they did not require a compile step.

Why didn't languages (even the interpretive ones) improve productivity more than they did? And, yes, people are still churning out new languages, but I believe that there are fundamental reasons why none of them are going to be what Fred Brooks called the "silver bullet".

Chap. II: Higher-Level Languages, 4GLs and Source Code Reuse

Well, I noticed fairly early on that these languages don't do much for *logic* (IF, THEN, ELSE, DO WHILE, etc.). For many kinds of business programming, what pushes up the development cost is the logic – there actually may not be much in the way of straight calculations. A logical choice can be thought of as a certain amount of work, whether you write it like this:

```
IF x > 2
THEN
    result = 1
ELSE
    result = 2
ENDIF
```

or like this:

```
result = (x>2) ? 1 : 2;
```

Figure 2.3

or

```
IF MARRIED AND FEMALE, DISPLAY MAIDEN-NAME    (sexist!)
```

Figure 2.4

or even draw the logic as a Nassi-Shneiderman or Chapin chart. One can argue that, because all of the above phrasings involve one binary decision, they involve approximately the same amount of mental work. The more complex the logic, the more difficult the coding. In fact, there is a complexity measure used quite widely in the industry called McCabe's Cyclomatic complexity measure, which is based very directly on the number of binary decisions in a program. In comparison, in our work, we discovered that the amount of logic in conventional programming *is* in fact reducible, because much of the logic in conventional programming has to do with the synchronization of data, rather than with business logic. Since FBP eliminates the need for a lot of this synchronization logic, this means that FBP actually does reduce the amount of logic in programs.

A number of writers have made the point that productivity is only improved if you can reduce the "gap" between the language of business and the language of computers. Now, one way to reduce the information requirements of a program is to pick options from a more limited universe. However, the user has to be willing to live within this more circumscribed universe. I remember an accounting package that was developed in Western Canada, which defined very tightly the universe in which its customers were supposed to operate. Within that universe, it provided quite a lot of function. If you asked the developers about adding some feature to it, their reaction was:

Chap. II: Higher-Level Languages, 4GLs and Source Code Reuse

why would anyone want to? Somewhat predictably, it didn't catch on because many customers felt it was too limited. The example that sticks in my memory was that of one customer who wanted to change a report title and had to be told it couldn't be done. Again, why would anyone feel that was so important? Well, it seems that customers, especially big ones, tend to feel that report headers should look the way *they* want, rather than the way the package says they are going to look. Our experience was that smaller customers might be willing to adapt their business to the program, especially if you could convince them that you understood it better than they did, but bigger customers expected the program to adapt to their business. And it was really quite a powerful package for the price! I learned a lot from that, and the main thing was that a vendor can provide standard components, but the customer has to be able to write custom components as well. Even if it costs more to do the latter, it is the customer's choice, not the vendor's. And that of course means that the customer must be able to visualize what the tool is doing.

As Higher-Level Languages (HLLs) were often referred to as 3rd Generation Languages (3GLs), languages which took advantage of frequently appearing application patterns to provide even more compact ways of describing applications were called 4GLs (4th Generation Languages). In general these worked by generating 3GL code. Many shops embraced particular 4GLs as they promised to reduce the amount of work programmers had to do, but the problem with these was that everything would go swimmingly for a while, and then the customer, like the customer above who wanted to change a report title, would want something that the 4GL did not provide. One alternative was to modify the generated code, but then you couldn't go back to the original 4GL code – unless you wanted to keep doing the same modifications to the 3GL code every time the 4GL code was modified! If the 4GL designer was very foresighted, the 4GL could provide "exits" (generally referred to as "callbacks" nowadays). A system which started out simple eventually became studded with exits, which required complex parametrization, and whose function could not be understood without understanding the internals of the product – the flow of the product. Since part of the effectiveness of a 4GL comes from its being relatively opaque and "black boxy", exits undermine its very reason for being.

It turns out that FBP can also capitalize on the same regularities as 4GLs do by providing reusable components (composite or elementary), plus standard network shapes. Instead of programmers having to understand the internal logic of a particular 4GL, they can be provided with a network and specifications of the data requirements of the various components: the programmer now has a single mental model based on data and its transformations, and is free to rearrange the network, replace the standard components by custom ones (provided they handle and generate the specified data formats), or make other desired changes.

Another common approach to reducing the amount of work involved in writing code that you may run into is "source code reuse". In this approach libraries of "raw" code are made available for developers to use in building their own applications. However, source code reuse suffers from a fundamental flaw: even if building a new program can be made relatively fast, once you have built it, it must be added to the ever-growing list of programs you have to maintain. It is even worse if, as is often required, the reusable source code components have to be modified before your program can work, because then you have lost the trail connecting the original pieces of code to your final program if one of them has to be enhanced, e.g. to fix a bug. Even if no modification takes place, the new program has to be added to the list of program assets your installation owns. Already in some shops, maintenance is taking 80% of the programming resource, so each additional application adds to this burden. In FBP, ideally all that is added to the asset base is a network – the components are all black boxes, and so a new application costs a lot less to maintain.

A related type of tool are program generators, similar to the idea of 4GLs – this is also source-level reuse with a slightly different emphasis. As above, an important question is whether you can modify the generated code. If you can't, you are limited to the choices built into the generator; if you can, your original source material becomes useless from a maintenance point of view, and can only be regarded as a high-level (and perhaps even misleading) specification. Like old documentation, the safest thing to do is often to just throw it away...

Some of my readers may have run into the design approach called "Structured Analysis". Even if you don't know it by that name, you may be familiar with other application design techniques which also show data flowing between functions. Here the application is shown as a network of nodes connected by paths across which the data flows. The nice thing about this type of design is that it can equally well describe departments within a company, applications, or components within an application. Unfortunately it is rather hard to convert such a design into von Neumann-style code. There is a chasm between the two mind-sets which nobody has been able to bridge in practice, although there are some theoretical approaches, such as the Jackson Inversion, which have been partially successful. FBP is the only technology which makes this problem go away completely, because the design and the working program use the *same* concepts.

FBP also forces designers to distinguish between a particular use of a component and its general definition. This may seem obvious in hindsight, but, even when documenting conventional programs, you would be amazed how often programmers give a fine generalized description of, say, a date routine, but forget to tell the reader which of its functions is being used in a particular situation. Even in old-style block diagrams I used to find that programmers often wrote the general description of the routine in a block and omitted its specific use (you need both). This is probably due to the fact that, in conventional programming, the developer of a routine is usually its only user as well, so s/he forgets to "change hats". When the developer and user are different people, it is easier for the user to stay in character.

To summarize, HLLs, code reuse, and 4GLs are all steps along a route towards the place we want to be, and all have lessons to teach us, and capabilities which are definitely part of the answer.

Chap. III: Basic Concepts

"Πάντα ῥεῖ (Panta rhei) – Everything flows" (Heraclitus of Ephesus, ca. 500 BCE)

In the middle years of the 20th century, it was expected that eventually computers would be able to do anything that humans could explain to them. But even then, some people wondered how easy this would turn out to be. A book first published in the 1950s, "Faster than Thought" (Bowden 1963), contains the following remark:

> "It always outrages pure mathematicians when they encounter commercial work for the first time to find how difficult it is." (p. 258)

and further on:

> "...it is so hard in practice to get any programme [sic] right that several mathematicians may be needed to look after a big machine in an office. ... It seems, in fact, that experienced programmers will always be in demand" (p. 259)

However, in those days, the main barrier was thought to be the difficulty of ascertaining the exact rules for running a business. This did turn out to be as hard as people expected, but for rather different reasons. Today we see that the problem is actually built right into the fundamental design principles of our basic computing engine – the so-called von Neumann machine we alluded to in Chapter 1.

The von Neumann machine is perfectly adapted to the kind of mathematical or algorithmic needs for which it was developed: tide tables, ballistics calculations, etc., but business applications are rather different in nature. As one example of these differences, the basic building block of programming is the subroutine, and has been since it was first described by Ada, Countess

Chap. III: Basic Concepts

Lovelace, Lord Byron's daughter, in the early 1800s (quite an achievement, since computers did not exist yet!). This concept was solidly founded on the mathematical idea of a function, and any programmer today knows about a number of standard subroutines, and can usually come up with new ones as needed. Examples might include "square root", "binary search", "sine", "display a currency value in human-readable format", etc. What are the basic building blocks of business applications? It is easy to list functions such as "merge", "sort", "paginate a report", and so forth, but none of these seem to lend themselves to being encapsulated as subroutines. They are of a different nature – rather than being functions that operate at a single moment in time, they all have the characteristic of operating over a period of time, across a number (sometimes a very large number) of input and output items.

We now begin to get some inkling of what this difference might consist of. Business programming works with data and concentrates on how this data is transformed, combined and separated, to produce the desired outputs and modify stored data according to business requirements. Broadly speaking, whereas the conventional approaches to programming (referred to as "control flow") start with process and view data as secondary, business applications are usually designed starting with data and viewing process as secondary – processes are just the way data is created, manipulated and destroyed. We often call this approach "data flow", and it is a key concept of many of our design methodologies. It is when we try to convert this view into procedural code that we start to run into problems.

I am now going to approach this difference from a different angle. Let's compare a pure algorithmic problem with a superficially similar business-related one. We will start with a simple numeric algorithm: calculating a number raised to the 'n'th power, where 'n' is a positive, integer exponent. This should be very familiar to our readers, and in fact it is not the best way to do this calculation, but it will suffice to make my point. In pseudocode, we can express this as follows:

```
/* Calculate a to the power b   */
     x = b
     y = 1
     do while x > 0
         y = y * a
         x = x - 1
     enddo
     return y
```

Figure 3.1

This is a very simple algorithm – easy to understand, easy to verify, easy to modify, based on well-understood mathematical concepts. Let us now look at what is superficially a similar piece of logic, but this time involving files of records, rather than integers. It has the same kind of structure as the preceding algorithm, but works with streams of records. The problem is to create a file OUT which is a subset of another one IN, where the records to be output are those which

Chap. III: Basic Concepts

satisfy a given criterion "c". Records which do not satisfy "c" are to be omitted from the output file. This is a pretty common requirement and is usually coded using some form of the following logic:

```
read into a from IN
do while read has not reached end of file
    if c is true
        write from a to OUT
    endif
    read into a from IN
enddo
```

Figure 3.2

What action is applied to those records which do not satisfy our criterion? Well, they disappear rather mysteriously due to the fact that they are not written to OUT before being destroyed by the next "read". Most programmers reading this probably won't see anything strange in this code, but, if you think about it, doesn't it seem rather odd that it should be possible to drop important things like records from an output file by means of what is really a quirk of timing?

Part of the reason for this is that most of today's computers have a uniform array of pigeon-holes for storage, and this storage behaves very differently from the way storage systems behave in real life. In real life, paper put into a drawer remains there until deliberately removed. It also takes up space, so that the drawer will eventually fill up, preventing more paper from being added. Compare this with the computer concept of storage – you can reach into a storage slot any number of times and get the same data each time (without being told that you have done it already), or you can put a piece of data in on top of a previous one, and the earlier one just disappears.... Although destructive storage is not integral to the the von Neumann machine, it is assumed in many functions of the machine, and this is the kind of storage which is provided on most modern computers. Since the storage of these machines is so sensitive to timing and because the sequencing of every instruction has to be predefined (and humans make mistakes!), it is incredibly difficult to get a program above a certain complexity to work properly. And of course this storage paradigm has been enshrined in most of our higher level languages in the concept of a "variable". In a celebrated article John Backus (1978) actually apologized for inventing FORTRAN! That's what I meant earlier about the strange use of the equals sign in Higher Level Languages. To a logician the statement $J = J + 1$ is a contradiction (unless J is infinity?) – yet programmers no longer notice anything strange about it!

Suppose we decide instead that a record should be treated as a real thing, like a memo or a letter, which, once created, exists for a definite period of time, and must be explicitly destroyed before it can leave the system. We could expand our pseudo-language very easily to include this concept by adding a "discard" statement (of course the record has to be identified somehow). Our

Chap. III: Basic Concepts

program might now read as follows:

```
      read record a from IN
      do while read has not reached end of file
         if c is true
            write a to OUT
         else
            discard a
         endif
         read record a from IN
      enddo
```

Figure 3.3

Now we can reinterpret "a": rather than thinking of it as an area of storage, let us think of "a" as a "handle" which designates a particular "thing" – it is a way of locating a thing, rather than the *storage area* containing the thing. In fact, these data "things" should not be thought of as being in storage at all: they are "somewhere else" (after all, it does not matter where "read" puts them, so long as the information they contain becomes available to the program). These "things" really have more attributes than just their images in storage. The storage image can be thought of as rather like the projection of a solid object onto a plane – manipulating the image does not affect the real thing behind the image. Now a consequence of this is that, if we reuse a handle, we will lose access to the thing it is the handle of. This therefore means that we have a responsibility to properly dispose of things before we can reuse their handles.

Notice the difficulty we have finding a good word for "thing": the problem is that this is really a concept which is "atomic", in the sense that it cannot be decomposed into yet more fundamental objects. It has had a number of names in the various dialects of FBP, and has some affinities with the concept of "object" in object-oriented programming, but I feel it is better to give it its own unique name. In what follows, we will be using the term "information packet" (or "IP"), coined, as we said above, by Herman van Goolen of IBM Netherlands. IPs may vary in length from 0 bytes to billions – the advantage of working with "handles" is that IPs are managed the same way, and cost the same to send and receive, independently of their size. Of course, this only works within shared memory – if you need to go from one machine to another, you will have to move the whole data chunk, but this happens relatively far less often than within-memory transfers.

So far, we have really only added one concept – that of IPs – to the conceptual model we are building. The pseudo-code in Figure 3.3 was a main-line program, running alone. Since this main-line can call subroutines, which in turn can call other subroutines, we have essentially the same structure as a conventional program, with one main line and subroutines hung off it, and so on. Now, instead of just making a single program more complex, as is done in conventional programming, let us head off in a rather different direction: visualize an application built up of many such main-line programs running concurrently, passing IPs around between them. This is very like a factory with many machines all running at the same time, connected by conveyor belts. Things being worked on (cars, ingots, radios, bottles) travel over the conveyor belts from one machine to another. In fact, there are many analogies we might use: cafeterias, offices with memos flowing between them, people at a cocktail party, and so forth. After I had been working with these concepts for several years, I took my children to look at a soft-drink bottling plant. We saw machines for filling the bottles, machines for putting caps on them and machines for sticking on labels, but it is the connectivity and the flow between these various machines that ensures that what you buy in the store is filled with the right stuff and hasn't all leaked out before you purchase it!

An FBP application may thus be thought of as a "data factory". The purpose of any application is to take data and process it, much as an ingot is transformed into a finished metal part. In the old days, we thought that it would be possible to design *software* factories, but now we see that this was the wrong image: we don't want to mass-produce code – we want less code, rather than more. In hindsight it is obvious – it is the data which has to be converted into useful information in a factory, not the programs.

Now think of the differences between the characteristics of such a factory and those of a conventional, single main-line program. In any factory, many processes are going on at the same time, and synchronization is only necessary at the level of an individual work item. In conventional programming, we have to know exactly when events take place, otherwise things are not going to work right. This is largely because of the way the storage of today's computers works – if data is not processed in exactly the right sequence, we will get wrong results, and we may not even be aware that it has happened! There is no flexibility or adaptability. In our factory image, on the other hand, we don't really care if one machine runs before or after another, as long as processes are applied to a given work item in the right order. For instance, a bottle must be filled before it is capped, but this does not mean that all the bottles must be filled before any of them can be capped. It turns out that conventional programs are full of this kind of unnecessary synchronization, which reduces productivity, puts unnecessary strains on the programmers and generally makes application maintenance somewhere between difficult and impossible. In a real factory, unnecessary constraints of this sort would mean that some machines would not be utilized efficiently. In programming, it means that code steps have to be forced into a single sequence which is extremely difficult for humans to visualize correctly, because of a mistaken belief that the machine requires it. It doesn't!

Similarly, an application can be expressed as a network of simple programs, with data (more usually their handles) travelling between them, and in fact we find that this takes advantage of developers' visual or "spatial" imagination. It is also a good match with the design methodologies generally referred to under the umbrella of Structured Analysis. The so-called "Jackson inversion model" (M. Jackson 1975) designs applications in this form, but then proposes that all the processes except one (the main-line) be "inverted" into subroutines. This is no longer necessary! Interestingly, Jackson starts off his discussion of program inversion with a description of a simple multiprogramming scheme, using a connection with a capacity of one (in our terminology). He then goes on to say, "Multi-programming is expensive. Unless we have an unusually favourable environment we will not wish to use the sledgehammer of multi-programming to crack the nut of a small structure clash." In FBP we have that "unusually favourable environment", and I and a number of other people believe he wrote off multi-programming much too fast!

How do we get multiple "machines" to run concurrently on a single computer? There are several ways of doing this : the most common are "threads" and "fibres" – all the early implementations of FBP ran on a single processor, so they ran what are now being called "fibres". More recently, we have started building threads-based implementations that also take advantage of multiple processors. In the case of fibres, we let our "machines" run until they are blocked, at which point they are suspended, and another "machine" gets to run. Dijkstra called such processes "sequential processes", and explains that the trick is that they do not know that they have been suspended. Their logic is unchanged – they are just "stretched" in time. In the case of threads, processing can switch from one thread to another at any point, but, provided the processor has plenty of work to do, this will usually happen when the first thread has nothing to do for a while, i.e. while it is suspended, waiting on some service. I should stress that, in the case of the threads-based implementations, the simplest technique is simply to allocate one thread per process – Sven Steinseifer, who has done a lot to improve JavaFBP and therefore indirectly C#FBP, has determined that, given the numbers of threads in a typical FBP application, this does not result in any degradation. However he says, "... the current threads-based JavaFBP implementation doesn't scale well beyond "typical" FBP applications. This may be a serious limitation for some applications." We will talk about the performance requirements of the newer, high data volume, applications that we are starting to run into, in Chapter 21, "Performance Considerations" (page 210).

What causes the suspension? Well, I/O is one reason, but the most common reason in FBP is when a process wants to receive data from, or to send data to, another process that it is communicating with. Processes are connected by means of FIFO (first-in, first-out) queues or connections which can hold up to some maximum number of IPs (called a queue's "capacity"). For a given queue, this capacity may run from one to quite large numbers. Connections use slightly different verbs from files, so we will convert the pseudocode in the previous example, replacing:

- "read" with "receive"
- "write" with "send"
- "discard" with "drop"
- "end of file" with "end of data"

Chap. III: Basic Concepts

A "receive" service may get blocked because there is no data currently in the connection, and a "send" may be blocked because the connection is full and cannot accept any more data for a while. Think of a conveyor belt with room for just so many bottles, televisions, or whatever: it can be empty, full or some state in between. All these situations are normally just temporary, of course, and will change over time. We have to give connections a maximum capacity, not only so that our applications will fit into available storage, but also so that all data will eventually be processed (otherwise data could just accumulate in connections and never get processed).

Now processes cannot name their neighbours, or connections either, directly – they refer to them by naming "ports", the points where processes and connections meet. More about ports later.

The previous pseudocode now looks like this:

```
receive from IN using a
do while receive has not reached end of data
    if c is true
        send a to OUT
    else
        drop a
    endif
    receive from IN using a
enddo
```

Figure 3.4

I deliberately used the word "using" on the "receive" to stress the nature of "a" as a handle, but "send a" seems more natural than "send using a". Note the differences between our file processing program and our FBP component:

- differences in the verbs (already mentioned)
- IPs "out there", rather than records in storage
- IPs must be positively disposed of
- port names instead of file names.

We said earlier that IPs are things which have to be explicitly destroyed – in our multi-process implementation, we require that all IPs be accounted for: any process which receives an IP has its "number of owned IPs" incremented, and must reduce this number back to zero before it exits. It can do this in essentially the same ways we dispose of a memo: destroy it, pass it on or file it. Of course, you can't dispose of an IP (or even access it) if you don't have its handle (or if its handle has been reused to designate another IP). Just like a memo, an IP cannot be reaccessed by a process once it has been disposed of (in most FBP implementations we clear the handle after disposing of the IP to prevent exactly that from happening).

To get philosophical for a moment, proponents of "garbage collection" tend to feel that IPs should disappear when nobody is looking at them (no handles reference them), but the majority of the developers of FBP implementations felt that that was exactly what was wrong with conventional programming: things could disappear much too easily. So we insisted that a process get rid of all of its IPs, explicitly, one way or another, before it gives up control. If you inject an IP in at one end of the network, you know it is going to get processed unless or until some process explicitly destroys it! Conversely, if you build a table IP, and forget to drop it when you are finished, many people might argue that it would be nice to have the system dispose of it for you. On the other hand... I could argue that such an error (if it is an error) may be a sign of something more fundamentally wrong with the design or the code. And anyway, all recent FBP implementations detect this error, and list the IPs not disposed of, so it is easy to figure out what you did wrong. So..., if we can do that, why not let garbage collection be automatic? Well, our team took a vote, and strict accounting won by a solid majority! It might have lost if the group had had a different composition! Theoretically, we could make this both an environmental decision and an attribute of each component, so we could detect if a "loose" component was being run in a "tight" shop, but we have never felt a strong need to do this (so far).

By the way, various types of protection have been implemented in the different FBP implementations, so IPs are fairly robust. One example is that (in the non-OO implementations) we added a "guard" character at the end of an IP's data area. If a receive detected that the guard character had been corrupted, then the IP must have been corrupted by "rogue" code; if the corruption was detected by a send, then it was the sending component itself that did the damage!

Now what are "IN" and "OUT" that our pseudocode receives IPs from and sends them to? They are not the names of connections, as this would tie a component's code to one place in the network, but are things called "ports". "Portae" means "gates" in Latin, and ports (like seaports) can be thought of as specific places in a wall or boundary where things or people go in or out. Weinberg (1975) describes a port as

> "... a special place on the boundary through which input and output flow... Only within the location of the port can the dangerous processes of input and output take place, and by so localizing these processes, special mechanisms may be brought to bear on the special problems of input and output.

Now doors have an "inside" aspect and an "outside" aspect – the name of the inside aspect might be used by people inside the house to refer to doors, e.g. "let the cat out the side door", while the outside aspect is related to what the door opens onto, and will be of interest to city planners or visitors. Ports in FBP have the same sort of dual function: they allow an FBP component to refer to them without needing to be aware of what they open onto. Port names establish a relationship between the receives and sends inside the program and program structure information defined outside the component. This somewhat resembles subroutine parameters, where the inside (parameters) and the outside (arguments) have to correspond, even though they are compiled separately. In the case of parameters, this correspondence is usually established by means of position (sequence number). In fact, in AMPS and DFDM, ports were identified by numbers rather than by names. While this convention gives improved performance by allowing ports to be located faster, our experience is that users generally find names easier to relate to than numbers – just as we say "back door" and "front door", rather than "door 1", "door 3", etc. For this reason, THREADS and its successors use port names, not numbers.

Some ports can be defined to be arrays, so that they are referenced by an index as well as a name. Thus, instead of sending to a single OUT port, some components can have a variable number of OUT ports, and can therefore say "send this IP to the first (or nth) OUT port". This can be very useful for components which, say, make multiple copies of a given set of information. The individual slots of an array-type port are called "port elements". Naturally you can also have array-type ports as input ports, which might for instance be used in components which do various kinds of merge operation. Finally, the component may need to find out how many elements an array-type port contains, and which ones are connected.

Now let's draw a picture of the component we built above. It's called a "filter" and looks like this:

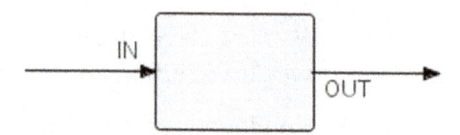

Figure 3.5

This component type has a characteristic "shape", which we will encounter frequently in what follows. FBP is a graphical style of programming, and its usability is much enhanced by (although it does not require) a good picture-drawing tool. Pictures are an international language and we have found that FBP provides an excellent medium of communication between application designers and developers and the other people in an organization who need to be involved in the development process.

Now we will draw a different shape of component, called a "selector". Its function is to apply some criterion "c" to all incoming IPs (they are received at port IN), and send out the ones that match the specified criterion to one output port (ACC), while sending the rejected ones to the other output port (REJ). The corresponding picture is shown in Figure 3.6.

Chap. III: Basic Concepts

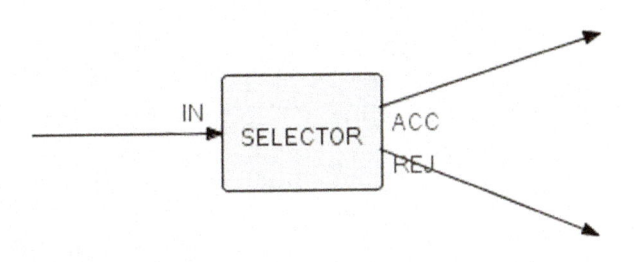

Figure 3.6

You will probably have figured out the logic for this component yourself. In any case, here it is:

```
receive from IN using a
do while receive has not reached end of data
    if c is true
        send a to ACC
    else
        send a to REJ
    endif
    receive from IN using a
enddo
```
- No drop?

Figure 3.7

Writing components is very much like writing simple main-line programs. Things really get interesting when we decide to put them together. Suppose we want to apply the filter to some data and then apply the selector to the output of the filter: all we need to record is that, for this application, OUT of FILTER is connected to IN of SELECTOR. You will notice that IN is used as a port name by both FILTER and SELECTOR, but this is not a problem, as port names only have to be unique within a given component, not across an entire application.

Let us draw this schematically in Figure 3.8.

We have just drawn our first (partial) FBP structure! FBP lets you reconfigure such networks in any way you like – add components, remove them, rearrange them, etc., endlessly. This is the famous "Legoland programming" which we have all been waiting for!

- 29 -

Chap. III: Basic Concepts

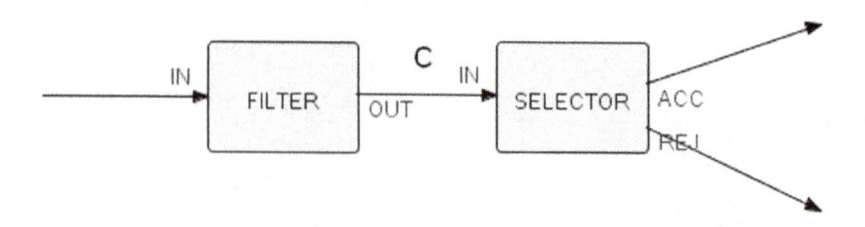

Figure 3.8

Now what is the line marked "C" in the diagram? It is the connection across which IPs will travel when passing from FILTER to SELECTOR. It may be thought of as a pipe which can hold up to some maximum number of IPs (its "capacity"). So to define this structure we have to record the fact that OUT of FILTER is connected to IN of SELECTOR by means of a connection with capacity of "n".

Now how do we prove to our satisfaction that this connection is processing our data correctly? In the early days of FBP there was a certain nervousness due to the fact that the timing of events isn't predetermined. So we came up with the following two laws or constraints that apply to IPs passing between any two processes, to ensure complete and accurate processing. Using the names in the above example, then:

- every IP must arrive at SELECTOR *after* it leaves FILTER

- any pair of IPs leaving FILTER in a given sequence must arrive at SELECTOR *in the same sequence*

The first constraint is called the "flow" constraint, while the second is called the "order-preserving" constraint. If you think about it using a factory analogy, this is all you need to ensure correct processing. Suppose two processes A and B respectively generate and consume two IPs, X and Y. A will send X, then send Y; B will receive X, then receive Y (order-preserving constraint).   Also, B must receive X after A sends it, and similarly for Y (flow constraint). This does not mean that B cannot issue its "receives" earlier – it will just be suspended until the data arrives. It also does not matter whether A sends Y out before or after B receives X. The system is perfectly free to do whatever results in the best performance. We can show this schematically – clearly the second diagonal line can slide forward or back in time without affecting the final result. This is shown in the following diagram.

- 30 -

Chap. III: Basic Concepts

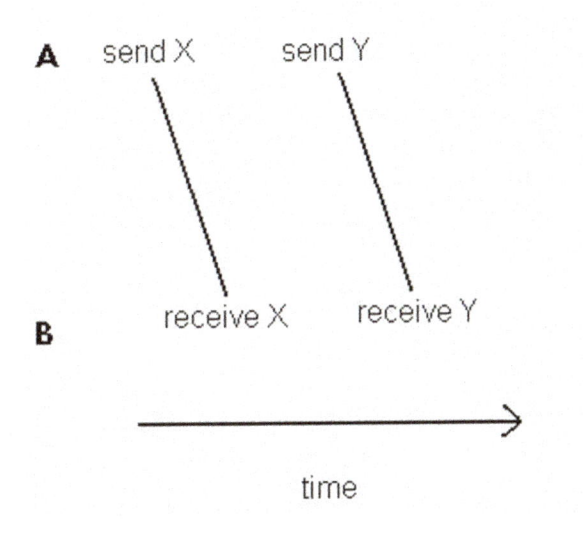

Figure 3.9

Connections may have more than one input end, but they may only have one output. IPs from multiple sources will merge on a connection, arriving at the other end in "first come, first served" sequence. It can be argued that by allowing this, we lose the predictability of the relationship between output and input, but it is easy enough to put a code in the IPs if you ever want to separate them again.

Up to now, we have been ignoring where IPs come from originally. We have talked about receiving them, sending them and dropping them, but presumably they must have originally come into existence at some point in time. This very essential function is called "create" and is the responsibility of whichever component first decides that an IP is needed. The "lifetime" of an IP is the interval between the time it is created and the time it is destroyed.

How does this apply to a business application? Well, most of the IPs in an application are created from file records: the file records are turned into IPs at file reading time, and the IPs are turned back into file records (and then destroyed) at file writing time. There are two standard components to do these functions (Read Sequential and Write Sequential). However, it often happens that you decide to create a brand new IP for a particular purpose which may never appear on a file – one example of these are the "control IPs" which we will describe in Chapter 9 (page 90), or another example might be a counting component which counts the IPs it receives using a "counter" IP, which will eventually be sent to a special output port when the component terminates.

This is the typical logic of a Counter component (by the way, the FBP convention is for this kind of component to try to send incoming IPs to an output port, and drop them if this port is not connected (the port should be specified as "optional" in the metadata):

- 31 -

Chap. III: Basic Concepts

```
        create counter IP using c
        zero out counter field in counter IP
        receive from IN using a
        do while receive has not reached end of data
            increment count in counter IP
            if port OUT connected
                send a to OUT
            else
                drop a
            endif
            receive from IN using a
        enddo
        send c to COUNT port
```

Figure 3.10

To show how natural this is in an object-oriented language, I will code this up as (most of) a JavaFBP component. Other minor parts of the code, e.g. metadata, will be described in the Appendix on JavaFBP. You will see a method containing the execution logic, and a separate one that initializes the component's port variables.

```
OutputPort outPort, countPort;
InputPort inPort;

protected void execute() {
  int count = 0;

  Packet p;
  while ((p = inPort.receive()) != null) {
    count++;
    if (outPort.isConnected()) {
      outPort.send(p);
    } else {
      drop(p);
    }
  }
  Packet ctp = create(Integer.toString(count));
  countPort.send(ctp);
}

protected void openPorts() {
  inPort = openInput("IN");
  outPort = openOutput("OUT");
  countPort = openOutput("COUNT");
}
```

Figure 3.11

Chap. III: Basic Concepts

In both JavaFBP and C#FBP, end of data on an input port is signalled by the `receive()` returning a null value. For reasons that hopefully will be clear later, no ports have to be explicitly closed.

To discover whether OUT is connected, we use the `isConnected()` method. If the send works, the IP is disposed of; if not, we still have it, so we dispose of it by dropping it. What if COUNT is not connected? Since the whole point of this component is to calculate a count, if COUNT is not connected there's not much point in even running this component, so we can just let it crash, or, perhaps better, test for this condition right up front.

As we said above, all IPs must eventually be disposed of, and this will be done by some function which knows that the IP in question is no longer needed. This will often be Writer components, but not necessarily.

At the beginning of this chapter, we talked about data as being primary. In FBP it is not file records which are primary, but the IPs passing through the application's processes and connections. Our experience is that this is almost the first thing an FBP designer must think about. Once you start by designing your IPs first, you realize that file records are only one of the ways a particular process may decide to store IPs. The other thing file records are used for is to act as interfaces with other systems, but even here they still have to be converted to IPs before another process can handle them.

Let's think about the IPs passing across any given connection. Clearly they must be in a format that the upstream process can output and the downstream process can handle. The FBP methodology requires the designer to describe the IPs first, and then define the transforms which apply to them. If two connected components have different requirements for their data, it is simple to insert a "transform" component between them. The general rule is that two neighbours must either agree on the format of data they share, or agree on data descriptions which encode the data format in some way. Naturally, if both components are written in Java and are running under JavaFBP, it is sufficient that the output of one and the input of the other specify the same class. However, even here, things may get a bit more complex.

Suppose, for instance, that process *B* can handle two formats of IP. In the OO world, the downstream component can simply test the class of the incoming IP. In a non-OO world, there will have to be a way for *A* to indicate to *B* for each IP what format it is in, e.g. by an agreed-upon code in a field, by IP length, by a preceding IP, or whatever. An interesting variant of this is to use free-form data. There may in fact be situations where you don't want to tie the format of IPs down too tightly, e.g. when communicating between subsystems which are both undergoing change. To separate the various fields or sections, you could imbed delimiters into the data. You will pay more in CPU time, but this may well be worth it if it will reduce your maintenance costs. XML is now a de facto standard for this kind of thing – warts and all!

The FBP implementation that actually went on the market, called DFDM, provided mechanisms

Chap. III: Basic Concepts

for attaching standard descriptions to IPs, called Descriptors, allowing them to be used and reused in more and more applications. Descriptors allowed individual fields in IPs to be retrieved or replaced by name – I will be describing them in more detail in Chapter 11 (page 110). In the later (OO) implementations (JavaFBP and C#FBP) this is not provided as part of the software, as this kind of thing can be done using reflection.

The next concept I want to describe is the ability to group components into packages which can be used as if they were components in their own right. This kind of component is called a "composite component". It is built up out of lower-level components, but on the outside it looks just like any other component. Components which are not built up of lower-level components are called "elementary", and can be written in any appropriate programming language.

To make a composite component look like other components from the outside, obviously it must have ports of its own. We will therefore take the previous diagram, and show how we can package it into a composite called *COMPA*:

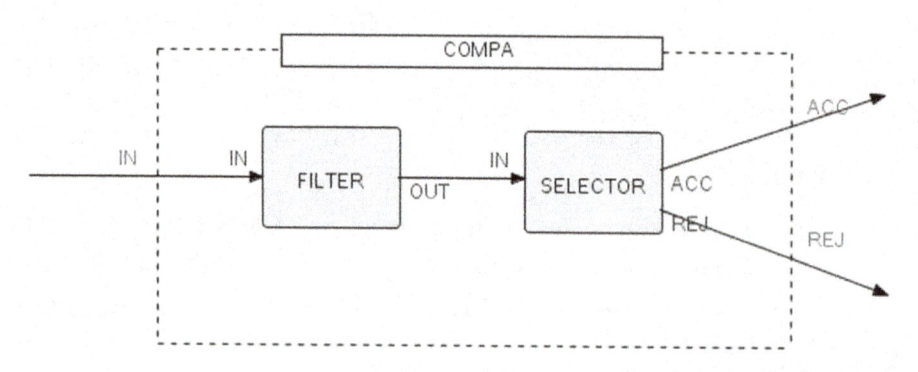

Figure 3.12

Once we have done this, *COMPA* can be used by anyone who knows what formats of data may be presented at port IN of *COMPA* and what formats will be sent out of its ACC and REJ ports. You will notice that it is quite acceptable for our composite to have the same port names as one of its internal components. You might also decide to connect the ACC port inside to the REJ port outside, and vice versa – what you would then have is a Rejector composite process, rather than an Acceptor. Of course *COMPA* is not a very informative name, and in fact we probably wouldn't bother to make this function a composite unless we considered it a useful tool which we expected to be able to reuse in the future.

Notice also that we have shown the insides of *COMPA* – from the outside it looks like a regular component with one input port and two output ports, as shown in Figure 3.13.

Now, clearly, any port on a composite must have corresponding ports "on the inside". However, the inverse is not required – not all ports on the inside have to be connected on the outside – if an

Chap. III: Basic Concepts

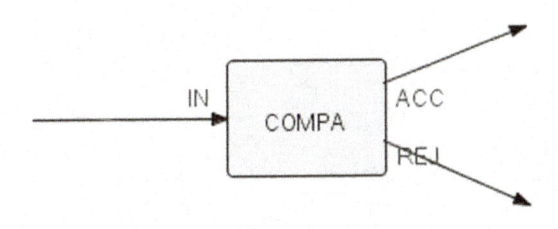

[Figure: COMPA component with IN port on left, ACC and REJ ports on right]

Figure 3.13

inside component tries to send to an unconnected composite port, it will get a return of "unconnected" or "closed", depending on the implementation.

We have now introduced informally the ideas of "port", "connection", "elementary component", "composite component" and "information packet".

At this point, we should ask: just what are the things we are connecting together? We have spoken as though they were components themselves, but actually they are uses or occurrences of components. There is no reason why we cannot use the same component many times in the same structure. Let us take the above structure (shown in Figure 3.8) and reverse it, as follows:

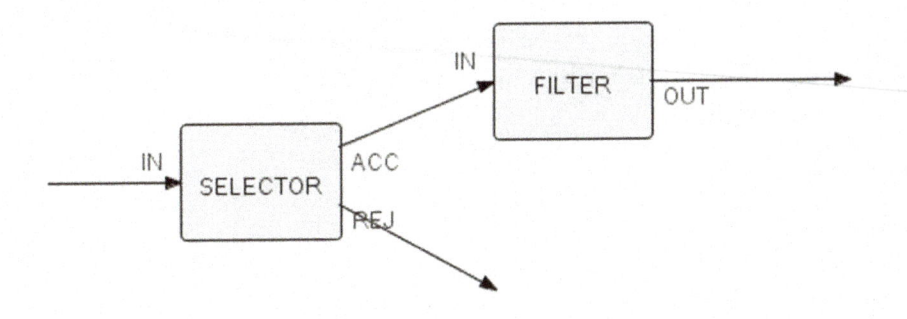

[Figure: SELECTOR with IN port, ACC port connecting to FILTER's IN port, FILTER has OUT port; SELECTOR also has REJ port]

Figure 3.14

Let's attach another FILTER to the REJ port of *SELECTOR*. Now the picture looks as follows:

- 35 -

Chap. III: Basic Concepts

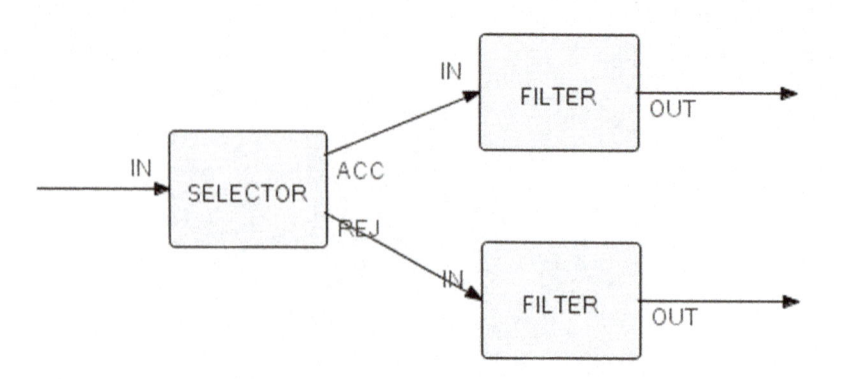

Figure 3.15

Here we have two occurrences of the *FILTER* component running concurrently, one "filtering" the accepted IPs from *SELECTOR*, the other filtering the rejected ones. This is no different from having two copiers in the same office. If we have only one copier, we don't have to identify it further, but if we have more than one, we have to identify which one we mean by describing them or labelling them – we could call one "copier A" and the other "copier B". Similarly, in most earlier FBP implementations, we took the name of the component and added a qualifier. However, in JavaFBP and C#FBP, we use OO conventions, and implement the component as a class, and the process as an instance of that class. We then give each process (component instance) a descriptive name, and use these names when specifying the connections between processes.

The following shows how this can be written in the simplest JavaFBP notation (omitting package name, imports and `main` method).

```
public class Xxxxx extends Network {

 protected void define() {
 component("Select", Selector.class);
 component("Filter1", Filter.class);
 component("Filter2", Filter.class);

 connect("Select.ACC", "Filter1.IN");
 connect("Select.REJ", "Filter2.IN");
 etc.
   }
}
```

Figure 3.16

- 36 -

Chap. III: Basic Concepts

In what follows, I will be referring to these component occurrences as "processes", even though, as we said above, this term could cause confusion. However, it seems the best option so far, and it is time to explain this concept in more depth. In conventional programming, we talk about a program "performing some function", but actually it is the machine which does the function – the program just encodes the rules the machine is to follow. In conventional, single-threaded, programming, usually we don't have to worry about this, but in FBP (as also in operating system design and a number of other specialized areas of computing) we have to look a little more closely at this idea. In FBP, the different components are executed by the processor in an interleaved manner, where the processor gives time to each component in turn. Since you can have multiple occurrences of the same component, with each occurrence being given its own series of time slots and its own working storage, we need a term for the thing which the processor is allocating time slices to – we call this a "process". The process is what the processor "multithreads" (some systems distinguish between processes and threads, but we will only use the term "process" in what follows). Since multiple processes may execute the same code, we may find situations where the first process using the code gets suspended, the code is again entered at the top by another process, which then gets suspended, and then the first process resumes at the point where it left off. Obviously, the program cannot modify its own code (unless it restores the code before it can be used by another process), otherwise strange things may happen! In programming terms, the code has to be "read-only".

Although this may sound arcane, it is not really that far removed from everyday life. Imagine two people reading a poster at the same time: neither of them needs to be aware of the point in the text the other one has reached. Either one of the readers can go away for a while and come back later and resume at the point where he or she left off, without interfering in the least with the other reader. This works because the poster does not change during the reading process. If, on the other hand, one person changes the poster while the other is trying to read it, they would have to be synchronized in some way, to prevent utter confusion on the part of the reader, at least.

We can now make an important distinction: composite components contain patterns of processes, not components. This becomes obvious when you think of a structure like the previous one – the definition of that composite has three nodes, but two of them are implemented by the same component, so they must be different processes. Of course, they don't become "real" processes until they actually run, but the nodes correspond one-to-one with processes, so they can be referred to as processes without causing confusion. Here is the same diagram shown as a composite:

- 37 -

Chap. III: Basic Concepts

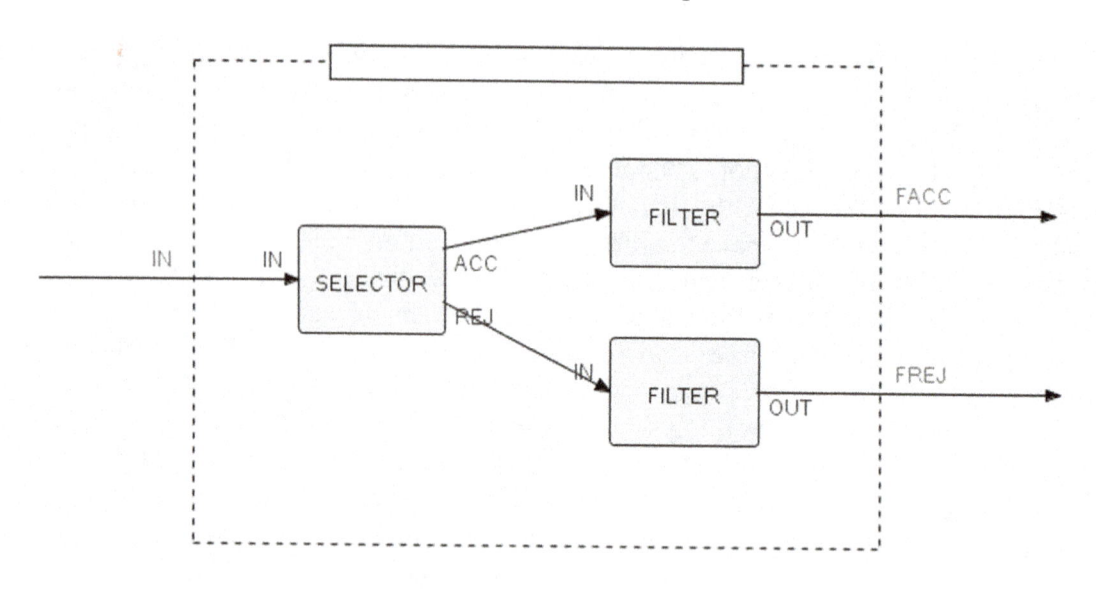

Figure 3.17

When this composite runs, there will be three processes running in it, executing the code of two components.

Lastly, I would like to introduce the FBP concepts of data streams and brackets. A "stream" is the entire series of IPs passing across a particular connection. Normally a stream does not exist all at the same time – the stream is continually being generated by one process and consumed by another, so only those IPs which can fit into the connection capacity could possibly exist at the same time (and perhaps not even that many). Think of a train track with tunnels at various points. Now imagine a train long enough that the front is in one tunnel while the end is still in the previous tunnel. All you can see is the part of the train on the track between the tunnels, which is a kind of window showing you an ever-changing section of the train. The IP stream as a whole is a well-defined entity (rather like the train) with a defined length, but all that exists at any point in time is the part traversing the connection. This concept is key to what follows, as it is the only technique which allows a very long stream of data to be processed using a reasonable amount of resources.

Just as an FBP application can be thought of as a structure of processes linked by connections, an application can also be thought of as a system of streams linked by processes. Up to now, we have sat on a process and watched the data as it is consumed or generated. Another, highly productive way of looking at your application is to sit on an IP and watch as it travels from process to process through the network, from its birth (creation) to its death (destruction). As it arrives at each process, it triggers an activity, much like the electrical signal which causes your phone to ring. Electrical signals are often shown in the textbooks like this:

Chap. III: Basic Concepts

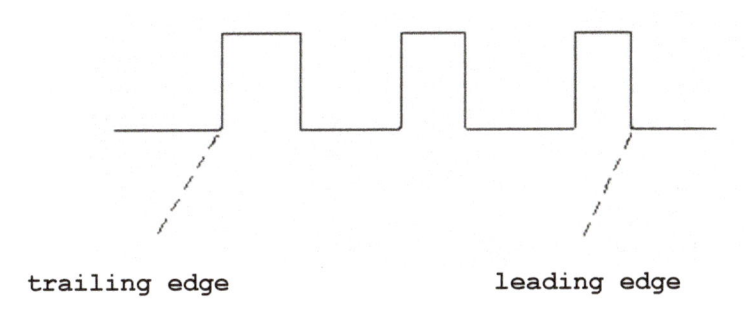

```
       ___      ___      ___
      |   |    |   |    |   |
      |   |    |   |    |   |
_____|   |____|   |____|   |_____
        /                /
       /                /
      /                /
     /                /
   trailing edge    leading edge
```

Figure 3.18

The moment when the leading edge reaches something that can respond to it is an *event*. In the same way, every IP has both a data aspect and a control aspect. Not only is an IP a carrier of data, but its moment of arrival at a process is a distinct event. Some data streams consist of totally independent IPs, but most streams are patterns of IPs (often nested, i.e. smaller patterns within larger patterns) over time. As you design your application, you should decide what the various data streams are, and then you will find the processes falling out very naturally. The data streams which tend to drive all the others are the ones which humans will see, e.g. reports, etc., so you design these first. Then you design the processes which generate these, then the processes which generate their input, and so on. This approach to design might be called "output backwards"....

Clearly a stream can vary in size all the way from a single IP to many millions, and in fact it is unusual for all the IPs in the stream to be of the same type. It is much more common for the stream to consist of repeating patterns, e.g. the stream might contain multiple occurrences of the following pattern: a master record followed by zero or more detail records. You often get patterns within patterns, e.g.

```
'm' patterns of:
    city record, each one followed by
    'n' patterns of:
        customer record, each one followed by
        'p' sales detail records for each customer
```

Figure 3.19

You will notice that this is in fact a standard hierarchical structure. The stream is in fact a "linearized" hierarchy.

To simplify the processing of these stream structures, FBP uses a special kind of IP called a "bracket". These enable an upstream process to insert grouping information into the stream so that downstream processes do not have to constantly compare key fields to determine where one group finishes and the next one starts. As you might expect, brackets are of two types: "open brackets" and "close brackets". A group of IPs surrounded by a pair of brackets is called a

Chap. III: Basic Concepts

"substream".

A very useful technique when processing substreams is the use of "control" IPs to "represent" a stream or substream. Almost all FBP implementations have the concept of a process-related stack, which is used to hold IPs in a LIFO sequence. In Chapter 9 (page 90), I will be describing how these concepts can be combined.

We have now introduced the following concepts: process

- component (composite and elementary)
- information packet (IP)
- structure
- connection
- port and port element
- stream
- substream
- bracket

Normally at this stage in a conventional programming manual we would leave you to start writing programs on your own. However, this is as unreasonable as expecting an engineer to start building bridges based on text-book information about girders and rivets. FBP is an engineering-style discipline, and there is a body of accumulated experience based on the above concepts, which you can and should take advantage of. Of course, you will develop your own innovations, which you will want to disseminate into the community of FBP users, but this will be built on top of the existing body of knowledge. You may even decide that some of what has gone before is wrong, and that is standard in an engineering-type discipline also. Isaac Newton said: "If I have seen further than other men, it is because I have stood on the shoulders of giants." Someone else said about (conventional, not FBP) programming: "We do not stand on their shoulders; we stand on their toes!" Programmers can now stop wearing steel-toed shoes!

Before we can see how to put these concepts together to do real work, two related ideas remain to be discussed: the design of reusable components and parametrization of such components (see the next chapter).

Chap. IV: Reuse of Components

"Reuse in DFDM [the 2nd FBP implementation] is natural. DFDM's technology is unsurpassed in its promotion of reuse as compared to other reuse technologies currently being promoted" (from an evaluation of DFDM performed by an IBM site in the US in 1988).

So far, we have spoken as though components are created "out of thin air" for a specific problem. You may well have suspected that I selected my components to illustrate certain concepts, without worrying about whether they would be useful in a real application. Well, the good news is that the kinds of components we have run into are in fact the ones which experience shows are very useful for building real applications. The bad (?) news is that it requires a large amount of experience in programming and a certain creative flair to come up with useful components. This should not be so surprising when you think about useful tools you are accustomed to using in real life. Where and when was the first hammer invented? Imagine a whole series of "proto-hammers", for instance reindeer horns, rocks attached to sticks, etc., gradually evolving into what we are used to today, with a claw on one side, and balanced just so.... Perhaps we should qualify that by saying "in the West". Different cultures will come up with different tools or different forms of the same tool. I seem to remember from my anthropology classes that the Australian aboriginals have a wonderful tool which is a combination of all the things they find most useful in their everyday life, and yet is highly portable. It is a combination spear-thrower, shield, dish and fire-starter. These kinds of tools are not invented overnight – they take time and experience, requiring progressive refinement by many creative people. The best tools will always evolve in this way. Tools may also pass out of use as the need for them diminishes, or they are replaced by something more effective – buggy whips are the classical example, but usually it happens without our even noticing! When did they stop putting running-boards as a standard feature on cars?

Chap. IV: Reuse of Components

Clearly, culture and the tools we use are closely intertwined – we have strong ideas about what is the right tool for a given job, but another culture may in fact have a different definition of what that job is.... In the West we consider using a knife and fork the "proper" way to eat food – a few centuries ago, we were spearing it with the point of a dagger. Knives and forks in turn mean that an acceptable Western meal might include some very large chunks of meat, or even half a bird. In the Orient, on the other hand, people have been using chop-sticks for a very long time, which requires that the food be served in bite-size pieces. Notice that the choice of tools also helps to determine what part of the serving is performed by the diner and what part by the cook behind the scenes.

One other thing we should consider is the need to be able to use the tool in unforeseen situations. A useful tool should not be too restrictive in the ways it can be used – people will always think of more ways to use a tool than its original designer ever imagined. Wayne Stevens (1991) used to tell a story about an airline attendant using a hearing set (that little plastic stethoscope you plug into the arm of your chair) to tie back some curtains. Elegant? No. Effective? Yes! We don't want to make a hammer so intelligent that it can only be used on nails.... Another example: why do some functions have non-obvious names? There are well-known cases where a tool was originally designed for one job, but people found that it was even more useful for some function the original designer did not foresee. This is in fact a testimony to the robustness of these tools.

Just as in the preparation and consumption of food there are the two roles of cook and diner, in FBP application development there are two distinct roles: the component builder and the component user or application designer. The component builder decides the specification of a component, which must also include constraints on the format of incoming data IPs (including option IPs) and the format of output IPs. The specification should not describe the internal logic of the component, although attributes sometimes "leak" from internal to external (restrictions on use are usually of this type). The application designer builds applications using already existing components, or, where satisfactory ones do not exist, s/he will specify a new component, and then see about getting it built.

Component designers and users may of course be the same people, but there are two very different types of skill involved. This is somewhat like the designer of a recent popular game, who admitted he was not particularly fast at solving it – his skill was in designing games, not in playing them. The separation between makers and users is so widespread in real life that we don't pay any attention to it unless it breaks down. In industry, as Wayne Stevens points out, we take for granted the idea that airplane builders do not build their own chairs – they subcontract them to chair manufacturers, who in turn subcontract the cloth to textile manufacturers and so on. In contrast, the world of conventional programming is as if every builder designed his own nails, lumber and dry-wall from scratch. Talk about "reinventing the wheel" – in conventional application development we reinvent the rubber, the nuts and bolts, and even the shape of the wheel!

Chap. IV: Reuse of Components

I'd like to talk a little bit about how useful components are developed. They are unlikely to emerge from a pure "top-down" approach, or from a pure "bottom-up" approach. In the first case, you do not discover dry-wall by progressively breaking down an architect's drawing of a house. In the second case, people who dream up useful components have to be willing to subject them to rigorous testing in real life situations. Even after this has been done, they still may not sell. Nobody in industry would bet the business on some untried tool which had never been evaluated in the field (well, usually not), and yet we do this frequently in application development. Another of Wayne Stevens' recommendations is not to build a generalized tool until you have found yourself doing the same job three or four times. Otherwise, you may find yourself investing a lot of time and effort in features that nobody will ever use, and you may find yourself unable to respond to customer requests for features they really do want.

In FBP a lot of the basic components have analogues in an area which is no longer well-known, but has been very productive of generalized components over a number of years – namely, Unit Record machines. The first data processing shops I worked in were cavernous rooms with machines scattered all over the floor, with operators carrying decks of punched cards from one machine to another. An application was defined by a (paper) diagram showing the flow of data (decks of punched cards) from one machine to another. In those days we had specialized machines, such as sorters, tabulators, collators, etc., and people learned to wire (parametrize) them and link them together into applications very effectively. And you didn't need a college degree to get applications working. In fact, I once figured how to solve a problem with a tabulating machine plug-board, straight out of the bath, over the phone, dripping wet, without even notes or a schematic to look at!

Just as Unit Record machines worked with streams of punched cards, the corresponding FBP components work with streams of IPs. Let's call these "stream-based" components. Examples of such components are:

- sort
- collate
- split
- replicate
- count
- concatenate
- compare

These all have the characteristic that they process data streams and that they require very little information about the format of their incoming data streams. They typically have well-defined application-independent functions.

We might expand the list with some general-purpose components which get down to the data field level, but still do not "understand" business processing. One such component might be a generalized transform component. I believe such a component, properly parametrized, could in fact do a lot of the processing in a given business application. Nan Shu of IBM in Los Angeles has written extensively about a language which she calls FORMAL (Shu 1985) – its function is to take descriptions of files and the transformations between them and use them to do the transforming automatically. She found that a large amount of business processing consists of moving data around, changing its coding, and doing table look-ups, e.g. one application might use a number for each US state, while another might use a two-character abbreviation. This suggests that another type of function in this same class is a generalized table look-up function.

There is another general class of components which we could call "technology-dependent". These components usually require specialized knowledge to build, but, once created, can be used by people who are not as technically skilled. They thus encapsulate specialized knowledge. They will usually be written in a lower level language. We had an interesting example of this some years ago at the IBM Montréal Data Centre: we had someone on our staff who was *the* expert on paper tape. Paper tape is a now largely obsolete medium which had its own quirks. It had special codes for various purposes, and in particular had a convention for correcting data (you punch all holes across the offending character, which is then treated as though there was no character there at all). Our expert was able to write some components which generated regular IPs, so that no other component in the application needed to know that the input was paper tape. You could build and debug an application using regular I/O, and then, after you had it working, you could unplug the reader module and replace it with the paper tape reading module. This meant in turn that testing could be done without the tester having to monopolize a scarce (and slow) piece of equipment.

The two most widely used technology-dependent components are "Read Sequential" and "Write Sequential". As you might expect, these convert file records into IPs, and IPs into file records, respectively. A matching Read/Write pair of components can be used to encode and decode any file format desired. For instance, you might decide that the medium you are using is so expensive that you want to compress the data as it is stored, and expand it as you retrieve it. Another useful function pair might be encryption/decryption. In fact, any Read/Write component pair can be thought of as embodying a data organization. Generalizing this thought, a sequential Read/Write component pair provides a conversion between a format suitable for processing and a linear format on some medium. For instance, we built a Read/Write pair which was specialized for dumping tree structures onto a linear medium and rebuilding them later.

In FBP you will often run into matched pairs of components: other examples are: split/merge, read/write, compress/expand, encrypt/decrypt, etc. This is characteristic of many FBP components – what one component does, another one undoes. In fact the combination of a component and its inverse should ideally result in a stream identical to the original input stream, just as in mathematics multiplying a number by its reciprocal results in unity, or composing a function with its inverse results in the Identity function.

Using separate Read and Write processes not only gives the separation between logic and I/O which is recommended by the majority of application development methodologies, but actually reduces elapsed time. The reason for this surprising result is that in FBP (even in fibre-based implementations) an I/O process which has to wait on I/O only suspends itself – other processes can proceed. This means that FBP applications tend to use as much CPU time as they are allowed to by the operating system. We will be talking more about performance later on, in Chapter 21 (page 210).

Another useful group of components deriving originally from Unit Record are those connected with report generation. These include such functions as pagination and generation of page headings and footings, as well as totalling and subtotalling, "cross-footing" (totalling rows and columns of numbers and comparing the sums), and other report generation functions. Reports are very often the main vehicle of communication between an application and the humans who use it, and the importance of these facilities to the average business is borne out by the remarkable longevity of IBM's RPG, which, while often regarded as old-fashioned, is still fulfilling a real need in the market-place. Later in this book, I will describe a Report Generation component which was used extensively in our shop (Chapter 10, page 105).

A good guideline for the functionality of a component is that its specification should not exceed about a page. Some FBP enthusiasts have gone so far as to say that the summary of a component's function should not exceed one paragraph, and should not have the word "and" in it. Another guideline we have found useful is that generalized components should not have more than 4 ports (array ports only count as one port). Of course, these are only guidelines – some components bring so much function together that their parameters are essentially mini-languages, but their usefulness may outweigh any awkwardness in parametrization.

The last category of component is that of "business components". These embody business rules, and should hopefully be relatively simple, especially if you have used the other categories of component as far as possible. We can imagine business components for different business areas – banking, oil and gas, and so on. Some will be more mathematical, others less so. In all cases they represent the knowledge of some business expert.

After functionality, one of the major considerations in connection with designing business components is the likelihood of change. There are some types of business logic which hardly ever change, and others which are changed every time they are run. An example of the latter might be the logic to generate employee taxable income statements at the end of the year. It is changed every year and run once a year. It would be very nice if our governments could send out a single reusable component every year which companies could then just plug into their own payroll programs. This also gets back to the question of roles: who installs the new module? Application development or operations staff? If the former, you have an ongoing need for application developers indefinitely; if the latter, can you be sure that the new component will be adequately tested? On the other hand, given the backlog of work that application development

Chap. IV: Reuse of Components

usually faces, something which can just be loaded up and run by operational staff is certainly attractive.

It would help if such a component does as much validation of its input data as possible to make sure it is being used in the right context. Ideally a component should never crash – in practice, of course, it is almost impossible to prevent one component from destroying another's data, but it is certainly possible to add validation logic to protect against (say) data format errors.

The above discussion is really another form of the old compile-time versus run-time debate. In FBP, compile-time comes in two flavours: component-level and network-level. Actually parameters can be specified inside a composite component and still be outside the elementary component which they control! I predict that eventually a lot of business logic will be embodied in rules held in rules databases. Such rules, written in a suitable language, can then be modified by people outside the normal application development group. These rules may not even be expressed in what a programmer would recognize as a programming language.

A forerunner of this was the IBM Patient Care System for hospitals, marketed in the early '80s, in which a surprising amount of the system logic (including screen layouts) was held in the form of tables, designed to be updated by senior clerical or nursing staff. This was very effective, as these were usually the people who had to use the system, and had the most operational experience with it. Again we see the separate roles of application-developer and application-user. If it bothers you to put so much control in the hands of end users, either implement authorization systems to make sure only the right people can modify key data, or specify the rules as tables hard-coded in the application definition, but outside the components that refer to them. This way, control remains in the application development group, but systems become much easier to modify and debug. However, we really should be moving away from requiring the DP department to do all systems maintenance.

If I am right that we will eventually see more and more business logic being either imbedded in reusable components or captured as explicit rules on disk, then the role of the current higher level languages (HLLs) in the future should diminish. We found in our experience that, given a powerful set of reusable components, people would go to enormous lengths to avoid writing HLL code. Much of the time, the resulting poorer performance does not matter – the Kendall Report (1977) contrasted the running time of the average program with the person-months required to develop it. Programs that took 6 person-months to develop might run for a few minutes of machine time over their entire lifetimes. So, most of the time, minor increases in the amount of CPU time really make no difference. Only in the case of long-running jobs run regularly is it worthwhile to do performance tuning, and, as we shall see in a later chapter, it is much better to instrument an FBP application to find out where your real bottle-necks are than to try to guess ahead of time and waste time optimizing code which doesn't affect your system's performance much. There are in fact a number of ways to do performance tuning in the FBP environments, once we figure out where the real leverage is.

Chap. IV: Reuse of Components

Far more important than CPU time is human time, and the fundamental question is really what is the best way to spend valuable human time. When deciding to develop a new component, you must take in account the expected return on your investment ("ROI" for short). Every new component must be documented, tested, supported, advertised and incorporated into educational material (well, ideally – sometimes not all of these happen!). Small wonder, then, that our experience with FBP shows that application developers using FBP avoid writing new code – being responsible people, they are aware of the burden they take on the moment they start coding a new component. However, this realization isn't enough – we have to change the economics of the situation. Code is a cost item, as Dijkstra and others have pointed out, and someone who adds to the total amount of code when it is not justified is costing your company money, now and into the future. I have started suggesting, only half in jest, that programmers should be "penalized" for each line of code they write! It has been pointed out many times that people will modify their behaviour according to how you measure them – and companies which still measure productivity in Kloc (thousands of lines of code) get what they deserve! In fact, some program improvements involve removing code – is this negative productivity?! Conversely, someone who produces a useful reusable component improves the productivity of all of its users, and deserves to be rewarded – some companies have already started trying that – the key word, of course, being "useful". N.P. Edwards, whom I mentioned in an earlier chapter, was a key player in getting IBM to move to reusable parts in the hardware area, and he has told me that the key breakthrough there also was in changing the economics of hardware development.

Someone who has talked and written extensively about the importance of reuse is T. Capers Jones (e.g. Jones 1992) – he has also been aware of my work for some years and has been supportive of it. He has been active in promoting the use of code-independent metrics, such as Allan Albrecht's Function Points, for measuring productivity, and has done a lot of work on the potential of reuse for reducing the costs of application development.

How do we know whether a tool is useful? The only way is to measure its use. Will people use it? They will if it fits the hand, and if you provide support and education for it. That in turn means you have to have the infrastructure in place to allow your company to take advantage of this new technology, and measures and incentives to get people moving in the right direction.

There is also the opposite question: what if the tool is "less than perfect"? Just as with real tools, there is no perfect tool – there are only tools which fit your hand more or less conveniently. Like many programmers who tend to be perfectionists, you may be tempted to postpone putting something on the market because you feel it isn't finished yet. The question should be: is it useful as it is? You can always enhance it as time goes on, provided you keep the interfaces stable (or provide "expansion hooks" but maintain upward compatibility). In fact, after it has been in use for a while, you may find that the extensions people really want are not at all what you expected. Since your reusable component will hopefully be in widespread use by this time, it is important that you allow extension while maintaining upward compatibility. In FBP, the fact that ports are

Chap. IV: Reuse of Components

named helps you to do this; also parameters (described in the next chapter) should be designed to be extensible. Parameters can be in string format, with delimiters, or, if fixed form, it is a good idea to insert a few zero bits – these can always to changed to one, to indicate that there is an extension portion.

Another kind of modification which will happen to your modules occasionally is error correction. It is certainly a pleasurable feeling to know that you have improved a component which many people are or will be using, and you might think that your users will welcome the change with open arms. Unfortunately some of your users may have adjusted to the error, and will need to be convinced that you know what is right for them. The other thing users do is take advantage of undocumented features. I talked about a tool fitting the hand – it may fit the hand, even with an error in it. One team found an error in a DFDM component, but instead of telling us about it, they carefully compensated for it. When we fixed it, their programs stopped working! I think they were quite indignant for a while until everybody realized what had happened. We had to spend some time explaining that everyone would be much better off if we fixed the bug rather than leaving it the way it was! There is a very important rule which you should impress on your users: If it isn't documented, don't trust it. IBM learned the value of this one by bitter experience, and has accepted its wisdom since the day some bright user discovered an undocumented instruction on one of the 700-series machines. When IBM started making invalid instructions result in exception conditions, I'm told quite a few programs in universities and other places stopped working!

The next question is: how will people find out about these components? There is a common misconception that reusable componentry doesn't work unless you have an elaborate catalogue, which people can interrogate to find the tool they want. On the other hand, Wayne Stevens has pointed out that most examples of reuse in everyday life are done very naturally without any catalogue. We know by heart most of the things we use commonly. Let's say you go into a hardware store because you want to attach a wood base onto a ceramic pot – you will be familiar with half a dozen types of fastener: glue, nails, screws, rivets, etc. Most of the time you will know exactly what kind of glue to use. In this case, let's say you are not quite sure what is best. You still don't have to scan the entire store – most of the time, you can go right to the shelf and start reading labels. What do you do if you are not sure where in the store to go to? You ask a store clerk, who may in turn pass you onto someone who is an expert in a particular area. If your requirements are really unusual, the clerk may have to consult a catalogue, but this is likely to be a rare case. The point is that effective reuse doesn't require catalogues, although they can certainly help.

To try to measure the productivity gains we were getting from DFDM within IBM Canada, we kept statistics on the amount of reuse taking place over a number of projects. The figures for three projects are shown in the following diagram (the numbers relate to components):

Chap. IV: Reuse of Components

PROJECT	Type	Unique	Occurrences	Reuse Factor	Productivity Factor
A	Project	133	184	1.4	3.7
	Gen Purpose	21	305	14.5	
	Total	154	489	3.2	
	GP/T	0.14	0.62		
B	Project	46	48	1.0	7.7
	Gen Purpose	17	306	18.0	
	Total	63	354	5.6	
	GP/T	0.27	0.86		
C	Project	2	54	27.0	135.0
	Gen Purpose	8	216	27.0	
	Total	10	270	27.0	
	GP/T	0.80	0.80		

In this chart, "Project" means components coded specifically for the project in question, while "General Purpose" means components that are off-the-shelf (already available and officially supported). "Unique" means separate components (separate pieces of code), while "Occurrences" means total number of processes (component occurrences or network nodes). Thus project A used 154 distinct components, of which 21 came off the shelf, but accounted for 305 of the 489 processes (about 3/5). GP/T means General Purpose as a fraction of Total, and it is interesting to compare the GP/T for unique components against the GP/T for component occurrences.

The "Productivity Factor" is calculated as follows: *total* number of processes divided by number of project-coded components. Since the first figure represents the amount of work the program is doing while the second figure represents the the amount of work a programmer has to do (apart from hooking together the network), we felt that this productivity factor was quite a good measure of the amount of real reuse going on. It is actually the reciprocal of what Bob Kendall

Chap. IV: Reuse of Components

called the "Figure of Merit" (Kendall 1988). Bob Kendall's "Figure of Merit" followed the convention that smaller is better, but in this edition I decided to use its reciprocal instead, as it seems more intuitive to have the larger number indicate better reuse.

DFDM had been in use about 2 to 3 years in that shop, and we had about 40 off-the-shelf components available, so quite a lot of the common tasks could be done without having to code up any new components. However, when the programmer did have to code up components, you will notice that quite often this code could also be reused, giving reuse factors greater than 1 (Project C had a factor of 27.0). In the third example in the above chart, the programmer only had to write 2 components, although there were 270 separate processes in his program. (You can probably figure out that this project involved running 27 different files through essentially the same 10 processes – so it did a lot of work, with very little investment of programmer effort!).

Although we thought at first that this last case was just a quirk, we turned up quite a few applications which were not that different from this one (e.g. Rej's letter quoted in the Introduction).

Here are some figures from an evaluation of DFDM quoted from at the beginning of this chapter (remember – coroutines are what we now call components):

> All of the function in the DFDM pilot application is performed by 30 unique coroutines (this is the number of coroutines that an individual would need to be familiar with in order to understand the function of the application).
>
> A total of 95 occurrences of these 30 coroutines make up the application ..... providing a 3:1 reuse ratio.
>
> These 95 coroutines are leveraged through the use of subnets and CNS [Compiled Network Specification] networks to perform the equivalent work of 225 unleveraged coroutines.

Some companies have tried to encourage people to write generalized code by offering them money or kudos. One counsel I would give them is that you need to monitor not how *many* components someone has written, but how *often* it is used. An appropriate analogy is the system of royalties in the publishing industry. Every time a module is used, the author should get some kind of token, be it money or recognition. This will ensure that your company will not accumulate a collection of wonderful, Rube Goldbergish gadgets sitting on the proverbial shelf, gathering dust.

Let us say that you are all convinced that reusable code is the way to go – how do we get it adopted in your particular shop? You will find (unless all your people are super-altruists) that the biggest enemy of reuse is not technology – it is human psychology. While many people will

Chap. IV: Reuse of Components

accept the new ideas enthusiastically, others will resist them, and for several different reasons. People who have become good at delivering applications under time pressure very often feel that they must at all costs maintain control of everything they use, and in fact all their experience has taught them that this approach works. Components developed by others will be on their critical path, and they will be pulled between the desire to reduce their own effort by using pretested components, and the fear that the components they are relying on will not be ready in time, will break or will not be maintained as the environment changes. They have to become convinced that someone will support these components – if necessary, on a 24-hour basis. This may not be necessary technically, but may be very necessary psychologically!

Another source of resistance is simply that some programmers love the bits and bytes and don't want to become mere combiners of precoded components. There is a role for these people, writing the components to specs. As we said above, two different roles seem to be emerging: component builders and component users. In my view the latter need skills very similar to those required by analysts. They need to be able to talk to users, gather requirements, and even build systems or prototypes of systems. For the more complex parts or parts which have to perform better, they can subcontract parts to the component builders. This is the domain where the programmer's programmers ("Merlins", as a friend of mine used to call them) can shine. In some senses, a component becomes an encapsulation of their particular skill or knowledge. I have found that it makes sense to get "tighter" about the external specs and "looser" about how the code is built internally. This lets them express their creativity, while still serving the needs of the organization as a whole. Of course, it must not be so poorly written that it doesn't perform well! And it absolutely must deliver the function according to the specs! Once those are assured, then your only concern is maintainability. Generalized code should be maintainable, but you probably don't have to control the format of every internal label!

A programmer once said to me, "I don't like DFDM because I don't get dumps" (I should explain that in the old days, a malfunctioning program just generated a pile of hexadecimal code and data, called a "dump", which the programmers then had to pore through)! At the time I took this to mean that because programs built using FBP tend not to crash, it is hard for programmers to get a feel of how they work. Does not knowing how the engine of your car works make you nervous? It probably does affect some people that way, but most of us don't care. Later, I realized that it also brings up the very fundamental question of trust – if the users of a package don't trust the package or its vendor (same thing, really), they are not going to be happy... And trust is fragile: hard to build up, and easy to damage.

Let us suppose that your company has become convinced that developers should not keep "reinventing the wheel", but that, like most companies, you have only reached the stage where you are maintaining a library of shared subroutines. How do we get formalized sharing of components in place? Suppose I find out that Julia is working on a module which is pretty close to what I want but it needs some tweaking to fit my needs. In most shops, we don't even know

Chap. IV: Reuse of Components

what to call it. Companies that have just started to grapple with naming standards often think it's neat for module names to start with the project code. For instance, if I am managing project ABC, then I can name all my modules ABC-something. This way, I don't have to worry about my module names conflicting with those of other projects. Even the library names will often have ABC built into them! So, even to be able to find the code, we usually have to have some kind of enterprise-wide naming convention. Next question: who does the modification of the code and who pays for it? What if Julia's schedule slips and starts to impact my schedules? Even if everything goes really well, who will maintain it, document it, and support it?

Many writers about reuse agree that the only solution is to set up an independent department to write and maintain components. This department must have enough resources to do the job properly, which also involves publicizing and selling their product. One tendency which must be resisted is that such departments often get tied up producing complex, generalized tools for a few users, or even for none – they just figure the component would be neat and they'll worry about selling them afterwards. Remember the principle of ROI: the company as a whole will get more bang for the buck out of a lot of simple tools, especially if they communicate well with each other, rather than from a few very complex ones. Since good tools will often start as special-purpose modules which some other group has found useful, there must be a path for promoting such ad hoc components to a place where other people can find them and rely on them. Our centralized software support department must have ways to beat the bushes for new and interesting components and must then have ways to evaluate whether potential customers are interested (otherwise why go to all that trouble?). It must also avoid getting sucked into writing or upgrading complex tools which have only a small market. It is a service organization, so it must be service quality oriented, not just a group of self-styled experts who know what is best for everyone else. It must become entrepreneurial, but not exclusively bottom-line oriented. In short, it must follow good financial and engineering practices. If this takes a major shake-up in the way your organization is structured, then you should really get started as soon as possible!

I believe that, unless companies start to bring engineering-type disciplines to application development, not only will they fail to take full advantage of the potential of computers, but they will become more and more swamped with the burden of maintaining old systems. You can't do a lot about old systems – I know, I've seen lots of them – but new systems can be built in such a way that they are maintainable. It should also be possible to gradually convert old programs over to the FBP technology piece-meal, rather than "big bang". A director I once worked for called this "converting an iceberg into ice-cubes"!

I believe all true disciplines follow a sort of cycle through time, which may be represented as shown in Figure 4.1.

- 52 -

Chap. IV: Reuse of Components

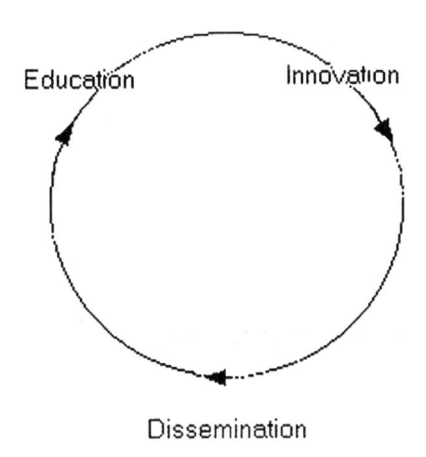

Education → Innovation → Dissemination (cycle diagram)

Figure 4.1

Innovation can only be founded on a base of solid knowledge of what went before – otherwise we are doomed to keep rediscovering the same old stale concepts. On the other hand, tradition without innovation cannot result in progress, and innovation is useless unless the word is gotten out to people who can make use of it. As I pointed out above, business application development has not really changed significantly since I started in the business in 1959 – but I really believe that now, at long last, we can start to see the promise of application development becoming a true engineering-style discipline.

Chap. V: Parametrization of Reusable Components

I would now like to describe the way generalized FBP components are made reusable, using one additional, very powerful FBP mechanism, the "Initial Information Packet" or "IIP". IIPs were proposed by E. Lawton of IBM in response to some of the problems we ran into using DFDM's parameter facility.

Let's say you have built a component like one of the ones described in the previous chapters. Let's call it "Select". It should be clear from the foregoing that this component can be used in a variety of contexts, as long as it is sent data in the format it expects. Because a component communicates with the outside world only through data being sent to or received from its ports, it can be held in object form, and never modified. Such reuse is often called "black box" reuse, to suggest the idea that the user cannot see the insides of the component. In addition, since the "black box" never needs to be modified, once its developer gets it working, it can be relied on to work correctly in any context. This is the converse of "white box" or "clear box" (source level) reuse, which is what most so-called reuse tools provide today. The latter type of reuse is easy to provide, but in my view doesn't buy its users much. It may reduce the cost of developing new code, but the amount of net new code which has to be maintained still increases. Furthermore, if a bug is found in the reused code, there is no easy way to tell whether it is safe to fix all instances of it – if you can even find them (with some reuse tools you can't even do that).

We will of course have to tell our black box Select component which fields to select on, as, otherwise, it will only be able to select on whichever fields were hard-wired into it. Suppose we want to tell it that it is to do its selecting on the contents of a field called `cust_id` in each incoming IP, and also want to give it a list of acceptable field values. In classical programming, we do this kind of thing by having the calling program specify parameters. In FBP we do something similar, but there is no user-written calling program in which to specify the

- 54 -

parameters. Instead there is a way for the application designer to specify this information, right in the application structure definition. This mechanism is called an Initial Information Packet (IIP). We also need an additional port on the component (let's call it OPTIONS, but of course it can have any name we want). An IIP is specified in the network definition and associated with the chosen port.

By the way, we are assuming that our generalized SELECT has some way of determining where in the record `cust_id` is to be found: in older languages, this would be converted via some kind of dictionary to an offset and length; in OO languages by reflection.

An IIP is turned into an ordinary IP by having the component issue a `receive()` call against the port the IIP is connected to. This has the added advantage that the OPTIONS port can also be fed by an upstream process instead of an IIP, so component options can either be decided at network definition time or deferred until execution time, without any modification of the component being required. In both cases, what the component sees when it does its receive from the OPTIONS port is an ordinary IP. In what follows, we will sometimes refer to this as an "options IP" – options IPs may start out life as IIPs or may be generated by upstream processes, but their function is primarily to control execution, rather than to carry data (obviously this is not a hard and fast distinction, and you may find a need for IPs which combine both functions).

One last point about options IPs: a major decision for the component designer is whether to make them free-form or give them a fixed layout – the former will generally be easier to specify, but is going to cost more processing time to scan for delimiters, convert numeric values, etc. However, since this processing is usually done just once, at the beginning of the run, it may not be significant in the context of total processing time.

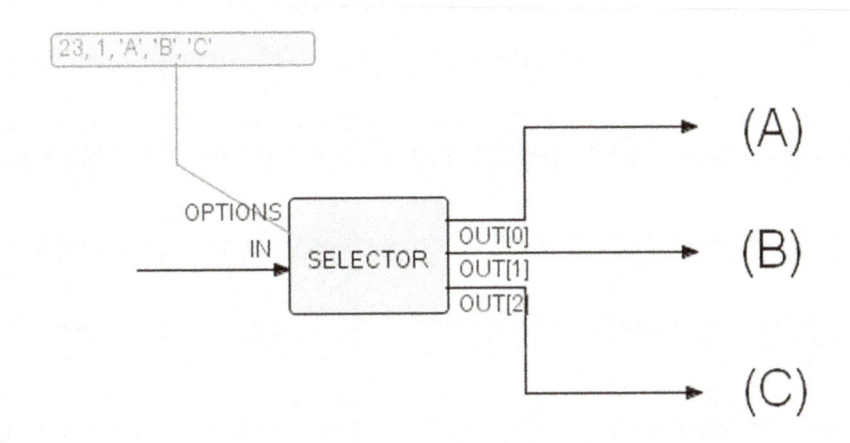

Figure 5.1

Chap. V: Parametrization of Reusable Components

The DrawFBP diagramming tool (described on page 340) is oriented towards free-form specification of IIPs.

Let's say we want to write a generalized selector where the field identification and permissible values are received from an OPTIONS port at execution time. Using a shallow rectangle to represent an IIP (by the way, you can't attach IIPs and regular processes to the same connection), we might represent our selector with its options IIP as shown in Figure 5.1. The field being selected on starts at offset 23, for a length of 1 byte. IPs with a value of A at that position will be sent to the zero'th element of port OUT, IPs containing a B go to the number 1 element, and so on.

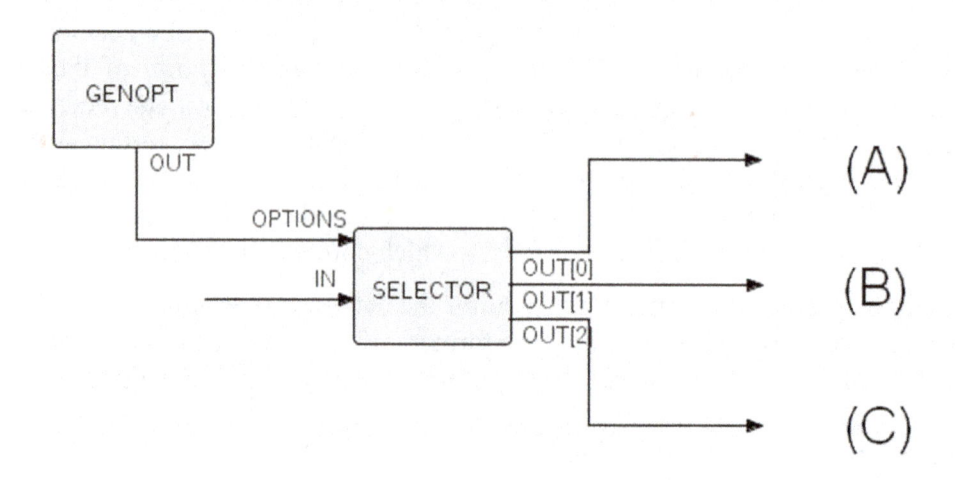

Figure 5.2

To convert the diagram shown in Figure 5.1 to use a connection instead of an IIP, simply change the block feeding OPTIONS to a component, and attach it to the OPTIONS port, as shown in Figure 5.2.

Parametrization of components may be thought of as a spectrum, running from low to high. Low parametrization (few or no parameters) occurs when a component has no variability – either because it is custom-coded for a particular application, or because it is so simple that it always does the same work in the same way. For instance, there is a very useful component in all existing FBP systems which simply accepts and outputs all the IPs from its first input port element, followed by all the IPs from its second input port element, and so on until all the input port elements have been exhausted, often called "Concatenate". This component is extremely useful for forcing a sequence on data which is being generated randomly from a variety of sources. One example might be control totals being generated by different processes which you then want to print out in a fixed order on a report. You know the sequence you want them displayed in, but you do not know the time at which they are going to be created. This is shown in Figure 5.3.

The function of this component is so simple that it doesn't need an options port. Now you may be asking, "Why not simply take all the incoming data streams and merge them into a single input port?". The answer is that you can do this, but the effect is somewhat different. What happens in that case is that the incoming IPs are merged in a "first come, first served" sequence, which is not what you wanted. However, there is a down side to this function: because the data from input port element 1 is held up until Concatenate knows that port element 0 has been closed, and so on for the remaining ports, there is the potential for deadlock. Deadlocks are not as bad as they sound, and there are well-established ways of detecting places where they might occur, and of preventing them before they can occur. In FBP, deadlocks are viewed as a design-time problem. We will be talking about the cause and prevention of Deadlocks in Chapter 16 (page 156).

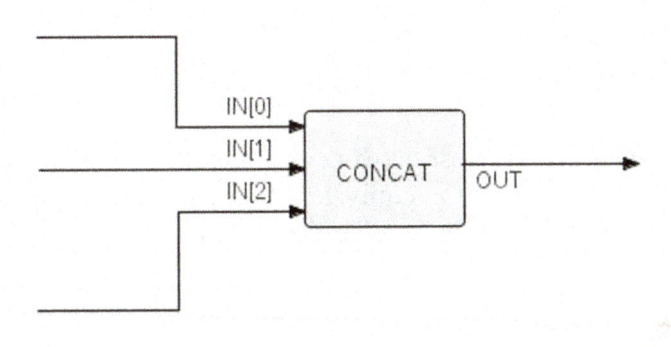

Figure 5.3

The Select component has a medium level of parametrization, and most of the components we will be talking about in this book are similar, but there are occasional components which have so many parameters that they can really be thought of as mini-languages. A later chapter (Chapter 17 – page 172) goes into more detail about the area of Problem-Oriented Mini-Languages, also referred to as Domain-Specific Languages (DSLs), and in Chapter 18 (page 178) we will be describing an approach to a generalized component of this type which in my opinion is interesting because it uses a non-procedural specification for certain types of business processing.

Chap. VI: First Applications using Precoded Components

"One of the things I like about AMPS [the first implementation of the FBP concepts] is that there are so many more ways to do a job than with conventional programming" (a programmer at a large Canadian company).

We will start this chapter with the simplest network imaginable – well, actually, a network with only one process is the simplest, but that is equivalent to a conventional program! The simplest network with at least one connection might be a Reader feeding a Writer, as follows:

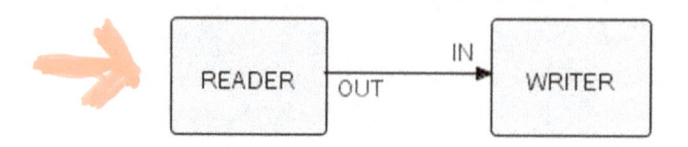

```
READER  OUT ──IN──>  WRITER
```

Figure 6.1

This network just copies one file to another, so it is equivalent to the kind of "copy" utility program which is provided by just about every operating system. The difference is that FBP lets you combine these utilities into more and more complex functions. Utilities in my experience provide a number of functions, but one always wants something a little different. The functions that they have coded into them are often not the ones one needs. This is quite understandable given the difficulty of predicting what people are going to find useful. One alternative is to combine a bunch of utilities by writing intermediate files out to disk. FBP effectively allows you to combine multiple utility functions without requiring any disk space, or the I/O to read and write from and to disk (so you also use less CPU time, and more importantly, less elapsed time).

Chap. VI: First Applications using Precoded Components

Suppose you wanted to combine a "copier" function with a selector, then sort the result before writing it to disk. Just string the functions you want together:

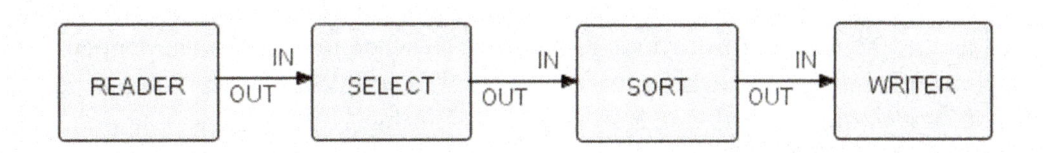

```
READER OUT → IN SELECT OUT → IN SORT OUT → IN WRITER
```

Figure 6.2

Actually, the network doesn't even have to be fully connected. For instance, the following is perfectly valid, and may even be useful!

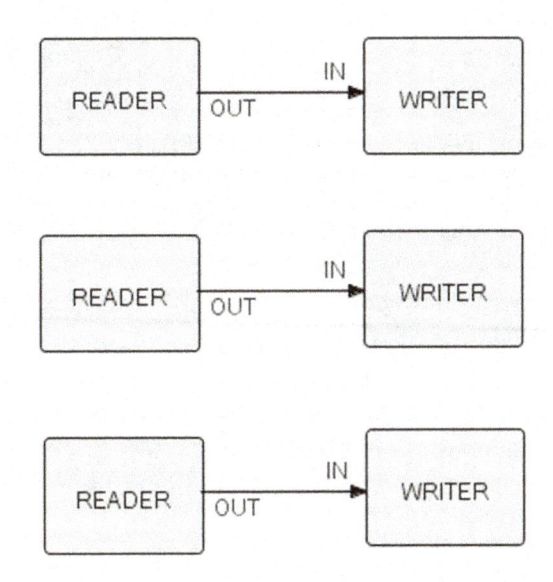

```
READER OUT → IN WRITER

READER OUT → IN WRITER

READER OUT → IN WRITER
```

Figure 6.3

I can remember a time when being able to write a program which would simultaneously read cards and write them to tape, read a tape and punch the records to punched cards, and do some printing, was considered the height of a programmer's ingenuity! With FBP, all you have to do is specify the connections between six processes as shown in the diagram!

Now, if you think about this diagram as a way to get something done, not to control *when* it

Chap. VI: First Applications using Precoded Components

happens, you will realize that the three pairs of processes shown above do not have to run concurrently. The point is that they can if there are adequate resources available, but they don't have to – it doesn't affect their correct functioning. Think of this network as three train-tracks, with a train running on each one. You just care that each train gets to its destination, not when exactly, nor how fast. In business applications it is correct functioning we care about – not usually the exact timing of events. Naturally, this makes old-guard programmers very nervous, accustomed as they are to controlling every last detail of when things have to happen. I will keep coming back to this point since it is so important: application development should be concerned with function, not timing control – unless, of course, timing is part of the function, as in some real-time applications. We have to decide what is worth the programmer's attention, and what can safely be left to the machine. Not knowing exactly when things are going to happen turns out to be liberating, rather than disorienting (for most people). But, yes, some programmers will find the transition rather hard!

By the way, when comparing 4GLs and FBP, I have been struck by the fact that you really can do anything in FBP! FBP's power does not come from restricting what programmers can do, but from encapsulating common tasks in reusable components or designs. Since a conventional program is in fact an FBP network consisting of a single process, the programmer is free to ignore all FBP facilities, if s/he wishes, and the result is a conventional program. This may sound glib, but it says to me that we are not taking anything away – we are adding a whole new dimension to the programming process. While some programmers do feel a sense of restriction with FBP, it comes from having to express everything as "black boxes", with well-defined interfaces between them, not from any loss of function.

In the rest of the chapter, we will put together some simple examples using reusable components, but first we should make a catalogue of some of the types of components which an FBP shop will probably have in its collection, a number of which we have already run into. The types which haven't been mentioned above are fairly obvious extensions of what went before. Some of the items in this list should be understood as representing types of component, rather than specific pieces of code. For example, a shop might have two or three Sort modules, with different characteristics.

- sort
- collate
- split
- assign
- replicate
- count

Chap. VI: First Applications using Precoded Components

- concatenate
- compare
- generate reports
- read
- write
- transform
- manipulate text (this might be a large group)
- discard

Let's also throw in some components which have proven useful during development and debugging: a "dumper" (which displays hex and character formats – in the case of Java and C# implementations I assume we will use reflection) and a line-by-line printer component.

We haven't mentioned "Assign" before. I am going to use this for some examples, so we will go into a little more detail on this type of component. Again this doesn't have an exact counterpart in the newer implementations, but could be implemented using reflection. This component (or component type) simply plugs a value into a specified position in each incoming IP, and outputs the modified IPs. It has the same shape as a "filter", and can be drawn as follows:

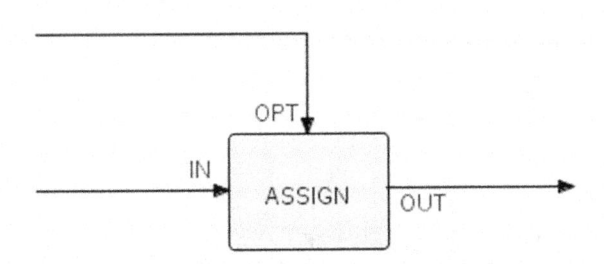

Figure 6.4

where OPT receives the specification of where in the incoming IPs the modification is to take place, and what value is to be put there. For instance, we might design an Assign component which takes option IPs looking like this:

                            3,5,ABCDE

This might specify that ABCDE is to be inserted in the 5 characters beginning at offset 3 from the

Chap. VI: First Applications using Precoded Components

start of each IP. This may seem to be overly simple, but it can be combined with other functions to provide a broad range of function.

By the way, this component illustrates the usefulness of IIPs: if Figure 6.5 is specified in an IIP, you have essentially defined a constant assign with the value defined outside the Assign process, but fixed in the network as a whole. Now, instead, connect the OPT port of Assign to an upstream process, and you now have a variable assign, where the values can be anything you want, and can be changed whenever you want.

Now let's use Assign to mark IPs coming from different sources. Let's suppose you want to merge three files and do the same processing on all of them, but you also want to be able to separate them again later. You could use Assign to set a "source code" in the IPs from each file, and use a Splitter to separate them later.

In an earlier chapter we have used the idea of a two-way Selector, looking like this:

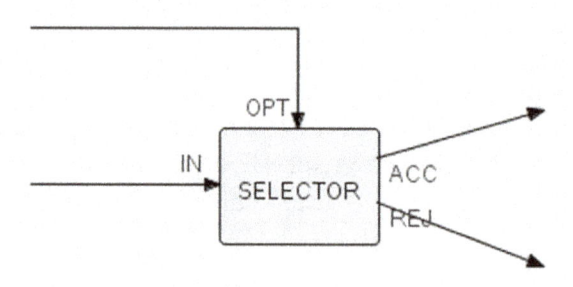

Figure 6.5

Now we can generalize this to an n-way Splitter, where, instead of two ports with specific names, we have an array port, which essentially uses a number to designate the actual output connection. Let us show this as in Figure 6.6.

Chap. VI: First Applications using Precoded Components

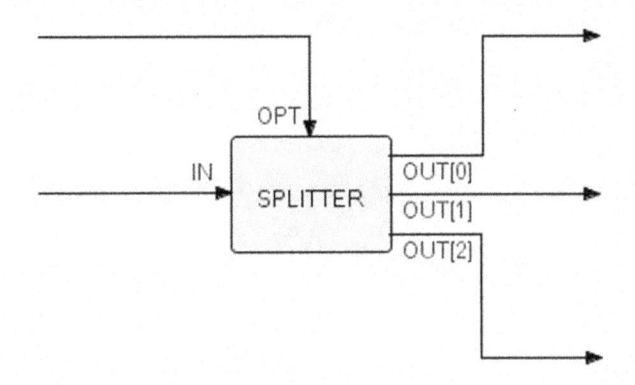

Figure 6.6

Combining the Assign components and a Splitter, we get the result shown in Figure 6.7.

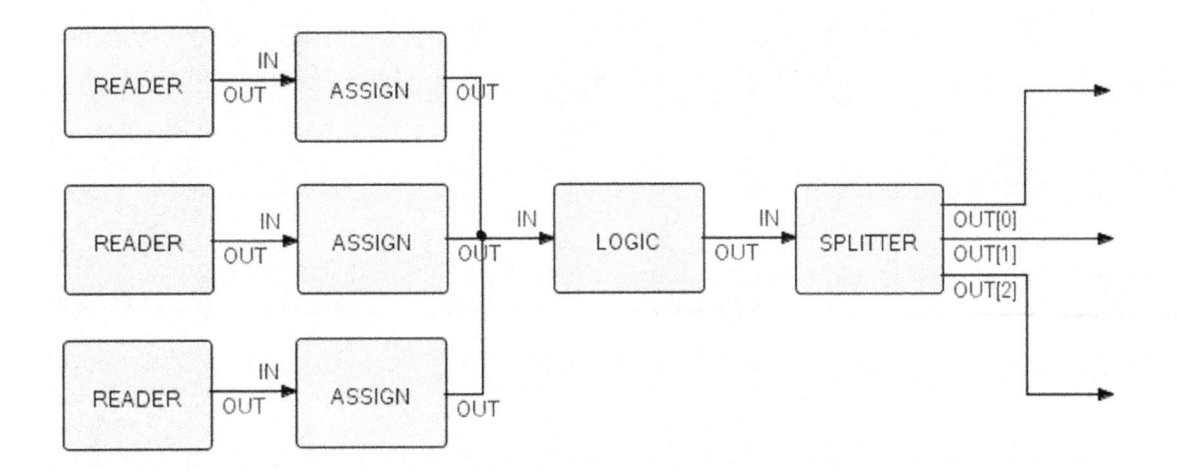

Figure 6.7

Splitters have to be parametrized by specifying a field length and offset, and a series of possible values. The above Splitter might therefore be parametrized as follows:

`54,1,'A','B','C'`

assuming the codes A, B and C were inserted into the IPs coming from the three readers, respectively.

- 63 -

Chap. VI: First Applications using Precoded Components

Let us construct a more complex example based on the provinces of Canada. Let's say we have a file of records with province codes in them. We want to arrange them by time zone, so that we can print them out and have a courier deliver them in time for start of business. The easternmost point in Canada is 4 1/2 hours ahead of the westernmost point, so most big Canadian companies have to wrestle with time zone problems.

Here we will also use a splitter to split the stream of IPs by province. Once the "province" streams have been split out, we could use Assign to insert appropriate codes into the different IP. This splitter might have an option IP looking like this:

`6,2,'ON','QC','MB','AB',...`

This will be read as follows: check the 2 characters starting at offset 6 from the incoming IP; if it is ON, route the IP to OUT[0]; if QC, to OUT[1]; if MB, to OUT[2]; etc. Of course, in both of the above cases, it would be much more friendly to be able to use field names, rather than offsets and lengths. We will talk about this idea in the chapter on Descriptors (page 110).

One other question we have to answer is: what does the Selector do if the incoming IP does not match any of the specified patterns? One possibility is for the splitter to simply send unmatched IPs to the next numbered array element. Another possibility might be to send unmatched IPs to a separate named port.

The application might therefore look like this (I'll just show two Assign processes, and assume all IPs find a match):

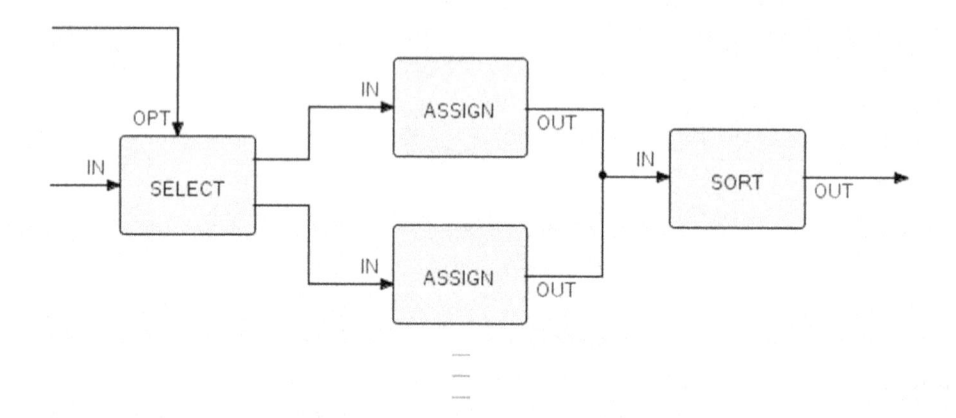

Figure 6.8

The Assigns can insert a code which ascends as one goes from east to west. Because Sort is going

- 64 -

Chap. VI: First Applications using Precoded Components

to rearrange all the data, we can feed all the modified records into one port on the Sort process. This also avoids the possibility of deadlock (I'll be talking more about why this should be so in a later chapter).

I didn't show the option ports on the Assigns, but they will be necessary to specify what codes should be inserted, and where.

Now let's add the logic to handle unmatched IPs. Since they should probably be reported to a human, we will add a printer component, and used the named port technique, as follows:

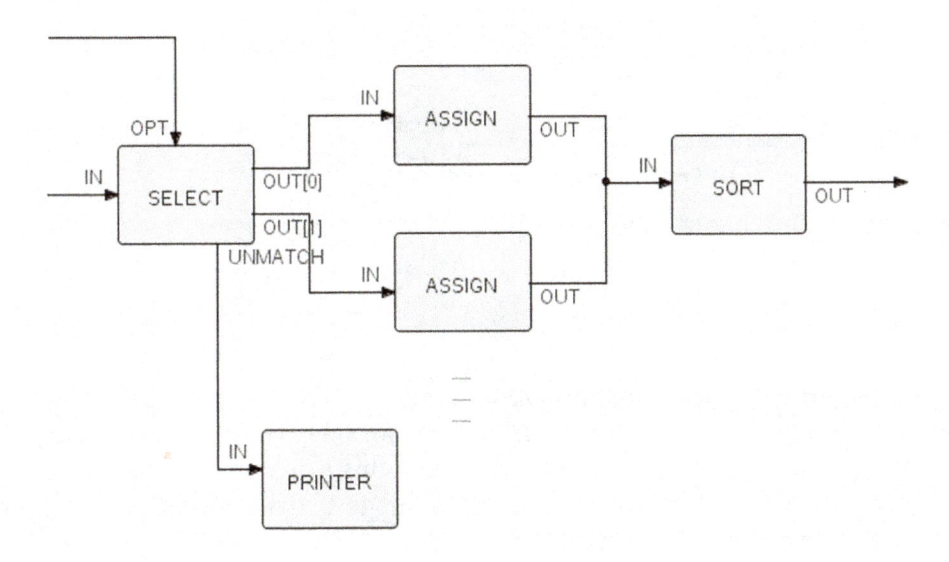

Figure 6.9

At this point we will simply have a list of unmatched IPs streaming out onto a print file. You will probably want to put out an explanatory title, and do some formatting. You will see later how to do this. For now, let's just say that you will probably need to change this network by inserting one or more processes where I have shown PRINTER above, as shown in Figure 6.10.

Let us suppose we now have our network working and doing what it is supposed to do – we have to ask the question: is this network "industrial strength"? There is a definite temptation, once something is working, to feel the job is finished. In fact, it is quite acceptable to use a program like the one shown above for a once-off utility type of application, or for a temporary bridge between two applications. But there is a fundamental question which the designer must answer, and that is (in this application), how long are there going to be exactly 13 provinces and territories in Canada? No, you did not suddenly jump into a book on Canadian politics!

Chap. VI: First Applications using Precoded Components

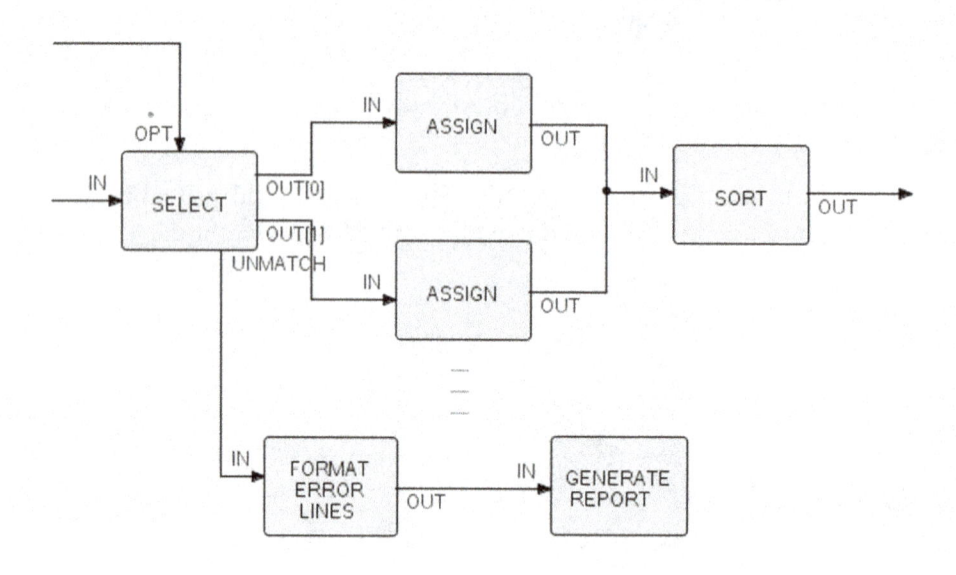

Figure 6.10

The problem is that we have made our program structure reflect a part of the structure of the outside world, and we have to decide how comfortable we feel with this dependency. Yes, there will always be programmers, and we can always change this program... provided we can find it! Nobody can make the decision for you, but I would suggest that if this program may have to survive more than a few years, you might want to consider structuring your code to use a separately compiled table or database, which can pull together all the attributes of provinces of interest to your application. Your application might then look like this (if you generalize SELECT to mean "determine which province it is", and ASSIGN to mean "insert the time zone code for each province"):

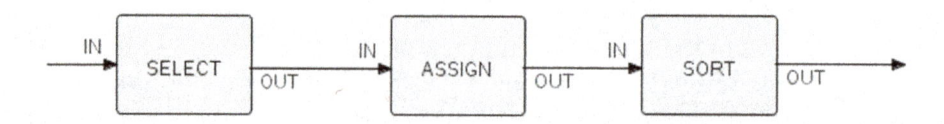

Figure 6.11

Note that this diagram has become simpler and the components more complex. It has the same general structure as the preceding diagram, but the shape does not reflect a (possibly changeable) political structure. Another approach might be to amalgamate the Select and Assign components shown above, using either special purpose code or a generalized transformer module.

A more subtle generalization might be to keep the parallelism, but not tie it to individual provinces at network specification time. Let us decide there will never be more than, say, 24 provinces, so we will extend the earlier diagram to have 24 Assign processes. Select will have 24 port elements on its output port, connected to the Assigns. Now, since both Assign and Select are option-driven, we can obtain their parameters from a file (being read by a Reader) or a table (using a Table Look-up component) and send them to their OPT ports. The possibilities are endless! The important decisions are not "how do I get this working?", but "what solution will give me the best balance between performance and maintainability?". When I was teaching FBP concepts, I used to tell my students that the machine will accept almost anything you throw at it – the real challenge in programming is to make your program comprehensible by humans (whether they are other people looking at your code years later, or your own self one week later)! This is far more of a challenge than simply getting the code working.

There is yet another way to look at this example: what we are really doing (in the last diagram) is converting one code to another under control of a table. One of the generalized component types that we found most useful was one (or several) table look-up components. The table could be held as a independently linked component (in MVS), in which case it would have to be maintained by the programming department, but a better technique is to hold it on a file. The table look-up component will then look like this:

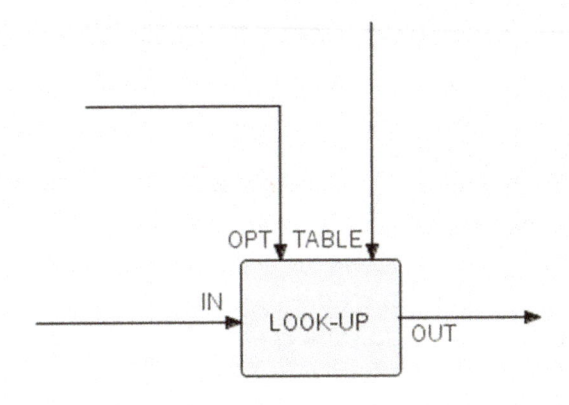

Figure 6.12

What will happen here is that at start-up time the component will read all the IPs from the port

Chap. VI: First Applications using Precoded Components

named TABLE and build a table in storage. It then starts a process of receiving IPs from IN, looking up a specified field in the table, inserting the found value into the IPs, and then sending them to OUT. Of course, this needs to be parametrized – probably we will need to specify the offset and length of the search field in the incoming IPs, and the offset and length of the field which is to be inserted. We will need a Reader to bring in the table IPs from a file, so the resultant network will look like this (partially):

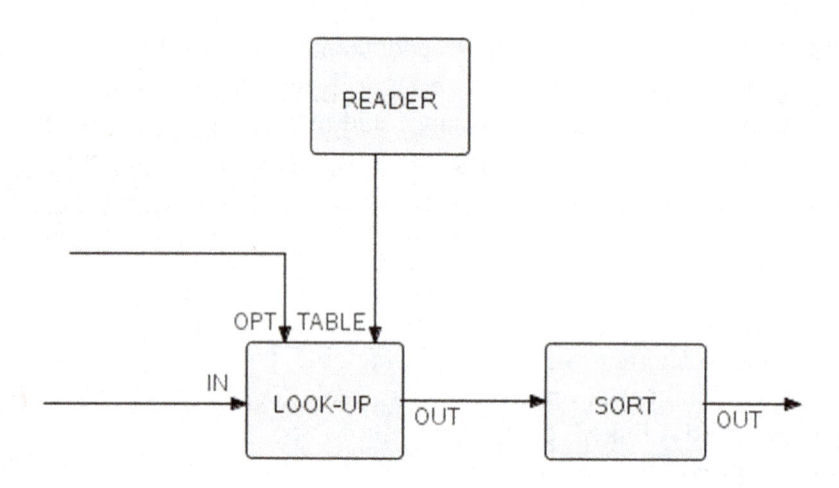

Figure 6.13

Table look-up components have been found to be very useful in the various dialects of FBP. In DFDM, the system was distributed with two "off the shelf" table look-up components. One of them was much like the one we've just described. However, the other one gives you some idea of what can be provided in the form of reusable code, with a little more imagination! It's pretty complex, but it is a "black box" piece of reusable code, and I am showing it just to indicate what can be done with a single component. Of course it violates some of the rules we gave above, so maybe this should sound some warning bells! However, I believe you will agree that it is still a "stream" process, rather than just a complex algorithm. Basically, it does table look-ups on a table which is being refreshed from some kind of backing store – it doesn't care what kind, so long as the other process conforms to a certain protocol. It therefore acts as both a table look-up component and as a buffering device, as shown in Figure 6.14.

This look-up component always works with another process (in this case called GET TABLE) which is used to access a direct access file or database. These two components work together as follows:

Chap. VI: First Applications using Precoded Components

- the top component builds the table, which starts out empty
- as each search request comes in, it is checked against the table; if a match is found, the search request goes out of OUT and the table entry out of MATCH
- if a match is not found, the search request is sent to the other process, which will either find it or not; if it finds it, the search request and the found table entry are sent back to the top component, to be respectively sent to OUT and added to the table
- if it does not find it, a zero-length IP is sent to the top component, together with the search request; the zero-length IP tells it not to add an entry to the table, and the search request is sent to UNMATCH

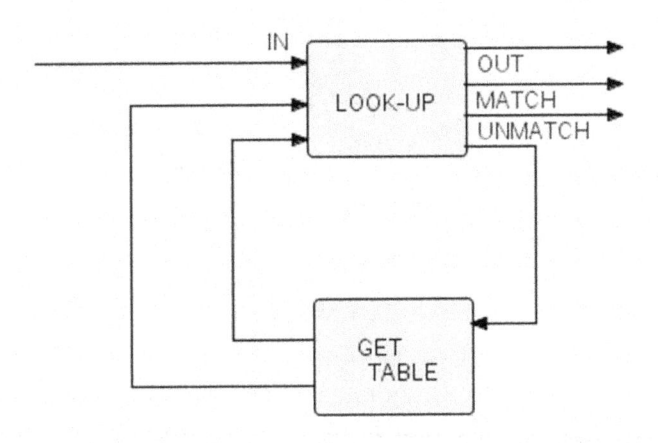

Figure 6.14

This may seem complicated, but once set up, it is very easy to use, and any process can occupy the "bottom" position, provided that it behaves as described. This component (the "top" component) only needed 4 parameters, of which one was the (optional) maximum number of entries in the table. If this limit was specified, and was reached, entries would start to be dropped off the table in FIFO sequence. Another possibility could have been to use an LRU (Least Recently Used) sequence, so that the table essentially becomes what is now called a "cache". .

This chapter has tried to give some idea of what can be done using only reusable components. Of course, the number of these is going to grow steadily, and, especially if you have made some of the organizational changes we suggested in an earlier chapter, you may wind up with a sizable number of useful, reusable tools. We don't know what this number is, but my guess is that it will taper off in the low hundreds. The amount these are used will probably follow a curve with the following general shape:

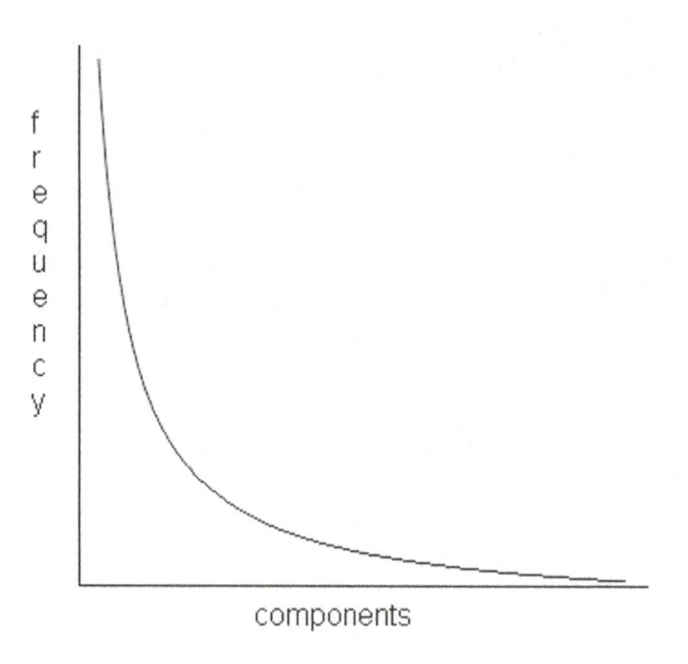

Figure 6.15

where the less frequently used components may be used only in a few applications. This shape is known nowadays as a "long tail", or "Pareto tail". Given this kind of distribution, you may wonder whether it is worth maintaining the low-frequency components in a support department, or whether they should be made the property of the using departments. The answer will depend on whether, and how much, specialized knowledge is encapsulated in them, how easy they will be to find if you need them again, whether you are trying to sell them outside the company, and so on.

This kind of rarely used component has similarities with what we have called "custom" components. Until all code is "off the shelf" (if that ever happens), there will be a need for customers to write their own components. This is not as easy as just hooking reusable components together, but it is also pretty straightforward. In the next chapter, I will talk about the idea of composite components, and then in the following chapter start to discuss some concepts for building systems by combining "off the shelf" and "custom" components.

Chap. VII: Composite Components

In Chapter 3 (Concepts – page 20), we talked about hierarchic structures of substreams – there is obviously another type of hierarchic structure in FBP, which has been alluded to earlier: the hierarchical relationship between components. Although the processes in an FBP application are all little main lines, cooperating at the same level to perform a job of work, it is easier to *build* the total structure hierarchically, with a "top" structure comprising two or more processes, most of which will be implemented using composite components. Each composite component in turn "explodes" into two or more processes, and so on, until you reach a level where you can take advantage of existing components, or you decide that you are going to write your own elementary components, rather than continuing the explosion process. Apart from the emphasis on using preexisting components, this is essentially the stepwise decomposition methodology of Structured Analysis.

The application of this approach to FBP is largely due to the late Wayne Stevens, arising from his work on Structured Programming and application development methodologies in general. Originally, from a hierarchy point of view, running FBP programs were "flat" – they had no hierarchic structure at all. People drew application networks on *big* sheets of drawing paper, and stuck them up on their cubicle walls. These drawings would then gradually accumulate an overlay of comments and remarks as the developers added descriptions of data streams, parametrization, file descriptors, etc. When the time came to implement the networks, the developer simply converted the drawing by hand into a list of Assembler macro calls.

Wayne realized that a better way to develop these networks was to use the decomposition techniques of Structured Analysis, but that, unlike in conventional programming, *there was no need to change your viewpoint as you moved from design to implementation*. In conventional program development there is a "gap" between the data flow approach used during design and

Chap. VII: Composite Components

the control flow viewpoint required during programming, which is extraordinarily difficult to get across. When designing DFDM we therefore provided a way for developers to grow their systems by stepwise decomposition, but at build time the hierarchy got "flattened" into a flat network. This approach turned out to be very successful – I alluded earlier to a colleague who built a 200-node network without once drawing a picture of a network!

So DFDM networks could be built up hierarchically, but were flat at run-time. This approach let developers build up their applications layer by layer. Just as a network links together black box modules, we felt it would be good if you could store a whole subnet (a partial network with "sticky" connections) as a black box, so that a vendor could sell a subnet as a product without customers being able to see the internal structure.

We then realized that another advantage of such a mechanism would be to improve the performance of interactive systems.

Consider an application comprising 200 processes – when you link all the code together into a single module, the result is a pretty big executable. The particular application mentioned above ran under IBM's transaction-oriented software, called IMS/DC, and the network was executed once for each transaction. However, when we started measuring performance, we found that, on each pass through the network, even though IMS/DC loads in the whole network for most transactions, only about 1/3 of the processes actually got executed for a given transaction. We wondered if we could just build a framework for an interactive application and load in the required chunks of logic dynamically. This would have the advantage that it would take less time to load in the application on each transaction, because the individual executables would be smaller, thus improving response time. Also, on each transaction you would only need the framework and the particular dynamic chunk involved, so the controlling framework could actually be made resident, improving response time even more. It should also make it easier to expand the application and even change it on the fly. The problem was: how do you run a network which modifies itself dynamically without losing track of your data?

For a long time, I resisted this idea, as I had a vision of a complex subway system like the London underground, but with the added complexity that stations would be appearing and disappearing at random. How would it feel to be a passenger in such a system?! I had earlier experimented with loading in individual components dynamically at run time: I was able to read in or load a piece of code, treating it as pure data, and let it travel through a network, until it arrived at a "blank" process (one which was connected to other processes but had no code assigned to it – a sort of *tabula rasa* process), at which point it would get executed, so I felt that dynamic process modification could work under controlled circumstances. Wayne Stevens had also proposed a particular case of dynamic network modification which is simpler than what we eventually landed up with, but we never got around to trying it out: his image was of engineers repairing a dam. The water has to keep flowing, so the engineers divert the water through a secondary channel. After the dam has been repaired, the water flow can be restored to its original channel. This seems like it would be a good way to do maintenance on an FBP system which has to keep running 24 hours a day, like a banking system.

I myself came up with a different and somewhat more complicated approach, which however was also safe and manageable, and which also solved the problem of executable size I described above. The trick was to have a "mother" process load a subnet, start up the processes in the subnet, and then go to sleep until all of her "daughter" processes had terminated. At subnet start time, the daughters are counted, so the subnet is finished when the count of active daughters has gone down to zero. While the mother is sleeping, some of the daughter processes can be given access to their mother's input and output ports. There will be no conflict over who has control of the ports, as the mother and the daughters are never awake at the same time.

We called these subnets in DFDM *dynamic subnets*. The "mother" was a generalized component called the Subnet Manager, which continuously iterated through the following logic:

- receive the name of a subnet in an IP,
- load the subnet module,
- "stitch" it into the main network,
- start it up and go to sleep,
- wake up when all the daughter processes have terminated,
- dispose of the subnet module and repeat these steps

In addition to the Subnet Manager, we added special precoded components (SubIn and SubOut) which were used for input and output handling by the subnet. Figure 7.1 shows a very simple dynamic subnet (with one input data port and one output port).

When *X* is given control, it behaves just like a mini-application: technically SubIn has no input ports, so it gets initiated. The other two processes have input ports, so they will not be initiated until data arrives. SubIn and SubOut have the ability to use their mother's input and output ports respectively. They have to be separate processes as they have to be independently suspendable. Thus, if the mother had two input data ports, the subnet would have to have two SUBIN processes to handle them. Of course, SubIn and SubOut are general-purpose components, so they have to have the mother's port names specified to them – this is done using IIPs.

Now we noticed a strange thing: normally, once a process terminates, it can never be started again. We saw that the Subnet Manager had to have the unique ability of being able to restart terminated processes. This was the only function in DFDM which had this ability, and it was in a very special off-the-shelf component.

Chap. VII: Composite Components

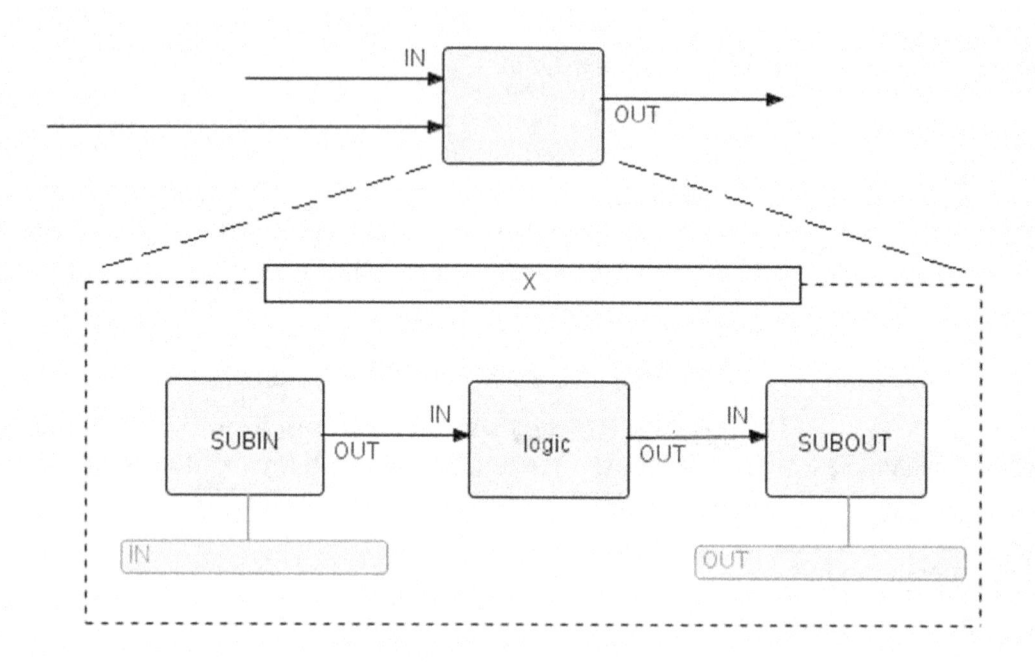

Figure 7.1

In the work which followed DFDM (we have referred to this as FPE), we realized that these characteristics of dynamic subnets could be extended to static networks as well. We moved this ability into the infrastructure (removing the subnet names port), so that all subnets had a built-in monitoring process. In JavaFBP and C#FBP, this is how subnets are implemented. This approach naturally coordinates the hierarchy of processes with the stream hierarchy. In addition, since the monitoring process's other job is to stitch the composite into the main network, we now have "black box" composite components. This facility allows subnets to be packaged as separate executable components for distribution, which can later be linked with other components by a developer to form the full application network. This seems very attractive, as a software manufacturer can now sell a composite component without having to reveal its internals. We will also see later (in Chapter 19 – page 185) that these concepts give us an intuitively straightforward way of implementing fairly complex functions such as checkpointing long-running applications. If we want to reintroduce the dynamic subnet capability, in JavaFBP or C#FBP, this will entail some work on different packaging approaches, e.g. OSGi. A nice little research project for someone!

We mentioned above how, in the present subnet approach, we have a "mother" process which monitors the execution of its daughter processes, and can "revive" them after they have all closed

Chap. VII: Composite Components

down. However, since the subnet cannot close down until all IPs have been received at all input ports, what would be the point of ever waking up the subnet again? Well, if that was all we could do, it would just be a performance improvement. However, we came up with an idea which we thought dovetailed in pretty neatly. Why not put markers in the data stream, such that the internal subnet thinks it is seeing end of data, and will terminate, but in fact there is more data to come, so it will be revived? We did this by adding an option to composite components called *substream sensitivity*. Initially this was implemented only for dynamic subnets, but eventually we saw its usefulness as an option on all composite components. Substream-sensitive composites have special SubIn processes which keep track of the bracket nesting levels at each of their input ports, and whenever this level drops to zero for a given port, the port involved is closed *(on the inside)*, resulting in an "end of data" indication next time the daughter process does a receive from that port. Essentially they make substreams on the outside look like streams on the inside. Since you can nest subnets within subnets, each level of nesting strips off one level of bracketing. The converse on output is to have a special SubOut which *restores* brackets. (In JavaFBP and C#FBP, the SubIn and SubOut components come in two flavours: substream-sensitive and non-substream-sensitive.)

For simplicity, we will just work with one input data port. Suppose we have a "substream-sensitive" composite subnet B, which contains C and D, as follows:

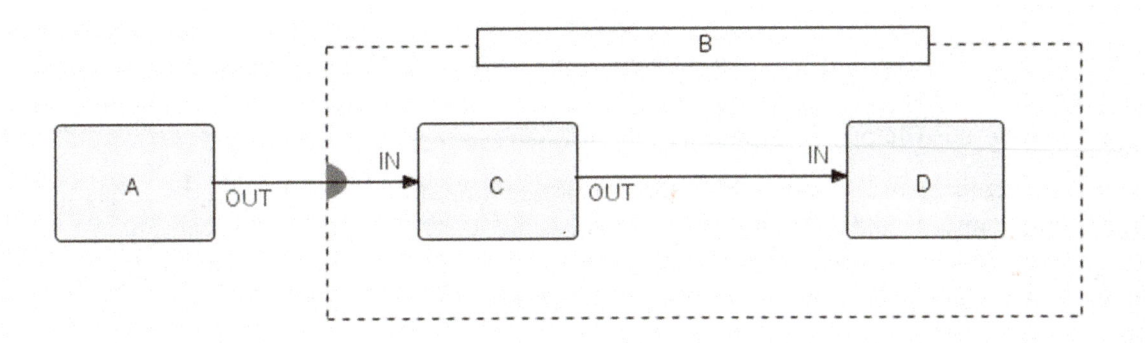

Figure 7.2

The point shown with a solid semicircle is a substream-sensitive input port on B. This is sort of a shorthand – the solid semicircle will actually be implemented as a SubIn process.

Suppose that A generates a stream as follows:

`(a b c d e f)   (g h i)   (j k l m)...`

Chap. VII: Composite Components

reading from left to right. Then C is going to see IPs *a, b, c, d, e* and *f,* and then end of data. At end of data it terminates, as it has no upstream processes at the same level *within its enclosing composite*, enabling D to terminate also. If D was a Writer, it would then close the file it was writing to. However, we know (although the subnet doesn't) that C and D are not permanently "dead" – when the next open bracket arrives at B's input port, they will both be revived. As far as C and D are concerned, IPs *a* through *f* constitute a complete "application", but, as far as B is concerned, each substream, e.g. *a* through *f* results in a single activation of the internal subnet.

What happened to the brackets? Well, we could add a process to remove the enclosing brackets of a substream, but it seemed a good idea to add the ability to substream-sensitive ports to drop the brackets if the designer wants. However, you may not always want this: for instance, if D was outputting IPs to B's output port, you might have to be able to put the brackets back on again.

In this example, you can see the insides of a composite working like a complete application within each activation of a composite. The power of this concept is that you can match levels of composite component to levels of nesting of substreams. So, *substream* structure can be related to *subnet* structure. I would like to record here the fact that this very powerful idea came from Herman van Goolen, of IBM Netherlands, and I feel it is very elegant. You can probably now see why we use brackets both to delimit substreams and as the delimiters which substream-sensitive composites respond to.

If we have more than one input port on a substream-sensitive composite component, as described above, our composite will process one substream from each input port successively until all the input ports are exhausted. Processing of these input streams will therefore be synchronized at the substream level. This kind of synchronization also ties in nicely with the requirements of Checkpointing (see Chapter 19 – page 185).

One last point: in JavaFBP and C#FBP, components contain *metadata* which describes their port requirements, and is used by their respective schedulers to check the validity of network connections. Since subnets are essentially a special type of reusable component, they also have to contain metadata. An example of a simple JavaFBP subnet is given in the Appendix.

Chap. VIII: Building Components & Some More Simple Applications

I am now going to describe some simple applications mixing reusable components and custom ones. We start with a fairly simple text processing application to make a few points about the design of applications in FBP. This is a classical programming problem, originally described by Peter Naur, commonly known as the "Telegram problem". This appears to be quite a simple task, namely to write a program which accepts lines of text and generates output lines of a different length, without splitting any of the words in the text (we assume no word is longer than the size of an output line). This turns out to be surprisingly hard to do in conventional programming, and therefore is often used as an example in courses on conventional programming. Unless the student realizes that neither the input nor the output logic should be the "main line" (highest level routine), but that the main line has to be a separate piece of code whose main job is to process a word at a time, the student finds him or herself getting snarled in a lot of confused logic. In FBP, it is much more obvious how to approach the problem, for the following reasons:

- words are mentioned explicitly in the description of the problem
- since we have to select our IPs between each pair of processes, it is reasonable for the designer to treat words as IPs somewhere in the implementation of the problem. It would actually be counter-intuitive to deliberately avoid turning words into IPs, given the problem description
- there is no main line, so the student is not tempted to turn one of the other functions into the main line.

Let us dig into the coding of this problem more deeply. We should have IPs represent words somewhere in the application. You will have realized also that we should have a Read Sequential

Chap. VIII: Building Components & Some More Simple Applications

on the left of the network, reading input records from a file, and a Write Sequential writing the new records onto an output file. Here is a partial network:

```
┌──────┐
│ RSEQ │ ── ?? ──────── ?? ─────▶ IN ┌──────┐
│  OUT │                              │ WSEQ │
└──────┘                              └──────┘
```

Figure 8.1

Now the output of Read Sequential and the input of Write Sequential both consist of streams of IPs containing words and blank space, so it seems reasonable that what we need, at minimum, is a component to decompose records into words and a matching one to recompose words back into records. Given the problem as defined, I do not see a need for any more components, but I want to stress at this point that there is no single right answer. Remember ROI? What you select as your basic black boxes depends on how much they are going to be used versus how much it costs to create them.

Let us add our two new components into the picture:

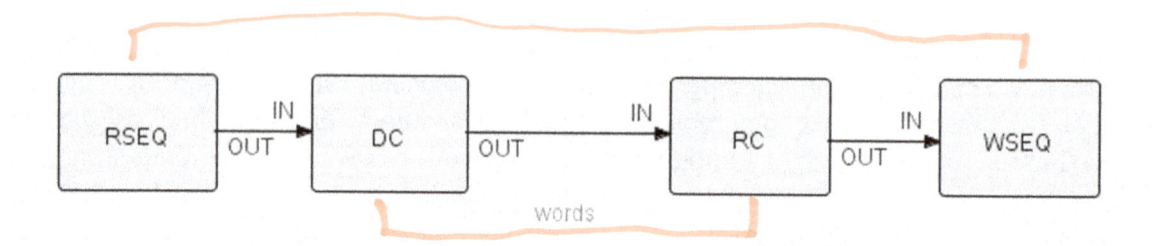

```
┌──────┐    IN ┌────┐      IN ┌────┐      IN ┌──────┐
│ RSEQ │──────▶│ DC │─────────▶│ RC │─────────▶│ WSEQ │
│  OUT │       │OUT │          │OUT │          │      │
└──────┘       └────┘   words └────┘          └──────┘
```

Figure 8.2

Now we have another matched pair of components – in the diagram I have labelled them DC (for DeCompose) and RC for ReCompose). Components can always find out the actual size of any IP, so we do not have to provide the size of the incoming IPs to DC as a parameter. However, RC cannot know what size of IPs we want it to create, so this size must be passed as a parameter to its OPTIONS port (I didn't have to call it that – but it is good a name as any). So let's show an options IIP on RC. RSEQ and WSEQ will also need to know the identifiers of the files they are working with, so our diagram now looks like this:

Chap. VIII: Building Components & Some More Simple Applications

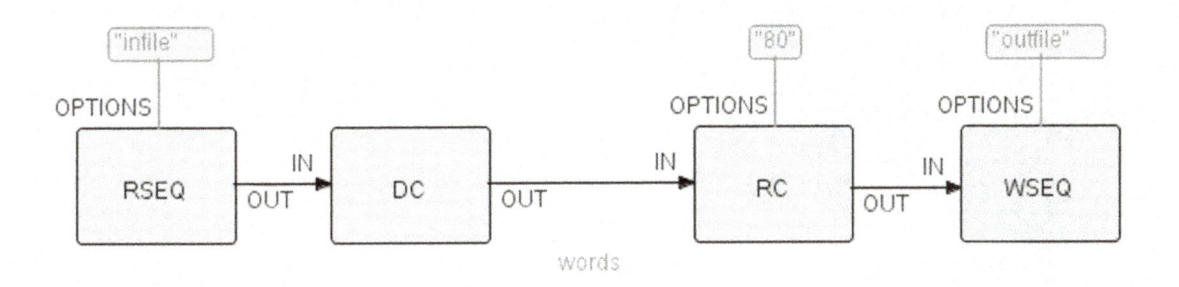

Figure 8.3

For completeness, I will give some possible pseudo-code for DC and RC. Remember that, once you have written and tested DC and RC, you have them forever. So it is worth the effort to get them "perfect" (as close to perfect as software ever gets!). On the other hand, if they are producing correct results, but you think you could make them prettier, with a bit more work, you could always distribute them to your users (with appropriate caveats), and deliver a new and improved version later. One of the great advantages of FBP is that you can simply insert a Display process on any connection, e.g. between DC and RC, to see if the IPs passing across that connection are correct. So testing is very easy. *← autologging?*

The logic for DC follows:

```
DC (Decompose into Words):

      receive from IN using a
      do while receive has not reached end of data
            do stepping through characters of input IP
                  if "in word" switch is off and current char non-blank
                        set "in word" on
                        save character pointer
                  endif
                  if "in word" on and current char blank
                        set "in word" off
                        build new string of length =
                              current pointer - saved pointer)
                        create IP using new string
                        send created IP to OUT
                  endif
            enddo
            drop a (original input IP)
            receive from IN using a
      enddo
```

Chap. VIII: Building Components & Some More Simple Applications

The Java code for this is given in the Appendix.

Here is the logic for RC:

```
RC (Recompose Words into Records):

        receive output record length from IIP port
        drop this IP

        create output IP and set it to all blanks
        start at beginning of output IP

        receive word IP from IN using a
        do while receive has not reached end of data
                if received word will not fit into output IP
                        send output IP to OUT
                        create new output IP and set to all blanks
                        start at beginning of output IP
                endif
                move contents of word IP into next space in output IP
                if there is room for 1 more character
                        move in single blank
                endif
                drop a
                receive word IP from IN using a
        enddo
        if output IP has at least one word in it
                send output IP to OUT
        else
                drop it
        endif
```

Maybe this logic can be simplified, but a component does not have to be simple on the inside – it should be simple on the outside, and above all it must work reliably! This point really illustrates a fundamental difference between conventional programming and FBP: I have just shown some pseudocode, and you may be feeling that we are back to conventional programming. However, another way of putting what I am trying to say is that, because we *can* program, it does not mean that we *should*. Most conventional programming, including a lot of the new Object-Oriented approaches, still stresses the production of new code. Many reuse approaches are based on finding what source code is available, and reusing it. Because code is such a malleable medium, and does not have an inherent component structure, we are always creating new stuff. We tend to forget that the results of our work may live long after us and that there is a cost to maintaining them, documenting and managing them. How many times have we heard, "It's less trouble to write my own version than to find out what's out there"? In FBP, the orientation is the exact

Chap. VIII: Building Components & Some More Simple Applications

reverse: use what's out there, and only build new if you can justify the effort in terms of ROI. This is where experience becomes valuable: after you have done the same job many times, you know whether other people will find components like DC and RC useful. If you know they won't, find another way to do the job!

Now we have a matched pair of useful components, but, of course, you don't have to use them together all the time. Let's suppose we simply want to count the number of words in a piece of text. We have already mentioned the Counter component in the Concepts chapter (page 20) – it simply counts all its incoming IPs and generates a count IP at the end. It could have an option which is substream-sensitive (i.e. generating one count IP for each incoming substream), but for now we will use it in its basic form. In this form, it simply sends the count it has just calculated out via one output port, while the original incoming IPs are sent out of another one if it is connected (this is an example of an optional port). This type of component is sometimes called a "reference" component, meaning that the original input IPs are passed through unchanged, while some derived information is sent out of another output port. So the resulting structure will look something like this (we won't bother to connect up Count's optional output):

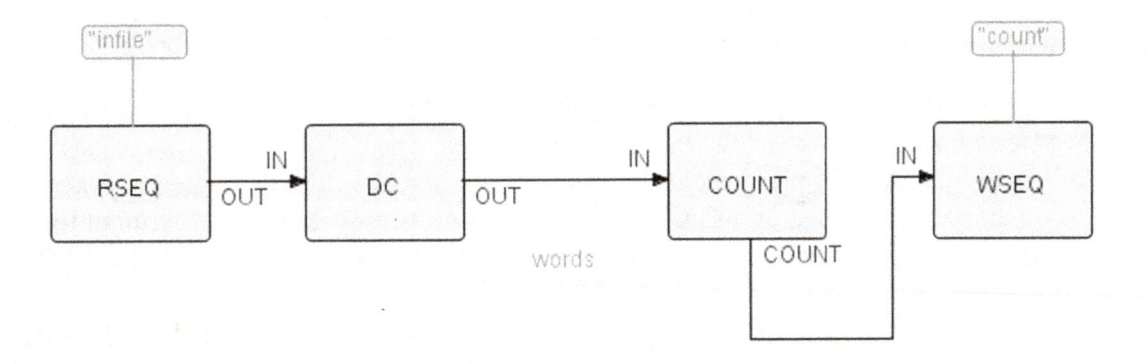

Figure 8.4

We can keep on adding or changing processes indefinitely! These changes may result from changing requirements, new requirements or simply the realization that you can use a component that was developed for one application on another. We talked in Chapter 4 (page 41) about some of the principles behind designing components for reuse.

As another more elaborate example, instead of counting the words, we could decide to sort them, alphabetically or by length. Once we have the words sorted alphabetically, it might be nice to be able to insert fancy heading letters between groups of words starting with the same letters, like some dictionaries.... Of course, once we have sorted them, we should eliminate duplicates. The resulting diagram would then look as shown in Figure 8.5.

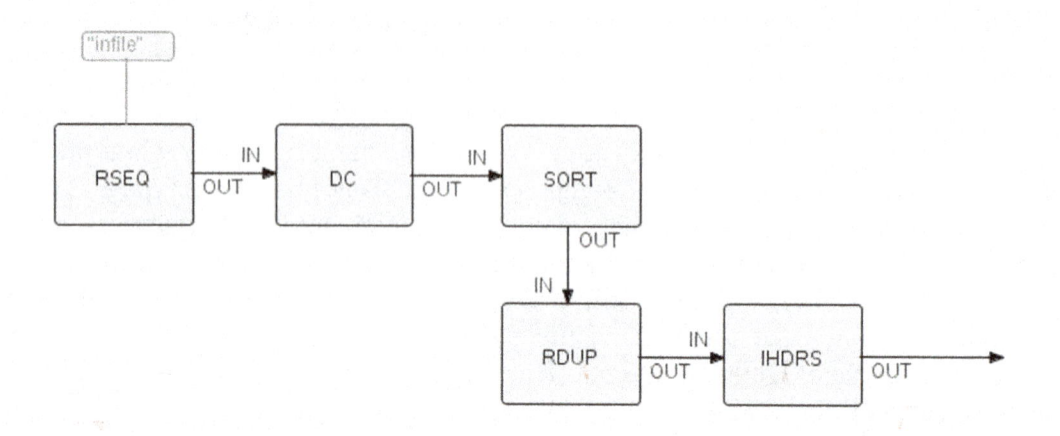

Chap. VIII: Building Components & Some More Simple Applications

Figure 8.5

where RDUP means "Remove Duplicates" and IHDRS means "Insert Header Letters".

It will come as no surprise that text processing applications have been very productive of generalized components. This is also the application area where the UNIX system has proven very productive. The UNIX pipe mechanism is very similar to FBP's data streams, except that UNIX communication is based on using streams of characters, whereas FBP's communication is by means of structured IPs. However, John Cowan (an early FBP enthusiast, and the "father" of JavaFBP) points out that at the level of the UNIX utilities (which correspond directly to FBP components), UNIX and FBP essentially share the same unit-record ancestry, with newlines as record separators and tabs, whitespace, colons or other characters as field separators. He also points out that most UNIX utilities let you specify the field separator as a command-line option.

An excellent example of this kind of text-processing application is P.R. Ewing's publication in the late '80s of a Concordance to the Ukrainian Bible (1988) – this was programmed using DFDM, and Philip found DFDM to be very well suited to this type of work. He later completed a Biblical Concordance for Xhosa (one of the languages of South Africa), using the C-based THREADS software (described in the Appendix). He reports that, after spending between 100 and 150 hours trying to develop this Concordance using conventional (non-FBP) software, he eventually had to abandon it unfinished. With THREADS he was able to produce a completed Concordance with about 40 hours of work (of course this does not include the time needed to input the Bible text). He told me that, as far as he was concerned, the big advantage of FBP is the fact that it simplifies the complexity of an application, and 40 hours (complete) vs. more than 100 hours (incomplete) certainly seems to bear this out.

Chap. VIII: Building Components & Some More Simple Applications

We have used the Sort function as a component a number of times in the foregoing examples. In conventional programming, Sort is usually packaged as a stand-alone utility, although various exits (they would be referred to as "callbacks" today) are provided to allow its behaviour to be modified. What are the advantages of packaging it as an FBP component? People very often have the reaction that Sort cannot be a good FBP component because it is too "synchronous" – all the input has to be read in before any of it can be sorted; then the sort proper takes place; then all the sorted records are output by a final merge phase. However, we have found a stream-to-stream sort to be a very effective FBP component for the following reasons:

- Performance: a Sort which is run as a separate job step has to use files for its input and output, and the control fields have to be in the same place in every input record. If we provide Sort as a stream-to-stream component, then data IPs which are to be sorted no longer have to be written to a file first and do not have to be retrieved from a file afterwards, but can simply be sent across a connection to the Sort, which in turn sends them on to the next process when it is finished, resulting in a considerable savings in I/O overhead. Actually, the "central" sort phase is the only part of the sort which cannot be overlapped with other processes (unless you are using a multithreaded implementation).

- Flexibility of positioning control fields: if the control fields are not in a standard place for all the input IPs, you can simply insert a transform process upstream of the Sort to make the key fields line up.

- Eliminating unnecessary sorting: sometimes, some of the IPs are known to be already sorted, in which case they can bypass the Sort, and be recombined with the sorted IPs later. This is often not practical when the Sort is a separate job step.

- Improved sorting techniques: if you know something about the characteristics of your keys, you may be able to build more complex networks which perform better than a straight sort. For instance, if you are sorting on a name field, it might make sense to split the data 26 ways, sort each stream independently, then merge them back together – I don't say it will definitely, but you can try it out. The sort process can thus be implemented with other components or subnets for purposes of experimentation.

Although some sorts are faster, a good rule of thumb is that the running time of most sorts is proportional to *n.logn*, where *n* is the number of records. Since this is a non-linear relationship, it may be more efficient to split your sort into several separate ones.

Figure 8.6 is a picture of a Sort with some IPs going around it, and with sort tags being generated on the fly by an upstream process (GTAG).

Actually Sort is an example of something I discovered quite early in the work on FBP: FBP enables you to tie together things which didn't expect to be tied together! If you can persuade something to accept and generate data packets, it can talk to other things which talk in terms of

Chap. VIII: Building Components & Some More Simple Applications

data. For instance, once you have converted Sort to a stream-to-stream component, it can talk to other utilities, HLLs, DB2, etc. They don't necessarily have to be callable – they just have to be able to accept and generate data once they are given control. I have written networks which contained Assembler, COBOL and PL/I programs, all in the same network.

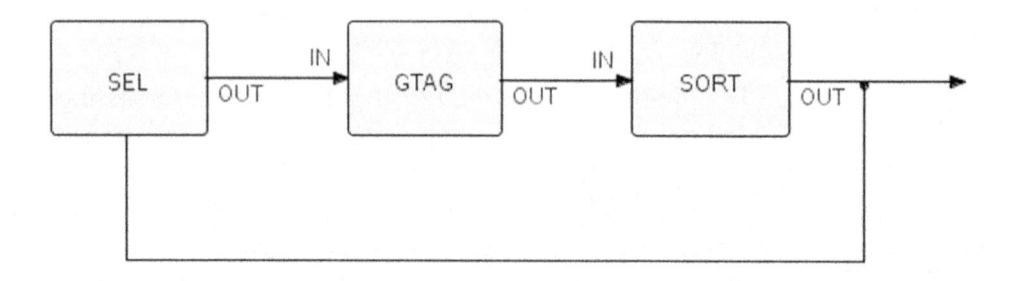

Figure 8.6

I also built an application which used a screen manager written in Assembler, REXX for all of its calculation logic, and IBM's GDDM/PGF (an early graphics package) for drawing some specialized chart types. Another network spanned two virtual machines, running on the same physical machine under control of what is nowadays called a hypervisor. This is a point we'll come back to later: you can design a big network, and then split it across different machines, processors, software systems, etc.

Incidentally, there is a flip side to this ability to tie things together 'without their knowledge': we alluded above to the fact that components have to be reentrant if they are going to multithread with each other. Strange things happen if you try to multithread processes which are not reentrant! After we had turned Sort into a stream-to-stream process, it seemed reasonable to want to run more than one Sort process in a single network. As long as one had fully completed before the other one started, we had no problems. When we tried to overlap two Sorts in time, strange things happened, so we decided that the safest thing to do was interlock the Sorts so that one couldn't start until the other had finished (this is not a great solution as it requires deciding which Sort should run first, which you will probably have realized by now runs counter to the philosophy of FBP). However, it is interesting to know you can do it in FBP, if you absolutely have to.

Now let's go back to the original Telegram problem, but first we are going to program it using conventional (control-flow) programming. Hopefully the reason for doing this will become clear soon.

From the above discussion, we see that *words* are the key concept needed to make this problem

Chap. VIII: Building Components & Some More Simple Applications

tractable. Once we realize this, we can go ahead and code it up, using something like the call hierarchy shown in Figure 8.7.

As we have said above, it is not at all obvious at first in conventional programming that this is the right way to tackle this job. Most people who tackle this problem start off by making GETWORD or PUTWORD the "boss" program, and promptly get into trouble. So we now realize that we have to "bring in a boss from outside" (call it MAIN), instead of "promoting" GETWORD or PUTWORD to boss.

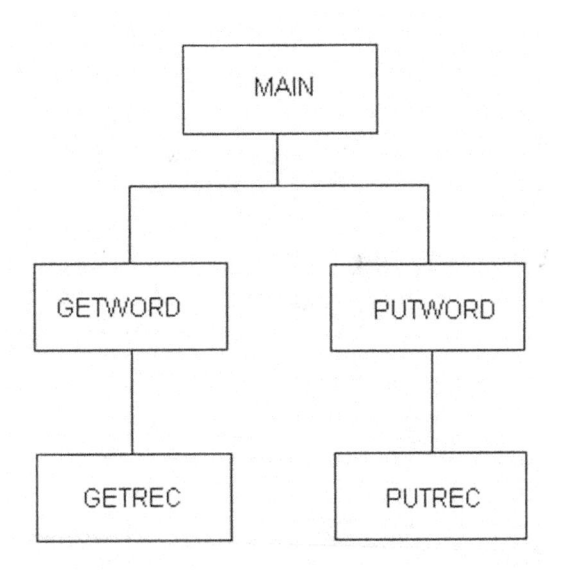

```
                    ┌──────┐
                    │ MAIN │
                    └──┬───┘
          ┌────────────┴────────────┐
     ┌────┴────┐              ┌─────┴────┐
     │ GETWORD │              │ PUTWORD  │
     └────┬────┘              └─────┬────┘
          │                         │
     ┌────┴────┐              ┌─────┴────┐
     │ GETREC  │              │  PUTREC  │
     └─────────┘              └──────────┘
```

Figure 8.7

Now MAIN can call GETWORD and PUTWORD to retrieve and store a single word at a time, respectively. To do this GETWORD must in turn call GETREC and PUTWORD must call PUTREC, to look after the I/O. Now note that all four of these subroutines have to "keep their place" in streams of data (streams of words or streams of records). In the bad old days we did this by writing them all as non-reentrant code, so the place-holder information essentially became global information. This is quite correctly frowned on as poor programming practice, as it has a number of significant disadvantages, so today we normally manage this kind of place-holding logic using the concept of "handles". The general idea (for those of you who haven't had to struggle with this kind of logic) is for MAIN to pass a null handle (in many systems this will be a pointer which is initially set to zero) to GETWORD. When GETWORD sees the null handle, it allocates a block of storage and puts its address into the handle. Thereafter it uses this block of storage indirectly via the handle, and at the end of the run, frees it up again. Although this block

Chap. VIII: Building Components & Some More Simple Applications

of storage is allocated and freed by GETWORD, it is considered to be *owned* by MAIN. This same logic is also used between MAIN and PUTWORD, between GETWORD and GETREC, and between PUTWORD and PUTREC.

At the basic level, our problem is that subroutines cannot maintain internal information which lasts longer than one invocation. In contrast, FBP components are long-running objects which maintain their own internal information. They do not have to be continually reinvoked – you just start them up and they run until their input streams are exhausted. There is an exception to this – namely, the type of component we describe as "non-loopers" (described in more detail in Chapter 9 – page 90), but these can be used in a network in exactly the same way as the long-running ("looper") type of component. Thus, FBP components can do the same things subroutines do, but in a way that is more robust and, something of considerable interest for our future needs, that is also more distributable. It is important to note that FBP does not prevent us from using subroutines, but my experience is that they are most appropriate for such tasks as mathematical calculations on a few variables, doing look-ups in tables, accessing databases, and so on – in other words tasks which match as closely as possible the mathematical idea of a function. Such subroutines are said to be "side-effect free", and experience has shown that side-effects are one of the most common causes of programming bugs. Hence subroutines which rely on side-effects for their proper functioning are a pretty poor basis on which to build sophisticated software!

At this point, to get you back in the data flow mood, let's talk about the text-processing example I talked about above. You remember the above example, where we want to take some text, split it into individual words, sort them, remove duplicates, insert fancy letters on every letter change, and print out the result. Oh, and let's print it out in two columns. Using FBP, this is quite simple – actually, we have just described the FBP network structure! I will leave this as an exercise for the reader. It also illustrates a point the late systems architect Wayne Stevens made frequently – namely, that we very often want to string a whole bunch of functions together in a serial manner. We say "do A and B and C and...", which is basically the same as "take the output of A and feed it to B; now take the output of B and feed it to C, and so on..." This is exactly the same as the pipelines of the UNIX system or MS DOS. This is such a natural and important function that a number of systems use a single character (|) to represent this. In the DFDM and THREADS interpretable notations we just used two key-strokes (->) to represent this relationship.

So far, we have worked with quite simple structures which either string together "filters" in what is sometimes called a "string of pearls" pattern, or we had one data stream generate more than one ("divergent" patterns). There is a point to be made about divergent flows: once two streams diverge, they will no longer be synchronized. Some software systems go to a lot of trouble to keep them synchronized, but our experience is that, most of the time, it is not necessary or desirable. There are ways to resynchronize them if you really have to, but you may find it's not worth the trouble! For one thing, in the chapter on deadlocks (Chapter 16 – page 156) we will find that resynchronization is a potential cause of deadlocks.

Chap. VIII: Building Components & Some More Simple Applications

People very often split data streams so that different parts of their networks can handle different IP types – this works best if you do not need to retain any timing relationships between the different types. If you do, there is a variant of the "string of pearls" technique that you may find useful: have each "pearl" look after one IP type and pass all the other ones through. Its (partial) pseudo-code would then look as follows:

```
receive from port IN using a
if type of 'a' is XXX
        process type XXX
endif
send a to port OUT
```

You can then string as many of these together as you want and each pearl will look after its own data type and ignore all the others.

Now it's time to talk about various types of Merge function.

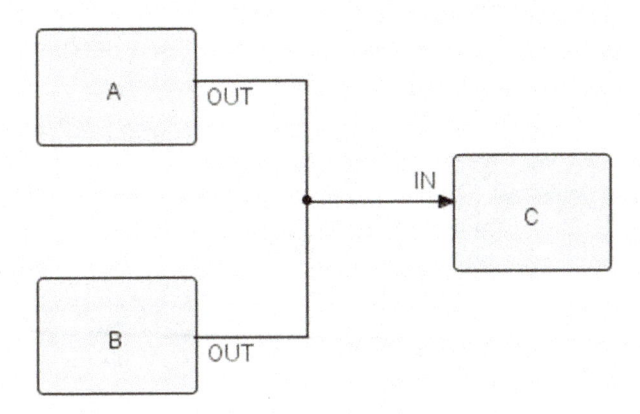

Figure 8.8

There is a basic merge built right into FBP: the first-come, first-served merge. This is done very simply by connecting two or more output ports to one input port, as shown in Figure 8.8.

The connection ending at *C*'s IN port is a single connection with two sources, and one sink – FBP does not support multiple sinks for a single connection. IPs being sent out along this connection will arrive at *C*'s IN port interleaved. The IPs sent out by *A* will still arrive in the correct sequence, but their sequencing relative to the output of *B* will be unpredictable. Why would you use this structure? Surprisingly often! *C* might be a Sort, so the sequence of its incoming IPs is going to be changed anyway. The IPs from the two output streams may be easily distinguishable, so we can always separate them out later. *C* may be interested in receiving its

Chap. VIII: Building Components & Some More Simple Applications

input data as fast as possible – any additional sequencing may cause delays, and in fact may even cause deadlocks.

Now perhaps the first-come, first-served merge may not be adequate, in which case we will need a process at the junction of the two streams. This may be a custom-coded merge component, or you may be able to use one of the ones supplied with the FBP software, for instance Collate or Concatenate. Both of these use one or more port elements of a single array port to handle their input streams, so we will use this convention. The reason for this is that they can handle any number of input streams up to the implementation maximum. Of course, custom components could call one input port JOE and the other one JIM – it's up to the developer (of course assuming the component's users will put up with it!).

Our diagram now looks like this:

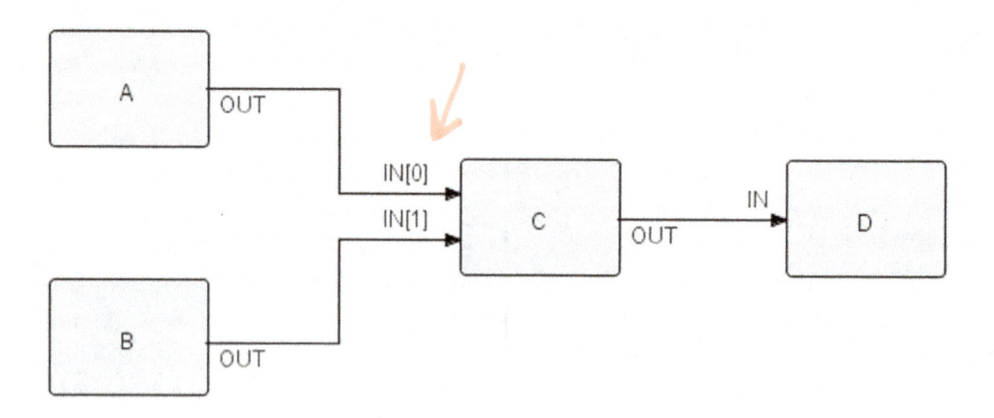

Figure 8.9

Now we have:

- OUT of *A* connected to IN[0] of *C*
- OUT of *B* connected to IN[1] of *C*
- OUT of *C* connected to IN of *D*

If *C* is a Collate, then the output of *A* will be merged with the output of *B* according to key values – usually the key fields are specified to Collate by means of option IPs. Alternatively the Collate may use one or more named fields which will be related to the IPs by means of descriptors (see page 110).

Now, if we were to use Concatenate instead of Collate, then what we are saying is that we want *C* to send all of *A*'s output on to *D* before it accepts any of *B*'s output. As we said above, there are

Chap. VIII: Building Components & Some More Simple Applications

some situations where this can be useful, too. Collate, however, is a very powerful component, and in conjunction with the ideas described in the next chapter, significantly simplifies application programs which would be extremely complex using conventional programming techniques. Collate also provides a natural mechanism for implementing the SQL join function – which is probably getting to be more familiar to today's programmers than the traditional batch update!

I recently came across what some consider the perfect example of the utility of coroutines (FBP processes) – it's called the Same Fringe Problem. It is described in a 1991 paper by Richard Gabriel: *http://www.dreamsongs.com/10ideas.html*, and a number of solutions in different languages are described on Ward's Wiki – *http://c2.com/cgi/wiki?SameFringeProblem*. Here is the definition:

> Two binary trees have the same fringe if they have exactly the same leaves reading from left to right.

If you look at the solutions in various languages, you can see that the FBP solution is far and away the simplest! Here is the picture:

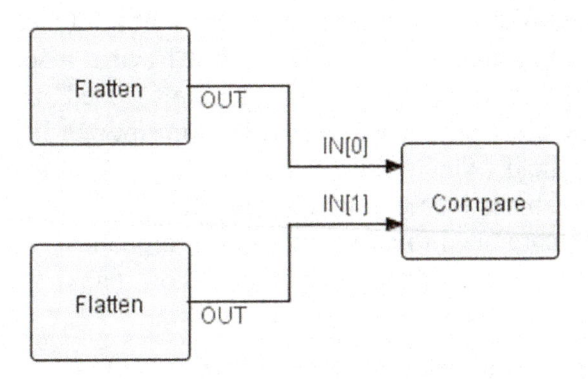

Figure 8.10

where each instance of *FLATTEN* walks a tree and sends out an IP for each leaf. *COMPARE* reads pairs of leaves, one from each input port, compares them and terminates with some kind of error message if a pair doesn't match up; otherwise *COMPARE* continues until all input IP pairs have been received and processed. Simple!

Chap. IX: Substreams and Control IPs

We are now going to expand on the use of the Collate component mentioned in the previous chapter. This chapter will also show how Collate, substreams and control IPs can be combined to address one of the most difficult types of conventional business batch application. The main function of Collate, just as it was for the Collator Unit Record machine from which it gets its name, is to merge the IPs in its incoming data streams based on values in key fields (the definition of these key fields is normally specified in an options IP). In most applications, we have more than one key field, which are used to specify different levels of grouping. As an example, let's take a file of bank accounts within branches. In this particular bank, we'll say that account numbers are not guaranteed to be unique across branches. Another way of saying this is that to make an account number unique across the whole bank, we must specify the branch number.

Suppose we have a batch application where a stream of banking transactions must be run against a stream of account records. This is often the most efficient way of updating the account records when you have to process millions of them every day. One might think that it would be simpler to just access each account record directly, but this will be extremely I/O-intensive, so the batch approach is still extremely heavily used, and it is one of the hardest types of application to code using traditional programming techniques, and is usually referred to as an "Update" program. I once figured that something like a quarter of all business programs running today are Updates! Whether or not that is the right figure, Update programs are hard to code and harder to modify, and yet the only assistance programmers ever received in pre-FBP days is a piece of paper, handed down from father to son, showing the basic logic for Updates, which is a pattern of moves and compares usually called the "Balance Line" technique. This logic then has to be modified by hand to suit the particular situation you are faced with. However, it is still only a description of an approach – to adapt it to a particular application you have to massively modify it. I once had the dubious pleasure of having to modify an update program (not FBP, obviously!) whose author had written the client an explanation of why his enhancement request could not be satisfied, which started, "Owing to the limitations of data processing,...."! My clear recollection is that modifying that program (and, for a conventional program, it was really quite well-written) was only *almost* impossible!

Now imagine what you could do if you had a prewritten, pretested component for collating data streams. Let us imagine that we have a file of transactions and a file of accounts, both sorted by account number within branch. We set up two Reader processes, and collate their output streams into a single one, specifying branch number and account number as "major" and "minor" control fields, respectively. When Collate finds two equal records from two different port elements, it outputs the one from the lowest-numbered element first. The resulting output stream might contain the following sort of pattern:

```
IP type     branch    acct #      date        amount    DEP/WD
account        1         1
trans          1         1      1992/3/12      12.82     DEP
trans          1         1      1992/3/12     101.99     WD
trans          1         1      1992/3/12      43.56     WD
trans          1         1      1992/3/26      54.77     WD
trans          1         1      1992/3/26      12.26     WD

account        1         2
trans          1         2      1992/3/03      34.88     DEP
trans          1         2      1992/3/03      10.00     WD
   .
   .

account        2         1
trans          2         1      1992/2/29      25.99     DEP
trans          2         1      1992/3/25      87.56     DEP
account        2         3
trans          2         3      1992/3/01      34.88     WD
trans          2         3      1992/3/17      88.22     DEP
   .
   .
```

Figure 9.1

Notice that the effect of Collate operating on sorted input streams is to give us a nicely sequenced and grouped data stream, consisting of two kinds of data IP. The job of the process downstream

Chap. IX: Substreams and Control IPs

of Collate is therefore much simpler than the conventional Balance Line, which has to do this grouping as well as implement the required business logic. A conventional Update also has to worry about what happens if one file is exhausted before the other. Instead, in our FBP solution, the actual business logic (as compared with all the logic of synchronizing the two data files) sees one IP at a time, determines its type, and decides what to do with it. In what follows, we will call this process *UPDATE_ACCTS*. One rule of thumb in conventional programming is that the complexity of a program is roughly proportional to the square of the number of input files. Just one reusable component, Collate, therefore can reduce the complexity of *UPDATE_ACCTS* significantly!

So far we have talked about the branch and account levels. Now let's assume we want to group transactions by date – bank statements often only show one subtotal per day. This then gives us three grouping levels, most of which are only recognized by changes in control fields. A change of account number is recognizable by the arrival of a new Account IP, but this cannot tell us when we have started a new branch. So a lot of the logic in a conventional Update is keyed to *changes in value* of control fields. Now, Collate has to look at all the control field values anyway, so it would be nice if we could have Collate figure out the groupings and pass that information to downstream processes, which would therefore be relieved of all this comparing to see when a given group starts or finishes. How does Collate pass this grouping information downstream? You guessed it! We use the "bracket" IPs mentioned in Chapter 3 (page 20).

Bracket IPs have a recognizable type which follows a special convention, so that they can never conflict with user-defined types. They also come in two flavours: open and close brackets. They may also contain real data (if their IP length is non-zero), which by convention we use for the name of the group they delimit. Let's get Collate to insert some brackets into its output data stream, resulting in a collated data stream that looks like the following diagram. I will use angle brackets to represent open and close bracket IPs, but this time we will show the names of the groups they refer to in the data part of the bracket IP ("date" means a group comprising all the deposits and withdrawals for a given date). To make things a bit clearer, I will use indentation to show the nesting pattern, and separate the fields using commas (CSV format). Figure 9.2 shows the first few IPs of the collated stream – the fields are: IP type (followed by a bar), branch no., account no., date, amount, and deposit vs. withdrawal (a boolean switch). Open and close brackets have an optional string to indicate the grouping they refer to, although that isn't really necessary in this example as there is only one type at each level.

Generally, the logic of *UPDATE_ACCTS* will consist of a "case" statement based on the type of the incoming IP. An open bracket will cause counters and totals for the correct level to be initialized to zero; a close bracket will cause an IP containing the counters and totals for that level to be sent to an output port. We won't even have to reinitialize the counters and totals at this point because we know that another open bracket will be coming along shortly (or end of data).

- 92 -

```
<  (branch)
  <  (account)
    account| 1, 1
    <  (same date)
      trans| 1, 1, 1992/3/12,  12.82,  DEP
      trans| 1, 1, 1992/3/12, 101.99,  WD
      trans| 1, 1, 1992/3/12,  43.56,  WD
    >  (same date)
    <  (same date)
      trans| 1, 1, 1992/3/26,  54.77,  WD
      trans| 1, 1, 1992/3/26,  12.26,  WD
    >  (same date)
  >  (account)
  <  (account)
    account| 1, 2
    <  (same date)
      trans| 1, 2, 1992/3/03,  34.88,  DEP
      trans| 1, 2, 1992/3/03,  10.00,  WD
    >  (same date)

. . . . .
```

Figure 9.2

We could either update the counters and totals at every level for every incoming data IP, or just "roll" the values into the next level up at close bracket time – it seems simpler to choose the latter. There is some redundancy in the data structure, as an account IP is always immediately preceded by an account open bracket, but this is much better than not having enough data! Since we will be needing information from the account IP, we can just ignore the account open bracket, or we can do a cross-check that they are both present ("belt and braces" programming – that's "belt and suspenders" for American readers!).

So far the main piece of logic for *UPDATE_ACCTS* (the process downstream of the Collate) is as shown in Figure 9.3.

Chap. IX: Substreams and Control IPs

```
    receive incoming IP
    begin cases based on IP type
        case: open bracket for branch
            initialize counters and totals for branch
        case: open bracket for account
            initialize counters and totals for account
        case: open bracket for date
            initialize counters and totals for date

        case: account
            pick up account info
        case: transaction
            increment counter for debit or credit
            add amount to debit or credit total

        case: close bracket for date
            output IP containing counters and totals for
              date
            roll these values to account level
        case: close bracket for account
            output IP containing counters and totals for
              account
            roll these values to branch level
        case: close bracket for branch
            output IP containing counters and totals for
              branch
    end cases
```

Figure 9.3

Notice that these groupings are perfectly "nested", and at any point of time we are only looking at one level or at most two adjacent ones. There is also considerable similarity in the "open bracket" logic for the various levels, and similarly for the "close bracket" logic. This suggests that we could handle this kind of logic more elegantly using a push-down or "last in first out" (LIFO) stack. We also have to have somewhere to hold these counters and totals in, so it make sense to hold them in IPs, and store (the references to) the IPs in the stack.. This kind of IP is called a *control IP*, and it can be described as an IP whose lifetime corresponds exactly to the lifetime of a substream, which it can be said to represent.

So the above logic now becomes much simpler:

Chap. IX: Substreams and Control IPs

```
receive incoming IP
  begin cases based on IP type
      case: open bracket
          create IP for this level
          initialize counters and totals for this level
          push IP onto stack

      case: account
          pick up account info, insert into account IP
      case: transaction
          increment counter for debit or credit in IP
             currently at head of stack
          add amount to debit or credit total in IP
             currently at head of stack

      case: close bracket
          pop IP off stack
          roll counters and totals in this IP into IP
             currently at top of stack (if any)
          output IP which was just popped off stack
  end cases
```

Figure 9.4

I happen to like stacks, and we shall see in Chapter 23 (page 235) that there are striking similarities between the way components like the one we have just described parse their input streams and the way compilers parse their input. In both cases stacks are the natural mechanism for keeping track of nested structures. We have accordingly provided a stack mechanism in most FBP implementations. This stack is outside of the component – in what we might call "IP space" – so that data in it is preserved even if the component logic exits (as long as the process is not actually terminated).

You may have noticed that Figures 9.3 and 9.4 did not have the familiar "do while receive has not reached end of data" – this is because they are written in a style which assumes that they end execution after processing each IP. In FBP an inactive process will be invoked the next time an IP arrives at any of its input ports, so this kind of component will be invoked once for each incoming IP. A result of this is that it cannot maintain continuity across multiple IPs, but this is where the stack comes in. Since the stack is outside the process's local storage, continuity can be maintained across the invocations using the stack. This style of component is called a "non-looper", as opposed to components written in the "do while receive has not reached end of data" style, which are referred to as "loopers". This is not an externally detectable attribute of a component, but just depends on when and how often the component decides to end processing –

- 95 -

Chap. IX: Substreams and Control IPs

as long as there is data to be processed, it will continue being reinvoked. Of course, this is not a hard and fast distinction, as you can have "partial loopers", e.g. where a component has decided to terminate after every *n* packets have been processed.

You may be wondering what the advantages of non-loopers are, if any. Well, for one thing, non-loopers end execution more frequently, so IPs which have not been disposed of are detected sooner, making such errors easier to find. Also, non-loopers' local storage is only used within one invocation, so there is less opportunity for one IP's logic to interfere with another's – in the case of the OO implementations (JavaFBP and C#FBP) this means that they should not use instance variables to hold application data. This is especially dangerous when the same code is being used for multiple users in an interactive application, as happens with a number of server architectures. Also we shall see in the chapter on Checkpointing (Chapter 19 – page 185) that there is an advantage to having processes yield control as often as possible, as this means that there will be more periods when the component is dormant – i.e. does not have active data that has to be checkpointed. As always, there are pros and cons.

Obviously, there is still some application logic left to be written for *UPDATE_ACCTS*, but I have tried to show that the approach of holding control IPs in a stack (together with a generalized Collate) does significantly simplify the remaining piece of logic you do have to write. One of the things that also makes this logic simpler is the fact that every action is associated with the arrival of a distinct type of IP (this is even more obvious in the case of non-loopers), rather than a change in value – this is what allows one to split up the logic of such a component into distinct self-contained cases. When talking about such logic, I often find it useful to refer to "open bracket time", or "detail time". An incoming IP triggers an action, which starts up and then finishes, readying the process for the arrival of the next IP (or end of data). In a later chapter, I will try to show that the code we still have to write has such a simple structure that we can begin to think about generating it semi-automatically from some kind of specification other than a HLL program.

By the way, as you work through this kind of logic, you may notice a characteristic flavour of FBP coding: very little of the data you will be dealing with actually resides in a process's working storage – the vast majority of it will be in IPs, very often control IPs like the ones we have just been discussing. When you think about it, this should not be that strange – in a real life office, most of your data is in files, memos or on the computer – how much data do you have to hold in your personal short-term memory? I don't know about you, but I try to hold onto as little data as possible, for as short a time as possible (after which I destroy it, pass it on it or file it – just like IPs).

Chap. X: Some More Components and Simple Applications

In this chapter, we will be working with a more complex example, the Sales Statistics application described in (Leavenworth 1977). The referenced paper describes an application in which a sorted detail file of product sales is run against a product master file, producing an updated master file and two reports: a summary by product and a summary by district and salesman. The figure on the next page, which originally appeared in (Morrison 1978), shows the FBP process network for this application.

In the conventional approach to building this application, we would first split off the district/salesman summary into a separate job step preceded by a Sort. This leaves us with a function which accepts two input files and generates three outputs (updated master, product summary and Sort input, also referred to as extended details). This function must pass details against masters, take care of the fact that one of the files will usually terminate before the other, handle control breaks, detect out-of-sequence conditions, etc., etc.

As we said in the previous chapter, the Collate component is key to simplifying this kind of application. The resultant diagram is shown in Figure 10.1.

The output of the Collate component consists of sequences of groups, called "substreams", each consisting of an open bracket, a master, zero or more details, and a close bracket. This is shown schematically in Figure 10.2 below.

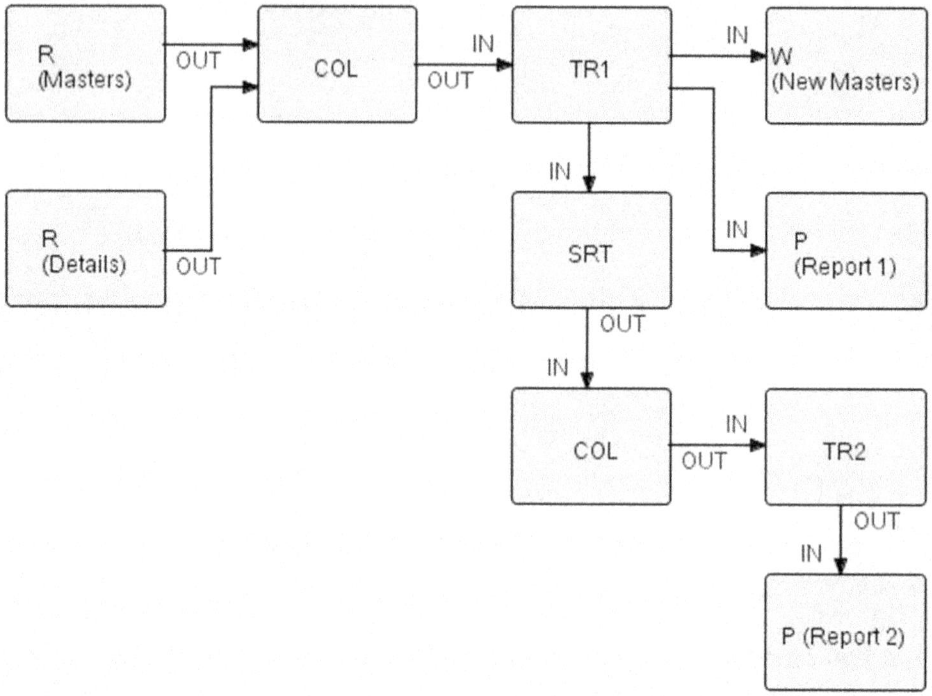

Chap. X: Some More Components and Simple Applications

Figure 10.1

where

- *R* is a Read component.
- *W* is a Write component.
- *COL* is a generalized Collate which merges two or more streams on the basis of specified control fields and inserts bracket IPs between IPs with different control field values. (If used with only one stream, it simply inserts bracket IPs – this is the case in the second occurrence of *COL*).
- *P* is a Print component.
- *TR1* and *TR2* correspond to Tran-1 and Tran-2, respectively, in B. Leavenworth's paper
- *SRT* is a generalized "Sort" component which sorts the Extended Details coming out of Tran-1, by Salesman within District.

- 98 -

Chap. X: Some More Components and Simple Applications

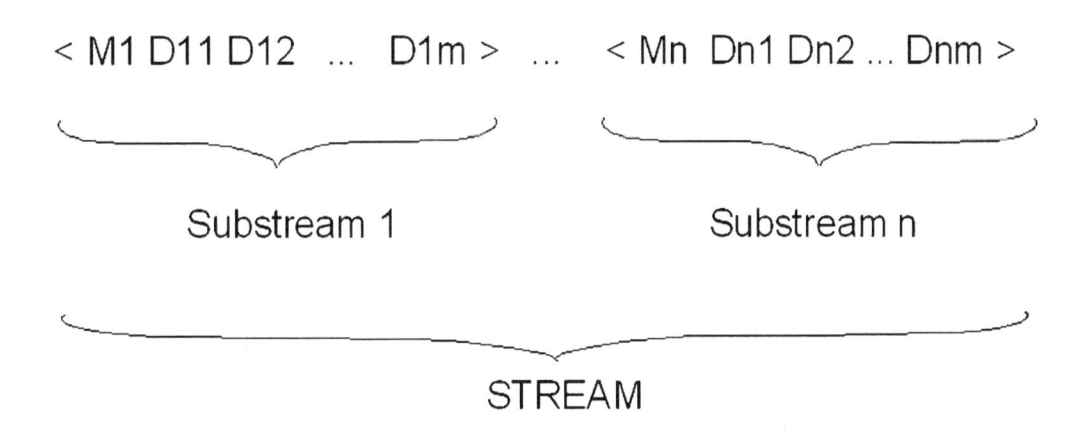

$$< M1\ D11\ D12\ ...\ D1m >\ ...\ < Mn\ Dn1\ Dn2\ ...\ Dnm >$$

$$\underbrace{\qquad\qquad\qquad}_{\text{Substream 1}} \qquad \underbrace{\qquad\qquad\qquad}_{\text{Substream n}}$$

$$\underbrace{\qquad\qquad\qquad\qquad\qquad\qquad\qquad\qquad\qquad}_{\text{STREAM}}$$

Figure 10.2

J-D. Warnier (1974) uses a vertical form of the above diagram to define the input and output files of an application, and uses this to determine the structure of the code which has to process them. Unfortunately, control flow programming requires that one of the files has to become the driver in terms of the overall program structure, so that, if there are any significant differences between the structures of the different files, the program structure becomes less and less easy to derive and understand, and hence to maintain. In FBP, this structure tells us important things about just those components which receive or send this particular stream structure, so it remains an extremely useful device for understanding the logic of the application.

Figure 10.3 shows the input stream for *TR1* as it might be expressed using an extension of J-D Warnier's notation.

Of course, in Warnier's book, this type of diagram is used to describe actual files, rather than FBP streams, but I believe it generalizes quite nicely to IPs, substreams and streams. The last column, of course, is fields within IPs.

Another methodology with close affinities to Warnier's is the Jackson methodology, already alluded to. He uses a horizontal version of this notation, using asterisks to indicate repeating items. Figure 10.4 shows how this diagram might look using his notation.

By the way, a given substream may not have a master IP – this would be a situation where the transactions refer to a non-existent master, or may in fact contain an "add" transaction to create a new one.

- 99 -

Chap. X: Some More Components and Simple Applications

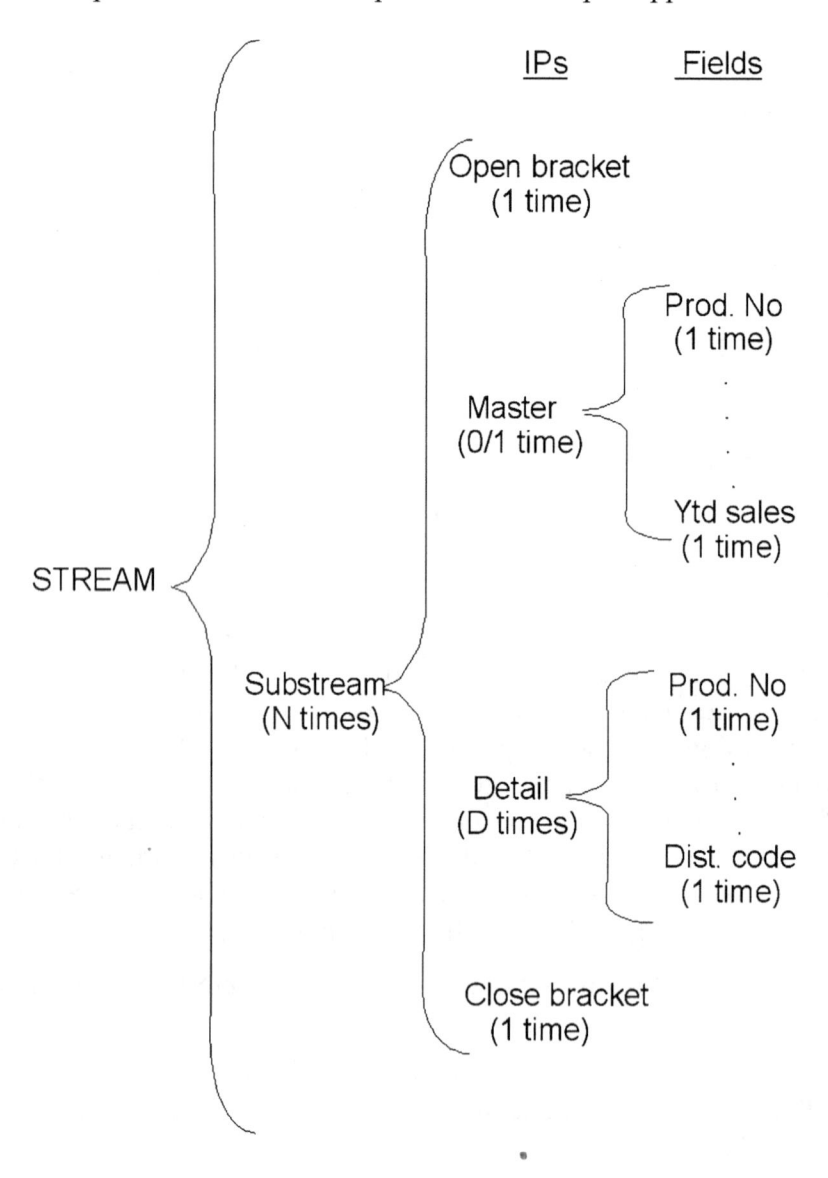

```
                                IPs              Fields

              ┌  Open bracket
              │   (1 time)
              │
              │                        ┌ Prod. No
              │                        │  (1 time)
              │        Master          │      .
              │       (0/1 time)       │      .
              │                        │      .
              │                        └ Ytd sales
              │                           (1 time)
STREAM  ┤
              │                        ┌ Prod. No
              │  Substream             │  (1 time)
              │  (N times)             │      .
              │        Detail          │      .
              │       (D times)        │      .
              │                        └ Dist. code
              │                           (1 time)
              │
              │  Close bracket
              └   (1 time)
```

Figure 10.3

The Jackson equivalent follows on the next page (Figure 10.4).

- 100 -

Chap. X: Some More Components and Simple Applications

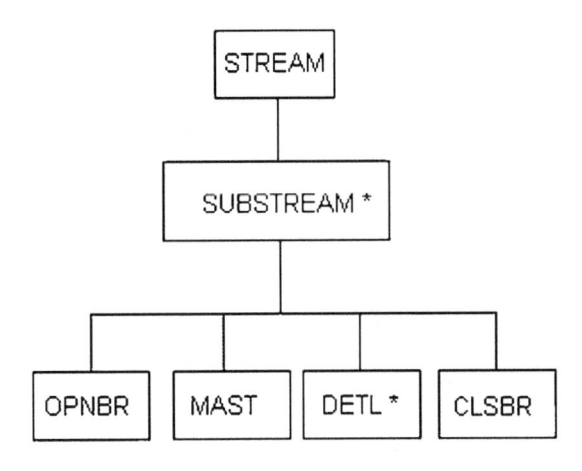

```
                    ┌────────┐
                    │ STREAM │
                    └────────┘
                         │
                  ┌─────────────┐
                  │ SUBSTREAM * │
                  └─────────────┘
                         │
        ┌────────┬───────┴───────┬────────┐
    ┌───────┐ ┌──────┐      ┌────────┐ ┌───────┐
    │ OPNBR │ │ MAST │      │ DETL * │ │ CLSBR │
    └───────┘ └──────┘      └────────┘ └───────┘
```

Figure 10.4

Now, going back to our example, *TR1* generates three output streams – one consisting of updated master records, one of summary records, which were similar to masters but had a different format (they were intended for a report-printing component), and one of "extended" details: detail records with an "extended price" field (quantity times unit price) added.

In the OO implementations, summary records need not be a different class from masters, as they contain the same data, but we will keep the same name for ease of understanding.

The following computations must be performed:

```
extended price (in detail) :=
   quantity from detail * unit price from corresponding
       master record

product total (in summary) :=
   sum of extended prices over the details relating
       to one product master

year-to-date sales (in summary and updated master) :=
    year-to-date sales from incoming master record +  product total
```

Figure 10.5

We have talked above about using non-loopers with stacks to handle nested streams and substreams. If we add a stack to our *TR1* components, we get the following "blown up" picture of *TR1* (the stack is not normally shown in a network definition – I just show it to emphasize that it is "external" to the process):

- 101 -

Chap. X: Some More Components and Simple Applications

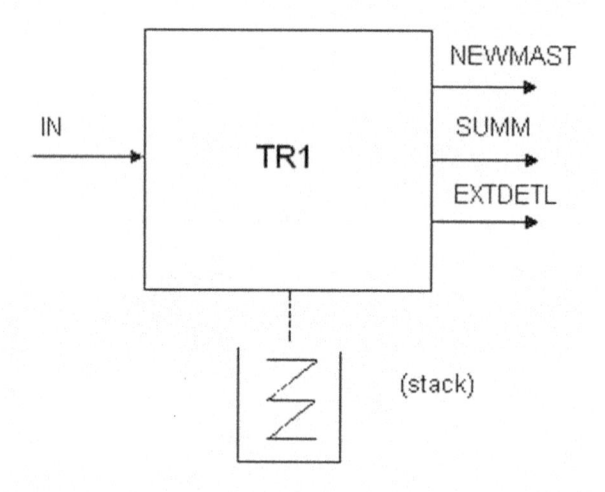

Figure 10.6

Here is the logic that needs to be performed for each incoming IP (as you can see, it is very similar to the logic we showed in the previous chapter):

```
• At "open bracket time",
    • create a control IP
    • store the IP in the stack
• At "master time",
    • obtain the control IP from the stack
    • copy the information from the incoming master into the control
      IP, such as unit price, year-to-date sales, etc.
    • clear the total quantity and sales total fields field in this new
      IP
    • discard the master IP
    • replace the control IP in the stack (you have to remove an IP
      from the stack before it can be processed)
• At "detail time",
    • obtain the control IP from the stack
    • update the total quantity by the quantity in the detail IP
    • calculate an "extended price" for the detail
    • update the total sales by the calculated value in the detail IP
```

```
                  • put out the extended detail to its own output port
                  • return the control IP to the stack
        • At "close bracket time",
                  • obtain the control IP from the stack
                  • create a summary
                  • calculate the product total (dollars)
                  • format the summary IP and put out to the summary port
                  • create a master IP with the information from the control IP,
                    and put to the "updated master" output port
                  • discard the control IP
                  • the stack is now empty, so that when the next open bracket
                    arrives, a new control IP can be "pushed" onto the stack,
                    preserving the stack depth
        • At end of data,
                  • the process closes down, resulting in its output ports being
                    closed, which in turn allows its downstream processes to start
                    their own close-down procedures.
```

Figure 10.7

Note that the updated master IP is not output until "close bracket time", as all the details for a given master have to be processed first.

FBP is chiefly concerned with dynamic IPs, rather than with variables. Although it might at first glance seem that this would result in undisciplined use and modification of data, in fact we have better control of data because each IP is individually tracked from the moment of creation to the time it is finally destroyed, and it cannot simply disappear, or be duplicated without some component issuing a specific command to do this. During an IP's transit through the system, it can only be owned by one process at a time, so there is no possibility of two processes modifying one IP at the same time. We in fact monitor this at execution time, by marking an IP with the ID of its owning process: the act of getting addressability to an IP, if successful, confers "ownership" of that IP on the process doing it.

In fact, in this example almost all modifiable data is in IPs, and there is no global data at all. FBP did not require a global facility during its earlier years, and, although it has been added to some dialects of FBP, it is still only used very occasionally.

We can also use Figure 10.1 to illustrate how easy it is to modify this kind of network, whether it is to satisfy business requirements, improve performance, or for whatever reason. Here is what I said in my article (Morrison 1978) about how this diagram might be modified (this article uses the term DSLM (Data Stream Linkage Mechanism) for the cluster of concepts which we now call FBP):

"A valid objection can be raised that sorting is just one way of arranging information

Chap. X: Some More Components and Simple Applications

into a desired sequence, and that the decision as to the exact technique should not be made too early. The point is that DSLM allows the designer to concentrate on the flow of data and in fact makes the available options more visible and more controllable. For instance, in the above example the designer may decide that, for various reasons, he prefers to construct a table of district and salesman codes and totals, which will be updated randomly as the extended details come out of TR1."

I then went on to suggest that the subnet demarcated by the dashed lines in the diagram below could be replaced by a network which updates totals at random, then signals a scan and report function to display the resulting totals, i.e.

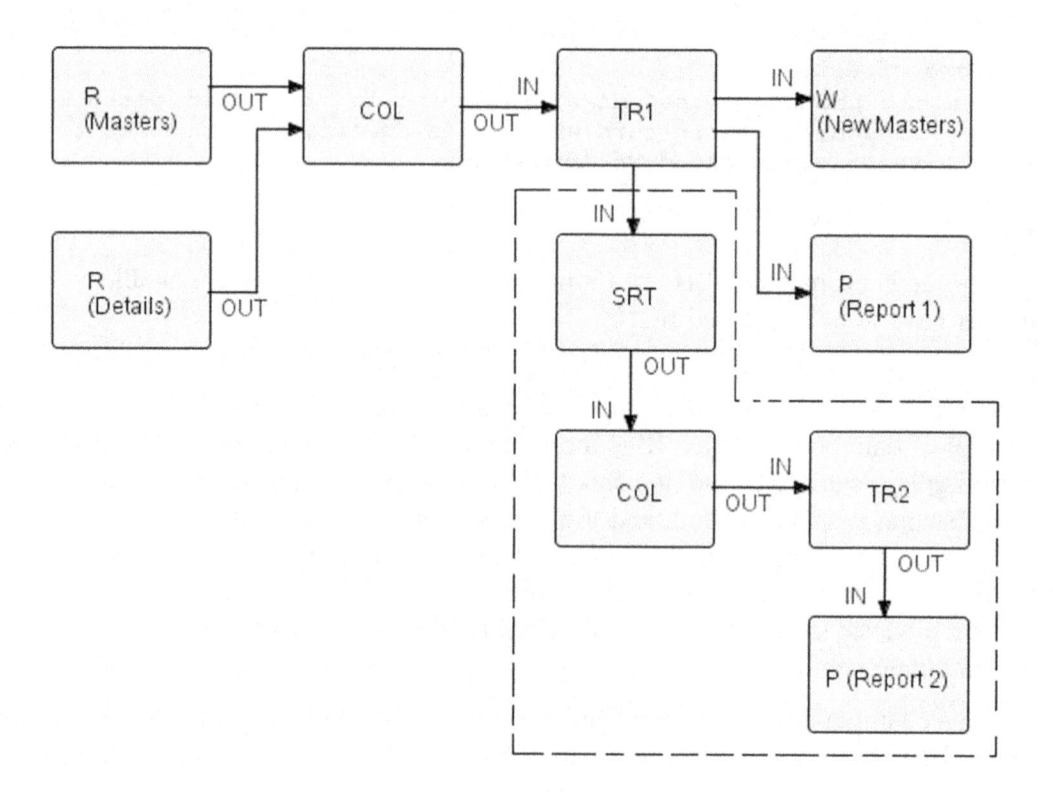

Figure 10.8

Figure 10.8 could be modified as shown in Figure 10.9.

Here RAND is a component which updates totals in a table using indexing, while SCAN goes through all the totals at end of job, generating report lines.

- 104 -

Chap. X: Some More Components and Simple Applications

How does SCAN get triggered and, once triggered, how does it get access to the table which has been built by RAND? Well, since, in FBP, all that moves through connections are the handles for IPs, why not have RAND just "send" the whole table? This ensures a) that SCAN doesn't start until RAND has finished, and b) it takes care of SCAN getting addressability to the table – *at the right time*! In conventional programming, tables don't move around – and, in fact, in FBP they don't either, but it is very convenient to make them appear to!

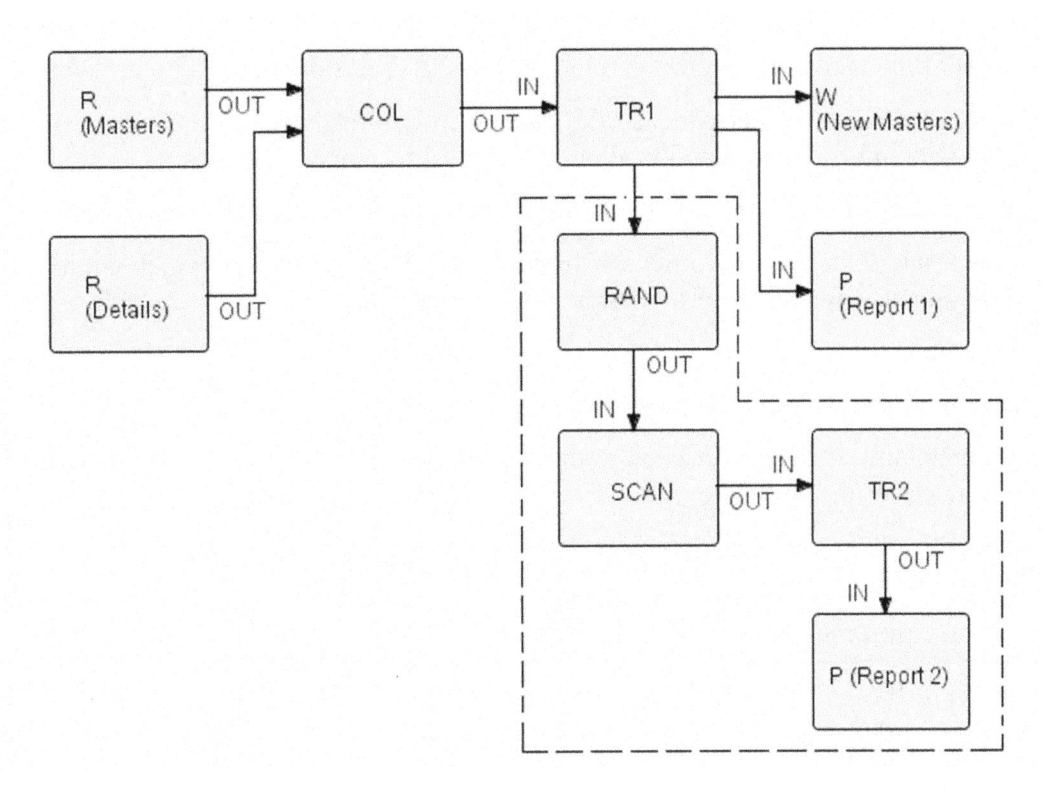

Figure 10.9

I mentioned a "report generation" component above. You will find this essential for your batch business applications, and it illustrates the power of FBP and also FBP's ability to help you divide function into manageable components. For almost all our business applications we found that we needed a component which would accept formatted lines and combine them into report pages. An upstream process can have the job of generating the formatted lines, and this type of function should be kept separate from page formatting. FBP is a "black box" reuse tool, and in fact your Report Generator component can be used as a black box by your applications. As such, it can implement the standards for reports in your installation, and it can make it easier for programmers to conform to your standards by making it less work (definitely the best way to

Chap. X: Some More Components and Simple Applications

encourage adherence to standards)! So far, so good. However, every shop has a different report standard, so you will have to build your own black box to embody your own standards. Luckily it is easy to build new components using the FBP API calls. If we decide that we want to distribute this kind of component more widely, it seems to call for a different distribution technique: either in source format, or implemented as a pure black box, but with installation-provided exits (callbacks), or as a black box supporting a mini-language. Perhaps we should call this a "grey box".

Here is a list of the facilities we provided in the Report Generator we used in our shop:

- accept two lines of permanent title information as run-time options, and combine these with date information in an installation-standard format
- accept two dates for the run: the actual date and the effective date ("as of" date)
- accept additional title information from an additional IP stream which could be changed dynamically (on receipt of a "change title" signal)
- generate page numbers
- accept a signal to reset the page number
- generate an "end of report" box at the end of the report (this lets the human receiving the report know it is complete)
- generate a "report aborted" box on the report on demand
- support all of the above features in English, French or bilingual English and French (under control of an option).

This may seem like a long list, but it basically embodied a preexisting set of shop standards, some of which were supported by subroutines, but some weren't. Now, instead of having to mandate a standard which people see as extra work, we had a component which did it "automagically". In our experience, it is much easier to enforce a standard which saves people work. If they use your component, their reports will follow shop standards, and your systems will also be more reliable and cheaper to build and maintain. You can tell your developers, "We don't mind if you don't follow standards, but it'll cost you, and, if you miss your deadlines, we'll be asking for an explanation!". The same philosophy was followed in the early days of hardware development. Designers were perfectly free to create new components, but they had to carry the whole cost of development, testing, etc., themselves. Today, it is no coincidence that the vast majority of personal computers are built around a very small number of different processor chips. This is a variant of a point we will come back to often – only by changing the *economics* of application development will we get the kind of behaviour we are trying to encourage.

One last point may appear obvious at first: this Report Generator assumes that its input IPs are fully formatted report lines. Formatting of these report lines may logically be split off into

Chap. X: Some More Components and Simple Applications

separate components. Now, programmers rooted in conventional programming may feel that such rigid separation is not possible, but they have not had the experience of using a separate component which makes such separation attractive economically, as well as logically. Once such a thing exists, people find that they can make intelligent decisions balancing esthetic considerations against economic ones. Without such a component, you don't even have a choice!

A component like the Report Generator can be added to your application incrementally – that is, you first get your application working with a simple line-by-line printer component, then replace that with the report generation component to produce a good-looking report. Although you are introducing more function into your application, you can predict very accurately how much time it is going to take to do this. As a development approach, I call this the "centre out" development approach – you can get the core logic working first, and then add formatting, input editing, etc., later.

In conventional programming, many writers have commented on the exponential relationship between size of application and resources to develop it. This graph typically has the following shape:

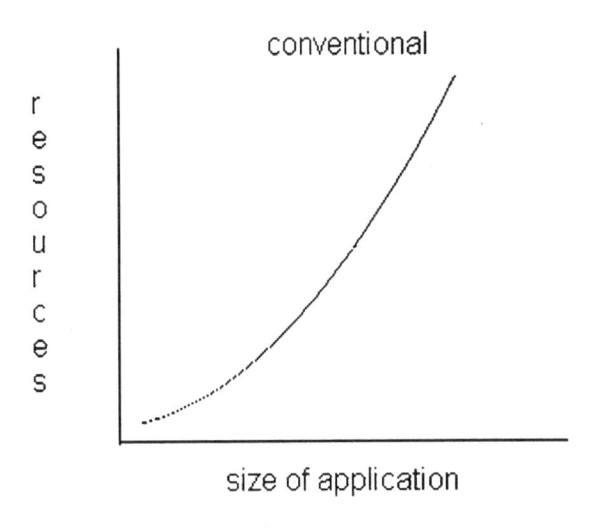

Figure 10.10

Development using FBP shows an essentially linear relationship, as follows:

- 107 -

Chap. X: Some More Components and Simple Applications

resources
                                  ....FBP
          size of application

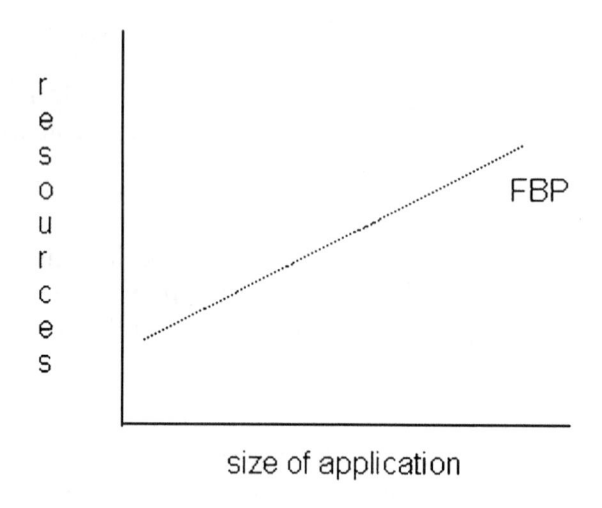

Figure 10.11

Superimposing the two graphs (even if we allow for the possibility that start-up costs may be slightly higher – in FBP you tend to do more design work up front), we get the following picture:

resources
              conventional
                            FBP
          size of application

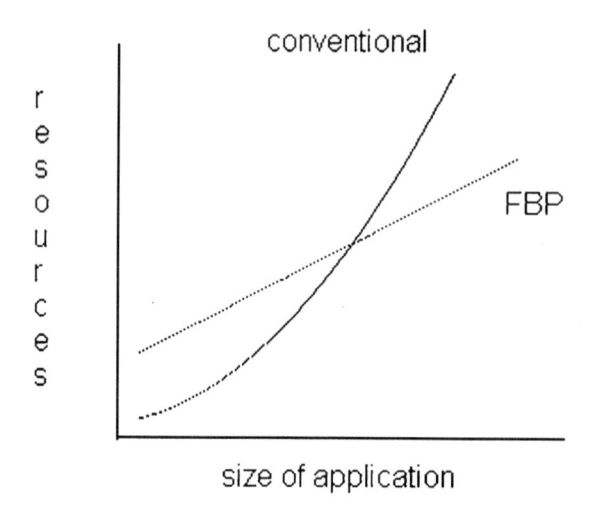

Figure 10.12

- 108 -

Chap. X: Some More Components and Simple Applications

Clearly at some point (and we have found this to occur even with surprisingly small applications), FBP's productivity starts to overtake that of control flow, and in fact gets better the larger the application. *FBP scales up!* My colleague Chuck (he of the 200-process application) didn't have to worry that his application was going to become harder and harder to debug as it got bigger – he just built it methodically, step by step – and it has since had one of the lowest error rates of any application in the shop. Finally, in case you think that this only worked because he was a single individual who could hold it all in his head, ask yourselves what are the requirements for successfully managing a big project. Surely, some of the more important ones are exactly what FBP provides so well: a consistent view, clean interfaces and components with well-defined functions.

Chap. XI: Data Descriptions and Descriptors

The reader will note similarities between this chapter and Object-Oriented (OO) concepts. The concepts described in this chapter are not really central to FBP, but we feel they are important for application development in general, and we were able to integrate them smoothly into our earlier FBP implementations, and a subset into the OO ones: JavaFBP and C#FBP. Even though a lot of the following discussion, especially when I use the term "layouts", applies to the non-OO implementations of FBP, a surprising amount of what follows will have counterparts in the OO world! In what follows, I will argue that using `int` or `float` for monetary amounts is dangerous in any language. Even though OO languages allow one to use more sophisticated data types, nothing prevents the programmer from using primitive data types for money or other dimensioned values – and I am not aware of any language that does! Since FBP is so heavily data-oriented, it makes sense to try to manage data as intelligently as possible.

Up to now, you will have probably noticed that we have usually been assuming that all components "know" the layouts (which includes encoding techniques) of the IPs they handle. The layouts of all IP types that a component can handle and the IP types that it can generate become part of the specification of that component, just as much as the overall function is. If you feed something raw material it can't digest, you are bound to have problems, just as in the real world!

In conventional programs, you usually use the same layout for a structure or file record in all the subroutines of a program, which reduces the portability of subroutines that could be shared across applications, but in FBP actually only each pair of neighbouring processes has to agree on the layout. This means that a process can receive data in one format and send it on in a different format. If two neighbouring processes (perhaps written by different suppliers) are using different layouts, all you have to do is add a transform process in between.

Chap. XI: Data Descriptions and Descriptors

Now suppose you at first wanted to have two neighbouring processes communicate by means of 20-element arrays. You then decide this is too restrictive, so you stay with the arrays, but allow them to communicate the size of the arrays at run-time. This is a type of "metadata", data about data, and can be as much or as little as the two processes involved want. For instance, their agreement might specify that the array size is to be positioned as a separate field (it could even be a separate IP) ahead of the array.

Now most higher level languages don't support metadata very well, so you are dependent on having the data formats imbedded in a program. Also, it is easy for old data to get out of step with the programs that describe them. There is a perhaps apocryphal story that somebody discovered several decades ago that the majority of the tapes in the US Navy's magnetic tape library were illegible. It wasn't that the tapes had I/O errors – they were in perfect shape physically – but the problem was that the layouts of the tape records were hard-coded within program code, and nobody knew which programs or copy code described which tapes!

In DFDM we extended the idea of metadata by providing run-time descriptions which could be attached to IPs passing across a connection. DFDM allowed the creator of an IP to attach a separately compiled descriptor to the IP, which was used by special DFDM services which accessed fields by name. Whenever an IP was created, the "allocate" function could optionally specify a descriptor which was to be permanently associated with that IP. All the IPs of the same type would share the same descriptor. This of course is very similar to what OO systems do today – FBP has in fact sometimes been described as "the first OO system".

In DFDM these access services were called GETV and SETV ("get value" and "set value"). They had the advantage that, if you ever wanted to move a field (call it AMOUNT) from one place to another in the structure containing it, you didn't have to recompile all the programs referring to it. Another advantage was that, with a single call, a component could access a field which might be at different offsets in different types of incoming IP. For example, the field called AMOUNT could be at different locations in different IP types, and the component would still be able to access it or modify it, as long as the IPs had descriptors. The DFDM GETV and SETV services (and their descendants) were designed to be called from S/370 Assembler or from the HLLs we supported. They also provided limited conversion facilities between similar field formats – for example, between 2-byte and 4-byte binary fields, between different lengths and scales of packed decimal (a format which encodes 2 digits in each byte, except for the rightmost one which holds a digit and a sign), or between varying and non-varying character strings. Thus you could specify that you wanted to see a binary field as 4 bytes in working storage, even though it was only 2 bytes in the IP.

Without such a facility, the layout of incoming IPs has to be part of the specification of all components. This points up another advantage of GETV and SETV: if a component is only interested in three fields, only those specific field names have to be mentioned in the specification for the component, rather than the whole layout of the IPs in question.

Chap. XI: Data Descriptions and Descriptors

When you add this facility to the idea of option IPs, you get a powerful way of building more user-friendly black boxes. For instance, you could write a Collator which specified two field names for its major and minor keys, respectively. It would then use GETV to locate these fields in the correct place in all incoming IPs. "Collate on Salesman Number within Branch" seems much more natural than "Collate on bytes 1-6 and 7-9 for IP type A, bytes 4-9 and 1-3 for IP type B," and so on. Thus it is much better to parametrize generalized components using symbolic field names, rather than lengths and offsets. The disadvantage, of course, is performance: the component has to access the fields involved using the appropriate API calls, rather than compiled-in offsets. However, the additional CPU time is usually a negligible cost factor compared with the cost of the human time required for massive recompiles when something changes, or, still worse, the cost of finding and correcting errors introduced while making the changes!

When we looked at the problems of passing data descriptions between components, we rapidly got into the problem of what the data "means": in the case of our conventional Higher Level Languages, the emphasis has always been on generating the desired machine instruction. For instance, on IBM mainframes, currency is usually held as a packed decimal field, and usually amounts are held with 2 decimal places (these usually have special names, e.g. cents relative to dollars, new pence relative to pounds, and so forth – are there any mixed radix currencies left in the world, like pounds, shillings and pence?). Since the instructions on the machine don't care about scale (number of decimal places), the compiler has to keep track of scale information and make sure it is handled correctly for all operations. (You could conceivably use floating point notation, but this has other characteristics which make it less suitable for business calculations).

Now suppose a component receives an IP and tries to access a currency field in it based on its compiled-in knowledge of the IP's layout. If the compiled code has been told that the field has 2 places of decimals, that's what the component will "see". So we can now do arithmetic with the number, display it in the right format (if we know what national currency we are dealing with), and so forth. But note that the layout of the IP is only defined in the code – the code cannot tell where the fields really start and stop. So we have a sort of mutual dependency: the only definition of the data is in the code, and the code is tightly tied to the format of the data. If you want to decouple the two, you have to have a separate description of the data which various routines can interrogate, which can be attached to the data, independent of what routines are going to work with that data. If this is powerful enough, it will also let you access older forms of your data, say, on an old file (the "legacy data" problem).

Apart from format information, you also have to identify what *type* of data a field contains. For instance, the number

```
19920131
```

might be a balance in a savings account ($199,201.31), but it could also be a date (31st January,

Chap. XI: Data Descriptions and Descriptors

1992). Depending on which it is, we will want to perform very different operations on it. Conversely a function like "display", which applies to both data types, will result in very different results:

```
$199,201.31
```

versus

```
31st January, 1992
```

The traditional HLLs PL/I and COBOL will see both data types as FIXED DECIMAL and COMPUTATIONAL-3 respectively. And, of course, you can do the same kind of thing in an OO language – nobody can *force* programmers to use business classes. Again, only the program knows which kind of data is in the field (by using the right operations). There is also the issue of which representation is being used. We have all (especially Canadians!) run into the problem of not knowing whether 01021992 is January 2 (American convention) or February 1 (British convention). So we have to record somewhere which digits represent the day, which the month and which the year. Thus a complete description of our field has what we might call "base type" (signed packed decimal, in this case), length (and perhaps scale), domain *and* representation. Some systems use a standard representation for "internal" data, or at least a format which is less variable than "external" formats, but the "data about data" (metadata) items which I have just described are pretty basic. (Base type could be treated logically as part of the more general domain information, but it turns out to be useful for designing such functions as "dumb" print processes). In some systems, domain is referred to as "logical type", and representation as "physical type".

Let us now look at another example of the pitfalls of programs not knowing what kind of data they are working with. Suppose that you have coded the following PL/I statement in a program by mistake:

```
NET_PAY = GROSS_PAY * TAX;
```

where TAX is a computed amount of tax, not the *tax rate*. The compiler isn't going to hesitate for a microsecond. It will blithely multiply two decimal values together to give another decimal value (assuming this is how these fields are defined), even though the result is perfectly meaningless. Remember: computers do what you tell them, not what you mean! We used to say there should be DWIM instruction on the machine (Do What I Mean)! A human, on the other hand, would spot the error immediately (we hope), because we know that you can't multiply currency figures together. The compiler knows that the result of multiplying two numbers each with 2 decimal places is a number with 4 decimal places, so it will carefully trim off the 2 extra decimal places from the result (maybe even rounding the result to the nearest cent). What it can't do is tell us whether the whole operation makes any sense in the first place!

Chap. XI: Data Descriptions and Descriptors

One other (real world) problem with currency figures is that inflation will make them steadily larger without increasing their real value. If 11 digits seemed quite enough in 1970, the same sort of information may need 13 or 15 digits in 1992. It is disconcerting to have your program report that you mislaid exactly a billion dollars (even though it is usually a good hint about what's wrong)! It would be nice if we could avoid building this kind of information into the logic of our applications. If we had an external description of a file, we could either use this dynamically at run-time, or convert the data into some kind of standard internal format – with lots of room for inflation, of course! The other place where this affects our systems in in screen and report layouts. As we shall see, these are also areas where it makes a lot of sense to hold descriptions separately, and interpret them at run-time. What we don't want to do is have to recompile our business systems every time some currency amount gets too big for the fields which hold it.

This is another legacy of the mathematical origins of today's computers – everything is viewed as a mathematical construct – integers, real numbers, vectors, matrices. In real life, almost everything has a dimension and a unit, e.g. weight, in pounds or kilograms, or distance, in miles or kilometres. If you multiply two distances together, you should get area (acres or hectares); three distances give volume, in cubic centimetres, bushels or litres. Currency amounts can never be multiplied together, although you can add and subtract them. Dates can't even be added, although you can subtract one date from another. There is a temptation with dates to just convert them into a canonical form (number of days from a reference date – for instance, Jan. 1, 1800) and then assume you can do anything with them. In fact, they remain dates, just represented differently, and you still can't add them.... On the other hand, you *can* do things like ask what day of the week a date falls on, what is the date of the following Monday, how many business days there are between June 30 and August 10, etc. (although holiday processing is not as straightforward, being region-dependent).

We have used the term "representation" quite a lot so far. Some of the above complexities come from confusing what the data is with how it is represented. The data is really a value, drawn from a domain (defined as a set of possible values). We really shouldn't care how the data is represented internally – we only care when we have to interface with humans, or a file is coming from another system. However, we do have to care every time we interface with current higher level languages. The requirements for interfacing with humans involve even more interesting considerations such as national languages and national conventions for writing numbers and dates, which should as far as possible be encapsulated within off-the-shelf subroutines.

Multilingual support is an increasingly important area. Some Asian languages involve double-byte coding, which differs from machine to machine, as well as from language to language. Computer users no longer feel that they should have to learn English to use an application, although most programmers are still willing to do so! This attitude on the part of programmers still sometimes laps over into what they build for their customers, but the more sophisticated ones know that we are living in a global market, and that computers have to adapt to people, rather

Chap. XI: Data Descriptions and Descriptors

than the other way around. In many ways, Canada has been at the forefront of these changes, as it is an officially bilingual country, and French Canadians have historically been very insistent, and rightly so, that their language be written correctly!

If we separate the representation from the content of the data, we can look at the variety of possible representations for any given chunk of data, and consider how best to support conversion from one to another. I once did a survey of data formats in use in our shop, and counted 18 different representations! These were all inter-convertible, provided you were not missing information (like the century). A lot of retired programmers were called back into harness around the year 2000, converting programs with 6-digit dates to make them able to cope with the 21st century – and I predicted this back in 1994, without much attention being paid! Lest there be any doubt among my readers, if it hadn't been for countless programmers working evenings and week-ends, poring through millions of lines of code, our vaunted technological civilization would have been lying in tatters! We did our job so well that some commentators still don't realize that there was ever any danger – believe me, there was!

As we said above, the representation of data inside the machine doesn't really concern us. The representation of data is of interest when we are talking about external uses of that data (being read by humans, being written to or read from databases, or being processed by HLLs). In some ways, this resembles the Object-Oriented view. When *displaying* data (e.g. numeric fields) we found that we needed "global" information to control how the data should be presented. In the case of currency, you need to know:

- currency symbol (whether required and, if so, which)
- whether currency symbol is floating or fixed
- separators between groups of three digits (whether required, and, if so, what symbol)
- separators between integer part and fractional part (what symbol)
- whether negative values should be indicated and, if so, how (DR, CR, preceding -, following -, etc.)

In addition, these options usually come in "layers": there may be an international standard, a national standard, and a company standard, and a particular report may even use one or more such representations for the same domain, e.g. amounts with and without separators. Today it is not enough just to provide one conversion facility in each direction. Representations occur at the boundaries between responsibilities and, I believe, require sophisticated multi-level parametrization.

With the older HLLs such as PL/I and COBOL, the best we can probably do is to describe fields and use smart subroutines as much as possible for all the conversion and interfacing logic. This will let us implement all known useful functions, but it cannot prevent illegal ones. Object-oriented and some of the newer High Level Languages with strong typing are moving in this direction, but they cannot force programmers to use "smart data". I suspect we have to go further, though, as some form of dimensional analysis will probably be necessary eventually.

So far we have only talked about static descriptions of data. DFDM also had another type of data description which proved very useful, which we called "dynamic attributes". Dynamic attributes were also a form of metadata, but were attached to IPs, instead of to their descriptions. The first example of this that we came up with was the "null" attribute. We took this term from IBM's DB2, in which a column in a table may have the attribute of "may be null". This means that individual fields in this column will have an additional bit of information, indicating whether or not the particular value is null or not, meaning either "don't know" or "does not apply". Some writers feel that these two cases are different, and in fact the latter may be avoided by judicious choice of entity classes, but the former is certainly very useful. In DFDM interactive applications, we often used "nullness" to indicate fields which had not been filled in on a screen by the end-user.

The "null" attribute also works well with another dynamic attribute which we also found useful: the "modified" attribute. Suppose that an application screen has a number of fields on it, some of which do not have values known to the program. It is reasonable to display "null" fields as blank, or maybe question-marks. If the user fills one or more fields in, their attributes are changed to "modified" and "non-null". This information can then be used by the application code to provide user-responsive logic. We found that this kind of logic often occurred in the type of application which is called "decision assist": here you often see screens with a large number of fields and it becomes important to know which ones have been modified by the user.

Many applications encode null as a "default" value, e.g. binary zeros, but there are a number of formats which do not have an unused value, e.g. binary, so how do you tell whether you have zero eggs, or an unknown number? Does a blank street name and number in an address mean that we don't know the house-owner's full address, or that she lives in a rural community, where the mailman knows everyone by name? Also, we saw no advantage to confusing the idea of null and default – what is an appropriate default number of eggs?

Where DB2 has specific handling for the "nullness" attribute only, DFDM generalized this idea to allow you to attach any kind of dynamic attribute data to any field of any IP, e.g. "null" and "modified", but also "colour", "error number", etc. Since we felt we couldn't predict what kinds of dynamic attribute data we might want to attach to the fields of an IP, we built a very general mechanism, driven by its own descriptor (called, naturally, a Dynamic Attribute Descriptor or DAD). It allowed any number of attributes to be attached to each field and also to the IP as a whole. Thus, we had a "modified" attribute on each field, but, for performance reasons, we had a "modified" attribute on the IP as a whole, which was set on if any fields were modified.

"Null" and "modified" are of course boolean, but we allowed binary or even character dynamic attributes. One character-type dynamic attribute which we found very useful for interactive applications was "error code". Suppose an editing routine discovered that a numeric field had been entered by the user incorrectly: it would then tag that field with the error code indicating "invalid numeric value". Any number of fields could be tagged in this way. When the IP containing the screen data was redisplayed, the display component would automatically change all the erroneous fields to some distinctive colour (in our case yellow), position the cursor under the first one and put the corresponding error message in the message field of the screen. Without leaving the component, the user could then cycle through all the error fields, with the correct error message being displayed each time. This was really one of the friendliest applications I have ever used, and it was all managed by one reusable component which encapsulated IBM's ISPF (Interactive System Productivity Facility) services, called ISM1 – it is discussed in more detail in Chapter 20 (page 195).

Some writers have objected to the "null" attribute on the grounds that it introduces 3-valued logic: yes, no and don't know. Our experience was that, in practice, it never caused any confusion, and in fact significantly reduced the complexity of the design of our end-user interfaces.

Just as in OO classes, IP types are often related in a superclass-subclass relationship. This comes up frequently in file handling: one may know that one is dealing with, say, cars, but not know until a record is read what kind of car it is. It would be very nice to be able to attach a "car" descriptor to each record as it is read in, and then "automagically" move down the class hierarchy for a given record, based on some indicator in the record. This is in turn related to the question of compatibility of descriptors: what relationships are allowed between the class of an IP being sent and what the receiver expects. In JavaFBP we tried including run-time checks, but this turned out to be complex, as e.g. the output of Collate, so class information is now optionally included in the component class metadata, allowing it to be checked by diagramming tools such as DrawFBP, if available.

Mike Beckerle, a long-time FBP advocate, considers type checking especially important when working with large data volumes. He says:

> FBP systems differ in the nature of the packets of information moving around between the components. How much reusability one can obtain from FBP components is very much affected by this, and the data handling overhead of components has a first-order impact on overall efficiency. In the case of parallel FBP systems, there is also a major impact on the ability to produce a good parallel execution of the flow. An FBP system can be given a robust type system which enforces composition properties and enables all sorts of interesting optimizations.

He has developed a scheme for checking that the output of one component is compatible with the input of the next, which he refers to as "type systems for FBP data". Here is how he describes his

Chap. XI: Data Descriptions and Descriptors

concept:

> ... each port has an interface schema – describes the structure of data arriving there. These are partial schemas – they describe the requirements the data must satisfy, not the exact structure. An input schema describes the requirements the incoming data must satisfy, an output interface schema describes the constraints the output structure obeys when data arrives there. Hooking such an operator [what we've been calling a "process"] into a flow requires you to say which actual data fields map to each aspect of the interface.
>
> Based on these interface schemas, the author of the operator code has APIs available for manipulating the data which work in terms of the interface, so for data where the interface says a field is mapped, on an input, the operator can read it. For a field mapped on an output, the operator author has an API to write it, and for a field which is transferred from input to output, a special API allows ONLY this behaviour to be expressed. You can move the data from input to output, but you can't look at it, nor modify it.
>
> One of the important things this can represent is what we call "transfer" or "polymorphic transfer" – so an operator with say 1 input and 1 output port can say that the input looks like X, Y, Z* – i.e., needs two fields mapped to names X, and Y, and a third Z can have any number of fields mapped to it. The output looks like W, Z*, so whatever was mapped to X, and Y is used to compute new field W, but Z* transports exactly to the output what was mapped to it from the input.
>
> The API the author of the operator uses to write the operator would in this case enforce the "contract" by not providing any way to look at or touch or modify what was mapped to Z*, so that it is dependable that it is transferred through without modification of any sort.
>
> If you cascade operators like this together into a flow, then an ordinary compiler-style dataflow analysis can tell you where each field of each record comes into existence, and where it is read, and where it disappears, along with where its value is preserved so that flow restructuring is allowed.
>
> Many benefits accrue to FBP systems that have this kind of type system. Probably the most important is to be able to move around "repartitioning" as is needed to spread out data sets to operate on them in parallel. This is an expensive operation, and to be avoided if at all possible. If the partitioning key fields are preserved by any operator, then the partitioning operation can be hoisted to be done before that operation. This

will often allow the partitioning to be hoisted to the beginning of a flow, thereby eliminating a separate basic round-robin or pseudo-random partitioning of data then followed by some key-based repartitioning later in the flow.

This partitioner-hoisting optimization is an important one because if you create black-box sub-graphs which include a partitioning operation, the flow optimizer really really wants to decompose them and hoist the partitioners up to earlier parts of the flow without affecting the result. Yet black box abstractions really do want to be able to be created which hide the fact that a repartitioning operation is part of their logic. If you want this black box algorithm hiding, you have to enable the hoisting optimization or the costs get out of hand.

To me the FBP potential is realized only when you have a quite strong polymorphic type system which allows easy creation of highly polymorphic operators, and provides the FBP system the information it needs to perform rich optimizations.

In a recent e-business application built around 2000 and 2001 using the Java implementation of FBP (JavaFBP), we designed and implemented a number of business objects, such as Monetary, which are described on the author's web site – *http://www.jpaulmorrison.com/busdtyps.shtml*. This is now a project on *SourceForge*, called JBDTypes, and has recently (2009) been picked up by Softpedia – see *http://www.softpedia.com/get/Programming/Components-Libraries/JBDTypes.shtml*. There is also a more general discussion of what he calls "smart data" on the author's web site, which contains an interesting description of the famous Canadian "Gimli Glider" – see *http://www.jpaulmorrison.com/datatyps.shtml*.

Chap. XII: Tree Structures

Up to this point, I have been talking about single IPs travelling through networks, like cars and buses in a system of highways. I have talked about how streams of IPs can be treated as higher-level entities, and how these can in turn be given more complex structures by the use of "bracket" IPs. I hope I have shown that, using these concepts, quite complex applications can be handled in a straightforward manner.

However, what if we want to build more complex structures and move them through the network as single units? Streams take time to cross a connection, and you may want a whole data structure to be sent or received at a single moment in time. Since, as we said before, only the handles travel through the net, it is just as easy for an IP containing one bit of data to be transferred from process to process as one containing a megabyte, so why not allow complex structures to move as a unit? It turned out that there was a natural analogue to this idea in real life (which always tends to reassure us that we are on the right track!). We mentioned before the idea that IPs are like memos – you can dispose of one in one of three ways: you can forward it (send), discard it (drop), or keep it (using the various methods of holding onto IPs, e.g. stacking, saving on disk, etc.). Well, of course there is a fourth thing you can do with a memo (no, not wad it up and throw it at a neighbour) – clip it to another piece of paper, and then do one of the previous three things with the resulting composite memo. Make that four things, actually, since you could clip the composite memo to another piece of paper, or to another composite memo, and so on.

Just as the composite memo can be sent or received as a unit, so the structure of linked IPs, called a "tree", can be sent or received as a single object. Once a process has received the tree, it can either "walk" it (move from IP to IP across the connecting links), completely or partially disassemble it, or destroy it. For instance, the receiver might walk the tree looking for a particular kind of IP, and, for each one it finds, it could unlink it and dispose of it in one of the standard

Chap. XII: Tree Structures

ways. The following diagram shows two processes, one assembling trees and one disassembling them again (in a different order):

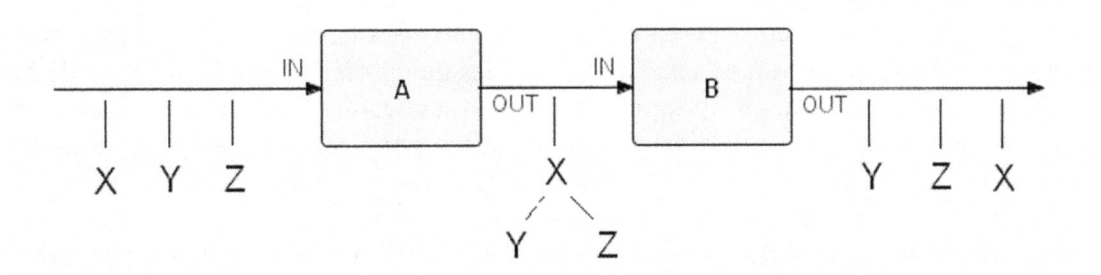

Figure 12.1

A converts a series of three IPs of different types and sizes into a tree of IPs, and *B* disassembles the trees and outputs the component IPs (in a different order).

In all implementations of this concept so far, no node could descend from more than one parent node, and we did not allow any loops – much like a real live tree! I do not believe we lost much expressive power by doing so. The main reason for doing this is to allow FBP's ownership and disposal rules for IPs to work.

You will probably have realized that we don't need any special mechanisms as long as the tree is assembled and disassembled within one activation of one process (activation is described in detail in the chapter on Scheduling Rules – page 126). In fact you could read in a set of IPs and build an array of pointers for sorting, say – this is in fact how a number of components work. It is only when a tree has to be passed from one activation to another, or from one process to another, that the IP disposition rules have to be taken into account. Thus, in the picture above, process *A* receives (or creates) three IPs, assembles them into a single tree of 3 IPs and sends it out – in this case *A* starts with an "owned IP count" of 3, and reduces it to 0 by attaching 2 IPs to the root (count is now 1) and then sending the tree as a whole out (count of 1 goes to 0). Obviously the "attach" function decreases the count by 1, or the arithmetic wouldn't work. *B* receives one IP (count goes from 0 to 1), and detaches the attached IPs ("detach" increments the count, so the count goes from 1 to 3). If we allowed any violations of the above rules about tree shape, we wouldn't be able to map so easily between trees and streams.

In one application we had a striking example of how useful trees can be in the FBP environment: in a batch banking application, bank accounts were represented by complex sequential structures (on tape). Each account record consisted of an account header, followed by a variable number of different trailer records belonging to a large number of different types, e.g. stops, holds, back

- 121 -

Chap. XII: Tree Structures

items, etc. The problem was that, most of the time one could just process these sequentially, but sometimes processing later in the stream resulted in changes which should be reflected earlier in the stream. For example, an interest calculation, triggered by a particular type of trailer record, might require the account balance in the header record to be updated. You could always hold on to the header and put it out later, but then it would have to collated back into its correct position. And anyway there was quite a lot of this "direct" access going on, including adds and deletes of trailer records. Using conventional programming, this application became fiendishly complex because all the logic had to be coordinated from a timing point of view, and there were timing conflicts between when things were required and when they became available! (We know this because originally it was coded using conventional logic, and it was very complex!) We were also talking about large volumes of these structures – we had to be able to process about 5,000,000 every night. When we did this application using FBP, we realized that we could implement this application very simply and naturally by converting each account record into a tree structure. Once the tree had been built, "direct access" processing could jump from one IP type to another within the tree structure, add or delete IPs, etc., and then the whole thing could be converted back to linear form when we were finished. This solution turned out to be simple to understand, easy to code and easy to maintain.

Figure 12.2 shows a simple tree of four IPs, where the top box represents the "root" IP, and all the other IPs are descended from it directly or indirectly. In this diagram (mixing our metaphors a bit):

- X is the root
- Y and W are the daughters of X
- Z is the daughter of Y
- Z and W are terminal IPs ("leaves")
- Y is a non-terminal IP

Now, within a single component, this type of connection can largely be done (in languages that support them) using pointers. However, for the Japanese DFDM product, our group felt that you should not have to preplan all the list structures an IP might have attached to it. For instance, an employee might have lists attached to him or her showing children, courses attended, departments worked for, salary history, etc., and it would very nice if this information could be added incrementally, without having to change the descriptions of participating IPs. Plus we wanted to have a structure that the infrastructure could work with, rather than having to rely on application code knowledge. We therefore introduced the idea of named chains, any number of which could be added to an IP, without that IP requiring any changes to its description.

Chap. XII: Tree Structures

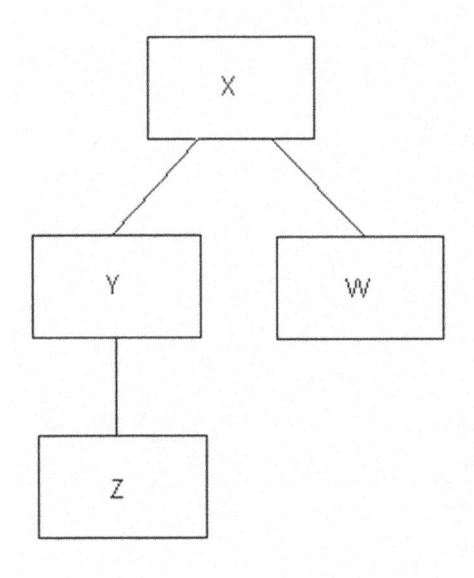

Figure 12.2

An employee IP could for instance have the following chains attached to it: *CHILDREN, SALARY_HIST, COURSES*, etc. We then of course needed to provide traversal services, and we in fact built some fairly powerful services, e.g. add an IP to a named chain (it is created if it does not yet exist), get next chain (so you could walk the chains without knowing their names), get the first IP of a named chain, get next IP in a chain, detach an IP from a chain, and so forth. You could attach a chain to an IP, or an IP to a chain, but not a chain to a chain, or an IP to an IP. These trees thus had a less uniform structure (chains alternating with data IPs), but we felt that this still provided a powerful paradigm, and a less "programmer-dependent" approach to tree manipulation and traversal. An employee IP with one child, Linda, and who has taken two courses, is shown in Figure 12.3.

Chap. XII: Tree Structures

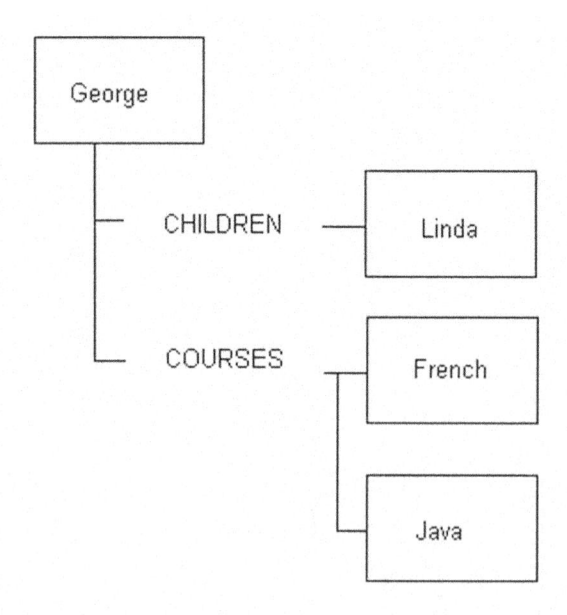

Figure 12.3

Just as in FBP we require application components to dispose of IPs explicitly, we also had to put certain constraints on how trees can be disassembled. This introduced the concept of "direct" and "indirect" descent. The root is owned directly by whichever process has just received it. IPs which are chained to that root are therefore owned indirectly by the same process (they are not owned directly by anyone, except possibly the root IP). You can only send or drop an IP you own directly – you have to detach a chained IP first, then send it or drop it. A process can however chain another IP (which it must own directly) onto an IP which it only owns indirectly, but that's the only service it can reference it with, apart from looking at it! We also added logic to check that a process did not try to chain a root IP onto one of its own descendants – that would have been allowed by the other rules, but would result in a closed loop!

One other point about trees is that hierarchic tree structures, no matter how they are implemented, can easily be converted into nested substreams like the ones described in the previous chapter. For instance, the tree shown in Figure 12.2 can be "linearized" as follows:

`<X <Y Z> W>`

Figure 12.4

where the convention is that the IP following a left bracket is the "mother" of the other IPs at the same level of bracket nesting. This kind of transformation will be familiar to LISP users. In fact we have just shown a LISP "list of lists".

- 124 -

Chap. XII: Tree Structures

In the "chain" implementation described above, we would have to capture chain identifiers, so we can just add chain information to the left brackets, as we did in Chapter 9 (page 90). Thus the tree shown in Figure 12.3 might look as follows after linearization (as in earlier chapters, the "group name" is shown as the data part of open and close bracket IPs):

```
IP type            data
<                  employees
employee           George
<                  children
child              Linda
>                  children
<                  courses
course             French
course             COBOL
>                  courses
>                  employees
```

Figure 12.5

This can then easily be converted back into tree format if desired. It also of course corresponds quite well to various database approaches: "children" and "courses" could be different segment types in an IBM DL/I database. In IBM's DB2 we could make "employee", "children" and "courses" different tables, where "employee" is the primary key of the "employee" table, and a foreign key of the other two. And of course this maps perfectly onto XML!

One last point: although we have stated several times our belief that IPs should be disposed of explicitly, it turns out to be very useful to be able to discard a whole tree at a time. The tree therefore has to have enough internal "scaffolding" to allow the `drop` service to find all the chains and attached IPs and discard them. The later versions of DFDM needed this anyway, so that they could provide services like 'locate next chain', but this ability to drop a whole tree turned out to be important even when we had no traversal services. Although at first it seemed that applications would always know enough about the tree structure to do the job themselves, we developed more and more generic components which understood about trees generally, but not about specific tree structures. This facility perhaps most closely resembles the "garbage collection" facility of object-oriented languages.

In JavaFBP, every packet contains a HashMap called `chains`, and IPs are attached to a particular named chain, or detached from one, using methods of the Packet class. In C#FBP, this facility is still under development (as of early 2011).

Chap. XIII: Scheduling Rules

So far, we have talked about processes running asynchronously, but have not discussed how FBP software manages this feat. This is a key concept in FBP and we need to understand it thoroughly if we are to design reliable structures, and debug them once they have been built. Although this subject may appear somewhat forbidding, you will need to grasp it thoroughly to understand how this kind of software works. After a bit it will recede into the background, and you will only need to work through it consciously when you are doing something complex or something unexpected happens. Of course you are at liberty to skip this chapter, but, if you do, you will probably find some of the later chapters a little obscure!

Let us start by looking at the following component pseudo-code (from a previous chapter):

```
receive from IN using a
do while receive has not reached end of data
    if c is true
        send a to OUT
    else
        drop a
    endif
    receive from IN using a
enddo
```

You will be able to see that the job of this component is to receive a stream of IPs and either send them on or destroy them, depending on some criterion. As we said above, this code must be run as a separate process in our application. We will use the term "component" when talking about the code; "process" when talking about a particular use of that code.

Chap. XIII: Scheduling Rules

Before, we were looking at processes and components strictly from a functional point of view. Now instead let's look at a component as a piece of code. Clearly it is well-structured: it has a single entry point and a single exit (after the "enddo"). Once it gains control, it performs logic and calls subroutines until its input stream is exhausted ("end of data" on IN). It is therefore a well-formed subroutine. Subroutines have to be called by another routine (or by the environment), and at a particular point in time. So.... what calls our Selector component, and when? The what is easy: the Selector component is called by the software which implements FBP, usually referred to as the "scheduler". The formal name for the action of calling the component is called its "initiation". The *when* is somewhat more complicated: the answer is that a component is called as soon as possible after a data IP arrives at one of its (non-IIP) input ports, or just as soon as possible if there are no input ports. When the component gives up control and there are no more IPs to process, it is said to have "terminated".

"As soon as possible" means that we do not guarantee that a process will start as soon as there is data for it to work on – the processor may be busy doing other things. Normally this isn't a problem – we want to be sure that our process has data to work on, not the reverse! If we really need very high responsiveness, we can use the component priority (supported in JavaFBP and C#FBP) to improve this. So far, the only other implementation of the FBP concepts that I am aware of that implemented a priority scheme was a system written in Japan to control railway electric substations (Suzuki et al. 1985). This software built on the concepts described in my Systems Journal article, and extended it to provide shared high-performance facilities.

The other possible start condition is what one would expect if the process has no input connections. In this case, one expects the process to be "self-starting". Another way of looking at this is that a process with at least one input connection is delayed until the first data IP arrives. If there are no input connections, the process is not delayed. Again, the process will start some time after program start time when the processor is available. A recent addition to the JavaFBP (and eventually C#FBP) scheduler is the "self-starting" attribute, which indicates that the component is to be invoked at the beginning of the run, *even if* it has input ports.

Note that Initial Information Packets (IIPs) do not count as input connections for the purposes of process scheduling – when a process starts is determined by the presence or absence of connections with upstream processes. IIPs are purely passive, and are only "noticed" by the process when it does a receive on an IIP port element.

Now we have started our process – this is called "activation", and the process is said to be "active". When it gives up control, by executing its "end" statement, or by explicitly doing a RETURN, GOBACK, or the equivalent, it "deactivates", and its state becomes "inactive".

Now remember that our component kept control by looping until end of data. Now suppose our component doesn't loop back, but instead just deactivates once an IP has been processed. The resulting pseudo-code might look like this:

- 127 -

Chap. XIII: Scheduling Rules

```
receive from IN using a
if c is true
    send a to OUT
else
    drop a
endif
```

We talked about this kind of component in Chapter 9 (page 90). They are called "non-loopers". The logic of non-loopers behaves a little differently from the preceding version – instead of going back to receive another IP, it ends (deactivates) after the "endif". A consequence of this is that the process's working storage only exists from activation to deactivation. This means that it cannot carry ongoing data values across multiple IPs, but, as we saw in Chapter 9, the stack can be used for this purpose. A non-looper becomes "inactive" after each incoming IP.

What happens now if another data IP arrives at the process's input port? The process is activated again to process the incoming IP, and this will keep happening until the input data stream is exhausted. The process is activated as many times as there are input IPs. The decision as to when to deactivate is made within the logic of the component – it is quite possible to have a "partial looper" which decides to deactivate itself after every five IPs, for example, or on recognizing a particular type of IP. This "looping" characteristic of a component is referred to as its "periodicity".

Let us consider an inactive (or not yet initiated) process with two input ports: data arrives at one of the ports, so the process is activated. The process in question had better do a receive of the activating IP before deactivating – otherwise it will just be reactivated. As long as it does not consume the IP, this will keep happening! If, during testing, your program just hangs, this may be what is going on – of course, it's easy enough to detect once you switch tracing on, as you will see something like this:

```
Process_A Invoked

Process_A Activated
  .

  Process_A Deactivated
  Process_A Activated
  .

  Process_A Deactivated
  Process_A Activated
  .
```

Chap. XIII: Scheduling Rules

```
  .
Process_A Deactivated
Process_A Activated
  .
```

and so on indefinitely!

Our group discussed the possibility of putting checks into the scheduling logic to detect this kind of thing, but we never reached a consensus on what to do about it, because there are situations where this may be desirable behaviour – as long as the activating IP does get consumed eventually. We did, however, coin a really horrible piece of jargon: such a component might be called a "pathological non-depleter" (you figure it out)! And besides, it's really not that hard to debug...

Returning to IIPs, we have said that in all recent implementations of FBP processes read in IIPs by doing a receive on their port. If they do a receive again from the same port within the lifetime of the process (between initiation and termination), they get an "end of data" indication. This means that a component can receive an IIP exactly once during the lifetime of the process. If a component needs to hold onto the IIP across multiple activations, it can use the stack (described in Concepts) to hold the IIP, either in the original form in which it was received or in a processed form.

So far, we have introduced two basic process states: "active" and "inactive". We have also introduced the terms "initiation" and "termination". Before initiation, the process doesn't really exist yet for the FBP software, so initiation is important, as the scheduler has to perform various kinds of initialization logic – e.g. starting the thread in a threaded implementation. Termination is important because the scheduler must know enough not to activate the process again. Termination of a process also affects all of its downstream processes, as this determines whether they in turn are terminated (a process only terminates when all of its upstream processes have terminated).

Processes may thus be thought of as simple machines which can be in one of a small number of different "run states". The four main run states are the ones we have just described:

- not yet initiated
- terminated
- active
- inactive

"Not yet initiated" is self-explanatory – all processes start off in this state at the beginning of a job step or transaction.

"Terminated" means that the process will never receive control again. This can only happen if all of a process's upstream connections have been closed – each of the input connections of a

- 129 -

Chap. XIII: Scheduling Rules

process can either be closed explicitly by that process, or will be closed automatically if all of the processes feeding it have terminated.

The underlying idea here is that a process only becomes terminated if it can never be activated again. It can never be activated again if there is nowhere for more data IPs to come from. Note that, while a component's logic decides when to deactivate, termination is controlled by factors outside of the process. The only way a component can decide to terminate itself is by closing its input ports. Processes that don't have input ports just return.

A simple example will show why this facility is needed: suppose you have a Reader process which is reading a file of a few million records, and a downstream process crashes: under normal FBP rules, the Reader keeps reading all the records and sending them to its output port. As each send finds the output port closed, the Reader has to drop the undeliverable IP. So it has to read all the records, requiring a few million each of "create", "send" and "drop". Instead, it is much better to bring the Reader down as quickly as possible, so it can stop tying up time and resources. If the "send" cannot deliver its IP, it crashes the application. To avoid this, the component can test if the output port is closed before issuing the "send". This takes care of any necessary housekeeping, and eventually the whole network can close down. By the way, this practice makes sense for all components, not just long-running ones – it is good programming style for components always to test for unsuccessful sends. If this condition is detected, they must decide whether to continue executing, or whether to just close down – this usually depends on whether the output port is related to the main function of the component, or whether it is optional. There is now also an `isConnected()` method for output ports.

When all the processes in a network have terminated, the network itself terminates. Now, it is possible for one process to block another process so that the network as a whole cannot come down gracefully. This is called a "deadlock" in FBP and is described in some detail in a later chapter. This is however a design problem, and can always be prevented by proper design. If the network is properly designed, it will terminate normally when all of its processes have terminated, and all resources will then be freed up.

In Chapter 7 (page 71), we talked about various kinds of composite components. DFDM's dynamic subnets and the composite components of FPE had the ability to revive terminated processes. In that chapter we explained why this ability is necessary, and we shall run into it again in Chapter 19 (page 185), when we talk about Checkpointing. Revived processes actually go from the "terminated" state back to the "not yet initiated" state – but this is the only case where this is allowed to happen.

If we had a separate processor for each process, the above-mentioned four states would be enough, although a component waiting to send to a full connection, waiting to receive from an empty one, or waiting on an external event, would have to spin waiting for the desired condition. To allow processes to share processors, we have introduced a "suspended" state, so we can split

Chap. XIII: Scheduling Rules

the active state into "normal" and "suspended", resulting in five states:

- not yet initiated
- terminated
- active normal
- active suspended
- inactive

At this point I would like to stress the point that a given process can only be in one of these states at a time, and, when suspended, a process can only be waiting for a single event – this can either be an external event or an FBP connection service. While you will occasionally feel that this is too much of a restriction, we deliberately made this decision in order to make an FBP system easier to visualize and work with. At various times in the development of FBP systems, we were tempted to allow a process to wait on more than one event at a time, but we always found a way round it, and never needed to add this ability to our model.

As an example of this, suppose you want to have a process, P, which will be triggered by a timer click or by an IP arriving at an input port, whichever comes first: the rule about processes having a single state suggests that you will need two processes, one waiting on each event type. One possible solution, therefore, is to have one process send out an IP on each timer click, and then merge its output stream with the IPs arriving from another source, resulting in a single stream which is then fed to P. The overhead of the extra processes is outweighed in our experience by the reduction in complexity of the mental model and the consequent reduction in software complexity and improved performance. Here is a picture of the resulting network:

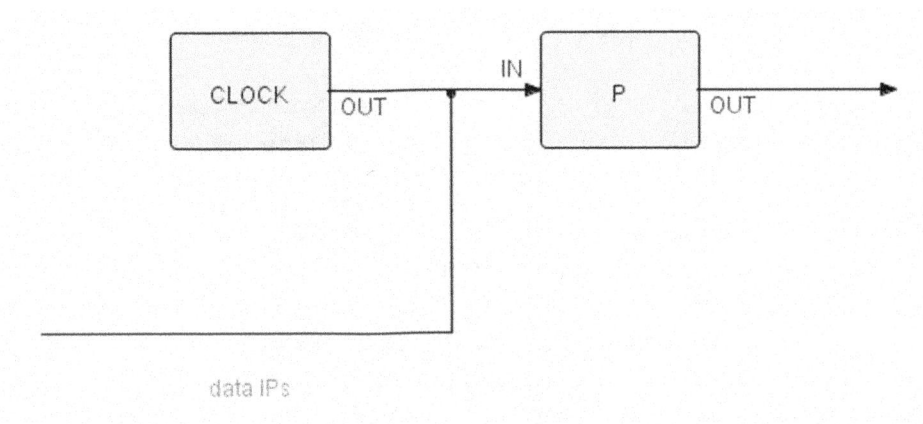

Figure 13.1

Chap. XIII: Scheduling Rules

Up to now, we have assumed that all ports are named. However, not all ports need to be known to the components they are attached to: sometimes it is desirable to be able to specify connections in the network which the processes themselves don't know about. These are especially useful for introducing timing constraints into an application without having to add logic to the components involved, and handling various kinds of error condition. One such type of port is what we call automatic ports, to reflect the idea that their functioning is not under the component's control.

Consider two processes, one writing a file and one reading it. You, the network designer, want to interlock the two components so that the reader cannot start until the writer finishes. To do this, you figure that if you connect an input port to the reader, the reader will be prevented from starting until an IP arrives on that port (by the above scheduling rules). On the other hand, readers don't usually have input ports, and if you add one, the reader will have to have some additional code to dispose of incoming IPs, looking something like this:

```
if DELAY port connected
    receive from DELAY port
    discard received IP (if any)
endif
```

Figure 13.2

Now, to avoid having to add seldom-used code (to receive these special signals) to every component in the entire system, the software should provide two optional ports for each process which the implementing component doesn't know about: an automatic input port and an automatic output port. If the automatic output port is connected, the FBP scheduler closes it at termination time.

The automatic input works like this: if there is an automatic input port connected, process activation is delayed until an IP is received on that port, or until the port is closed. This assumes that no data has arrived at another input port.

Figure 13.3 shows the Writer/Reader situation, where the solid line indicates a connection between *W*'s automatic output port and *R*'s automatic input port. The solid circles at each end of the line indicate automatic ports. Since *W* only terminates when it has written the entire file, we can use the automatic output signal to prevent the Reader from starting too early. An automatic port need not only be connected to another automatic port – it can always be connected to a regular port, or vice versa. Any IP that has been received (by the scheduler) at an automatic input port is automatically discarded (better not use any important data for this job, unless you have taken a copy)!

Chap. XIII: Scheduling Rules

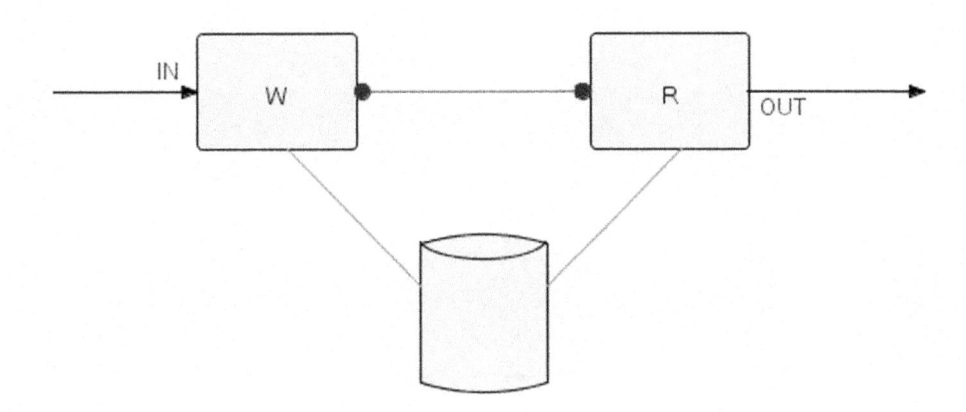

Figure 13.3

Here is how this (partial) network might be coded in JavaFBP – as before, omitting package name, imports and `main` method:

```
public class Xxxxx extends Network {

 protected void define() {
 component("Write", WriteFile.class);
 component("Read", ReadFile.class);

 connect("Write.*", "Read.*");
 etc.
   }
}
```

Figure 13.4

Figure 13.5 shows a network where the automatic output signal gates an IP from another process. Assuming that C receives from I1 before it receives from I2, then C will not process the input at I2 until A has terminated. If we made I1 automatic, we would have essentially the same effect, except that C would not have to do a receive, but conversely, it would not have the option of processing the input at I2 first.

- 133 -

Chap. XIII: Scheduling Rules

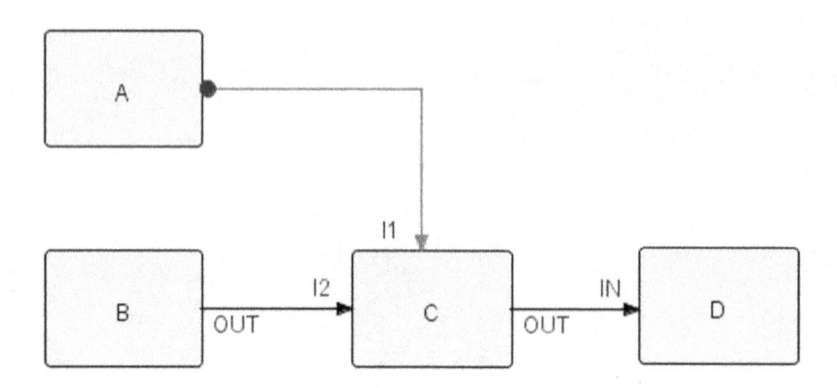

Figure 13.5

One last topic we should mention is the problem of the "null" stream: in DFDM a component receiving a null stream (a stream with no data IPs) was invoked anyway. This logic, while consistent with the regular scheduling rules, tended to increase run-time costs. In one interactive application, we found that 2/3 of all the processes were error handlers, and so should really never get started if no errors occurred.

We then thought of providing an option to change this behaviour for a whole network. But then we had the problem of Writers and Counters. Consider a Writer component writing a disk file: when it receives a null stream, you want the Writer to at least open and close its output file, resulting in an empty data set. If it doesn't do this, nothing gets changed on the disk, and another job reading that file would see the data from the previous run! "Counter" components which generate a count IP at end of data have a similar problem – how can they generate a count of zero if they are never invoked? A better way to handle these conflicting requirements was to introduce the concept of "must run at least once". This is an attribute of the component, not of the process, and means simply that the component must be activated at least once during each run of the network. So Writer and Counter components can do their thing, even when receiving a null data stream. This seems much simpler! In the case of THREADS, attributes are specified currently using a separate file, with extension `.atr`. In the case of the Java and C# implementations, MustRun is now a component attribute, specified right in the class using metadata.

Chap. XIV: Loop-Type Networks

All of the network shapes we have encountered so far have been of the kind we call "batch", and have generally had a left-to-right flow, with IPs being created on the left-hand side and disposed of on the right of the network. Sometimes we need to use a different kind of topology, which is a *loop-type* network. Note this should not be confused with "loopers", which are a type of component. Several of the later chapters contain examples of loop topology, so it is worthwhile spending some time talking about this type of network at a general level. Many networks will in fact be a mixture of the two types, but, once you understand the underlying principles, hopefully they won't present any problems. Here is a very simple example of a loop-type network:

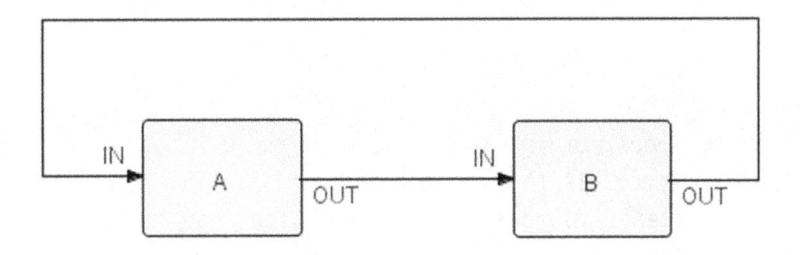

Figure 14.1

The first question we need to answer about this type of network is: how does it get started? You may remember that the only processes which get started automatically are those with no input connections (IIPs don't count). If you look at Figure 14.1, you will see that there are no processes which have no input connections (double negative intended!). *B* has an input connection coming from *A*, but *A* has an input connection coming from *B*! The simplest thing to do is just to add an extra process which has no input connections and then use it to start *A* or *B*. So the picture now looks like this:

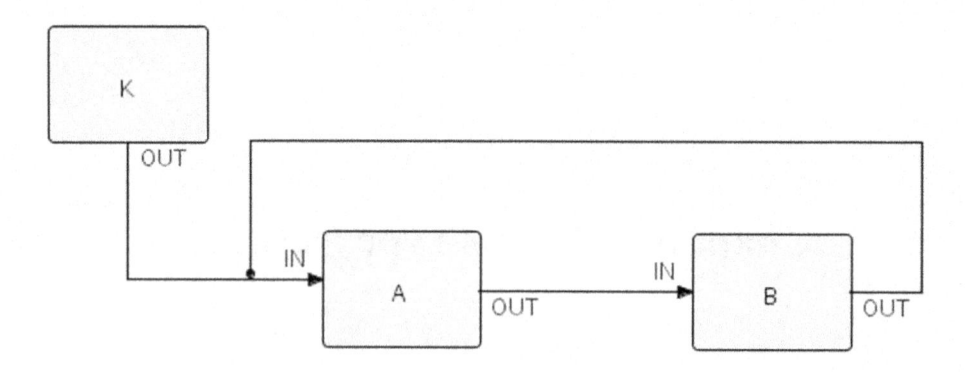

Figure 14.2

where *K* is the starter ("kicker") process, that emits a single packet containing a blank. *K* can be connected to either *A* or *B* as the logic demands.

With the recent addition of the "self-starting" attribute, another solution would be to make at least one of these components "self-starting".

Now that we have started our loop-type network, not surprisingly, there is another problem: how does it close down? The problem here is in the definition of close-down of a process – a process closes down on the next deactivation after all of its upstream processes have closed down. In the above diagram, since *A* is upstream of *B*, but *B* is also upstream of *A*, we get a "catch-22" situation: *A* cannot close down because *B* cannot close down until *A* closes down, and so on. The solution is to provide a special service which makes a process look to its neighbours as if it has closed down. One of the processes involved must then decide to close down and will use this service to notify the other processes. In the batch situation, closedown of the network as a whole was typically initiated by readers closing down (because they had finished reading their files or had run into problems). In loop-type networks, one of the processes – usually one which is interacting with a user – has to decide that no more data is going to arrive, so it closes down.

The service which tells a process's neighbours that it has closed down is one we have mentioned casually before: "close port". FBP lets a component close an input port or close an output port. The function of this service is to close ports before they would normally be closed (this would normally happen automatically at process close-down time, but there are cases, like this one, where we just can't wait that long). A process closing an output port has the same effect on its downstream processes as if the process had terminated. A process closing an input port has the

Chap. XIV: Loop-Type Networks

same effect on its upstream processes; also if all of its input ports are now closed, it automatically terminates.

So, to close down the network, *A* or *B* in Figure 14.2 simply closes its input or output port – it doesn't matter which one. Suppose *B* closes its input port and ends execution: it will now terminate because no more input data can now arrive. *B* is in fact *A*'s upstream process, so *A* will also be able to close down, thus bringing down the whole network (the "kicker" process will have closed down long ago).

Now that we know how to make loop-type networks start and stop, why would we want to use them? This usually has to do with synchronization, which we will also be talking about in a later chapter. In a regular left-to-right network, the left side of the network will be processing the last IPs, while earlier IPs are being processed further to the right in the network. This asynchronism gives this technique a lot of its power, but there are situations where you have to coordinate some processing with a specific external event, or make sure that two functions cannot overlap in time. One such example is that of an interactive application supporting one user. Here *A* in the above example might be an interactive I/O component and *B* might be a component to handle the input and generate the appropriate output, e.g.:

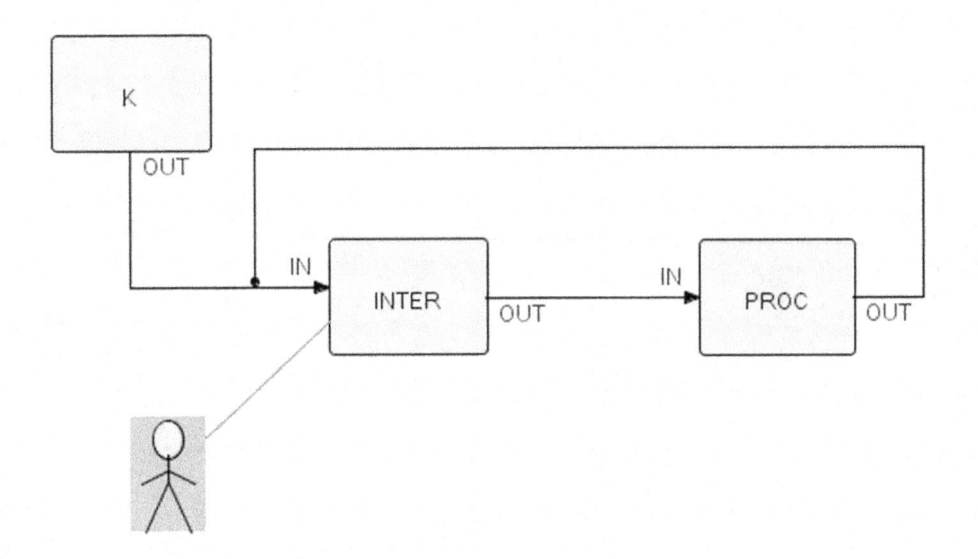

Figure 14.3

where *INTER* controls a screen. In this figure, *INTER* displays a prompt, then waits for some action on the part of the end user, and then sends information to *PROC*, which in turn will send some results back for display, and so on. Waiting for input need only suspend *INTER*, allowing

Chap. XIV: Loop-Type Networks

other processes to be working on their input while *INTER* is suspended.

If, on the other hand, this were a left-to-right flow, and *PROC* were preceded by an input process and followed by an output process (without the "back flow"), input and output to and from the same screen would no longer be synchronized. You therefore have to synchronize at least one component to the pace of the user, so that she can act on the data presented on a screen before getting the next screen.

Since the IPs from which a screen is built must fit into the connections in the loop and/or the working storage of the processes, we have to make sure there is enough capacity in these connections. One way to make sure we don't have to worry is to use the tree structures described in Chapter 12 (page 120). A tree of IPs can be used to represent the screen data and can be sent around the loop as a unit. Alternatively, the screen data can be represented as one or more substreams, and then we just have to make sure the total queue capacity is set high enough.

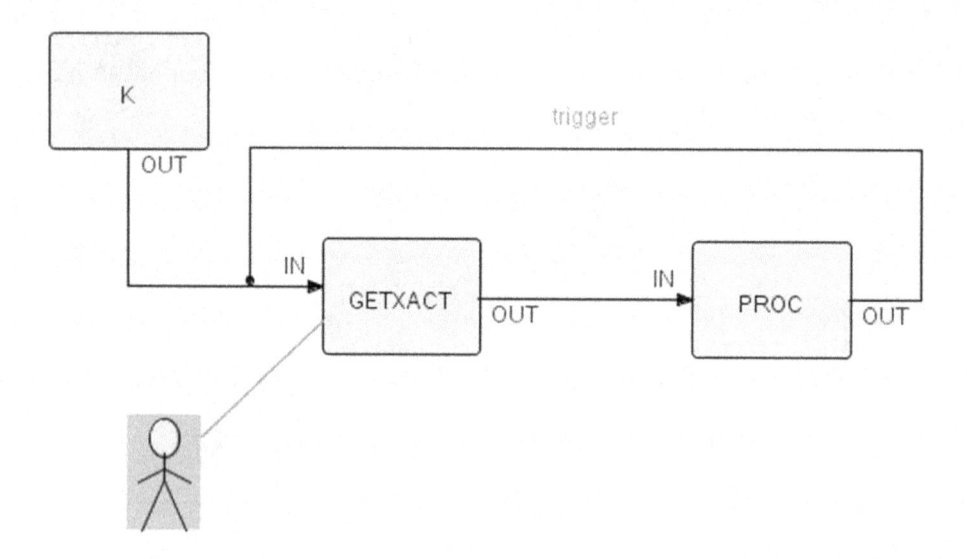

Figure 14.4

In IBM's IMS on-line software, you also have a loop structure, but with a different purpose. IMS is a queue-driven on-line environment, and an IMS program (at least the kind called Message-Processing Programs – MPPs) keep obtaining transactions from the IMS message queue until there are no more for that MPP, or until certain other conditions are met which cause the MPP to close down. Each time a transaction is obtained from the queue, IMS takes what is called a "synchronization point (syncpoint)", which allows databases to be updated, etc. IMS is a transaction-based system, so, if a transaction fails, any changed data is backed out to the previous syncpoint. This is an approach to Checkpointing, which we will be discussing in detail in

Chap. XIV: Loop-Type Networks

Chapter 19 (p. 185). In FBP, the diagram for an MPP would be the same as the previous one, except that *INTER* is replaced by a "transaction getter", as shown in Figure 14.4.

In this kind of situation, each time around this loop the program will be dealing with different users, so, unlike the previous example, you cannot use the working storage of the processes to save user data across multiple transactions. The flip side of this is that it is actually somewhat dangerous to allow data to persist in a process's working storage from one user to the next. This is therefore an argument for using non-loopers as much as possible in this situation. Although IMS has been around for a number of decades, the approach it follows for its MPPs makes sense for a variety of environments, and we will see a very similar design in Chapter 20 (page 195), in connection with multi-user servers.

Another use for loop networks is for "explosion" applications, of which the classical example is the Bill of Materials explosion, where components of some complex assembly will be "exploded" into subcomponents progressively until they reach ones which cannot be broken down any further.

If you know that the largest possible explosion would not fill up storage, you could use a loop of two or more processes with very high capacity queues connecting them (it is dangerous to use a loop with only one process as you could end up getting deadlocked, and no current FBP implementation allows it). Of course, the IPs for composite parts must be removed from the data stream when their subcomponents are added to it, or when they are found not to be further reducible, so eventually the looping data stream will go empty.

This type of logic can also be useful when parsing other kinds of recursive structures, e.g. lists of lists or expressions in a language. A colleague, Charles Douglas, used it very effectively in a text processing application, where the user needed to be able to name lists of databases and in turn use those names in other lists. He implemented this very similarly to a Bill of Materials explosion. His application went through all the lists, progressively exploding them until it got down to the actual database level. Thus, suppose we have the following lists:

```
A:   B, C, D, E
B:   D, E, G
D:   E, F
```

Figure 14.6

Then, if you feed in A, the successive stages of explosion are as follows:

```
A
B, C, D, E
D, E, G, C, E, F, E
E, F, E, G, C, E, F, E
```

Figure 14.7

- 139 -

Chap. XV: Implementation, Network Splitting and Client-Server

"A complex system which works is invariably found to have evolved from a simple system which works", John Gall (1978)

"Systems run better when designed to run downhill. Corollary: Systems aligned with human motivational vectors will sometimes work. Systems opposing such vectors work poorly or not at all", John Gall (1978)

"Loose systems last longer and work better", John Gall (1978)

A colleague of mine, Dave Olson, has been studying the application development process in particular, and large organizations in general, and has realized that the budding science of chaos has a lot to tell us about what is going on in this kind of complex process and what we can do about it. In the study of chaos one frequently runs into feedback loops, and, in our business, just as one example, we have all experienced what happens when a project starts to run late. Fred Brooks described this kind of thing in his celebrated book, "The Mythical Man-Month" (1975).

Chaotic systems also are characterized by areas of order and areas of apparent disorder. Dave's 1993 book, *"Exploiting Chaos: Cashing in on the Realities of Software Development"*, describes these concepts and also describes how they can be applied to explain and handle many of the problems we run into in our business (Olson 1993). In a section on techniques for reducing disorder, he talks about DFDM and its relationship to the Jackson Inversion methodology (mentioned elsewhere in this book). He later gives more detail on DFDM, and describes how you would approach designing an application with it as follows:

Chap. XV: Implementation, Network Splitting and Client-Server

To use DFDM, you first define the data requirements of the application, defining how the data flows and is transformed during the application process. Then you create transform modules for the places in the flow where data must be merged, split, transformed or reported. The full application definition consists of the data definitions and data flows, defined to DFDM, and the transform modules that are invoked by the platform.

In a personal communication to me, he expanded this into the following set of recommendations:

- View the application in terms of the information that needs to move from place to place.
- Create transform modules for the places where data must be merged, split, transformed, or reported.
- Separate data definitions from transform code so that transforms can be reusable code. Transforms thus care more about what has to be done, not so much about how individual pieces of information are represented.
- Provide certain building block transforms that will be needed by most applications, including file storage, file retrieval, file copy, printing, user interaction, etc.
- Build a systems framework so that an application can be defined in terms of its data flows and transforms; the framework handles scheduling, concurrency, and data transfers between transforms.

Doesn't sound much like conventional programming, does it? However, viewing an application in terms of data and the transforms which apply to it underlies many design methodologies. The problem has always been how to get from such a design to a working program. This is the "gap" I have referred to above. With FBP, you can move down from the highest level design all the way to running code, without having to change your viewpoint.

The first stage of designing an application is to lay out our processes and the flows between them. This is pretty standard Structured Analysis, and has been written about extensively by Wayne Stevens and others. Of course the scope of your application is sometimes not obvious – we can draw our network of processes as large or as small as we want. A system is whatever you draw a dotted line around. By this I mean that the boundary of any system is determined by an arbitrary decision that, for practical purposes, part of the world is going to be considered and part is going to be ignored. In the astronomy of our Solar system, we can treat influences from outside the Solar system as effectively negligible, and this works fine most of the time, even though theoretically every object in the universe affects every other. You may think that your skin separates a well-defined "you" from the rest of the universe, but biochemistry teaches us that all sorts of molecules are constantly passing in and out through this apparent barrier. Indeed all the

Chap. XV: Implementation, Network Splitting and Client-Server

molecules in our bodies are totally replaced over a period of a few years. This is rather a Zen idea – taken to the extreme it says that objects don't have an objective existence (pun intended), but are just the way we "chunk" the universe. And we should also be aware of the way the words we use affect the way we view the universe. As an amateur linguist, I find a number of B.L. Whorf's examples quite striking: in one example (Whorf 1956), he gives a word in one of the Amerindian languages that describes people travelling in a canoe, in which there is no identifiable root meaning "canoe". The canoe is so much an assumed part of their experience that it doesn't have to be named explicitly.

Thus, to design systems, we have to delineate the system we are going to design. This first decision is critical, and may not be all that obvious. So consider the context of the system you are designing: have well-defined (and not too many) interfaces with the systems outside your chosen system.

You can now lay out the processes and flows of your system. Explode the processes progressively until you get down to the level where you start to make use of preexisting components. In FBP, you will find these starting to affect your design as you get closer to them. This is one of the points where FBP design differs from conventional programming, but it should not really surprise us as we do not design bridges or houses purely top-down or purely bottom-up. As I said before, how can you "decompose" the design for a house so that it results in the invention of dry-wall? But conversely, you have to know where you're going in order to be able to determine whether you're getting closer to it. Ends and means must converge. Design is a self-conscious process of using existing materials and ideas or inventing new ones, to achieve a desired goal.

On the way to your goal, like any hiker, you have to be willing and able to change your plans as you go. The nice thing about programming using FBP is that you can move between a "real" program and its simulation very easily, so you can try something and modify it until you're happy with it. In fact, with FBP we can realize an old programming dream of being able to grow an application from its simulation. You can replace processes by components which just use up x seconds of time, and vice versa.

In programming I believe there should be no strong distinction between a program and a prototype that you use along the way during development. If something in the environment or in your understanding changes, so that an old assumption is no longer true, you have to be able to change your design. While I am very aware that the cost of change goes up the further back you go in the development process, you have to know when to cut your losses, and go back and do some redesign. If it helps, consider how much harder it is for, say, a surgeon to do this!

If you combine FBP with iterative development, I believe that you have a very powerful and responsive application development technology. You can try different approaches, it's cheap to make changes, and when it is time to dot the *i*'s and cross the *t*'s, it is essentially a linear process.

Chap. XV: Implementation, Network Splitting and Client-Server

By way of comparison, I believe that the chief failing of the "waterfall" methodology was that it was so awkward to go back that development teams would press forward phase after phase, getting deeper and deeper into the swamp, or they would in fact do some redesign, but pretend they were doing development (or even testing!). Here is Dave Olson again: "Programmers know that highly detailed linear development processes don't match the way real programming is done, but plans and schedules are laid out using the idea, anyway." He goes on to stress that, while there are some projects for which the "waterfall" process will work fine, you cannot and should not shoehorn every project into it.

Apart from the iterative explosion process for networks we have just described (vertical), in FBP I have found there is another process which is orthogonal to it. This is the process of cutting up networks horizontally, to decide how and where they are going to run. In this process, we assign parts of our network to different "engines" or environments. Since FBP systems are designed in terms of communicating processes, these processes can run on all sorts of different machines or platforms – in fact anywhere that has a communication facility.

When you think about the ways a flow can be chopped up, remember you can use anything that communicates by means of data, which in data processing means practically any piece of hardware or software. I call this process "cleaving". Networks can be "cleaved" (apparently you can also say "cleft" or "cloven", but I think I will stay with "cleaved") in any of the following ways (in no particular order and not at all mutually exclusive):

- multiple computers (hosts, mid-range, PCs or mixture)
- multiple processors within one computer
- multiple tasks
- different geographical sites
- multiple job steps within a job
- secondary transactions
- client/server
- multiple virtual machines
- etc.

All of these have their design considerations, but that's just like the real world, where there are many different processes and they all communicate in different ways. Today I can call up a friend by phone, mail him or her a hand-written letter, fax it, communicate by e-mail, text, send a telegram, or stick a note in a bottle, throw it into the Atlantic and hope it gets delivered eventually! Each one of these has areas where it is stronger or weaker.

Let us take as our starting point one common network cleaving techniques: multiple job steps in a

Chap. XV: Implementation, Network Splitting and Client-Server

job (this is a mainframe batch concept). Suppose you have decided that your network is going to run as a batch job under MVS. Here is a high-level picture of the network:

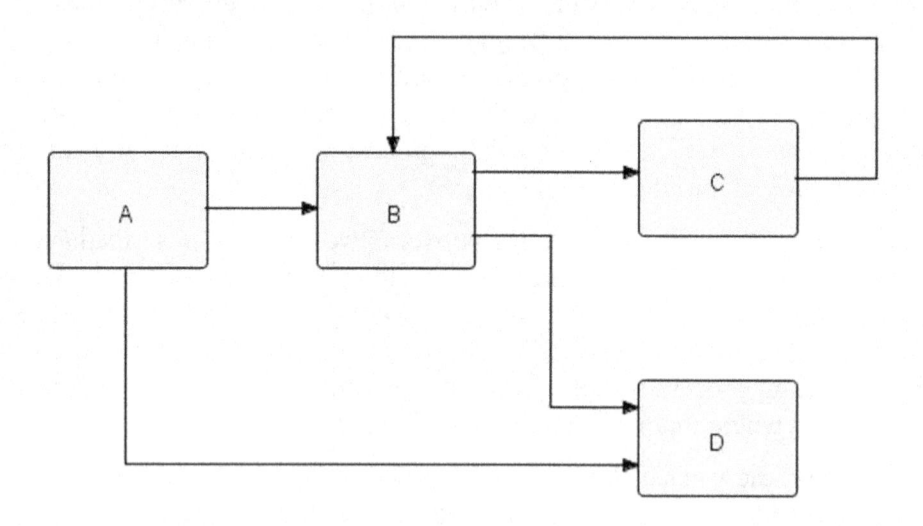

Figure 15.1

Let us suppose that, for whatever reason, we want to run this as multiple job steps of a single batch job. Now job steps can only run sequentially, and they communicate by means of files. While they can be skipped, they cannot be repeated. This means that *B* and *C* basically have to be in the same job step. However *A* and *D* can be split off into different job steps if desired. Suppose we decide to make both *A* and *D* separate job steps – this will result in 3 job steps in total.

Data files are really just another kind of data flow, so in FBP we can replace any connection with a sequential file. So let's change the connections leading out of *A* and those leading into *D* to files. Once we separate two processes into different job steps, of course all connections between them must be replaced by files. Each one of these will in turn require a Writer and Reader. Using dotted lines to show step boundaries and [X]'s to indicate files, our diagram now looks as shown in Figure 15.2.

I have shown the Writers and Readers around the files as *W*'s and *R*'s to keep the similarity between the two previous figures. These are proper processes even though they are not shown as full-size boxes. Steps 1 and 3 thus have 3 processes each; step 2 has 4.

Chap. XV: Implementation, Network Splitting and Client-Server

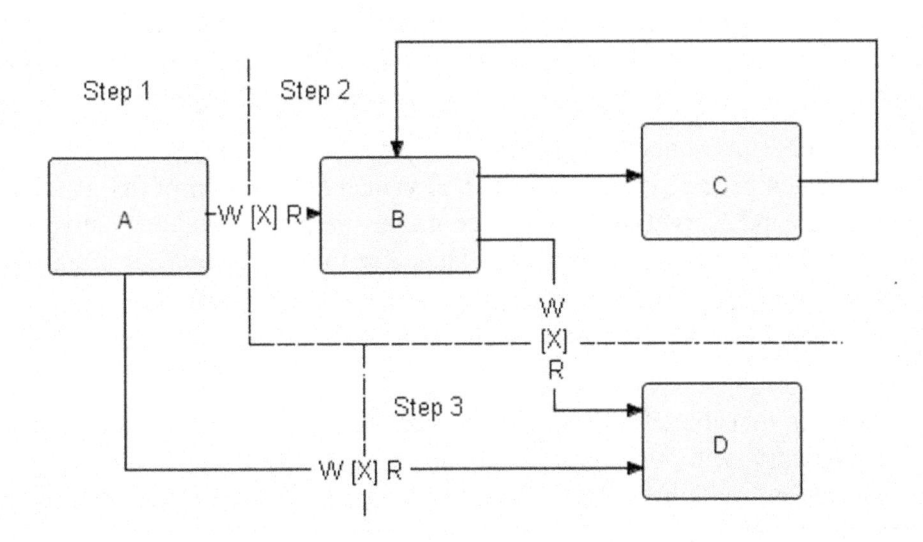

Figure 15.2

If we show this picture at the job step level, as in Figure 15.3, we see that we *could* have designed it this way earlier in the process, and then exploded it to get Figure 15.2. However, it is much better to design a complete application and then cleave it later, as other considerations may affect our decisions on how the network should be split up.

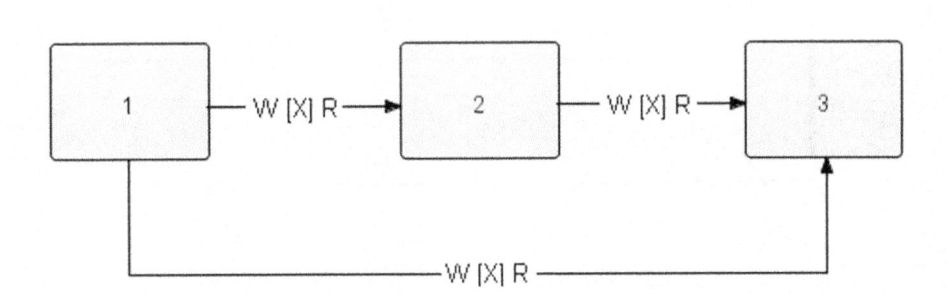

Figure 15.3

In fact, since it is so easy to move processes from one job step to another, there is no particular point in splitting up our network early – you can just as well leave it to the last minute. In conventional programming, moving logic from one job step to another is very difficult, due to the

Chap. XV: Implementation, Network Splitting and Client-Server

drastic change of viewpoint when you move from data flow design to control flow implementation, so the decision about what are going to be the job steps has to be made very early, and tends to affect the whole implementation process from that point on.

I'd like to make another point about this rather simple example: in Figure 15.2, you notice that communication between process A and process B is managed by two processes and a file. In FBP, this "two processes and something" is a common pattern whenever any two processes communicate other than via FBP connections. Thus a communication line might be "managed" by a Send process at one end, and a Receive process at the other. I will give a few examples later in this chapter of other kinds of communication between networks, and you will see this pattern in all of them.

A more subtle point is that the transition from Figure 15.1 to Figure 15.2 was made entirely by manipulating the network, without having to add any complexity to the underlying software. This point is related to the principle of what are called "open architectures": simple systems that can talk to each other are much better than large, opaque, non-communicating systems.

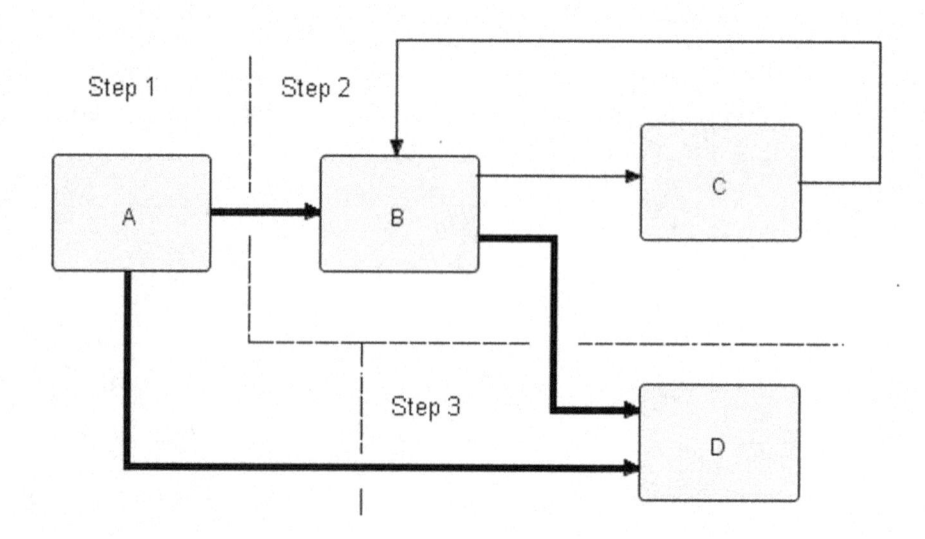

Figure 15.4

Our experience is that it is much better to implement subsystems like file handling and communications as visible processes under the developer's control than to bury them in the software infrastructure. Since the latter is common practice among software developers, all I can say is that this preference is based on solid experience. But consider the advantages: Write-file-Read becomes just one mechanism supporting a particular way of cleaving networks – we could

Chap. XV: Implementation, Network Splitting and Client-Server

have used many others, and in fact could change from one to another during project development.

To try to show what happens if we go the other way, consider what would have happened if we had decided to have two kinds of connections: an intra-step connection and an inter-step connection. Let's take Figure 15.1 and assign each connection to one of these two categories depending on whether it crosses a step boundary or not (we'll assume you do this at the same time you divide the network up into job steps), as shown in Figure 15.4.

Now, I claim that we have made both the implementation and the mental model more complex, without providing any more function to the developer. Not only will the added complexity make the system harder to visualize and therefore harder to trouble-shoot, but we may have made some useful operating system features inaccessible or only accessible through still more complexity in the interface. And if a programmer wants to replace the inter-step connections with, say, a DB2 database, s/he is going to have to add extra processes anyway, and change the inter-step connections back to intra-step connections....

A similar point can be made about the proposal a number of people have made: to allow IPs to be removed from connections out of sequence, based on priority. I would argue that this also makes the mental model much more complex – and such a facility would have to be built into the scheduler at a deep level. On the other hand, a case could be made for doing the FBP "first come, first served" merge on a priority basis – this has not been implemented yet, but could probably be added fairly easily at some time in the future.

Let's take another look at Figure 15.2. We could draw a box around each of the patterns shown as

```
----W [X] R----
```

to make it a process in its own right. This process can run perfectly well within a job step, and in fact we have met this pattern before in Chapter 13 (Scheduling Rules – page 126), where we drew it as shown in Figure 15.5.

As you will recollect, we used automatic ports to ensure that the reader did not start until the writer had finished writing the file. Taken as a whole, this process is rather like a sort without the sorting function! It writes a whole data stream out to disk, then reads it back and sends it on. We can also state this a bit differently: it keeps accepting IPs, storing them in arrival sequence, until it detects end of data; it then retrieves them and sends them on. During the early history of FBP, this was called, slightly fancifully, an "infinite queue" – however, I now realize that FBP connections (the old name was "queues") are by definition finite, and the previous name is really rooted in the old batch applications. A better name for this structure might be "file buffer". We will run into this technique again in the chapter on Deadlocks (page 156), and you will find that it is one of the most useful techniques for preventing deadlocks.

Chap. XV: Implementation, Network Splitting and Client-Server

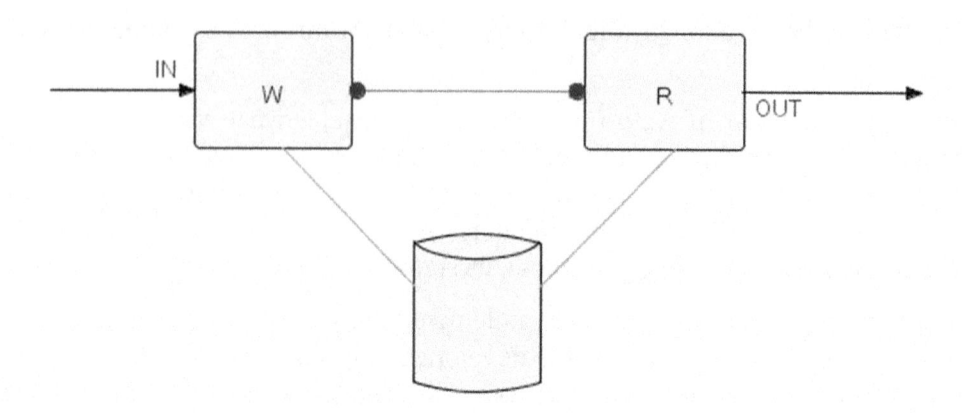

Figure 15.5

I would like to discuss the "granularity" of processes at this point. We suggested at the beginning of the chapter that processes can be as large or small as you like. For pragmatic purposes, we have chosen to pick a certain "grain" of process as the one we will implement, and connect them with a different mechanism, the connection. There are higher-level processes, which we call subnets, and the highest subnets are programs. Above programs you will find still higher processes referred to as jobs, applications, workflows, and so on. Different levels of this hierarchy will tend to be implemented by different mechanisms, but, if we need to, we can always move processes up or down the hierarchy. We can also treat a connection as a special type of process – this is is like using a magnifying glass to zoom in on a part of our network. Any time we want a connection to behave differently from normal connections, we simply replace it by a process (plus the connections on either end). We could also use this technique if we wanted to have another type of connection between processes, say, a connection supporting "priority mail". However this will require additional port names – a number of writers have described processes implementing FBP's connections (also known as "bounded buffers"), but we have found it more convenient to put them in the infrastructure.

As I read the ever-growing body of literature on parallel processes, I have been struck by the variation in granularity across the various implementations, from fine-grained to very coarse-grained. And in fact you will have noticed that FBP processes vary from very simple to quite complex. However, they do seem to agree on a certain "grain size". In the chapter on Performance (page 210), we will talk about how granularity affects performance, and how this fact can be used to obtain trade-offs between maintainability and performance.

In addition, we do not claim that the level of granularity described in this book is the best or the final one for all purposes – only that it is a level which we have found to provide a good balance between performance and expressive power. It is productive of useful components and

Chap. XV: Implementation, Network Splitting and Client-Server

developers seem to be able to become comfortable with it! Figure 15.6 shows a network which implements what used to be called a "half adder", using IPs to represent bits and FBP processes to model boolean operations – while this worked fine as a simulation, I do not suggest that we could build a real machine on it (although we might be able to build a *slow* simulation of a machine)!

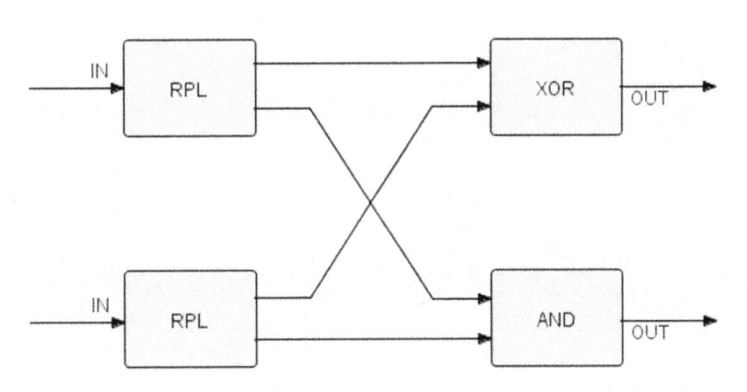

Figure 15.6

where *RPL* means Replicate, *AND* is the boolean AND operator, and *XOR* is the boolean exclusive OR.

We alluded above to "managing" a communication line by means of matching processes. Here we could distribute a network of processes between multiple computers, which may or may not be in the same room, building, city or country. This is "distributed" processing, which is gaining more and more attention. Instead of each computer labouring away by itself in splendid isolation, people today are accustomed to having computers be able to talk to each other around the world, using a wide variety of different communication techniques. The Internet of today was foreshadowed within the IBM Corporation by the internal network called VNET. I once impressed the heck out of a visitor by showing him how, from a terminal in Toronto, by using a one-line command, I could display the VNET file traffic between Australia and Japan!

Suppose we want to have two computers, each with multiple processes running on it, communicate asynchronously, then the two computers could simply exchange data by using two dedicated processes at each end of the link. A high-level schematic is shown in Figure 15.7.

This diagram shows two systems, each with a Sender and a Receiver process. The Sender of one system sends to the Receiver of the other, and vice versa.

Chap. XV: Implementation, Network Splitting and Client-Server

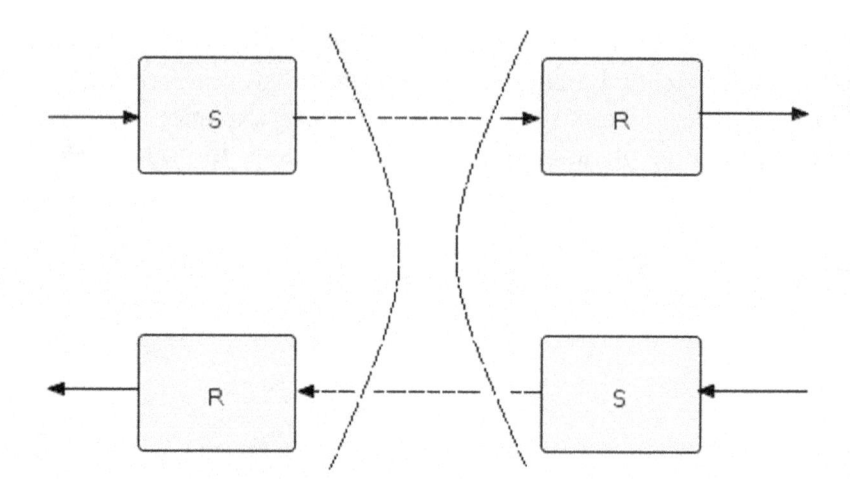

Figure 15.7

One of the things that FBP has always been good at is allowing different programming languages to "talk" to each other. Communication is by means of data, which is a universal language in data processing. Unfortunately, two of the most popular current languages, Java and C#, both use virtual machines, Java executing "bytecode", and C# the Microsoft Intermediate Language, so Denis Garneau has suggested that the best way to allow Java and C# to communicate is to use *sockets* – this would allow one to have a large network, where in fact different parts are written in different languages. This idea could in fact be extended to allow multiple languages to participate in a single extended network. So a large network could be designed, and then split into portions using different languages, with the different portions communicating via sockets – this process would be very like the "cleaving" process described earlier on in this chapter. Recently (April 2009) we were able to pass data experimentally between separate FBP networks, one written using JavaFBP, and one using C#FBP, running concurrently on my desktop. I consider this an important milestone, with all sorts of interesting implications!

There is a lot of interest these days in what are called client-server relationships. You may in fact have realized by now that, in FBP, every process is a server to its upstream processes. So the client-server paradigm is a very general one, from the level of FBP processes as high up as you care to go. However, it is important to stress also that FBP processes are peers, and peer-to-peer, which is more general than client-server, is a very natural match with the FBP approach. The FBP model is cooperative rather than hierarchical.

One major addition we have to make to the above schema is to allow for the possibility of asynchronous flows from multiple sources. If a machine in Toronto can have data flowing in from Montréal and/or Edmonton, it has to be able to accept data on a first-come, first-served basis (subject, perhaps, to a priority scheme if there is a need to handle express messages). We

Chap. XV: Implementation, Network Splitting and Client-Server

have already seen in FBP a mechanism which provides this – namely, multiple output ports feeding one input port. If you have this situation, you must have some way of routing the response back to the right source, so the data must be tagged in some way. In FBP, one way is to arrange for the incoming data to contain a "source index", which we could use as an output port element number. Figure 15.8 shows just two clients.

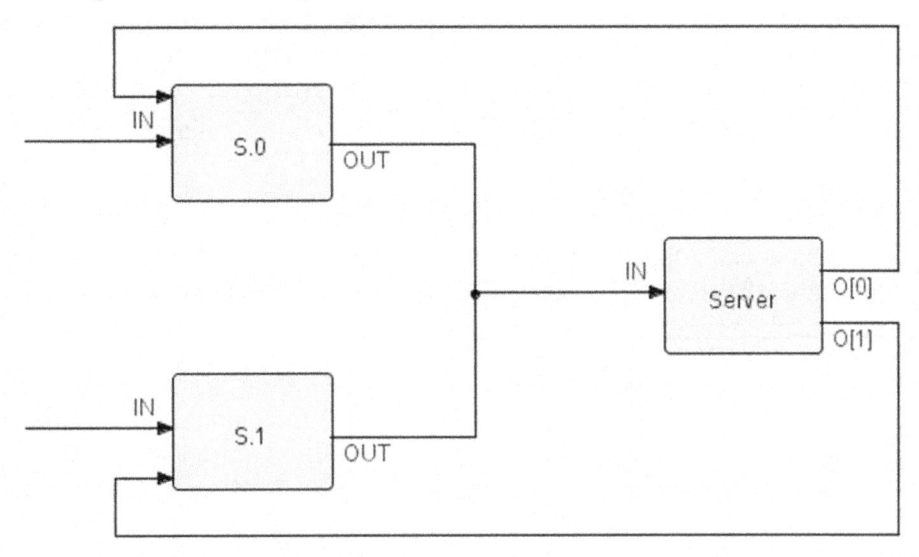

Figure 15.8

In this configuration "S.0" sends an IP to the server, and then waits for the response to arrive back, after which it can send another request. Meanwhile, "S.1" is going through the same cycle. You can see from the diagram that IPs from "S.0" and "S.1" will arrive at the server in "first come, first served" sequence. Of course, the server can only handle one request at a time, so it has to be able to process requests as fast as possible, relative to the arrival rate. Otherwise, a queue builds up which will in turn slow down all the processes requesting service. As in the above discussion of "cleaving" networks, any line in the above diagram can be replaced by other forms of communication, including the above-mentioned "Send-line-Receive" pattern, resulting in various kinds of distributed network. The "n to one" connection in the middle of Figure 15.8 would be implemented very naturally as multiple Senders sending to a single Receiver process. In FBP, the reverse situation, a "one to n" connection, is not implemented directly in network notation, but can be implemented simply by a Replicate process. In a distributed network, this would correspond naturally to a "broadcast" communication function, where one process sends the same message to multiple receivers. This is the kind of arrangement used by many taxi dispatching systems, where the dispatcher sends in broadcast mode, but individual taxis reply on their own wavelength.

We mentioned that the server in Figure 15.8 can only handle one request at a time. This would be the simplest way of implementing its logic. Another wrinkle might be to add an "express" port, like the express lane at some banks. However, unless the express port has its own server, this scheme can still be degraded by a low-priority request which is tying up the server. So it might be better to have two processes running concurrently, one handling express requests, and the other low--priority requests. Of course, this adds logical complexity, especially if the two servers are competing for resources. One possible solution is to implement an enqueue/dequeue mechanism to resolve such conflicts – this actually fits quite well with FBP, and was implemented experimentally in DFDM. The above-mentioned article (Suzuki et al., 1985) also describes a similar feature its authors developed as an alternative communication mechanism between processes.

Generalizing still further, we may multiplex the server by having multiple instances of the same component. For instance, suppose the server is doing I/O which may be overlapped with processing – you could have many instances of the same component serving the client queue. This is like many bank branches today, where several tellers are servicing a single queue of customers.

In the bank branch situation, the tellers "pull" customers off the queue. FBP however is a "push" environment, so we need a "load balancing" process to ensure that queues don't build up more in front of some servers than others. The resulting diagram might look as shown in Figure 15.9.

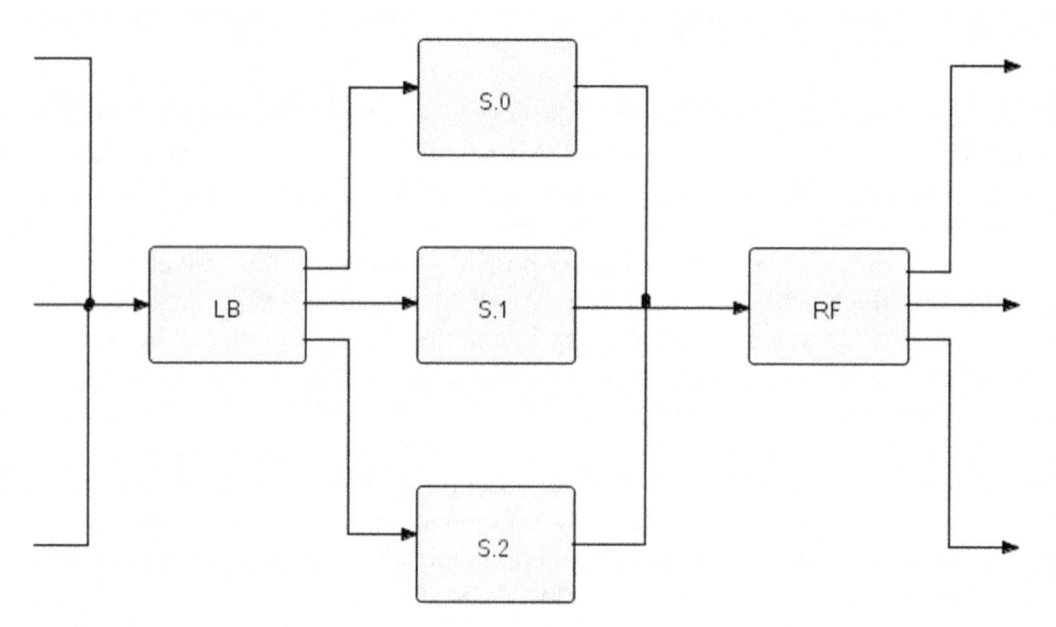

Figure 15.9

In this figure, requests are assumed to be coming in at the left side, tagged with an indication as to their source. They merge into *LB* which performs load balancing, sending the incoming

Chap. XV: Implementation, Network Splitting and Client-Server

requests to whichever server has the shortest input queue (number of IPs in its input connection). From the servers, the IPs then travel to *RF,* which is a redistribution facility. From there they eventually travel back to their original requesting processes. You will find a description in Chapter 21 (page 210) of how the load-balancer technique was used very effectively to reduce the run-time for a disk scanning program from 2 hours down to 20 minutes (a reduction of 83%!).

One topic which has been getting a lot of attention recently is that of portability of code. This is certainly one of the appeals of HLLs, but my personal feeling is that their disadvantages outweigh their advantages. While clearly you cannot port Assembler language from one type of hardware to another using a different instruction set, I believe a better solution is to port at the *function* level. A Collator can be defined to do the same job on two or more input streams, independent of what language it was coded in. So we can move Collators from one machine to another and expect that our function works identically. Not only does this approach take advantage of the strength of the black box concept, but it removes the necessity for code to be white boxes written in a portable language (which usually results in lowest-common-denominator languages, or frustrating and time-consuming negotiation about standards).

We have now seen how to decompose designs vertically, cleave them horizontally, and some other concepts such as client-server relationships. But in what order should you develop your application? I don't think there is a fixed sequence, but I have found two sequences productive: along the lines of bottom-up and top-down, I call them "output-backwards" and "centre-out". "Output-backwards" means that you start with the outputs intended for human consumption, and work backwards deciding how this data is going to be generated. If it's an interactive application, output is the screen, and you will eventually work back to the screen, which closes the loop. "Centre-out" means that you start with the core processes, usually the ones which do business logic, together with any required Collators and Splitters, and get them working using the simplest Reader and Display components. Fancy output formatting, input editing, etc., can then be added incrementally working out from the centre. This approach is really a kind of prototyping, as you can develop the main logic and check it out first, before investing effort in making the output pretty, making the application more robust, etc. At selected points along the way, you can demonstrate the system to potential customers, prospective users, your manager, or whomever.

Last but not least, during this whole process of development you will want to test your developing product. You can test a single component by just feeding it what it needs for input and watching what comes out as output. You generate its input using Readers and its output using some kind of Display component. In the early stages, the simpler these scaffolding components are, the better. The trick, as in prototyping, is to only introduce one unknown at a time. The more you can use precoded components, and the simpler they are, the fewer unknowns you will be dealing with. Any time you want to see the data that is travelling across a connection, just insert a Display process, like a probe in an electrical circuit. So testing is very simple.

As I have tried to emphasize in what went before, I feel that, while FBP is great for developing

Chap. XV: Implementation, Network Splitting and Client-Server

applications, it is perhaps even more effective in improving maintainability. After all, all attempts to make programs more maintainable after the fact have failed, so maintainability has to be designed in from the start. As some of the anecdotes above attest, FBP seems to have it designed into its very fabric. Given that your program will change constantly over the years, you will need a simple way to verify that the logic which you didn't change still works. Testing that a system still behaves the way it used to is usually called "regression testing". Wayne Stevens came up with an FBP-based technique for doing this. You take the original output of the system to be tested and store it in a file; you then imbed your system in a network as shown in Figure 15.10.

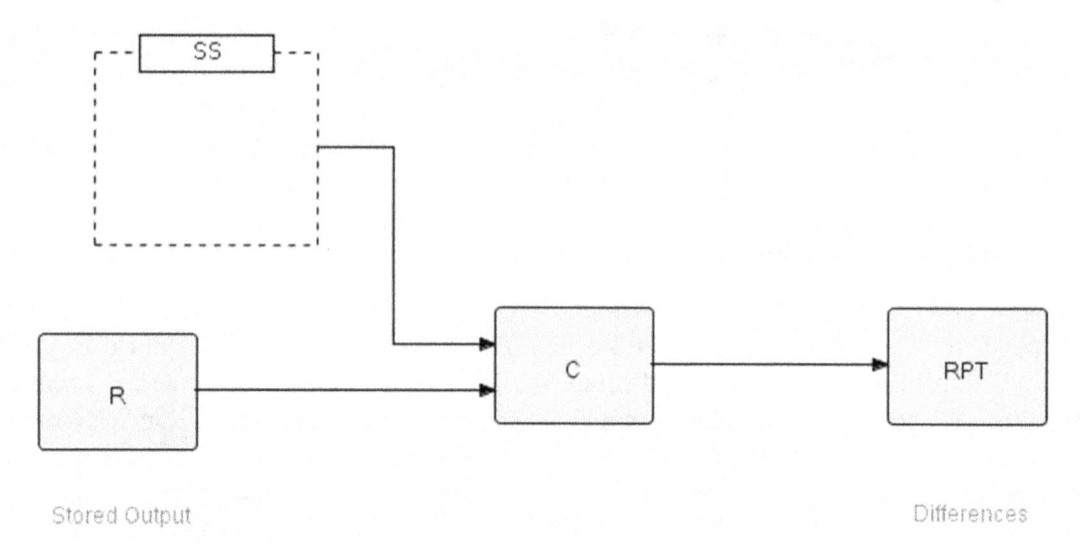

Figure 15.10

where

    SS represents the Subject System

    R is a Reader for the previously stored output

    C compares the stored output against current output

    RPT generates a report on the differences

This network is clear while also being generic. For instance, you might need to insert filters on *C*'s two input streams to blank out things which will vary between the two runs, e.g. dates and times. You might want to display the differences in different orders, so you can insert a suitable Sort upstream of *RPT*.

Chap. XV: Implementation, Network Splitting and Client-Server

A related (FBP-specific) problem comes up if C's input streams are not in a predictable sequence, say, because they are the result of a first-come-first-served merge, or if overlapped I/O has been occurring, so some IPs may have overtaken others. The simplest solution is probably to sort them before C sees them, but a better one, if it is feasible, is to mark the IPs at a point where they still have a fixed sequence, so that they can be split apart again before doing the compare. Of course, any processing you do to the differences (after the compare) will be cheaper than processing you do before the compare process (assuming that most of the data has compared equal).

I have given you a very high-speed description of some methodology and implementation techniques which are characteristic of FBP. You will doubtless come up with your own procedures, guidelines and "rules of thumb", and I hope that eventually there will be a community of users of FBP all exchanging ideas and experience (and experiences).... and more books!

Chap. XVI: Deadlocks: Their Causes and Prevention

Deadlocks are one of the few examples in FBP of problems which cannot involve only one process, but arise from the interactions between processes. They occur when two or more processes interfere with each other in such a way that the network as a whole cannot proceed. I know some programmers feel that they have traded the known difficulties of conventional programming for a new and exotic problem which seems very daunting, and they wonder if we have not just moved the complexity around! Although deadlocks may seem frightening at first, I can assure you that you will gain experience at recognizing network shapes which are deadlock-prone, and will learn reliable ways to prevent deadlocks from occurring. I know of *no* case where a properly designed network resulted in a deadlock during production.

First, however, I think we should look a little more deeply at the question I mentioned above: if FBP is as good as I claim, why does it give rise to a new and exotic class of problem which the programmer would not encounter in normal programming? Well, actually, it's not new – it's just that a conventional program has only one process, so you don't have to worry about deadlocks. In FBP we have multiple processes, and multiple processes have always given rise to deadlocks of various kinds. Actually anyone who has designed on-line or distributed systems has had to struggle with this concept. For instance, suppose two people try to access the same account at a bank through different Automatic Teller Machines (ATMs). In itself this doesn't cause a problem – one just has to wait until the other one is finished. Now suppose that they both decide to transfer money between the same two accounts, but in different directions. Normally, this would be programmed by having both transactions get both accounts in update mode (Get Hold in IMS DL/I terms).

Consider the following sequence of events (call the accounts X and Y):

Chap. XVI: Deadlocks: Their Causes and Prevention

- trans A – get X with hold
- trans B – get Y with hold
- trans B – try to get X with hold   (1)
- trans A – try to get Y with hold   (2)

At point (1), transaction B gets suspended because it wants X, which is held by A. At point (2), transaction A gets suspended because it wants Y, which is held by B. Now neither one can release the resource the other one wants. If A had not needed Y, it would have eventually finished what it was doing, and released X, so B could have proceeded. However, now that it has tried to grab Y, the result is an unbreakable deadlock. This is often referred to as a "deadly embrace", and in fact it has similarities to one kind of FBP deadlock. Usually on-line systems have some kind of timeout which will cancel one or both of the transactions involved.

Normally, the chance of this kind of thing happening is pretty small, so a lot of systems simply don't worry about it. It can be prevented completely by always getting accounts in a fixed sequence, but this may not possible in all situations, so it is probably true to say that some proportion (even if a tiny one) of transactions will deadlock in an on-line system, so you have to be able to take some kind of remedial action.

In FBP, we can also get deadlocks between the processes of a network. Of course, in an FBP on-line system, each transaction would be a network, so you can get deadly embraces between separate networks requesting the same resources, but we will assume these are handled in the normal way for the underlying resource management software. However, because a network has multiple processes, we can get deadlocks *within* a network. In all these intra-network cases, we have discovered that it is *always* a design issue.

This type of deadlock can always be detected at design time, and there are tried and true techniques for preventing them, which we will be talking about in this chapter. Wayne Stevens also has a very complete analysis of deadlocks and how to avoid them in Appendix B of his last book (Stevens 1991).

The general term for deadlocks like the deadly embrace is a "resource deadlock". There is a classical example of this in the literature called the "dining philosophers problem", which has been addressed by many of the writers on multiple processes. Imagine there is a table in a room, on which are 5 chopsticks, spaced equally around the table, and a bowl of rice in the centre. When a philosopher gets hungry, he enters the room, picks up the two chopsticks on each side of his place, eats until satisfied and then leaves, replacing the chopsticks on the table (after cleaning them off, I hope). If all the philosophers go in at the same time, and each happens to pick up the chopstick to his right (or left), you get a deadlock, as nobody can eat, therefore nobody can free up a chopstick, therefore nobody can eat! Notice that the dining philosophers exhibit the same loop topology which I have been warning you about in earlier chapters. The dining philosophers

Chap. XVI: Deadlocks: Their Causes and Prevention

can also suffer from the reverse syndrome, "livelock", where, even though there is no deadlock, paradoxically one of the philosophers is in danger of starving to death because there is no guarantee that he will ever get the use of two adjacent chopsticks. Kuse et al. (1986) proved that, although a network with fixed-capacity connections (like the ones in FBP) can suffer from deadlock, it can never suffer from livelock.

We will use Figure 14.2 from the chapter on Loop-Type Networks (page 135) to introduce an FBP version of a resource deadlock. I'll show it again here for ease of reference:

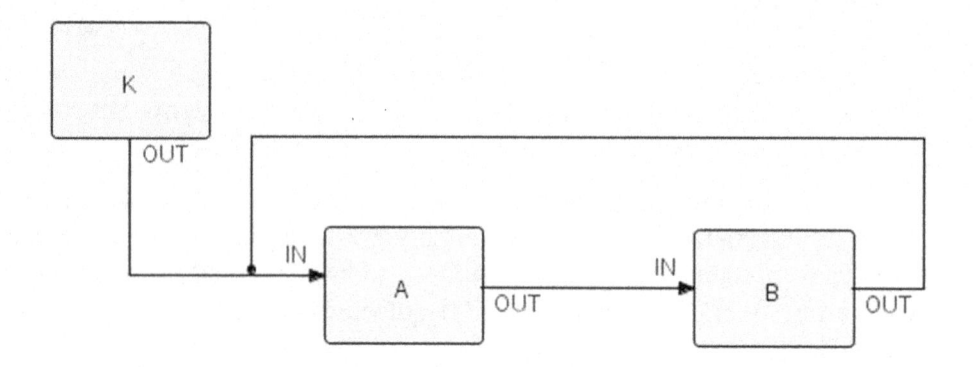

Figure 16.1

Suppose that *A* is a simple filter, with the following logic:

A's logic:

```
/* Copy all IPs from IN to OUT */
        receive from IN using a
        do while receive has not reached end of data
                send a to OUT
                receive from IN using a
        enddo
```

Figure 16.2

And suppose that *B* is similar, but its **send** function is conditional, as shown below.

Chap. XVI: Deadlocks: Their Causes and Prevention

B's logic:

```
/* Copy c-type IPs from IN to OUT */

      receive from IN using a
      do while receive has not reached end of data
            if condition c is true
                  send a to OUT
            else
                  drop a
            endif
            receive from IN using a
      enddo
```

Figure 16.3

We'll begin by starting *A*. *A* sends an IP out of its OUT port. It next does a `receive` on IN, but there is nothing there, so it suspends. The connection between *A* and *B* now has something in it, so *B* starts up. Let's say condition *c* is false, so *B* receives the IP, but fails to send it out. *B* then goes on to its `receive`, and suspends. *A* is also suspended on a `receive`, but it is going to wait indefinitely as *B* hasn't sent the IP that *A* is waiting on. *B* is suspended indefinitely since *A* cannot send what *B* is waiting on. This is very like the deadly embrace: two processes, each suspended waiting for the other to do something. Since *A* and *B* are suspended on `receive`, there is nothing active in our network (*K* has terminated). So no process can proceed. The program as a whole has certainly not finished normally, but nothing is happening! This is in fact how the driver recognizes that a deadlock has occurred.

AMPS and DFDM add a wrinkle to this: it is possible to have one or more processes suspended waiting for an external event (such as I/O completion) to occur. In this case, this is not a deadlock as the wait will eventually complete, so the network as a whole goes into a "system wait", waiting on one or more external events. When one of these completes, the scheduler regains control, and gives control to the process in question, allowing all the other interlocked processes to start up as needed. This feature is one of the important performance advantages of FBP: unlike conventional programming, if a process needs to wait for an event to occur, it is usually not necessary with FBP to put the whole network into wait state.

To take advantage of this feature, AMPS and DFDM had to handle I/O using the MVS "basic" or asynchronous access methods. If any process in the network was waiting on I/O, you didn't have a deadlock. This was also the case if a component was waiting on a timer.

A big advantage of the preemptive threading used by JavaFBP and C#FBP is that we no longer have to use asynchronous I/O, but we realized that a process could still be suspended waiting on some non-FBP event, so we recently introduced a "long wait" indication, where the component

- 159 -

Chap. XVI: Deadlocks: Their Causes and Prevention

could specify a maximum time for a non-FBP function, and time out if that is exceeded. Also, if any process is in the "long wait" state, you don't have a deadlock. Here is an example of a component using "long wait" (minus package name and imports):

```
@ComponentDescription("Writes a stream of packets to an I/O file")
@InPorts( { @InPort(value = "IN", description = "Packets to be written",
                type = String.class),
            @InPort(value = "DESTINATION", description = "File name",
                type = String.class) })
@OutPort(value = "OUT", optional = true,
          description = "Output port, if connected", type = String.class)
@MustRun
public class WriteFile extends Component {

  InputPort inport;
  InputPort destination;
  static String linesep = System.getProperty("line.separator");

  double _timeout = 10.0; // 10 secs

  OutputPort outport;

  @Override
  protected void execute() {
    Packet dp = destination.receive();
    if (dp == null) {
      return;
    }
    destination.close();

    String s = (String) dp.getContent();
    try {
      Writer w = new BufferedWriter(new FileWriter(s));
      drop(dp);
      Packet p;

      while ((p = inport.receive()) != null) {
        longWaitStart(_timeout);

        try {
          w.write((String) p.getContent());
           } catch (IOException e) {
          System.err.println(e.getMessage() + " - component: " +
                 this.getName());
        }
        w.write(linesep);
```

- 160 -

Chap. XVI: Deadlocks: Their Causes and Prevention

```
      longWaitEnd();

      w.flush();
      if (outport.isConnected()) {
        outport.send(p);
      } else {
        drop(p);
      }
    }
    w.close();
  } catch (IOException e) {
    //do nothing
  }
}

@Override
protected void openPorts() {
  inport = openInput("IN");
  destination = openInput("DESTINATION");
  outport = openOutput("OUT");
}
```

Figure 16.4

Let's redraw Diagram 16.1, showing the states of each process shown in the top left corner of the process, resulting in Diagram 16.5. You'll find this pattern of states is quite common, and is quite characteristic of a certain kind of deadlock. The drivers of all FBP implementations always list the process states as part of their diagnostic output in the event of a deadlock.

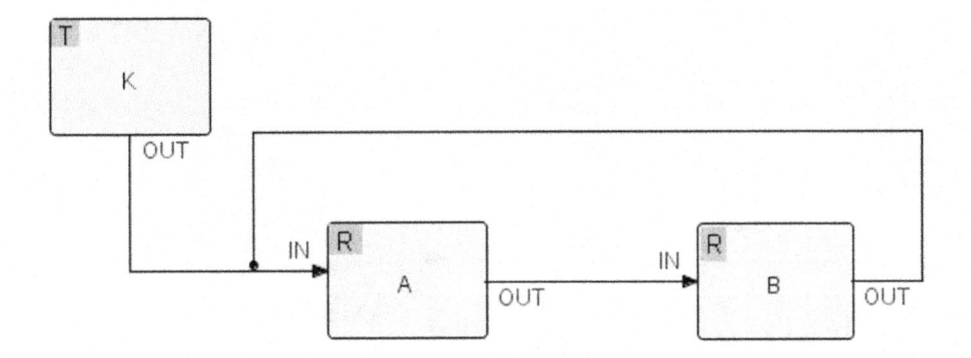

Figure 16.5

- 161 -

Chap. XVI: Deadlocks: Their Causes and Prevention

where T means terminated,

and R means suspended on receive

Since the only kind of resource "native" to FBP is the IP, the only problem can be non-arrival of IPs. So thorough testing will detect it. We could also have "infrastructure" or "hybrid" (FBP plus infrastructure) deadlocks, where, say, one process is waiting on an external event which never happens, and another on an IP that the former is to send out. There is nothing to prevent two processes from interlocking each other by both issuing explicit locks on the same resource, but in different orders. Old-style deadlock considerations still apply here, but, as I've said, this is a well-understood area of computing.

The other class of deadlock familiar to systems programmers is the "storage deadlock". In this kind of deadlock, the deadlock occurs because one process does not have enough storage to store information which is going to be needed later. This type of deadlock, unlike the resource deadlock, can usually be resolved by providing more storage (not always, because some variants of this continually demand more storage...).

Here is an example of a storage deadlock: suppose you are counting a stream of IPs, and you want to print out all the IPs, followed by the count. The components for doing this should be quite familiar to you by now: the IPs to be counted go into the *COUNT* process at the IN port and emerge via the OUT port, while the count IP is generated and sent out via the COUNT port at close-down time. So all we have to do is concatenate the count IP after the ones coming from OUT. This is certainly very straightforward – the network is shown in Figure 16.6.

Code this up in whatever dialect of FBP you like, and run it, and you get a perfectly normal run. Now, however, suppose that, for some perverse reason, you want to see the count IP *ahead* of the ones being counted. Since we're using a Concatenate function, you might think all we have to do

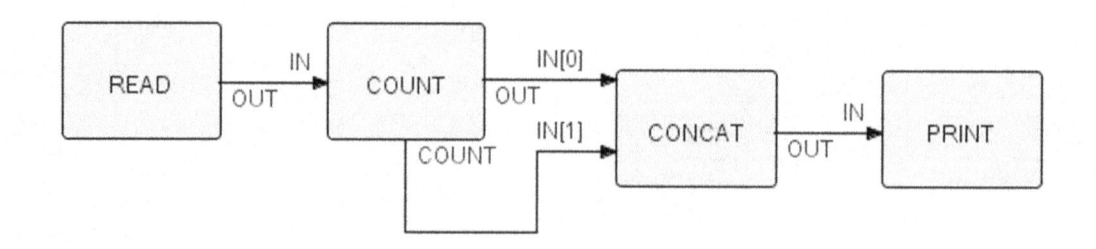

Figure 16.6

is concatenate the count ahead of the IPs coming out of OUT. So we change the picture as

Chap. XVI: Deadlocks: Their Causes and Prevention

follows:

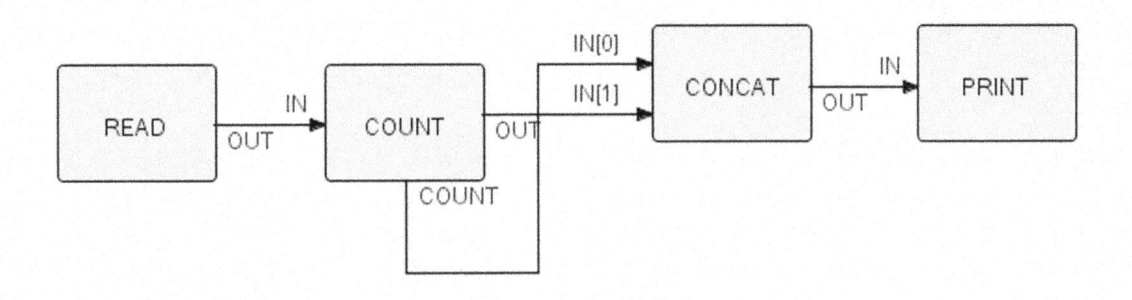

Figure 16.7

When we run this, to our surprise the result of this is a little different: we get a display along the following lines:

```
Deadlock detected
 Process Print Not Initiated
 Process Concatenate Suspended on Receive
 Process Count Suspended on Send
 Process Read Suspended on Send
```

Figure 16.8

This is definitely not the result we wanted! As before, let's try taking the process states and inserting them back into the diagram:

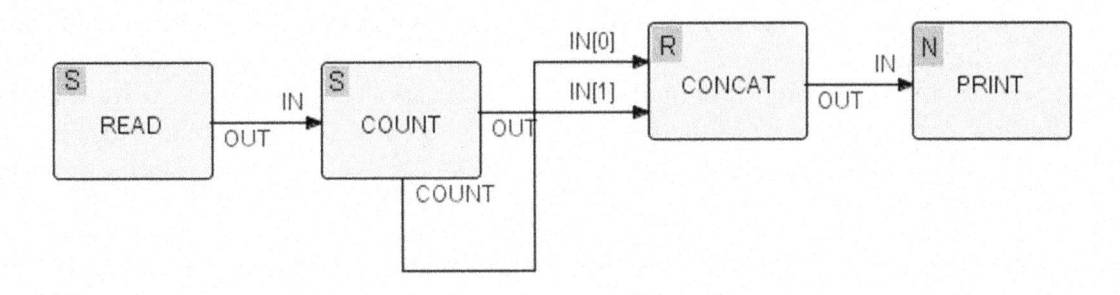

Figure 16.9

where S means suspended on send,

R means suspended on receive,

and   N means not initiated

Chap. XVI: Deadlocks: Their Causes and Prevention

You will find that in this kind of deadlock there is always a "bottleneck", or point where the upstream processes tend to be suspended on `send`, and the downstream processes are suspended on `receive`. As we saw before, some processes may have terminated – these can be excluded from this discussion. Processes which are inactive or not yet initiated can be treated as if they are suspended on receive.

If *COUNT* is suspended on `send` and *CONCAT* is suspended on `receive`, but they are adjacent processes, then clearly COUNT is sending data to a connection different from the one *CONCAT* is waiting on! Although there is data on the connection labelled OUT, *CONCAT* insists on waiting on a connection where there is no data, and, at this rate, there never will be! The problem is that the count IP is not generated until all of the input IPs have been processed, and the connection labelled OUT has a limited capacity, so there is nowhere to store the IPs after they have been counted.

Although this kind of deadlock resembles a resource deadlock (because each process is waiting on the other to do something it can't do), it can be resolved by giving one or more connections more storage, so it is of the class of storage deadlocks. You will remember that we don't make all our queues "infinite" because then you can't guarantee that everything will get processed in a timely manner (or ever, if you want to allow 24-hour systems). But if you visualize the OUT connection bulging like a balloon as IPs are pumped into it, you can see that, eventually, *COUNT* is going to have processed all its input and will generate the count IP, and we can start to let the balloon deflate back to normal!

What's the best way of doing this? Unfortunately, the question depends on how many IPs are being counted. If you knew absolutely how many IPs there were, you could just make the capacity of the connection big enough (provided you have enough storage). We can do this in any FBP implementation by adding a capacity number to a `connect` statement or method call. Depending on the amount of data, this may well take care of the problem. However, how do you know what is the magic number of data items? Remember the provinces of Canada – the process has already started which should eventually lead to the creation of a new one (or several). It's a fair bet that there will always be 7 days in a week, or 365 1/4 days in a year, but most other "constants" are subject to change, not to mention really variable numbers like the number of departments in a company.

Now suppose we follow the balloon analogy a bit further – what we could do is allow connections to bulge only if you would otherwise get a deadlock (i.e. no process can proceed), and let them bulge until we run out of storage. This initially seems attractive, but it makes error determination more complex. Remember that we allocate storage for IPs when they are created, not when we put them into a connection, so if you run out of storage somewhere, you won't know who is the culprit... However, if we put limits on the amount of storage we use, and perhaps slow down upstream processes, there may be situations where this is a practical solution. In his work dealing with large amounts of data, Mike Beckerle has effectively used a related

Chap. XVI: Deadlocks: Their Causes and Prevention

technique – described later in this chapter under "Parallelism issues" (page 169).

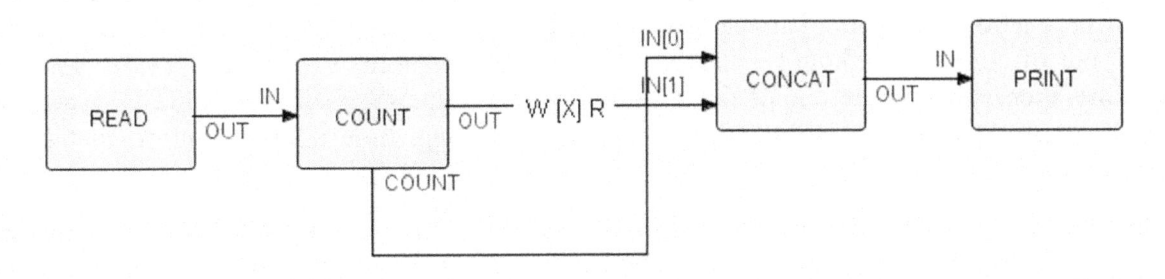

Figure 16.10

So far, the simplest general solution we have come up with is still to use a sequential file. You will remember from Chapter 15 (page 140) that we can replace any connection with a file. Let's change the network as shown in Figure 16.10, using the notation we used in Chapter 15. In that chapter we used

---W [X] R---

to indicate a "sandwich" with the file being the meat, and a Writer and Reader being the bread on each side. In Chapter 15, we used automatic ports to ensure that the Reader does not start until the Writer is finished.

Now, if you step this through in your head, or try it out on the machine, you will find that the file soaks up IPs until it gets end of data. Meanwhile *CONCAT* is waiting for data to arrive at IN[0]. The "meat" file's Reader can start at some point after this, but will only run until its output connection is full. At this point, the only thing that can happen is for *CONCAT* to receive the count IP, then end of data, then switch to receiving from IN[1]. From this point on, the data IPs will just flow through IN[1] to *CONCAT*'s output port.

We have seen that you can set capacities on all connections. What would happen if we gave all connections a standard capacity of, say, 20? Then examples like the above (the situation before we added the sequential file "sandwich") would work fine as long as there were only 13 Canadian provinces and territories. Add a few more provinces one day, and your nice production program goes boom! Since amounts of test data tend to be smaller than production amounts, we would never be sure that programs which worked fine in test would not blow up in production. We have therefore adopted the strategy during testing of making connection capacities as small as possible, to prevent this kind of thing from happening. Once we go into production, however, we can safely increase connection capacities to reduce context-switching overhead. A propos, my son, an experienced programmer, has suggested the following aphorism: "During testing, better

- 165 -

Chap. XVI: Deadlocks: Their Causes and Prevention

to crash than to crawl; in production, better to crawl than crash!" The second half of this doesn't mean, of course, that you should put poorly performing systems into production – it just means that in production, when problems arise, it is better to try to keep going, even if in a degraded mode, but of course you should make sure someone knows what's going on! There is a story (possibly apocryphal) about one of the early computers (either SAGE or STRETCH) which did such a good job of correcting storage errors, that for some time nobody noticed that it was running slower and slower!

In Chapter 15, we talked about the Writer/Reader sandwich, which I am referring to as a "file buffer". This is a general solution for storage deadlocks, and the only slightly tricky thing about such deadlocks is figuring out which connection has to be expanded. If you bear in mind that it must be a connection which is full (i.e. its upstream process is suspended on `send`) while its downstream process is suspended trying to receive from a different port, you'll find it pretty easily.

This dependency on number of IPs occurs in conventional programming, and you are probably familiar with the problem of having to make design decisions based on number of items. Michael Jackson gives an example in his 1975 book of a file which consists of two types of groups of records (we would call them substreams), where the substream type is determined by the type of the last record, rather than the first. He gives as an example a file consisting of batches, each with a control record: if the control record agrees, you have a "good" batch; if it doesn't, it is a "bad" batch. The problem of course is: will the batch fit in storage? If it will fit safely, there's no problem. If not, you either use a file, or provide some form of backtracking (going ahead with your logic, but being prepared to undo some of it if it turns out to be a bad batch). In the foregoing I have tried to stress that it's not good enough if the batch fits into storage now – you have got to be sure it will fit in the future!

There is one final type of deadlock which again involves a loop-type network, but where most of the processes are suspended on `send`. This is more like a resource deadlock than a storage deadlock, and usually arises because one or more processes are consistently generating more IPs than they receive. In this kind of deadlock, giving them more storage usually doesn't help – the network just takes longer to crash. However, in the case of a loop structure like a Bill of Materials explosion, some processes are consistently generating more IPs until you reach the elementary items, so you have got to think pretty carefully about how many IPs may be in storage at the same time. When in doubt, use a file!

If all this seems a trifle worrying, in most cases you will find that you can recognize deadlock-prone network topologies just by their shape. In fact, the very shapes of the above networks constitute a clear warning sign: any loop shape in your network diagram, whether

Chap. XVI: Deadlocks: Their Causes and Prevention

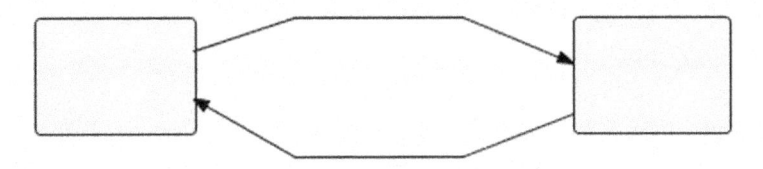

circular

Figure 16.11

or divergent-convergent,

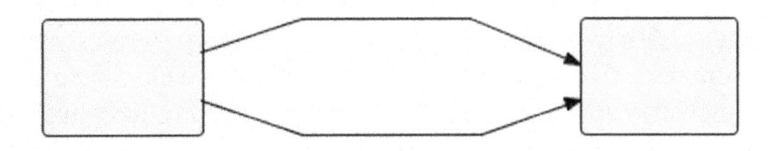

Figure 16.12

should be treated with caution, as they are possible sources of deadlocks.

In case some people may have read the previous paragraph as saying that they should avoid these deadlock-prone topologies completely, I should reiterate that it is often a perfectly adequate solution to just add one or more "file buffers" into the network.

In an earlier chapter (Chapter 8 – page 77), we talked about how, after you have split a stream into multiple streams, the output streams will be "decoupled" in time. If you decide you want to recombine them, you will usually land up with a variant of the above diagram. Unless you are willing to use the "first come, first served" type of merge (by connecting multiple output ports to one input port), you are creating a very fertile environment for deadlocks. Generally speaking the split and merge functions have to be complementary, but that may not be enough. Let's set up an example. Suppose we want to spread a stream of IPs across 3 servers, and then combine them afterwards. One approach might be to use a "cycling" splitter, which sends its incoming IPs to its output port elements *0* to *n-1* in rotation. We will also need a merge which takes one IP from each port element in rotation and outputs them to a single output port. The picture looks like this (setting *n* to 3):

Chap. XVI: Deadlocks: Their Causes and Prevention

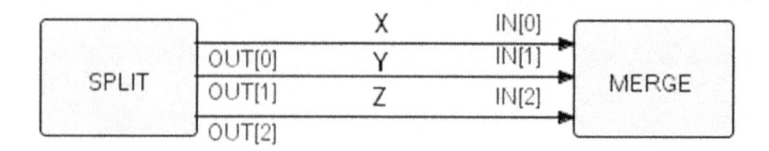

Figure 16.13

Now we can add any processing we like at the spots marked X, Y and Z. Well, not quite, as a number of people have discovered. For one thing, MERGE must see 0's, 1's and 2's in strict rotation. If you want to drop an IP, you had better make sure there is a "place-holder" IP in its place, unless you can arrange to drop one or more entire sets of 0, 1 and 2. If you don't do this, at the least your IPs will be out of order, and you may eventually get a deadlock (actually that might be better from a debugging point of view!). The same thing applies if you want to add extra IPs, except that the place-holders will have to be in the other streams. We have found that this impulse to split up streams into multiple ones is a common one among programmers, and it can be very useful. I give this example as a warning of some of the pitfalls which await you when you try to recombine them. In fact, it may not even be necessary! You may find that the assumption that data has to be kept in strict sequence is just a hold-over from the old synchronous style of thinking! Humans usually like to see data in sort sequence, but computers often don't care.

I am going to show one more deadlock example, because it illustrates the use of the "close port" service, which has been required by all FBP dialects. Consider Figure 16.14.

You know that *CONCAT* receives all IPs from [0] until end of data, and then starts receiving from [1], and so on. What can you deduce about the upstream process *Q*? Well, it should somehow be able to generate two output streams which overlap as little as possible in time.

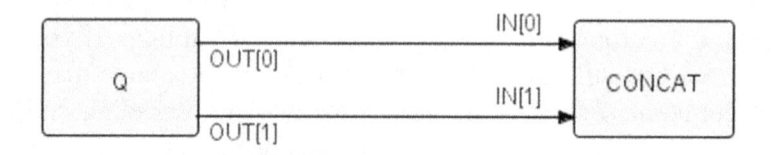

Figure 16.14

We also notice that this (partial) network has a divergent-convergent topology, which suggests it is deadlock-prone. What might cause it to deadlock? One possibility is if *Q* starts to send IPs to [1] while *CONCAT* is still expecting data at element [0]. What causes *CONCAT* to switch from [0] to [1]? *CONCAT* switches every time it detects end of data on an input port element. But...

Chap. XVI: Deadlocks: Their Causes and Prevention

end of data is normally caused by the upstream process terminating, and *Q* has not terminated. So *Q* has to have some way to signal end of data on [0] to *CONCAT*, so *CONCAT* can start processing the data arriving at [1] – otherwise *CONCAT* will still be waiting on [0] while data build up on [1]. What *Q* has to do is close each of its output ports before it switches to the next one. This will send a signal downstream enabling *CONCAT* to switch to its next input port.

I feel the example shown in Figure 16.14 is interesting as it illustrates a useful technique for subdividing a problem: what *Q* is really doing is subdividing its input stream into "time domains", which *CONCAT* can then safely recombine into a single stream. A lot of sequential files in the business world have this "time domain" kind of structure – e.g. a file might have a header portion, perhaps a list of cities followed by a list of sales staff, followed by a trailer portion. This kind of structure can be handled nicely by splitting the input stream into separate "time domains".

Parallelism issues

Mike Beckerle says the following:

> The FBP systems used inside many commercial data processing frameworks exploit data partitioning and so generate a much larger FBP processing flow for execution from a logical FBP graph or drawing. Each FBP component/operator logically may produce many instances of that component/operator in the graph that is actually executed so as to divide and conquer large sets of data. Key to this is the introduction of partitioning operators into the flow to divide up the data, and merge operators when it must be reassembled.

In connection with deadlocks, Mike makes the point that, when large volumes of data are involved, you naturally want to keep processing going in parallel to the greatest extent possible. Unfortunately, under certain circumstances it is very hard to avoid getting deadlocks. In a diagram like Figure 15.9 (p. 152) you can see that the IPs going through *RF* will be processed one at a time. To make even better use of multiple cores, you want to keep processing as parallelized as possible. This results in the type of structure shown in the left-hand side of Figure 16.15.

This part of this diagram works fine, with good processor utilization by the parallel streams. Unfortunately, as Mike points out, there is often a need to do a join of the separately processed streams, as shown in the diagram. If the amounts of data to be joined are relatively small, you could bring the streams together into a single input port, on what is called a "first-come, first-served" basis, and use a Sort component to sort the data together into the desired sequence. Mike tells me that Sorts that are multithreaded and also overlap sorting with the receipt of data from the flow (as the AMPS Sort did) are now "standard fare". The problem when using OO

Chap. XVI: Deadlocks: Their Causes and Prevention

languages is that efficient sorting of large volumes of data is hard to do with OO languages, so most of this has to be done using C/C++, which gives you much better control over data representation. There is a big difference between sorting in Java and C/C++, and when you are working with very large amounts of data, it is well worth putting the extra human effort into tuning the software.

You will immediately recognize this diagram as an example of the "convergent" network topology.

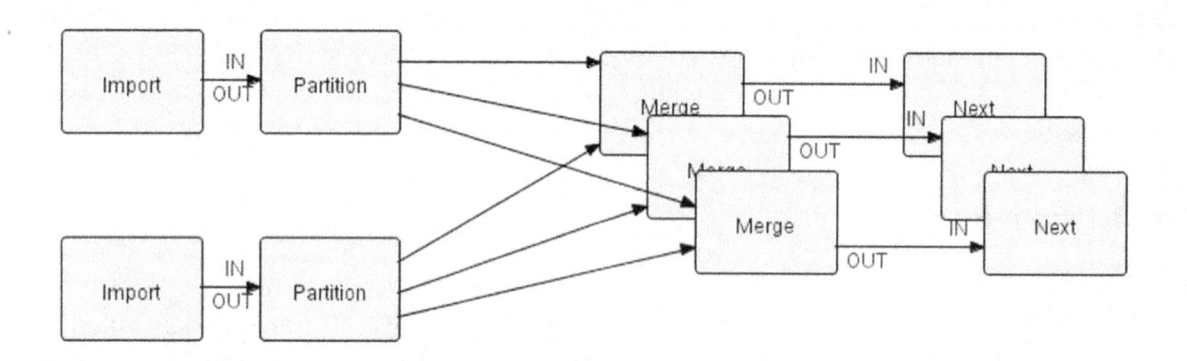

Figure 16.15

Here is Mike again:

> The merge operators are typically algorithmic here. They are not feeding data together on a first come first served basis, but are, for example, examining the incoming streams of data, and merging based on maintaining order by a key field so as to avoid the need to sort again. This creates a hazard for deadlock any time there is a long-enough stream of packets with the same key value. One side of the merge will back up the flow back to the partition operators, and beyond that to the Import components at which point the flow is deadlocked.
>
> This deadlock can be avoided with large enough buffers on the flow arcs, but unfortunately, we never know how big is enough because it depends on the data we are processing. In the worst case we need to buffer the entire input data set being imported. But we don't want to put these kinds of unbounded buffering everywhere in the flow.

Mike has come up with the following solution: First you find all the convergent arcs of the flow. In the figure this would be those entering the Merge components. Each of these arcs is changed

Chap. XVI: Deadlocks: Their Causes and Prevention

to implement what Mike calls "reluctant buffering", which basically works like this: First, you need processes which are able to monitor their own outputs. If they cannot deliver records to output, even if slowly, they wait for a period and then try again. If still not successful, they start allowing inputs to build up until (hopefully) they are able to deliver their output, in which case they revert to the normal situation.

You will see that this is a modification of the "ballooning out" approach that we mentioned above as a possible solution to the problem of deadlocks. There will certainly be topologies where this is inadequate, but for the diagram shown above, which represents a common situation in high-volume applications, it seems to be a workable solution.

I asked Mike about tuning the "reluctant buffering", and here is what he had to say:

> ...I used a trick I have found useful in many situations which is to adjust the parameters dynamically but to include a pseudo random factor. The behaviour that you really have to avoid is oscillation where the system drives itself back and forth between bad behaviors. The pseudo random factor eliminates this pretty well. I learned this trick from Ethernet actually which has an exponential backoff and retry algorithm but they also toss in a randomness factor.

If you remember the "file buffer" sandwich described above, this can be implemented as a subnet containing two components, but it could also be implemented as a single component, writing to the file, and then reading it back. To implement ballooning, you could replace this sequential file by a large FIFO queue, and have one component that writes to it, and one that reads from it. This would involve two threads – one writing and one reading, asynchronously. To make this work well, we should also make the reading thread higher priority than the writer, and also provide a way of slowing down the writer when the FIFO queue gets too big. This might have to be done at several levels, i.e. provide different writer sleep times for different numbers of packets in the queue – and possibly overflow to a file, if necessary. This is also where Mike's tuning suggestion could be used. This approach definitely looks promising, and could eventually become a standard part of JavaFBP and C#FBP, and future FBP implementations.

Chap. XVII: Problem-Oriented Mini-Languages

"One of the greatest advantages of little languages is that one processor's input can be another processor's output" – Jon Bentley (1988)

"Another lesson we should have learned from the recent past is that the development of 'richer' or 'more powerful' programming languages was a mistake in the sense that these baroque monstrosities, these conglomerations of idiosyncrasies, are really unmanageable, both mechanically and mentally. I see a great future for very systematic and very modest programming languages" – E.W. Dijkstra (1972)

Problem-oriented mini-languages can be thought of as essentially an extension of the types of parametrization we talked about in Chapter 5 (page 54). Jon Bentley, like many other writers, has pointed out the importance of finding the right language for a programmer to express his or her requirements. This language should match as closely as possible the language used in the problem domain. If you view the programmer's job as being a process of mapping the user's language to a language understood by the machine, then clearly this job becomes easier the closer the two languages are to each other.

You may have gathered, correctly, that I am not overly excited about the HLLs (Higher-Level Languages) of today. They appear to me to occupy an uncomfortable middle ground between more elegant options at each end of the spectrum. At the low end: machine code – Assembler is fine for a certain problem domain; at the high end: reusable "black box" modules. Some jobs can really only be done in Assembler, although C (now C++) is moving in on its turf – the problem is portability. Black box modules solve the portability problem much more effectively than HLLs – you just port at the function level, rather than at the code level. Historically, HLLs evolved out of

Chap. XVII: Problem-Oriented Mini-Languages

"small" languages like FORTRAN by the gradual accretion of features as people tried to extend the languages to new application areas. Most of them are on firmest ground when dealing with arithmetic because here they had traditional notations and experience to build on.

In my opinion, there are three major problem areas common to almost all HLLs:

- the data types of variables ("smart" data not being enforced),
- constants
- the basically synchronous nature of these languages.

We have already talked about variables in the context of the usual computer concept of storage. Data types we have talked about in the chapter on Descriptors (page 110). Now let's talk about constants.

Constants are usually not (constant, that is)! Constants are vastly overused, mostly because it is so easy to hard-code a constant into a program. To take an extreme position, I would like to see constants only used when they reflect the structure of the universe, such as Planck's constant or π, or conversion rates between, say, kilometres and miles – they're not likely to change. A case can also be made for allowing metadata (data about data), e.g. number of bytes in an *int* field, although much of this can be avoided by judicious use of descriptors and generalized conversion routines. I also vote for zero and one – they're too useful (for things like clearing and incrementing counters) to give up! Also to one and zero let's add their boolean cousins, "true" and "false". But that's the lot!

An ex-colleague of mine *claims* that he knew someone who wrote a program for a company which had exactly 365 employees. You guessed it – an employee left the company, and all the date calculations were off! While this story is probably apocryphal, there is an interesting point here: the only way it could have happened is if the program used the same constant for both numbers. Many shops ban the use of literals, in an attempt to reduce this kind of thing, whereas, of course, it only helps if people are also encouraged to use *meaningful* symbol names. If, as many programmers do, the constant in question was labelled F365, it would actually make this kind of error *more* likely.

Literals would actually have prevented this kind of thing from happening, whereas calling a constant F365 works the other way! One of the constants should have been NUMBER_OF_DAYS_IN_YEAR (that's non-leap, of course), and the other one shouldn't have been a constant at all! Remember: *most constants aren't!*

So far we have mostly talked about numeric values. There is another class of constants that one runs into quite often in programs: strings which identify entities or objects. Consider a test like

```
IF PROVINCE = 'ONT'.....
```

I would argue for two reasons that this shouldn't be used: the first point is that in HLLs we are

Chap. XVII: Problem-Oriented Mini-Languages

forced to compare two character strings – whereas what we would like to ask is (in English):

```
If this province is Ontario,....
```

This may not look very different, but in the first case we are dealing with how affiliation with Ontario is *encoded* in a particular field; in the second, we are asking if the entity being referenced is the *entity* Ontario (with all its connotations). OO languages are better in this regard: `province` could be an instance variable within one object which contains the handle of another object (`ontario`) belonging to the class Province, and you can ask if two objects are the same object (==). However, when this information is stored in a file, Ontario might be represented by the value 2, so you tend to spend all sorts of machine resources converting back and forth between 2 and 'ONT' (or the object `ontario`). Nan Shu has identified conversions between codes as one of the most common functions performed by business application code (Shu 1985).

The second point is more subtle: even if you can refer to unique objects as a whole, rather than by an indirect encoding, should you? Consider the following sort of code, which we often find in business applications:

```
IF PROVINCE = 'NB' OR PROVINCE = 'PEI' OR PROVINCE = 'NS'...
```

If Canada adds a new province, how do you find all the lists like the above, and how do you decide if the new province should be added to that list or not? What is the concept that makes this set of provinces different from all the others? This is an example of a very common problem with code which is probably responsible for significant maintenance costs in shops around the world. At this point you will probably realize that we haven't done anything yet in FBP to prevent people from doing this. And as long as we are stuck with today's computers as the underlying engine, we probably can't, unless we ban constants entirely! What we can do is provide tools to help with this kind of situation (i.e. support the logic which people are trying to implement), and raise programmers' consciousnesses by means of walk-throughs, inspections, apprenticeship or buddy systems, or whatever.

The general concept which I would like to see known and used more widely is what IBM's Bucky Pope calls "class codes". He suggests you first ask what is the underlying concept behind the list; you then build a table or database, and implement the concept as an attribute of the entities (in this case, provinces). So the above test becomes something like:

```
FOR ALL PROVINCES P IN PROVINCE_TABLE,
IF P IS MARITIME, .....
```

The overhead goes up a bit, but maintenance costs go down drastically, and since it is now generally accepted that human time is a lot more expensive than machine time (Kendall 1977), it seems short-sighted to keep on perpetuating this type of code, and incurring the resultant costs. By the way, this principle applies equally if only one province happens to be mentioned in a particular list: how do you know that a new province won't show up which shares attributes with the one you've picked?

If we are going to (almost) ban constants from code, put entity attributes and what might be called "variable constants" on disk, why not put logic on disk as well? This gets us into the domain of rules-driven systems. Remember we said above that FBP gets rid of a lot of the non-business logic, so most of the remaining logic in code should be either general-purpose, e.g. the logic to Collate two data streams, or it should be business-related, e.g.

```
IF INCOME > $50,000, CALCULATE SURTAX USING FORMULA .....
```

Now, both the criterion and the formula are certainly going to change, and on a regular basis, so why put them in code which requires programmers to change it, after which the changed programs have to be recompiled, approved, promoted, the old ones archived, and so on and so on? It seems much better to put the whole thing somewhere where it can be maintained more easily, and perhaps even by non-programmers. I believe that much business logic, perhaps almost all, can be put on disk and interpreted using simple interpreters.

One important question remains: whether to put our attribute tables, rules, etc., in separately loadable code modules or in data files. The former are really a half-way house, as you still need programmers to maintain them, but at least the information is separate from your program code, so it can be shared, and is much easier to manage and control than when it is buried in many different code modules. However, I believe putting this kind of information into databases is a still better solution, as it can be updated by non-programmers, e.g. clerical staff, and it can have separate and specific authorization.

In rules-driven systems, straight sequential logic may not be the best way to express the rules. Prolog – see *http://en.wikipedia.org/wiki/Prolog* – and its derivatives provide a very interesting approach to expressing logic. It should be stressed that logic programming is not incompatible with FBP – I once wrote an experimental FBP component which drove a Prolog set of rules to perform some logic tests on incoming IPs. The effect was like having a friendly database, because you could ask questions like "list all the mothers older than 50" even when you had not stored the attribute "mother" explicitly in the database (just tell Prolog that a "mother" is anyone who is female and has offspring). The logic programming people have independently explored the possibilities of combining logic programming with parallelism, e.g. such languages as Parlog.

Now, if we can put our rules out on disk, avoiding such perilous traps as variables and constants, and restrict the code proper to non-business-related logic, then it seems that there really isn't much of a role for today's HLLs!

On the topic of parallelism in languages, a recent paper by Guy L. Steele Jr., a Sun Fellow, argues (*http://research.sun.com/projects/plrg/Publications/ICFPAugust2009Steele.pdf*), as do a number of the thinkers about parallelism, that we should be focusing on algorithms and data structures

Chap. XVII: Problem-Oriented Mini-Languages

that are intrinsically parallel. Here is what Richard Harter has to say in the FBP Google Group (started by Justin Bozonier – see *http://groups.google.com/group/flow-based-programming*) about this approach:

> I am inclined to believe that it is based on a flawed approach towards parallelism that ultimately will lead nowhere. ...
>
> What Steele suggests in the talk is that the game is to focus on data structures and algorithms that are intrinsically parallel. Implicit in this approach is the thought that the actual splitting of the execution of code will be done in the background by a run time system. (I opine that by now we have learned that this kind of splitting should not be done in the code.)
>
> My view is that Morrison has the right idea. Instead of focusing on parallelism in data structures and algorithms, focus on parallelism in program structure. In other words Steele is thinking at the wrong level.
>
> Here are some key points as I see it:
>
> (a) Use mini-processes instead of functions. The problem with functions is that their execution is inherently serial ; the execution of mini-processes is inherently parallel.
>
> (b) Don't use shared memory [FBP *can* use shared memory, but the concept doesn't *rely* on it – PM]. More generally, don't use shared resources. Locks, mutexes, and semaphores are not your friends.
>
> (c) Data partitioning is good; do it [at] the mini-process level.
>
> (d) Have the concept of data objects that are passed from mini-process to mini-process. Morrison emphasizes that his "information packets" are objects that only have a single conceptual location at a time.
>
> (e) Different languages/software representations should be used for the inter and intra mini-process levels. At the upper level coordination languages are appropriate; at the lower level classical programming languages.

So far, we have talked about the basics of most programming languages as being arithmetic and logic, but there exist languages today which address quite different domains. Over the years, we have seen a number of other kinds of specialized languages, such as SNOBOL (pattern-matching), or IPL V (list processing) appear and sometimes disappear. Since in conventional

Chap. XVII: Problem-Oriented Mini-Languages

programming it is hard to make languages talk to each other, it is generally the richer ones which have survived. FBP, on the other hand, makes it much easier for languages to communicate, which suggests that what we may see is a larger number of more specialized languages communicating by means of data streams. Based on our experience with human languages, what would be very nice is if they could all share the same syntax, but work with different classes of objects (semantics). It has been found that humans have a lot of difficulty switching from one syntax to another, whereas we can hold many sets of words independently without getting them confused. This is supported by recent work with bi- and multi-lingual communities – people tend to use one syntax for both languages, or a hybrid, but they can keep the vocabularies quite well separated.

A colleague of mine makes the interesting point about the above scenario that it ties in with the new science of Chaos. If you consider the total application space as chaotic, then you will get areas of order and areas of disorder (Olson 1993). Each mini-language can handle its own area of order, and can communicate using standard interfaces (IPs) with other areas of order. Each mini-language defines its own paradigm – while no paradigm should be expected to do the whole job, judicious combination of many paradigms is often highly effective.

I would argue that, any time a set of parameters reaches a certain level of complexity, you are approaching a mini-language. The parameters to the IBM Sort utility almost constitute a language about sorting, and in fact IBM added a free-form, HLL-like syntax to the older-style pointer list which it used before. Since decoding the sort parameters is relatively fast compared with the sort itself, it is reasonable to make the sort parameters as human-convenient as possible. The semantics of a set of sort control statements are quite simple, just referring to objects of interest to the sort (and its user).

If you have spent years labouring with a conventional HLL, by now you may be wondering how one can do anything without using variables or constants! Well, quite a bit, as it turns out. In Chapter 24 (Streams and Recursive Function Definitions – page 240), we will talk about a style of programming which is called "applicative" or "functional". When you combine the idea of functions with recursive definition, it turns out that you can express quite complex computations without ever using a variable (Burge 1975)! I shall try to show in later chapters that the application structuring supported by FBP has characteristics in common with applicative/functional programming – without requiring application developers to become symbolic logic experts!

In the next chapter I am going to describe some work I did on a possible approach to a mini-language for describing business processes running in an FBP environment, taking advantage of the fact that there are other precoded FBP components (such as Collate) to do a lot of the heavy lifting. This is not supposed to be a definition of a complete language, but more of a sketch of how a language might look which breaks with many time-honoured but rather shop-worn traditional solutions.

Chap. XVIII: A Business-Oriented Very High Level Language

The following is a sketch for a different kind of language – one that describes business logic descriptively, rather than procedurally. I was reading an article by M. Hammer et al. (1977), describing a system which they called the *Business Definition Language* (BDL), and I started thinking that some of BDL's basic ideas were really complementary to FBP – FBP doesn't have a native way to express business logic, while FBP provides simple solutions to some of the awkwardnesses that I spotted in BDL. BDL might be described as a tabular/functional approach to expressing business applications, which embodies a number of desirable program attributes listed by B. Leavenworth in his 1977 paper:

- elimination of arbitrary sequencing (sequencing not dictated by the data dependencies of the application)
- pattern-directed structures (non-procedural specification)
- aggregate operations
- associative referencing

Of course, these are embodied in BDL, which I will describe in this chapter, but it seems to me that FBP can make BDL even more natural.

I want to expand on these four points a bit. The following are my interpretations, but I hope that I don't depart too far from the spirit in which Leavenworth intended them!

Leavenworth sees the first point, "arbitrary sequencing", as one of the serious problems with procedural languages, and of course it has come up frequently in various forms in this book. As we have said before, the von Neumann machine forces you to fix the sequence of every

Chap. XVIII: A Business-Oriented Very High Level Language

statement, *whether it matters to the logic or not*. Consider the two statements

```
MOVE A TO B
MOVE C TO D
```

Clearly it makes no difference to the logic what order they are executed in, but change the first statement to refer to C or D, and you reverse them at your peril! Thus,

```
MOVE A TO C
MOVE C TO D
```

is totally different from

```
MOVE C TO D
MOVE A TO C
```

It is also worth noting that much of the optimizing logic in compilers involves trying to determine which statements can be moved and which ones cannot.

It should also be clear in the light of what has gone before why "pattern-directed structures" are desirable. Humans are much better at working with descriptions (especially visual ones) than lists of instructions.

"Aggregate operations" – this is closely related with trying to avoid procedural solutions. We have found that the higher level the constructs the language deals with, the more powerful it is, and the less of a barrier there is between the programmer's concept and its expression in the language. Of course, higher-level constructs require higher-level operations.

An example I have always found interesting is the APL language. It is highly expressive and a lot of its power derives from the foundation work that Ken Iverson did investigating the basic theory of matrices. While most of us were taught to treat matrix multiplication as an atomic operation, Iverson found a simple yet powerful way to make visible the fact that it is really a particular relationship between two binary operators, which he represented using the "dot" symbol. This is a second-order operator, as it works with other operators, rather than variables. Not only did this allow other binary operators to be combined in the same way (like "or" and "and", or "min" and "max"), but it freed up the simple "multiply" operator so it could be generalized smoothly from scalars to vectors to matrices.

As an example of aggregate operations, let's compare the way PL/I and APL handle matrices. In PL/I you can write the following statement:

```
A = A + A(2,3);
```

Figure 18.1

Chap. XVIII: A Business-Oriented Very High Level Language

This is implemented in a very procedural manner. PL/I executes this statement one element at a time, and does it in such a way that the rightmost dimension is the one which cycles most rapidly. So the sequence will be `A(1,1)`, `A(1,2)`, ..., `A(1,n)`, `A(2,1)`, `A(2,2)`, ..., and so on. When these additions hit `A(2,3)`, all "later" elements (those following `A(2,3)`) will have the new (doubled) value added to them, rather than the original one. In APL, on the other hand, matrices are treated as "aggregates", which are conceptually handled all at the same moment of time. Thus, you can write

`A ← A + A[2;3]`

Figure 18.2

and it behaves almost like the PL/I example, but `A[2;3]` does *not* change halfway through execution. This of course means that APL has to be able to manage matrices as more or less opaque objects, while PL/I treats matrix operations as if they were explicit loops of code. In FBP, although for performance reasons we have to process a stream one IP at a time, you very often can *think* of it as a single object. If you really have to process a whole stream as a single object, we have seen in the earlier chapters that you can turn it into a tree, and then turn it back later. In the chapter on Streams and Recursive Functions (page 240) we will see how one can use recursive function definitions to effectively treat a whole stream as a single aggregate object.

"Associative referencing" means the ability to locate an object by content, rather than by location. On most modern machines, this is done by means of a look-up of some sort, although there have been machines designed which did it by hardware. A few years ago there was a lot of interest in associative or "content-addressable" memory. While it is certainly nice to be able to find things that have moved, my feeling is that "handles" are fine, provided you have a way to find new things which you have never searched for before. Once they are found, they shouldn't have to move again, and their handles can be passed from process to process. An additional wrinkle is to leave a trail in the rare event that things do move (of course in both cases we are talking about a single shared memory). It is interesting that the main difference between Carriero and Gelernter's Linda (1989) and FBP is that the former is associative, while FBP, at least when running in one computer, as we have seen, uses connections and handles. We will be looking at Linda in more detail in a later chapter, but it seems to me that Linda's design should increase its overhead considerably over FBP, without a corresponding advantage in expressiveness. An example in one of the articles about Linda describes how to simulate an FBP connection, and it would be trivial to write matching FBP components which store and retrieve Linda tuples! Of Leavenworth's four points, this last seems to me the least exciting, but it should certainly be borne in mind as a design technique.

To give you a flavour of BDL, here is a portion of the definition for the "extended details" file (or stream) in Leavenworth's paper.

Chap. XVIII: A Business-Oriented Very High Level Language

Specification		Glossary	
Name	Derivation	Name	Definition
1 Ext Detail's	ONE PER Detail	Detail's	INPUT
2 Ext price	Unit price x Quantity	Unit price	IN Product Master
		Product Master	Master WITH Master product number = Detail product number
		Master product number	IN Master
		Detail product number	IN Detail
		Detail	CAUSE OF Ext detail
		Master's	INPUT
		Quantity	IN Detail
2 Salesman	Old Salesman	Old Salesman	IN Detail
		Detail	CAUSE OF Ext detail
2 District	Old District	Old District	IN Detail
		Detail	CAUSE OF Ext detail

Figure 18.3

This is the same *TR1* that was used in Chapter 10 (page 97). In this diagram, "'s" is the BDL notation denoting a collection or group. I shall continue to use their term "extended price", although a better term would be something like "extended monetary value".

I have labelled the columns as shown to give an indication of their purpose and interrelationships (BDL proper does not do this). The first two columns express the hierarchical structure of the file in question and the derivations of each of the entries, while the last two columns give definitions of all names appearing in the second column, and of any new names introduced in these definitions. The fourth column uses some reserved words to describe relationships between words in the first column and their sources. Thus, the derivation of "Ext price" is shown in the second column, and uses "Unit price" and "Quantity", whose definitions are in turn shown in the

Chap. XVIII: A Business-Oriented Very High Level Language

third and fourth columns. The whole approach is based on *definitions*, rather than *procedures*, which I find very appealing.

The structure shown in the first column is considered to repeat indefinitely through the "Ext detail's" file.

If a job step produces more than one output file, a BDL "program" similar to that shown above must be given for each one separately. Clearly, since each one is driven by the same input file, there is unnecessary duplication of logic here. In fact, in an attempt to avoid uncontrolled "global" definitions, the BDL language is considerably more redundant than one would like, and every duplication increases the risk of one or more of the copies getting out of step.

A more subtle problem arises from the lack of an explicit stream concept: in column three of the referenced diagram, "Product Master" is defined as that Master record (hopefully unique) whose "Master Product number" field is equal to the "Detail Product number" in the Detail record. WITH is an example of what Leavenworth calls "associative referencing" – it describes an implicit matching process. However, there is no indication of *how* the appropriate master record is located. While this is to some extent deliberate, when we actually come to build an application, we will eventually have to choose between various techniques for relating details and their corresponding masters, e.g. direct access, sort and merge, and perhaps others, which will have a profound effect on the basic structure of our design. It is true that the software could be allowed to select the technique automatically, but in our work with FBP we tend to feel that it is better to leave developers free to choose whichever technique seems most appropriate. Remember there will be prewritten, "black-box" code available to support whatever approach they select.

Assuming that the master and detail streams have been sorted, and then merged using Collate (described above), it is astonishing how succinctly we can specify the processing that needs to be applied to the merged stream to generate the desired output streams.

Three types of non-procedural information are really all you need:

- a description of the input and output streams, down to the IP level, and the creation and output criteria for the output IPs (let's call it an IP Relationship Diagram)

- descriptions of the various IPs involved (IP Descriptions) – this is basically the same as the list of instance variables in an OO class definition

- description of the calculation basis for "derived" fields – fields not present in the input IPs, or whose values are changed by the component (Derivation Descriptions).

Chap. XVIII: A Business-Oriented Very High Level Language

Here is the IP Relationship Diagram (IRD for short):

```
INPUT STREAM {
 Product Substream: REPEATING {
  Product Master OPTIONAL
  Sales Detail: REPEATING
  }
}

OUTPUT STREAMS {
New Masters {
 Product Master: ONE PER Product Substream
 }
Sort Input {
 Sales Detail: [ONE PER Sales Detail]
 }
Report-1 {
 Product Summary: ONE PER Product Substream [,NEW]
 }
}
```

Figure 18.4

This table describes relationships among IPs, so the lowest level items at any point always describe IPs – all higher level items are substreams, while the top level items are streams.

Only one input stream may be specified in the IRD, but there may be any number of output streams.

The quantifier phrases (REPEATING, OPTIONAL or ONE-OR-MORE) are pretty much self-explanatory. ONE PER x indicates that the substream in question is to be generated once for each occurrence of substream x (like BDL we can call x the "cause" of the substream being described). You will realize that the quantifiers on the input stream elements are exactly the same as those described in connection with the Warnier and Jackson notations (Chapter 10 – page 97).

The other things we have to specify are the contents of the various IP types, and the derivations of any derived fields. The following diagram shows the logic for those fields which are changed or created by the action of the component in question. Fields which are unchanged from the values they had on entering the component are not shown. It would be helpful to have some notation to relate fields to the IPs they are part of, so the tabular format shown below is probably not ideal. Finding a better notation will be left as an exercise for the reader!

Chap. XVIII: A Business-Oriented Very High Level Language

Name	Derivation
New Master	
Year-to-date Sales	Year-to-date Sales [IN Product Master] + Product Total
Extended detail	
Extended Price	Unit Price * Quantity
Product Summary	
Product Total	SUM of Extended Price [OVER Product Substream]
Year-to-date Sales	SAME as IN New Master

Figure 18.5

When a field in a "new" IP is not mentioned, it is assumed to have the same value as the field with the same name in the "cause" IP.

The function "SUM of A OVER B" sums all occurrences of field A within higher-level substream B (which is called the "range" of the OVER). Thus, Product Total is defined as the sum of Extended Price OVER Product Substream. The OVER-clause is shown in square brackets in this example, as it becomes redundant if the following rule is added: if OVER is omitted, the "range" is taken to be the "cause" (in the BDL sense) for the field being computed.

This is just a rough sketch for a mini-language that might do some of what people use HLLs for today. Because FBP allows us to mix languages freely, no one language has to be able to do everything, so we can design languages to specialize in different subject areas. By the same token, the same mental model is not valid for all possible uses – if you want to do *some* logic by pattern-matching, you do not have to do all of it by pattern-matching! Similarly, while mathematics is a great foundation for some types of programming, that does not mean that all programmers must become mathematicians. Lastly, a language can be expressive and still be rigorous. If the mental model is one that people find easy to grasp, it should enhance productivity, rather than just becoming an extra burden on the developer. It is absolutely crucial that we shift a certain amount of the work of developing applications to people who are not necessarily professional programmers, both to reduce the DP bottleneck, and also to take advantage of their expertise.

Chap. XIX: Synchronization and Checkpoints

We will start off this chapter by talking about how to synchronize events in an FBP application. After having stressed the advantages of asynchronism so heavily, it may seem strange to have to talk about strategies to control it, but there are times when you simply have to control the timing of events precisely, so it must be possible to do this. It is just that we don't believe in forcing synchronization where it isn't required. We have already seen various kinds of synchronization, such as loop-type networks and composites, so let us look at synchronization a bit more generally.

Typically we synchronize something in a process to an event elsewhere in the processing logic, or to an event in the outside world. Only certain events in certain processes need this treatment – it would be against the philosophy of FBP to attempt to synchronize a whole network.

The most basic kind of synchronization is when a point in the logic of a process is synchronized with a point event in time. In IBM's MVS operating system, an event was represented by a control block called, not surprisingly, an Event Control Block (ECB). Only one task could be waiting on it, but any task could post it complete. This was probably the ancestor of today's "semaphores".

The IBM main-frame dialects of FBP (AMPS and DFDM) implemented an event-type wait service to suspend a single process. This means that you could have one or more processes suspended on events without the whole application being suspended. You get this feature automatically when each process is a thread (preemptive multithreading), but these systems were fibre-based, so this was a necessary addition. In turn, in these systems, you could not afford to have I/O suspend a whole program, so most I/O was handled using asynchronous APIs. The application as a whole was only suspended if no process could proceed and at least one process

Chap. XIX: Synchronization and Checkpoints

was waiting on an event (if there were no processes waiting on events, you had a deadlock). We found that applications with many I/O processes often took less elapsed time than if they were coded conventionally using buffered I/O, for the reason given above.

Instead of a point event, we might instead have to synchronize an application to a time of day clock, e.g. "run this job at 5:00 p.m." All you need is a process which sends out an IP at 5:00 p.m., every day (or you could arrange for it to send out IPs every hour on the hour, or every five minutes, or every 20 seconds). Such a process can act as a clock, like the clock in a computer that sends out pulses on a regular schedule. These IPs can then be used to start or delay other processes.

Similarly to the "wait on event" service available to its components, DFDM also had the ability to suspend a process for a specified amount of time or until a particular time of day. This used a facility provided by MVS to post an event at a particular time. In the case of DFDM, this function was only provided as an off the shelf component: it could either delay incoming IPs by a certain amount of time, or generate a stream of IPs at given intervals. Where multiple time intervals were required, you could have as many of these processes as you liked in a network. This was reminiscent of the "future events queue" used by simulation programs – remember we talked about how in FBP you can evolve a simulation of a program into the program itself.

Another kind of synchronization referred to already is the need to delay something until a process has completed. As we said above, you can use what we call an "automatic output port" for this.

If you need to delay a process until two or more others have completed, a simple way of doing this could be to use Concatenate, as in the following diagram:

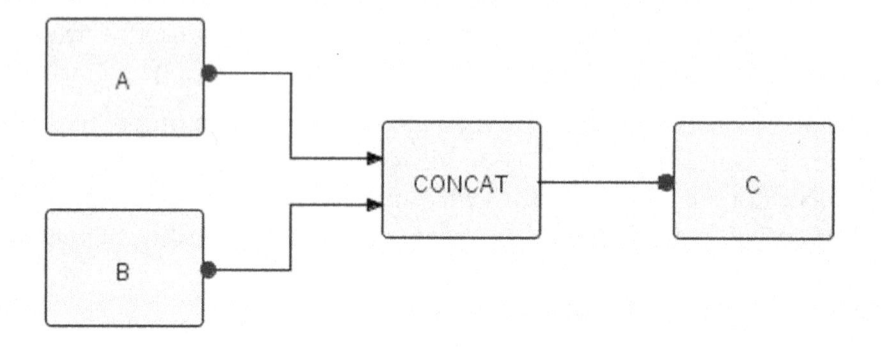

Figure 19.1

In this figure, processes *A* and *B* close their automatic ports when they terminate. *CONCAT* will not close down until both *A* and *B* have terminated, so the end of data signal from *CONCAT* (when *it* closes down) can be used to delay process *C*.

Chap. XIX: Synchronization and Checkpoints

Another kind of synchronization is built into the "dynamic subnet" mechanism of DFDM. We said before that a composite component monitors the processes within it. In particular, if the composite is substream-sensitive, it handles exactly one substream from every input port on each activation. These input ports are therefore also synchronized, so you can visualize the composite component advancing, one substream at a time, in parallel, across all of its input streams.

Of course, most often such substream-sensitive composite components only have one input port, in which case they process one substream per activation. We have described in some detail how they work in the chapter on Composite Components (Chapter 7 – page 71).

Now let's talk about checkpointing, and how we might tackle it in FBP. Most interactive systems and systems which share databases have to wrestle with the problem of *checkpointing*. For those of you not familiar with this, it is used for a number of disparate functions. Perhaps the most basic is to cut up a long-running batch job in such a way that, if it fails at some point, the whole thing doesn't have to be rerun. Checkpointing is also used in the case of interactive mainframe systems to ensure that data records are not held for too long. Suppose you have a transaction that needs to get exclusive control of two or more data records, do some processing, and then update them. During this period, no other transaction can be allowed to access the records. There is also the possibility of a failure during this period – to allow for this, you either postpone committing the changes until a certain point of time, or go head and make the changes, but be prepared to undo them if there is a problem. This requirement is also addressed by checkpointing, and different systems combined this with input transaction handling in different ways. This general type of processing is called OLTP (On-Line Transaction Processing). All of these situations can be addressed in FBP using the very powerful concept of "subnets".

In the old days, "checkpointing" just meant saving *everything* about the state of a program, and "restart" meant loading it all back in and resuming execution. Well, for one thing, a program had to come back to the same location and this might not be available. It became even harder as systems were distributed across multiple tasks or even multiple systems. In FBP, the states of the processes aren't in lock-step any more, so it becomes harder still! In general, as the environment becomes more complex, checkpointing needs more information to be provided by the programmer. However, we would very much like to be able to write a general checkpoint component which we could use across a wide range of applications, and we feel it should be possible to develop useful generalized components for this.

In the following paragraphs I will describe an approach which seems to fit the requirements. Rather than trying to create an enormously intelligent and complex module, our approach is to provide a series of points in time where as many processes as possible are quiesced, so that they do not require as much data to be saved about them.

The following three interactive mainframe environments all service different types of users. They are different options in the IBM IMS environment, and they illustrate different

Chap. XIX: Synchronization and Checkpoints

combinations of the above ideas. I am including them as they show the possible range of uses of checkpointing, and therefore suggest areas that we need to address in our solution.

a) IMS MPPs (Message Processing Programs), which service interactive users, are written as a loop handling multiple transactions sequentially until some number is reached (the loop may be terminated for other reasons as well). An MPP takes a checkpoint every time its goes back to the input queue for another transaction. This "commits" the updates, and unlocks the records involved so other users can access them. If the system crashes before the checkpoint, the updates have logically not been done, and IMS has to ensure that this is logically true (even if it has happened physically).

b) IMS Batch supports long-running batch applications, which should checkpoint about every half an hour, so that the amount of the job that has to be rerun is never more than half an hour's worth (this rule applies both to programs updating databases and to regular batch jobs using ordinary sequential files).

c) IMS BMPs (Batch Message Processing) are batch-type programs that need to access the files also being used by MPPs. This kind of program should checkpoint perhaps as often as every few seconds – otherwise, online users of the same data may become hung waiting for the BMP to release data which they need.

The common idea in all these cases is that the system saves the logical state of the system, so that it can be restored if required, and then releases data records locked by transactions (transactions have to indicate intent to update a record, which will lock that record), so other programs can access them. The information needed to restore a process to an earlier state is often called its *state data*. Clearly, the less data we can get away with saving, the less time checkpointing will take, and the faster any restart can occur if it is needed.

Since checkpointing needs a stable base with as little going on as possible, we will have to quiesce as many of the processes in our application as possible, and have as few IPs in flight between processes as possible. The more we can do this, the less state data we have to save.

Here's an analogy: a number of people are swimming in a pool, and a member of the staff decides it's time to put some chlorine into it. Now the first thing to do is to get all the swimmers out of the water. So the staff member blows the whistle – s/he now has to wait until everyone is out of the water, which might take a little while as everyone has to finish what they are doing. She now puts the chlorine in, waits some amount of time and then blows the whistle again to indicate that it is safe to go back in.

Let's reuse a diagram from Chapter 7:

Chap. XIX: Synchronization and Checkpoints

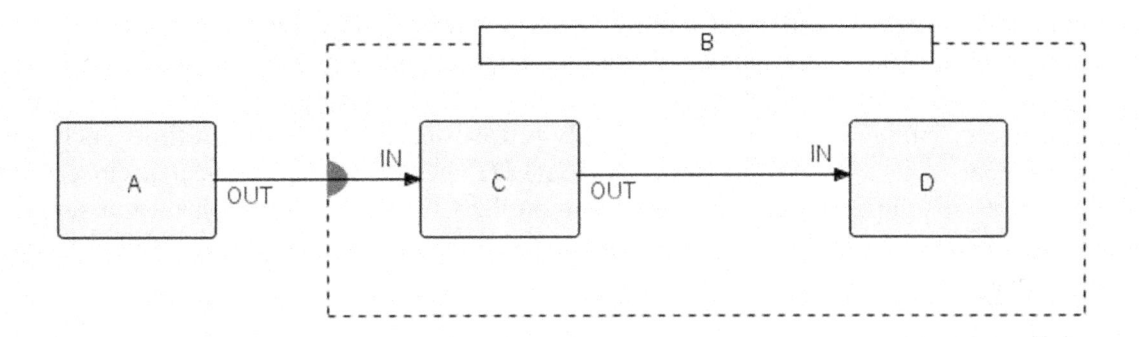

Figure 19.2

This shows a substream-sensitive composite B, containing two processes C and D. You will recall that, provided the data coming from A is grouped into substreams using bracket IPs, the inside of B will behave like a little batch job, starting up and closing down for every incoming substream. The composite deactivates each time its inside processes close down, and it restarts them when the next IP arrives from outside. During the times when C and D have closed down, there will be no IPs in flight, and C and D will not even have any internal storage allocated. The composite itself will be inactive. This then provides a rather neat mechanism for "getting everyone out of the water", because, remember, processes cannot be closed down until they themselves decide to allow it.

There is another idea which is suggested by the swimming-pool analogy: a swimmer who will not get out of the water will hold up the whole process! Remember the term "periodicity", referring to whether a component is a "looper" or a "non-looper" – non-loopers are quiesced between every invocation, so the more often a component gives up control, the more flexible it will be from the point of view of fitting into the checkpoint process. So, within the subnet, components that deactivate frequently are preferable to long-running ones.

We have provided a mechanism to clear the swimmers out of the pool, but we also need a way to ensure that they *stay* out until the chlorine has had time to dissolve!

At this point I should make a confession: this chapter in the original edition of my book talked about concepts that were never tested in real life. It now seems that there were logical inconsistencies in what I wrote then – my deepest apologies to anyone whom I may have confused. That will teach me to violate my own rules about only writing about things I have tried out!

With that off my chest, I now invite the reader to consider Figure 19.3.

In JavaFBP and C#FBP, subnets have an "automatic" port called *SUBEND. When this is

Chap. XIX: Synchronization and Checkpoints

connected up, the subnet will send a null packet to the *SUBEND port as soon as all the components within B have terminated. So in this diagram, we connect the subnet's *SUBEND port to a component called *SSGATE*, to let the subnet know it can accept another substream. *SSGATE* is a very simple component, and simply releases one substream at a time, each time it receives a signal at its CONTROL port. All *SSGATE* needs to do is inject a close bracket periodically into its output stream, do a `receive` on the CONTROL port (which will suspend it until the signal comes from the *SUBEND port), and then emit a open bracket, followed by the next set of data IPs.

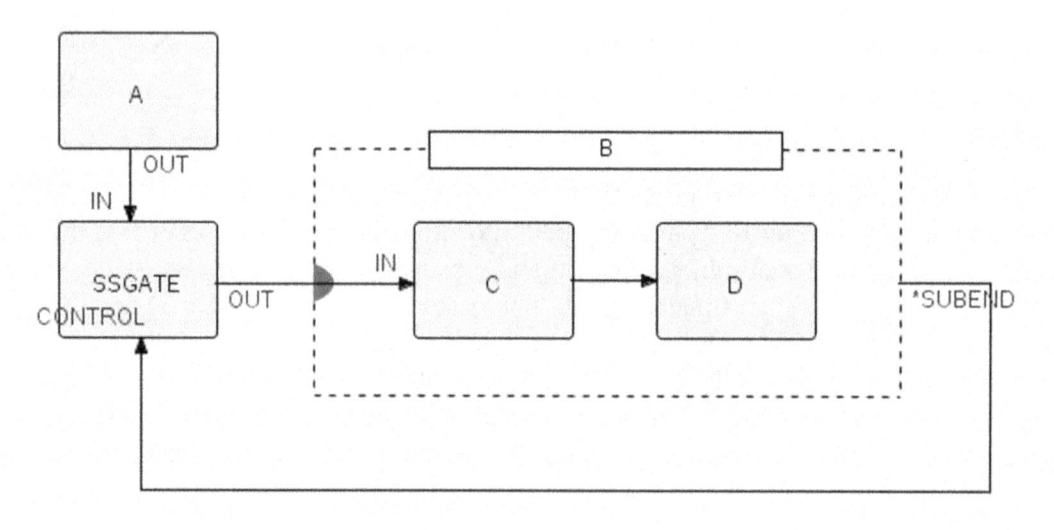

Figure 19.3

This seems pretty straightforward, but readers of the first edition raised the reasonable objection that it seems a bit strange to have to control this whole process from outside. So another approach would be to insert a special-purpose component upstream of C which simply terminates after *n* IPs have been processed, or after *x* minutes have elapsed, where *n* and *x* are specified by IIPs. You will remember that the symbol we have shown as a solid semicircle is really an independent process which recognizes open and close brackets, so B really contains 3 processes. So, instead, we can make this explicit, and reconnect the processes slightly, as shown in Figure 19.4. The main difference is that the *SUBEND signal is brought to an input port of the subnet itself, rather than to a separate process – except that a process's output port cannot be connected back to an input port, so we have to go via a *PASSTHRU* component (self-explanatory).

In Figure 19.4, component *SEP* uses some criterion to terminate every so often, effectively

Chap. XIX: Synchronization and Checkpoints

splitting its input stream into segments. The first thing the subnet does is do a receive from its input port called *CONTROL: as this is a loop structure, we will need a *KICKER* process to get the subnet started in the first place, as described in Chapter 14 (Loop-Type networks – page 135).

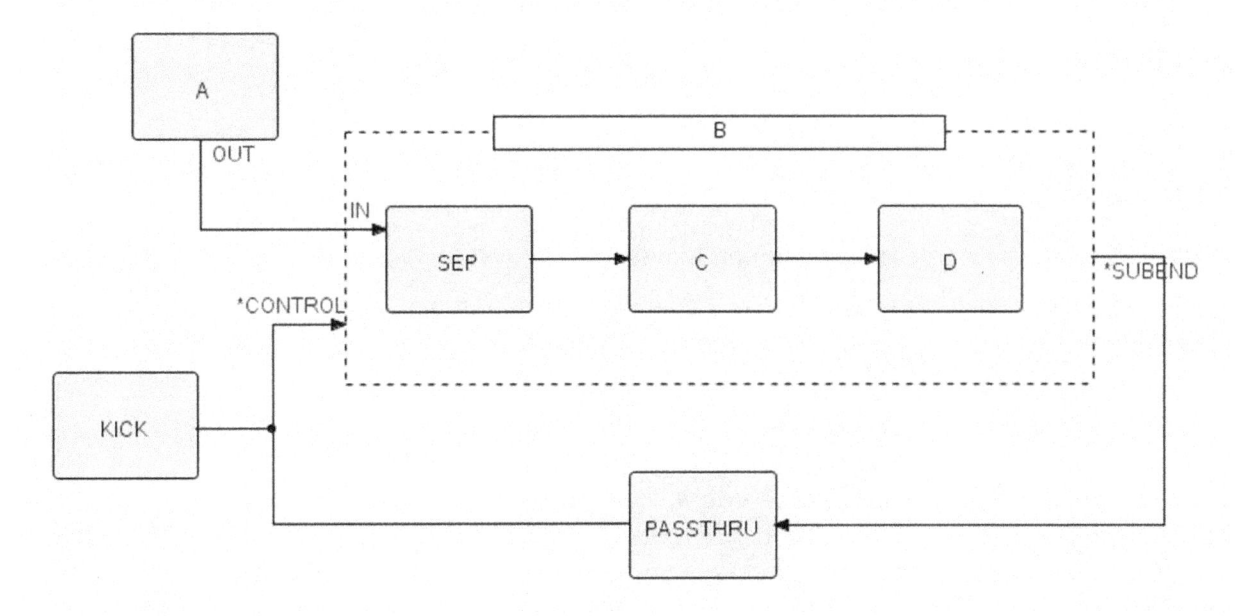

Figure 19.4

One last clarification required with this solution is that there is still an External Input Port process (*SUBIN*) buried in the diagram – right where the solid line crosses the dashed line! You don't want this process to be left holding an IP when *SEP* closes down, so *SUBIN* must check whether its downstream connection is closed before doing a `receive` from its upstream connection. The Java implementations of *SUBIN* (substream-sensitive and non-substream-sensitive) have been modified to do this.

Whichever of the two above solutions we use, there are two main criteria for when to take checkpoints: amount of I/O and time. In general, we will want to take checkpoints more frequently if there has been more update activity. Conversely, if the activity is low, we want to take checkpoints occasionally anyway to make sure that other programs are not hung for too long waiting for records to be unlocked. How can we drive checkpoints on both these criteria? Well, a close approximation to the amount of I/O is to count transactions, and do a checkpoint after every n transactions, where n is specifiable in an IIP. In addition, we want to trigger a checkpoint if t seconds or minutes have elapsed without a checkpoint.

To do the transaction counting, we might have some kind of Count process which counts off every n IPs, where n is specified in an IIP. However, there may be long gaps between the arrival

Chap. XIX: Synchronization and Checkpoints

of IPs, so suppose that, during the "quiet" times, we decide that we also want to recognize when *t* seconds or minutes have elapsed without a checkpoint. Let's take a Clock process, referred to at the beginning of the chapter, which generates an IP on every clock tick (again obtaining the interval from an IIP), and merge its output with the incoming data stream.

So, if the data stream looked like

```
a b c d e f g h i j k l m n o p q r s ...
```

Figure 19.5

The merged stream might look something like this:

```
a b c t0 d e f g h i j t1 t2 k l t3 m t4 n o p q r t5 s ...
```

```
where tn represents a clock tick
```

Figure 19.6

Now, the present FBP implementations do not *guarantee* that these clock ticks will ever get into this data stream unless there are simply no data IPs coming in. This is because we have always concentrated on making sure *that* all data is processed, but not *when*. And in fact this is probably adequate in this case, since we only care about the clock ticks when the frequency of incoming data IPs is low. To absolutely guarantee that the data IPs are inserted "in the right place", we would need to implement some kind of priority scheduling – this requirement seems to come up from time to time in different areas, and will probably have to be added to FBP schedulers eventually (see e.g. Mike Beckerle's discussion of Parallelism in Chapter 21 – page 225).

Clearly when there are fewer data IPs between a pair of clock ticks, e.g. between *t1* and *t2*, there is less activity; when there are more IPs, there is more activity. So a simple algorithm might be to drive a checkpoint on every incoming clock tick, and also after *n* IPs following the last clock tick IP. We might want to fancy this up a bit, by preventing checkpoints if a previous one occurred within some minimum interval, but the simple algorithm should do fine for most purposes. A lot of applications use a time interval only, especially in batch applications, where the problem is to reduce the cost of reruns, rather than releasing locked records.

We have talked about *when* to take checkpoints – we now need to discuss *what* should be saved when we take a checkpoint. In the example shown in Figure 19.3, process *A* is still active at checkpoint time – since it has no input connection, it won't terminate until it has generated all its output IPs. None of the helper components that we have mentioned (like the Clock process) have any internal state information which needs to be saved in case a crash occurs. So in our diagrams above, *A* is the only one which needs to be restartable, and there must be a way to make sure that it only generates IPs which have not been processed completely. If *A* saves state data on a

Chap. XIX: Synchronization and Checkpoints

database or file, the checkpoint mechanism of the OLTP environment itself has to ensure that the state data gets saved when it should, and rolled back when it should. The exception to this is that data IPs which caused errors should not get reexecuted, so you should store information about them in a non-checkpointable store.

Apart from such oddball cases, we can generalize across the different environments and say that *A* and processes like it should save their state data on a checkpointable backing store, be able to be restarted using it, and that this whole process should be as automatic as possible. Let's say that the state data has some recognizable empty state – then the state information on the backing store should start off in that empty state, it should be updated for each incoming IP or substream, and the program as a whole should reset the state data to empty when it finishes. This way, when the application is (re)started, *A* can determine if a restart is required and, if so, at what point.

I have put down here some ideas for an architecture and some reusable components which address, and hopefully simplify, this fairly complex area. This is just a sketch, and even though it may seem a bit complicated, many of the components can be off the shelf, so they won't have to programmed from scratch for every application. At this point, I'm sure you can all come up with better solutions which draw on your own expertise – the point being to design generalized utility components which encapsulate expertise, but which still are easy for other, less expert programmers to use. When you consider the potential cost of reruns to your shop, clearly some standard, easy to use, checkpointing approaches and components would be well worth the effort that goes into developing them. I have tried to show how FBP's powerful modularization capabilities could make that job significantly easier.

For another view on checkpointing, I would like to mention a recent paper (2009) by Sebastian Ertel at IBM, Mike Beckerle, and Christof Fetzer at the Technical University in Dresden, Germany, with the title, "ETL data streaming with EAI-style transactional data delivery guarantees, and transparent checkpoint/restart capability" – *http://ohua.sourceforge.net/ohua-paper.pdf* . ETL stands for "Extract, Transform and Load", and will be described in more detail in Chapter 27 (page 281). EAI stands for "Enterprise Application Integration". Ohua is an open source FBP-like methodology plus supporting software, and can be found at *http://ohua.sourceforge.net/*. Ohua grew out of Sebastian Ertel's thesis project, and has come up with some interesting improvements over Mike's earlier "Orchestrate" software – in particular, a concept that might be called "two-layer" components, which allows a number of powerful functions to be added between the component level (which stays simple) and the scheduler.

In connection with checkpointing, the authors of Ohua were concerned to avoid having to quiesce components before taking checkpoints, so their approach was to introduce a type of metadata (we could call it a special IP) called a "Checkpoint Marker", which tells a process (they use the term "operator", as do many of today's FBP practitioners) to start the checkpointing logic. In their approach, it is the operators that are responsible for storing their checkpoint data, so, when an operator has received a Checkpoint Marker among all its input ports, it stores its state

Chap. XIX: Synchronization and Checkpoints

data. It then propagates the Checkpoint Marker to its output connections. They felt that, in the context of ETL applications, which deal in huge amounts of data, it was not reasonable to have to quiesce sections of the network, and then have to start them up again after taking the checkpoint. So the FBP world can now add this technology to its bag of tricks!

In their paper they say, "Note that we assume that the write operation to save the state of an operator checkpoint uses a *transaction* [my italics] so that it is possible to positively determine if any operator has completed writing of a specific checkpoint or not." This idea of a "transaction" describes a piece of logic which is either complete or not started – if it crashes before completion, it is necessary to undo any intermediate results. The state data can itself be "rolled back", as we described above. Mike Beckerle tells me that the biggest contribution of Ohua is that it achieves the following things simultaneously:

1) writing data transforming components is still simple

2) data is delivered from sources, through transformations, to destinations transactionally, not in the end-to-end atomic sense, but in the sense that even in the presence of checkpoints, failures, and restarts, data is input and output once-and-only-once. The behaviour of a flow that is interrupted by failures and restarts, and the behaviour of a flow that runs without such interruptions is identical in terms of what data is transacted out of sources, and transacted into destination systems.

3) it retains other FBP benefits (available parallelism, asynchrony, efficiency, etc.)

As we move to distributed systems, it becomes more and more unwieldy as we try to coordinate events over more and more systems. If all of the database I/O in an application is being managed by a single process, or perhaps on a single computer, then you can visualize being able to issue some kind of "rollback" that will undo *all* database changes since the last checkpoint. However, imagine that you want to transfer funds between two different computers – obviously you have to withdraw funds from an account on one node and deposit them into an account on the other one. Either of these operations can go wrong, and the communication between the computers can fail, so you need some hand-shaking to either delay both operations until you know they are both complete, or you have to be prepared to undo an earlier operation if a later one goes awry. The latter approach seems more real-world, even if less general: you do the withdrawal first; if that works, you send an IP representing a sum of money to the other node, specifying both source and destination accounts. If the receiving end for some reason cannot accept the transfer, it gets sent back to be redeposited. You might call this the "optimistic" strategy, while only committing when you know both ends are OK is the "pessimistic" strategy. There is a growing body of work on "optimistic" checkpointing: some of the earliest work was done by Rob Strom's group at IBM, in connection with the NIL project, which will be described in Chapter 26 (page 268).

Chap. XX: General Framework for Interactive Applications

An increasing number of computer applications are interactive – in fact, today almost every application that the average computer user runs into is interactive. When this book was first written, such applications were rarer, and generally harder to write. Today everyone can knock off a simple interactive application, using standard tools.

The basic difference (and in fact the only difference) between batch and interactive applications is that the latter have to communicate with an end-user, with the result that some (but not necessarily all) application processes must be geared to the pace of the end-user. An end-user will enter commands and data on a screen, select among options, etc., and results will be displayed on the screen. Usually these events alternate, but some displays occur unexpectedly, and the user must also be able to interrupt processes or switch to other activities.

I make this point because historically there was a split between the systems supporting "batch" applications and those supporting interactive applications – however in FBP there is no real basis for such a distinction, and in fact we were able to share code between the two environments very productively, as I will describe later in this chapter.

Hardware and software environments vary: in the old days, users used what were called "dumb" terminals, where the computer did almost all of the formatting; nowadays, users have powerful computers on their desks (or in their laps), and these computers are able to do a great deal more of the work.

Let us consider the path from user back to user as a large network, which can be cleaved as described in Chapter 15 (page 140), anywhere that makes sense from a programming logic and performance point of view.

Let us start by making a distinction between one-user systems and multi-user systems. In the

Chap. XX: General Framework for Interactive Applications

case of mainframes you could have multiple one-user systems coexisting on a single computer by using what was called "time-sharing". IBM's Time Sharing Option (TSO) and CP/CMS were both examples of this approach – TSO supported multiple users under MVS, while CP was "hypervisor", supporting multiple virtual systems; CMS was a simple one-user operating system running on one such virtual system. TSO applications typically used a screen management tool called ISPF (Interactive System Productivity Facility), while CMS applications typically used less powerful screen management tools. In comparison, IMS and CICS were examples of multiple users sharing one application, though they used rather different approaches, and each had their own ways of describing screen formatting, and transmitting data to, and receiving data from, the user's screen. Now, with today's powerful PCs, the user's machine takes care of much of the display formatting, and the servers typically service multiple users – again using a variety of different approaches.

In this chapter I am going to build on the generic loop structure to create a general framework for interactive applications, and try to build on that logically. We will start off with a *very* high-level diagram, shown in Figure 20.1.

In this network, we show a single process, the Screen Manager, which controls the user's screen, and an IP (or group of IPs), conceptually similar to the token in a token-ring type of LAN, travels around the network triggering processes to execute. I am assuming that monitoring key-strokes has already been taken care of – we will only send out an IP (or group of IPs) when there is something significant for the rest of the network to work on. Bracket IPs provide a convenient way of grouping IPs for this kind of function – typically, we use the first IP of each substream for such information as screen name, name of key struck, position of cursor, etc., and the remaining IPs, if any, for the data fields. When this substream arrives back at the Screen Manager process, it triggers the display of data on the screen, waits at that process until the user responds, then proceeds to the next process in the loop. The data IPs, if any, will hold the data to be displayed on the screen, and will receive any data that the user enters on the screen.

This diagram, of course, shows the simplest possible interaction with the user – where the user requests alternate exactly with system responses – and this is the structure which is embedded in most interactive software systems. If you are going to relax that constraint, then you have to figure out a way of allowing asynchronous responses to come back to the user when he or she is working on something else, without destroying all that useful work, or breaking the train of thought... You also have to leave the keyboard unlocked for input, which opens up the possibility of the user getting frustrated and starting many copies of some application! I seem to recall that IBM's IMS system suffered from that problem – and, of course, the more frustrated the users became, the more times they hit the ENTER key, the more transactions got started, and the more backed-up the system became!

Chap. XX: General Framework for Interactive Applications

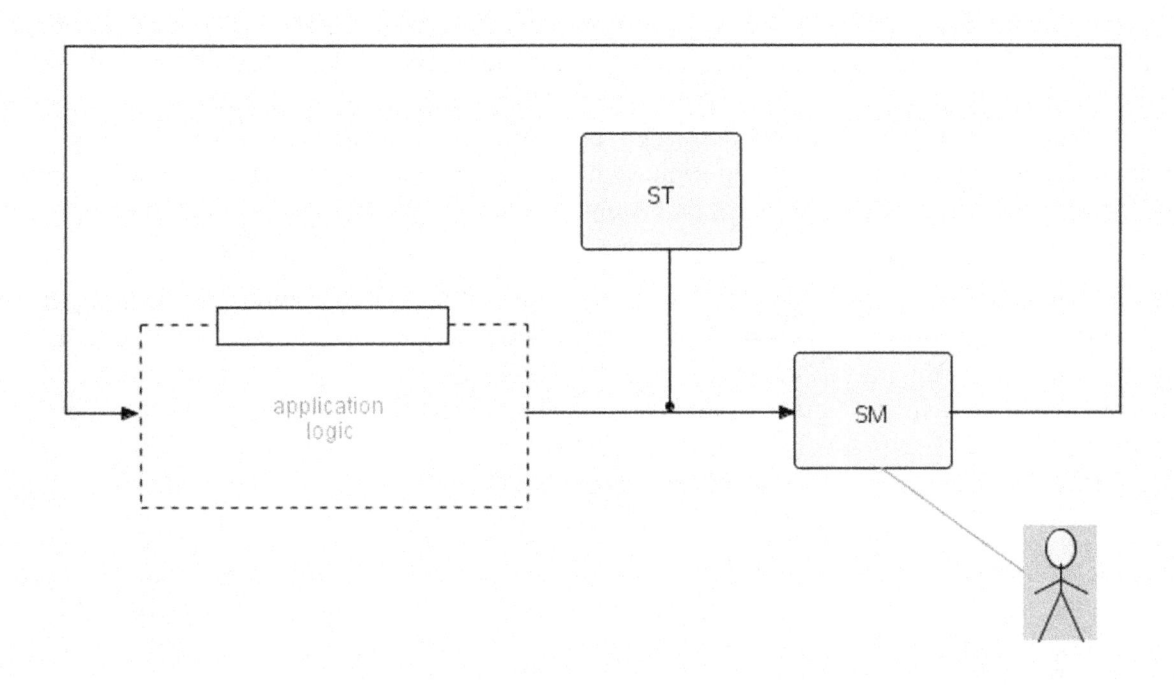

Figure 20.1

```
where SM   is a Screen Manager
      ST   starts the network as a whole
```

However, FBP doesn't care about what is going on with the user's screen, so we should be able to assume that *SM* will display a screen any time data arrives at its input port – obviously the application logic doesn't have to wait for an incoming IP substream to trigger more logic – everything in FBP is asynchronous, right? We'll also assume that by that time we will have solved the problems described in the previous paragraph.

In the first section of this chapter, though, we won't need this added flexibility. In fact, the general design I will describe next was used for a number of CP/CMS applications, and was later extended to other environments. It used a single generalized Screen Manager component, called ISM1 (ISPF Screen Manager 1), which used ISPF both to write to and read from a terminal. Although ISM1 was synchronous, because the underlying ISPF software was also synchronous, I think it's worth starting with this one, because it helped us discover some interesting things about interactive applications, and the kinds of components they need, and can lead to.

For simplicity let's assume that every application starts by putting up a "What do you want to do?" type screen. So *ST* (which is a self-starting process) causes *SM* to output a menu screen. *SM* has a place where the user's answer can be stored, so we can assume that *ST* sends out a

Chap. XX: General Framework for Interactive Applications

substream consisting of at least three IPs: open bracket, "request" IP, zero or more data IPs and close bracket. The brackets are needed so we can have a variable number of data IPs in the substream. The request IP will have, among other data, the name of the screen to be displayed. This substream then arrives at ISM1, which puts up a menu; the user enters a choice; the substream goes through the processing logic (which may change the contents of the IPs, or even add or remove IPs from the substream); and eventually we get back to ISM1 which puts up a new screen.

Now let's look a bit more closely at ISM1. This component accepted an input substream, put any variable data into position on the screen using the data descriptors associated with the data, and waited for action on the part of the user. When that occurred, the modified data was placed back into the right places in the data IPs, and the substream was then sent on to the next process downstream. ISPF identifies fields on the screen by name, and ISM1 used the field names from the descriptor to determine where to put each variable field.

In addition to this substream, referred to as the "fixed substream", ISM1 also accepted an additional, optional substream, called the "repeating substream". The mental image supported was that the screen has a fixed part, normally describing one or a small number of individual entities, and an optional list. Thus we could show a person's family on the screen: his or her personal information, the spouse's information (a separate IP), these providing fairly complete information, and zero or more children, showing just name, age and gender, say. If the user wanted more information on a child, he or she could select the child, and get a full screen devoted to that child, which might have further lists, e.g. education. One of the really neat things about being able to use IPs in this way is that both the list of children and the full screen describing a single child can be driven by the same IP – we just decide how much information we are going to show from that IP. By the way, since each screen was built using two substreams, we bracketed them together so that ISM1 would think of them as a unit – so ISM1 was in fact using a substream of substreams.

We used a run-time table describing which fields from each IP went where in the repeating section. This had some interesting capabilities – ISM1 allowed you to specify more than 1 line per repeating IP, and the developer could also specify whether a "select" column (used in ISPF to select one or more items from a list) was required or not.

ISM1 also used the dynamic attributes which we talked about in Chapter 11 (page 110) to keep track of which fields had been modified, and which were null. As I mentioned in that chapter, ISM1 also provided a special display for fields which had been "tagged" with error codes, and would let the user step through these errors using a reserved function key. ISM1 actually would not allow the user to go on to the next screen until all these "tags" had been removed one way or another! There has been lots of debate about whether this is a good idea or whether systems should be more forgiving! However, the important thing to remember is I am talking about the design of a single component – this is independent of the basic architecture of FBP.

Chap. XX: General Framework for Interactive Applications

So far, ISM1's abilities might seem about what you would need if you were "black boxing" a display function. However, it also provided the capability of converting numeric fields between the display format and the computational format, which dramatically simplified the logic in the other components of the application: we have discussed this in Chapter 11 under the title of "representations". As I said in that chapter, representations mainly come into play when you need to present data to humans, or port it across systems.

In a prototype of an interactive application using straight ISPF (where the ISPF functions were called directly from PL/I) I found the language forced us to have *three* PL/I fields for every numeric field on the screen:

- the field in a computational format
- numerals in fixed-layout character form (e.g. '000001234') for display
- a free-form character field for input in case the user wanted to modify the field

When we converted this prototype to use ISM1, the number of fields we had to declare in the HLL portion of the application dropped by 2/3! We also discovered a number of additional bonuses:

- you could send an IP with an attached descriptor to ISM1 and it would automatically be displayed in the desired format
- the user could enter the data in free-form, but you could be sure that it wouldn't get into the system unless it was a valid representation
- you could implement a standard input convention for your whole shop
- you could send an IP to ISM1 for interactive handling, or you could send it to a file writer, and you didn't need to make any changes to your data IPs. The effect of this was enormously improved testing and regression testing, because you could test a lot of your logic in batch mode.

On one project in IBM Canada, this last technique was used very effectively by a colleague, Philip Ewing. Later in this chapter I will share with you what he has written about that project.

We have now sketched out a screen management component ISM1, which accepts one or two substreams as input, and outputs them again after the user has responded. Now let's go back to Figure 20.1. We need to fill in the logic between SM and the application logic. To do this, the first step is to interpret the user's action. Even restricting ourselves for simplicity to "dumb" terminals, the user may decide to:

- modify any data field, including Select fields of a list as a special case

Chap. XX: General Framework for Interactive Applications

- enter a command in the command area
- hit a function key
- hit Attention (or Escape)
- position the screen cursor to a particular field

All these actions have to be encoded so that downstream processes can decide what is the appropriate response.

In the main-frame world, in particular in the ISPF and IMS/DC environments, function keys are usually treated as commands, so one of the standard outputs of our Screen Manager was a "command". These could be the very frequent ones like UP, DOWN, END and HELP, or more application-specific ones. It turns out that these commands are convenient bases for the decision about what to do next. Always remember that each of the components described here can be used independently of any other. Now, in Chapter 7 (page 71) we described DFDM's dynamic subnets – subnets which were linked as independently linked components and were loaded in dynamically and given control by a special component called the Subnet Manager. These provide a convenient way of subdividing and managing our application. The Subnet Manager is driven by IPs containing dynamic subnet names, so we need a component which will take the output of the Screen Manager and generate the subnet names for the Subnet Manager. Let's call this the User Response Analyzer (URA).

The URA component's job is to look up in a table patterns consisting of screen + action, screen only or action only, and decide what to do about them. As we said, since it sits upstream of the Subnet Manager, its main job is to select subnet names to be sent to the Subnet Manager, but you might decide to have it bypass the Subnet Manager, and send its input IPs directly to the Screen Manager. In this case, you could have it decide screen names. You could also have it do both.

You will notice that we haven't said where this table should be held: it could be compiled as a independently linked component, stored as a flat file, or held in a database. Perhaps a file would be appropriate during development, and a component in production. You will perhaps notice our predilection for tables – this is one of the most important ways of achieving portable code (remember Bucky Pope's "class codes", alluded to in an earlier chapter – Chapter 17, page 172).

The URA table might therefore look something like this:

Chap. XX: General Framework for Interactive Applications

Old Screen	User Action	Subnet	New Screen
A	CHOICE1	SUBNET1	B
B	END		A
A	HELP		HELP_FOR_A
HELP_FOR_A	END		A

Figure 20.2

Obviously this table is very easy to modify – in fact, if you add a comment capability, it really becomes self-explanatory.

The last component I am going to describe is the List Manager, which although fairly general, was one of our less successful ideas, and is included mainly because it illustrates some things to avoid in writing componentry (I feel it makes sense to include some failures in this book – as well as successes)! Its fundamental metaphor was sets of lists which persisted in storage, organized by "levels" – thus employees might be on one level, their children, departments worked in and courses taken might be three different lists at the next level. It could accept commands to do various things with these lists and levels, such as "create a new level", "insert a list at the current level", "jump to the next lower level", "pop up one level", "output a list (non-destructively)", "delete a level", and so on. Although (because?) this component was very powerful, in actual use it turned out to be very error-prone. Its design was a natural programmer's reaction to a particular set of requirements, but in hindsight it violated a number of the principles described in the foregoing. Its structure seemed to match our perception of what was going on in the prototypical interactive application – i.e. the user would display an employee, then ask to go down one level to find his or her children, pop back to the previous level, and so on. Because it was a single long-running process, we would just be able to manage these lists by working with IP pointers – we didn't have to pay the overhead of chaining or unchaining IPs. Also, it provided a focal point, in case we needed to store really big lists, where lists could overflow to disk. We also expected that, when we implemented this design on IMS, it would be very easy to dump all our lists to disk at the end of a transaction, and retrieve them when they were needed again.

In hindsight, the problems we ran into with the List Manager were probably to be expected, but at the time they came as somewhat of a surprise! I believe we were still thinking of interactive applications as sequential, so the command-driven single store made sense. However, it was so convenient to stash things away in the List Manager's storage that we had more and more processes sticking stuff in there and taking it out. The more complex our networks became, the harder it became to control the exact sequence in which the commands arrived at the List Manager. What we had done, of course, was to implement a somewhat more complex array of pigeon-holes, and the non-destructive read-out which seemed so attractive at first caused the same problems FBP was trying to avoid! Strange sequencing problems started to show up – lists would get attached to the wrong level, lists would show up on two different levels, and so on. In

Chap. XX: General Framework for Interactive Applications

turn, the sequence of the command IPs had to be controlled more tightly, introducing still more complexity. In hindsight, I believe we would have been better off using tree structures flowing between processes, rather than complex data structures within a process. Alternatively, a List Manager should only be fed by a single process, and this is the way I have shown it in the next diagram. Lastly, I believe that the underlying metaphor may not have been quite correct. For instance, suppose the user is stepping through an employee's employment history and decides to start looking at her courses. Should this be made another level? Or are all these lists at the same level? A better metaphor might have been to be able to pop up new windows as new lists are requested. It's also useful to be able to open multiple windows on the same list (but you have to be careful about updates!).

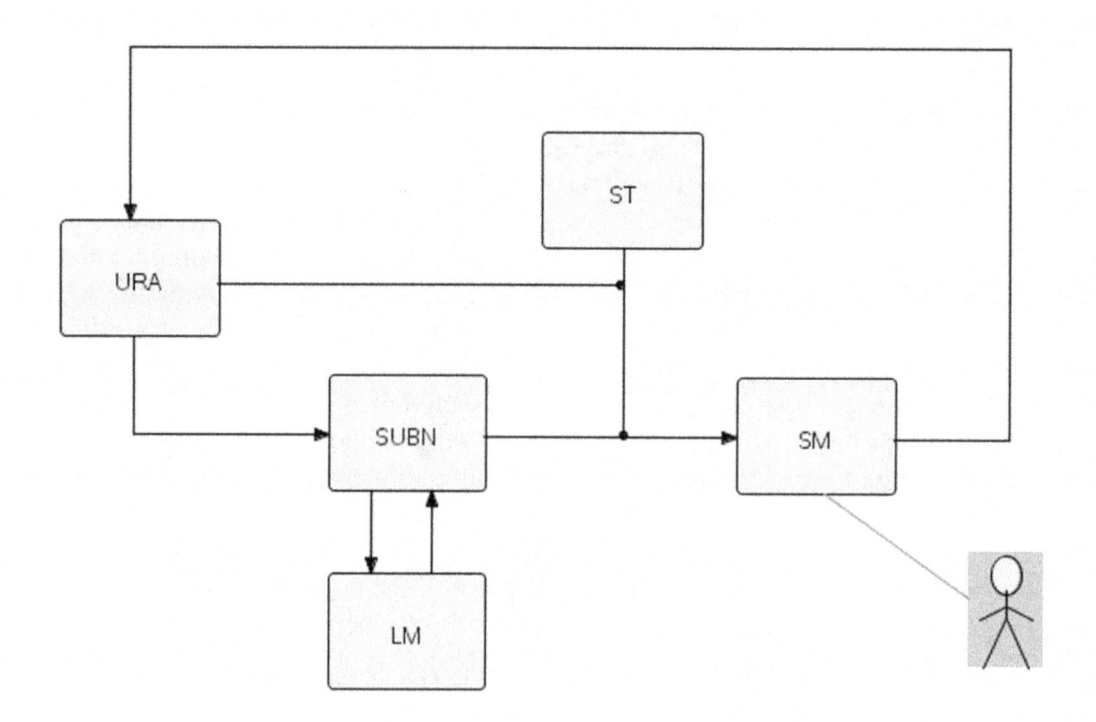

Figure 20.3

where SM is a Screen Manager
      ST starts the network as a whole
      URA is the User Response Analyzer
      SUBN is the Subnet Manager
      LM is the List Manager

Chap. XX: General Framework for Interactive Applications

We can now show the final picture, shown in Figure 20.3. Remember that this is only a skeleton – you can add additional processes to the diagram, and extend it in other ways also. And remember also that the List Manager, although shown in the diagram, is not the only way to manage storage of data.

What we have described here is the structure we called the DOEM, pronounced "dome", (DFDM On-line Environment Manager), still fondly remembered by some of the people who worked on it! It was at the same time a skeleton structure, a set of components and an approach to designing interactive applications. This is reuse at a higher level than the level we have been mostly talking about up until now, and from that point of view perhaps a precursor of the way interactive systems will be built in the future.

While the DOEM was a very powerful set of concepts, some of its components were more satisfactory than others in terms of their encapsulation of useful function and the simplicity of the underlying mental image. In some ways, the DOEM fell into the pitfall I have warned about elsewhere in the book – we tried to make it very general, based on our ideas of what a DOEM should provide, without frequent consultations with real users. Or we may have been talking to the "wrong" users. We never did build it for the IMS/DC platform, although we basically knew how to go about it. As it turned out, we didn't need that implementation anyway, for the reasons I am about to relate. This story is salutary, so I am going to tell it in some detail, as a cautionary tale for those embarking on developing reusable code.

Most of the time we were working on the DOEM, we were supporting two projects – let's call them A and B. The intent was to provide team A with an IMS/DC version of the DOEM, and team B with a CMS version. This seemed reasonable because a number of the components could be shared, and, although the CMS version was certainly simpler (single Screen Manager module, etc.), we understood pretty much how to build the DOEM on IMS/DC. However, the two teams' approaches to working with us were very different. The A team tended to be demanding and critical, frequently asking for specialized modifications of components or new facilities just for their own application, while B was more willing to work with us and to stay within the facilities that were already available or in plan. Both projects had the potential to be very important products, for different reasons, and both groups felt that they were getting benefit from DFDM, but both of them required quite a bit of our time, both to provide general support and to code and test the reusable components being supplied for the two environments.

Our development team was a small one and, under the circumstances, was getting stretched very thin trying to support both projects! Finally, management decided that we could only support one of these projects, and, after much soul-searching, they picked B. We started working intensively with B to make sure that the CMS DOEM worked well with their product, and as the two started to come together, we all realized that this had been a good decision. This product sold well in its own right in the Latin American market.

Chap. XX: General Framework for Interactive Applications

The A team were told that they could continue to use DFDM, but not the DOEM, and that we could no longer afford to give them special support. We really expected them to decide to drop the use of DFDM altogether, and while this would have been disappointing, we felt that this would have been a pragmatic decision on their part. However, at this point, a very strange thing happened: faced with the possibility of losing the use of this productivity tool and having to redesign and rewrite a lot of their code, the A team turned right around and started to solve their own problems using basic DFDM! Instead of having us build complex generalized components, they found simpler ways of doing what they needed, and the result was a less complex, more maintainable system. Their product also became a success and saved the company a fair amount of money.

Strangely, an additional project using the DOEM appeared suddenly on the scene one day, rather to our surprise! It seemed that a bright young contractor had been given the job of building a small interactive system, and had built it in a matter of a few weeks, using the DOEM, without telling any of the DOEM development team! We were very conscious that our documentation was nowhere near adequate at that time, but he said he had no trouble understanding and using it! Of course, he is very bright, but how often does something like that happen using conventional programming tools?

Since fairy tales usually have morals, let me propose the following: "Sometimes it is better to redesign a squeaky wheel than just put more oil on it".

The Screen Manager, ISM1 (actually an earlier version of it) was also used all by itself, before we even thought of the DOEM, on an earlier project within IBM Canada, and this project became very successful, not least because its developer, Philip Ewing, was excited by the concept of FBP (I believe he still is!), and was discovering neat new uses for it all the time. As you may have gathered, ISM1 was a very powerful component, and all by itself considerably simplified the development of interactive applications. Its development predated the rest of the DOEM by several years, so we had used it for several small projects. Here is what Philip has written about our experience on this project (called BLSB).

> DFDM was selected for use on the BLSB project because of the significant productivity improvements that were anticipated. The development team was not disappointed. Significant savings were realized in the following ways:
>
> 1. We were able to prototype more easily, beginning with a simple screen display, and adding functions one by one until the user was satisfied. The full function prototype could be modified to add a new edit or data-base lookup in a matter of hours, without disrupting the existing code.
> 2. Testing was made simpler because we were able to unplug the online screens and feed in test SCREEN REQUEST ENTITIES [abbreviated to SREs – these correspond to the "request IPs" referred to above] from files, and save the

returned SREs into separate files based on type of error. In this way all of the application function in the online system could be tested in batch.
3. Building on the experience gained in the function testing, the legacy data was converted to the new database format by feeding in the old data in SRE format (simulating re-keying all of the previous 3 years of data through the new system). The errors were saved in separate files based on the ERROR CODE that the application put into the SRE before returning it to the screen. Each file was known to contain only one type of error. In three iterations through this process we were able to convert and load 64,000 history records with only 12 records needing to be re-keyed manually. In addition to not having to write a separate conversion program, we were also assured that all of the data that was now in the database had passed all of the rigorous editing that had been built into the new application logic.
4. A great deal of effort in the design stage was saved because we could decompose functions to very granular levels before implementing. This meant that less thought needed to be put into the way different functions might affect each other, because different functions were now completely decoupled.
5. The "off the shelf" screen display function alone saved about 700 lines of application coding to handle ISPF panel displays. We did know ISPF before starting this project, but would not have needed to, since all of the ISPF specific code was in a DFDM-supplied function.

Less than 24% of the functions needed to be coded by the project, the rest came off the shelf. Furthermore, of the ones that we did have to code, the most complex was about 100 lines of code.

Here is a comment one of its developers made to me at that time about the BLSB project: "We allowed 3 weeks for testing, but it worked the first time."

It seems appropriate to include in this chapter a brief description of a brokerage application we built several years later, using the Java implementation of FBP (JavaFBP). In this case, this was only the server side of the application – communication between the client and server was handled by IBM's WebSphere, while the server was a RS/6000 running IBM's AIX software. The server code again used the familiar loop structure, but with requests from different users travelling around the loop, similar to the situation described above in connection with IMS/DC. Of course, as each process is handling data from multiple users, care must be taken to ensure that no data slops over from one user to another – this is facilitated by making the processes non-loopers, or by making sure user data is restricted to method-local storage. Trades were sent to remote processing sites, called "back-ends", where choice of back-end sites depended not only on the type of trade, but also even on the time of day. A simplified version of the network is shown in Figure 20.4.

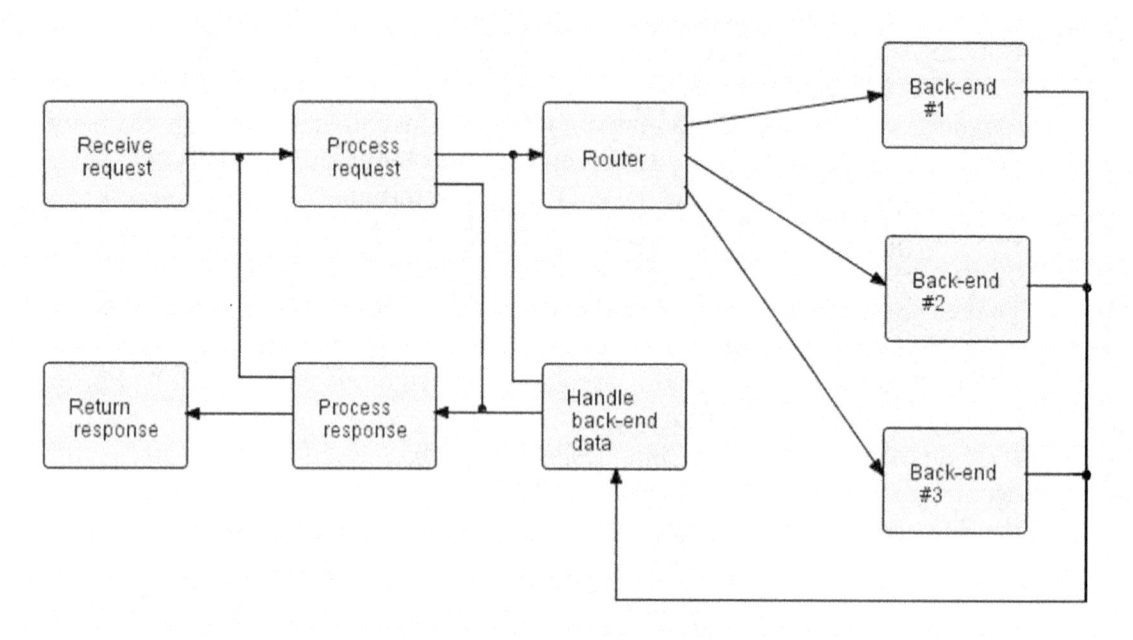

Figure 20.4

Communication with the back-end sites was via CORBA or MQSeries, both of which interface to FBP processes very simply and naturally. Figure 20.4 is only a high-level schematic and omits a number of caching processes that we used both for database access performance and also for data consistency. Obviously, Figure 20.4 only shows 3 back-ends, although in fact there were more than that.

The cross-connections represent requests that don't need to go to the back-ends, or requests that have to cycle through the network more than once before being returned to the user. Since the back-end processing is asynchronous, and may actually be batched up at the processing sites, transactions are identified by a unique ID, stored on a database, and removed from the data stream, so that they can be related to the responses coming back from the back-ends at some later time. At this point the transaction information is retrieved from the database, and the transactions reinserted into the stream going right-to-left in the bottom line.

Adding a couple of clients to Figure 20.4, we get the following (still seriously simplified) diagram shown in Figure 20.5. Communication between the computers (i.e. between the rightmost subnet and the others) could then use any of the standard inter-computer communication techniques.

Chap. XX: General Framework for Interactive Applications

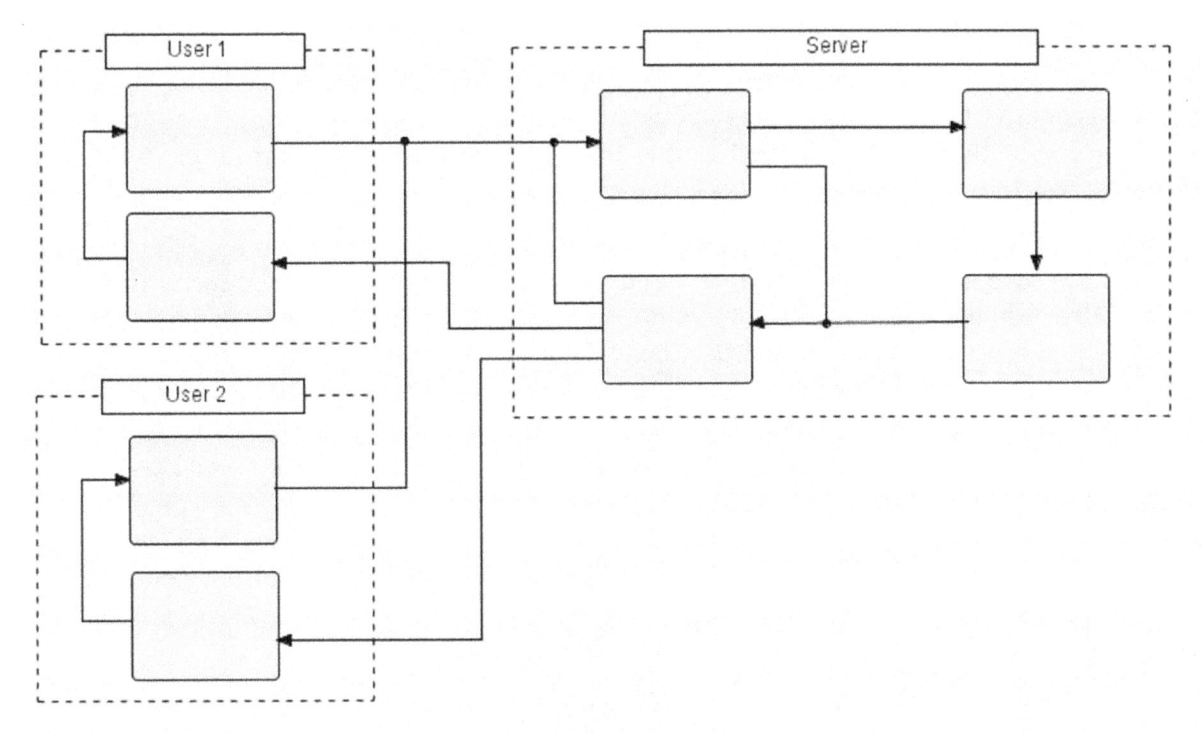

Figure 20.5

Now visualize a service request zipping round this loop (or at least the part marked "server"): the diagram as shown will work fine for a single user, but, when you have more than one, any delay at one process will delay processing for all users. We therefore used multiplexing at various points in the diagram, as described in Chapter 15 (page 140), to improve responsiveness. We also used caching processes, as I said above, for performance and data consistency. The latter issue arises, for instance, when handling share prices – although you need to keep refreshing share prices asynchronously, you don't want them to change in the middle of calculating a client's account balance.

I would also like to mention that this project used a fairly well-developed set of Java business types – they are described in on the author's web site under "Business Data Types" (*http://www.jpaulmorrison.com/busdtyps.shtml*), and can in fact be obtained from *SourceForge*, using the project name JBDTypes. This code has recently (late 2009) been picked up by Softpedia. The brokerage application described here underwent quite exhaustive testing, and we were just starting to do some performance testing when it was unfortunately terminated for non-technical reasons.

You will notice that the network shown in Figure 20.4 (or Figure 20.5) does not prejudge how many responses are passed to a user for a given request. However, current interactive technologies seem to be somewhat synchronous – i.e. they assume requests and responses

Chap. XX: General Framework for Interactive Applications

alternating rigidly for a given user. This seems to be true even for JavaScript. Ajax (shorthand for asynchronous JavaScript and XML) is one approach that promises relief from this purely synchronous approach. However, it was not clear to me how this could be interfaced to an FBP network, so I recently posted a question to the StackOverflow programming forum, as follows (*http://stackoverflow.com/questions/1308177/multiple-replies-from-server-for-one-client-request*):

> I want to send a request for data from a client to a server program, and the server (not the client) should respond with something like "Received your request – working on it". The client then does other work. Then when the server has obtained the data, it should send an asynchronous message (a popup?) saying "I've got your data; click on ... (presumably a URL) to obtain data". I have been assuming that the server could be written in Java and that client is HTML and JavaScript. I haven't been able to come up with a clean solution – help would be appreciated.

I received four answers, of which I felt the most interesting was the following from Zoidberg:

> Most of the work involves the server being asynchronous. To do this you must
>
> 1. Have an Ajax call to the server that starts a job and returns a confirmation the job has been started.
>
> 2. A page on the server that will return whether or not any jobs are complete for a user.
>
> 3. Have an Ajax widget on your client side that pings that page on the server every so often to see if any jobs have been completed. And if so make a pop up.
>
> This is the only way unless you use Flex data services.

Adobe Flex Data Services are now called Adobe LiveCycle Data Services (see *http://en.wikipedia.org/w/index.php?title=Adobe_Flex&oldid=341291076*) and provide:

- Remoting, which allows Flex client applications to invoke methods on Java server objects directly. Similar to Java remote method invocation (RMI), remoting handles data marshalling automatically and uses a binary data transfer format.

- Messaging, which provides the "publish" end of the "publish/subscribe" design pattern. The Flash client can publish events to a topic defined on the server, subscribe to events broadcast from the message service. One of the common use cases for this is real-time

Chap. XX: General Framework for Interactive Applications

streaming of data, such as financial data or system status information.

- Data management services, which provides a programming model for automatically managing data sets that have been downloaded to the Flex client. Once data is loaded from the server, changes are automatically tracked and can be synchronized with the server at the request of the application. Clients are also notified if changes to the data set are made on the server.

- PDF document generation, providing APIs for generating PDF documents by merging client data or graphics with templates stored on the server.

Maybe we should add the "ping" that Zoidberg describes to Figure 20.5...

The Wikipedia article on Comet seems relevant here: *http://en.wikipedia.org/w/index.php?title=Comet_%28programming%29&oldid=356340292*.

I have recently been informed that this problem has been addressed by HTML5, specifically *Websocket*.

I'd like to close this chapter by addressing an argument which you sometimes hear – namely that batch is dead, and that everything can now be done on-line and therefore must be done synchronously. As you have been reading the foregoing pages, you may have been wondering what the relevance of data streams and components like Split and Collate is to today's interactive applications. For a while I also believed that FBP was less relevant to interactive systems than to batch, but as we built more and more on-line systems, we found that the benefits of reusability and configurability are just as relevant to on-line as they are to batch, if not more so. In fact, by removing many of the old distinctions between on-line and batch, not only do programmers move more easily between these different environments, but we have found that code can be shared by batch and on-line programs, allowing large parts of the logic to be tested in whatever mode the developer finds most convenient. We have even seen cases where data was validated in batch using the same edit routines which would eventually handle it in the on-line environment.

Once you remove the rigid distinction between batch and on-line, you find that batch is just a way of trading off the cost of certain overheads, just as it is in a factory, and therefore it makes a lot of sense to have systems which combine both batch and on-line. Batch actually becomes necessary in really big applications, and some of today's biggest ones, such as data mining, are almost entirely batch. Batching can be defined as a way of reducing per-item costs by factoring out common costs to the beginning and/or end of the batch. If a batch is a substream, FBP allows you to have substreams that range from one IP to a whole file! As we have said before, FBP provides a consistent paradigm that applies equally well to a number of different environments – what is more, in many cases it allows the environment-dependent parts of an application to be factored out, so what is left is truly universal.

Chap. XXI: Performance Considerations

I cannot stress too strongly that FBP is intended for building *real* systems, and indeed the various dialects I have been describing in this book have been successfully used for this purpose many times. To achieve this, we *have* to keep performance in mind – not only must a system do what it is supposed to do, but it must do it in a "reasonable" amount of time. While admitting that this is a subjective measure, I submit that, at a given point in time, we generally have an image in our heads of what constitutes a reasonable amount of time for a particular function. While there will almost certainly be disagreements, say between users and developers, we see the use of SLAs (Service Level Agreements) becoming more and more widespread, which force the parties involved to reach some sort of compromise between what one wants and the other will commit to. Response time is another area which is highly subjective, but studies have shown that there are observable differences in behaviour as response time changes, which match the users' subjective impressions. Once people get used to subsecond response time, anything worse is highly frustrating. If it gets really bad, their whole style of interacting with the machine is forced to change.

Now a system which has to deliver function to real life users has to be reliable, and also has to perform. A system may provide wonderful function, but if you cannot produce adequately performing systems, it will only be of academic interest. Suppose you decide that you are going to interpret English descriptions of function using a natural language parser – it may be a great research project, but, *given present-day (2010) technology*, you probably can't run a bank on it! Can you "run a bank" on an FBP implementation? Yes, as of 2010, we've been using it for a large chunk of the batch processing of a bank's bread and butter transactions for almost 40 years! In fact, we were doing it on a 2 MIPS (2 million instructions per second) machine 40 years ago – which is probably less than what your cell-phone is running at today!

Chap. XXI: Performance Considerations

Now, not only must the infrastructure be fairly fast, but it must be *tunable*. Key to this, I believe, is being able to form a mental model of what is going on, and where a performance or logic problem may be occurring. If a developer or debugger cannot do this, the reaction may be to want to throw the baby out with the bathwater. Adequate performance is important even when a new system is in the evaluation stage. At this point, overall impressions can be very important. The system has to have knobs and levers that let the developers tune the system, and the system has to behave in a linear manner. Linearity means that systems must "scale up". As you add function, not only should you not get sudden breaks in continuity – crashes, unexpected results – but ideally the curve should not even be exponential. In conventional programming environments typically complexity, and therefore development time, goes up exponentially as program size. Humans tend to have difficulty grasping the implications of exponential curves.

While it is possible that software could automatically balance two variables, I believe performance is a multiple variable problem. In any given application, a programmer has to juggle resources, algorithms and whole design approaches. Given this complexity, the software should be made as transparent as possible. In FBP, although there are many possible solutions to a problem, the developer can select a solution and then see the results, and can in fact iterate quickly through a large number of possible solutions.

In my experience, the single most important factor affecting performance is the design. In general, shaving a few microseconds off a subroutine will not make much difference, unless it is being performed billions of times. But a different approach to a design can often save seconds, minutes or even hours. Stories of massive speedups due to the advantages of FBP-style software composition, and the different ways of looking at applications it provides, are commonplace among FBP adherents. Consider this story from Mike Beckerle:

> In 1998 we recoded a complex data-intensive application that had been written in C with embedded SQL for a direct-mail marketing company. We used our FBP system (Torrent Systems' Orchestrate – an FBP engine now found inside the IBM InfoSphere DataStage product). The system this was running on had exactly 1 CPU with 1 core, and was talking over a network to the RDBMS which was an Oracle instance.
>
> The C program with embedded SQL ran in 23 hours. The recoded FBP ran in 27 minutes on the exact same computer.
>
> What the FBP approach did is change the design of the algorithm entirely. The original was a single-threaded and very I/O-bound program. The FBP version was a multi-threaded compute-bound *workload*. It naturally made excellent use of all aspects of the computer system, multitasking to cover I/O delays with useful computation in other parts of the flow. FBP naturally does this transformation without

Chap. XXI: Performance Considerations

any particular effort on the part of the user.

That's pretty impressive!

However, to be able to take advantage of these changes of viewpoint, you have to have a modular system. With FBP, as we saw elsewhere in this book, you can replace a sort by a table look-up, or a file by a connection; you can move function from one job step to another, or from one system to another, and so on. As the programmer I quoted earlier told me, "One of the things I like about AMPS is that there are so many more ways to do a job than with conventional programming". *There is never just one way to do a job*. And an FBP developer is continually making conscious trade-offs between different factors. For instance, she might decide to favour response time over throughput, so that might tilt the scales towards direct access instead of sorting. Or the old storage vs. CPU time debate. Or within a component, you can trade off state data against code: boolean switches can either be held in a variable, or can be implemented by choosing between two code paths. It is important to know what options are available to you, and the system must allow you to choose the one you want.

The fundamental trade-off we make in FBP is that we have decided to spend a certain amount of CPU time to get improved programmer productivity and program maintainability. Of course the industry has been doing this since HLLs and operating systems were invented, so this is nothing new, but you always have to decide how much you are willing to pay. But the amount also has to be controllable – a certain cost may be appropriate for one type of application, but wildly inappropriate for another.

In the case of FBP, the cost is closely related to the number of processes, which in turn is related to what is called "granularity". In general, the finer the granularity, the more CPU time gets used, so you can afford smaller "grains" in an infrequently used part of our application network. Conversely, 5,000,000 IPs going through a path of 12 processes will cost at least 120,000,000t units of CPU time, where t is the cost in CPU time of one API call (each process is going to cost at least $2t$ units per IP – for a receive and send). Depending on the speed of your machine and what t is, you may decide that 12 is too many. Reducing this number will probably entail some sacrifice in terms of reuse or modularity, as you will be combining smaller, reusable functions into larger, more ad hoc components.

Periodically, people will write an FBP network and a PL/I program which do the same thing and then compare their performance. This is really comparing chalk and cheese! The maintainability of the two programs is totally different, as a PL/I program adds far more maintenance load to your DP department than does an FBP network. Furthermore, if a bug in a generalized component is fixed, everyone benefits, while if a PL/I program bug is fixed, usually there is no lap-over to other applications.

Susan came to us with a program which she felt was slow compared with a "reasonable"

Chap. XXI: Performance Considerations

execution time. I noticed that she was using the Assign component (described above) to set a 1-byte field in every IP, and there were a *lot* of IPs. She had been told to make her program very modular, but also she probably felt that Assign was a neat function, and it meant that much less PL/I that had to be written and maintained. I suggested that she add a single statement to each of a couple of her hand-coded PL/I components. There were other things we could do which together improved the running time significantly. Although we "improved" her program to the point where its performance was acceptable, we probably reduced its maintainability slightly. But this is another trade-off for which no general rules can be given – each situation has to be decided on its own merits. I mention this example mainly to stress that it's a complex decision whether to use a separate generalized component or add function to custom components, involving issues of maintainability, performance, predicted use, ROI and so on. There is a strong element of the aesthetic here – nobody *should* make the decision for you, just as nobody can tell you which paintings to like. Maybe someone *will*, but that's life!

The bottom line is that we have to give application designers as many choices as possible, and as much control as possible, and systems which won't or can't do this won't survive. Why has COBOL survived when so many more sophisticated products have fallen by the wayside? Because, even if you don't like it aesthetically, COBOL does provide this control, even if it takes years to write a system and, once written, it's even harder to maintain. However, COBOL systems degenerate over time, as the developers lose knowledge of, and control over, what's going on under the covers; FBP systems don't.

Now let's talk about specific techniques for tuning the performance of FBP applications.

When the same program was written in, say, PL/I and in DFDM, we quite often found that the elapsed time of the DFDM run would be less than that of the PL/I run, but the CPU time would be somewhat greater. It becomes obvious why this should be so if you visualize an FBP network with 6 processes all doing I/O: provided the I/O is using different channels, drives, etc., it can all be happening concurrently, while the scheduler will always be "trying" to find processor work to do to fill available CPU time. FBP programs tend to be CPU gluttons, but that is also the designer's choice – if he or she is concerned about this, I/O processes can be prevented from overlapping by synchronization signals. Usually, however, programmers want to reduce elapsed time, e.g. to fit into a processing "window" (time-slot). Today processing windows are getting shorter and shorter, so there is pressure to reduce elapsed time, even at the cost of more CPU time.

As we described above, using FBP connections in place of intermediate files definitely saves elapsed time, as all the records no longer have to be written out to disk and read back in again, but it will save CPU time as well, due to the reduction in the number of I/O commands issued. In the mainframe operating system, MVS, as probably in most systems, I/O is expensive in terms of CPU time as well.

Chap. XXI: Performance Considerations

Here are some statistics recorded during an evaluation of DFDM against an existing PL/I application, done by an IBM site in the US (EXCP means "EXecute Channel Program"):

```
I/O EXCP requests:            53.6% reduction
CPU Usage:                    16.8% increase
Elapsed execution time:       37.7% reduction
External DASD requirements:   84% reduction
```

Here is what *they* said about those figures:

> We attribute the above reductions in resource usage to the improved design of the application (as a result of using structured analysis which is promoted in conjunction with DFDM). The slight increase in CPU usage is a small trade-off when you take into consideration the improved design of the application which should significantly lower future maintenance.

Let's say that you have tuned your I/O as well as possible, and that you are now trying to estimate how much CPU time your application will take. I have found that a good predictor for CPU time is the number of API calls. On the IBM Model 168 in the 1970s (this was about a 2 million instructions per second (2 MIPS) machine, programmed in IBM mainframe Assembler language), each API call took approximately 10 microseconds. Of course later machines are much faster, but later implementations of FBP are typically written in higher level languages, have more features and do more checking.

Just for comparison, I did some measurements on THREADS, running on a 33 MHz 80486DX, in 1994, and the time per API call was approximately 50 microseconds.

In measurements done on my desktop machine (2 Intel® Pentium® 4s) on Nov. 2009, using JavaFBP, time per API call was 15 microseconds – almost back down to the 1970s Assembler value! Interestingly, running the same test on that same machine using the latest version of THREADS (which now uses Microsoft fibres, instead of `longjmp` and `setjmp`), time per API call is down to 3 microseconds.

Now, in most networks, there is usually a "back-bone": a path where most of the IPs travel. You could think of this back-bone as much like a critical path in a Critical Path Network. Let us suppose that this path consists of 12 processes, each sending and receiving: then, taking the figure of 10 microseconds, we get a cost of 240 microseconds per IP. If 5 million IPs travel this path, you get a total CPU time for API calls alone of 1,200 seconds, or 20 minutes. You may therefore decide that you want to consolidate some of the number of processes in the application "back-bone" into larger, less generalized ones – as we said above, this will reduce maintainability, but you may well decide that it is worth the price. Of course, you don't have to consolidate all the processes in your network – areas of the network which are visited less frequently, like error handling logic, may be left more granular.

Chap. XXI: Performance Considerations

It is common wisdom nowadays to concentrate on developing function first, and then worry about performance afterwards. This is quite valid as long as you don't squander performance up front by poor design. And here of course is where aesthetics comes in – I started my programming career on an IBM 650, which had 2000 10-digit words stored on a spinning magnetic drum, and I believe that it became almost an instinct to make programs as lean in terms of time and storage as possible. But, even in those far-off days, there was wide variation in the performance of code by different programmers. I believe the most successful ones never lose sight of the performance requirement, so that it is a constant undertone to their program designs. If you ignore performance and expect to add it back in later, you will generally be disappointed in the results!

Having said that, I must also warn against the other extreme – Wayne Stevens repeatedly stressed that you will generally not be able to predict where is the best place in your application for you to focus your tuning efforts. You may spend lots of time trimming a few seconds off some code which turns out only to be used occasionally. It is much better to run a performance tool on your application, using representative data, and find out where you should really be putting tuning effort. You can actually use the time you have saved by using an improved methodology to tune the parts of your system which make a real difference. One of the satisfying things about FBP is that, once you have improved the performance of a component, all future users of that component will benefit.

Similarly, you may decide to create a variant of a component to exploit a trade-off, and again you have increased the range of choices for future users. An example of this is a process I built whose function was to read disk files faster than the standard reader, but at the cost of more storage. We had a large direct-access data set which had to be read as fast as possible. I just read in a full track at a time, and figured out the order the records should be output in, based on the physical record tags. On the minus side was the fact that this approach took up a track's worth of storage, and the code was tied to the device's characteristics; on the plus side, it was fast! In our case, this Read Track component was definitely worth it – it didn't get used widely, but, when we needed it, there was nothing like it! Remember also that in FBP there is never just one way to do a job, so nobody is forced to use your component. This component can just be added to the tools available for your programmers to use – they just have to understand its behaviour, not how it works inside. By the way, training programmers to think like users is not that easy! This example has apparently been obsoleted by new hardware design of DASD, but I still think it's a valid example of a certain type of thinking.

Another kind of trade-off can be made in FBP by varying the capacity of connections. FBP's connections provide a powerful way of trading off CPU time against storage. All FBP schedulers (at least the fibre-based ones) have followed the strategy of having a process continue running as long as possible, until it is suspended for some reason. Now the more IPs there are in a process's input connection(s), the longer that process can go on before a context switch has to take place

Chap. XXI: Performance Considerations

(assuming there is room in its output connections to receive the output). So, in general, larger capacity connections reduce context switches, and therefore CPU time. But, of course, larger capacities mean more IPs can be in flight at any point in time, so your application will take up more storage. Another way of looking at this is that you are effectively loosening the coupling between processes, so larger capacity connections equals looser coupling, whereas smaller capacity connections equals tighter coupling. For instance, we discovered that sequential readers perform best if their output connections can hold at least a physical block's worth of records.

The Read Track process described above was used in conjunction with some other techniques to reduce a disk file scanning job from 2 hours to 18 minutes. The original running time of 2 hours was a cause for concern as we knew that the data we would eventually have to process was several times the amount we were using in the 2-hour run. It therefore became imperative to see what we could do to reduce the running time of the job. We achieved this significant reduction by changing the shape of the network and adding one new component. This example used AMPS and is described in my Systems Journal article (Morrison 1978), but for those of you who may not have access to it I think it's worth repeating here, as it embodies some very important principles. This is of course very similar to the situation Mike Beckerle described above.

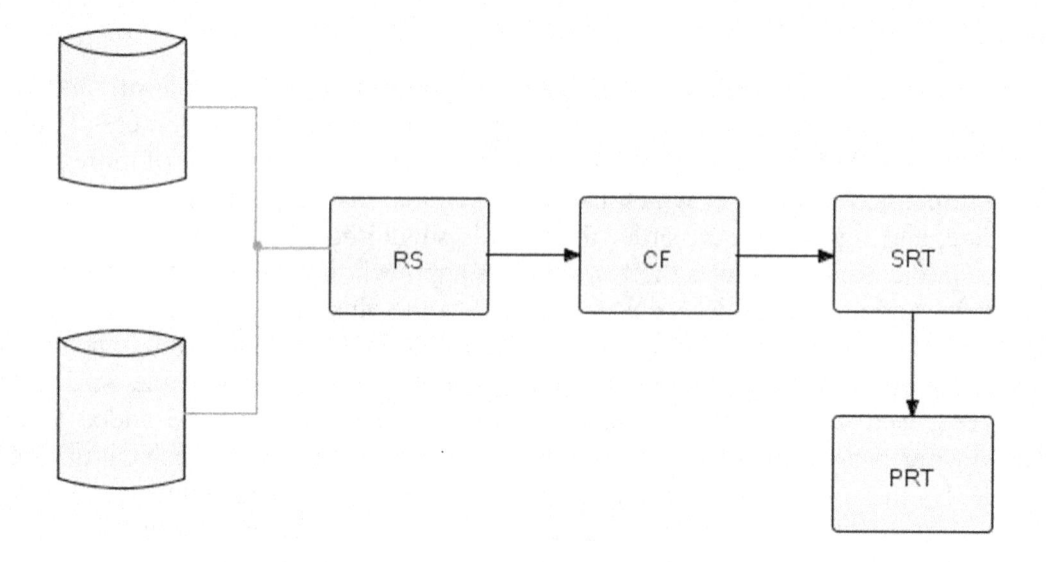

Figure 21.1

The application scanned chains of records running across many disk packs. One set of packs contained the "roots" of the chains, while another set of disk packs contained what we might call "chain records". Each root contained pointers to zero or more chain records, which in turn might

Chap. XXI: Performance Considerations

contain pointers to other chain records, which could be spread over multiple packs. The problem was that our insert and delete code was occasionally breaking chains, so I was given the job of running through every chain looking for broken links – but obviously the scanning program could not use the same code that was causing the problem! So I had to write all new programs to do the scanning job. These programs understood our pointer structure, and there was enough internal evidence that I could always detect a broken chain.

My first approach is shown in Figure 21.1, where *RS* means Read Sequential. This was the standard reader – we just concatenated its input files together, so its disk packs were read one after another. *CF* was the Chain Follower which follows chains from one record to the next and outputs diagnostic information only when it finds a broken chain. *SRT* sorts the output of *CF* to put it into a sequence which is useful for humans, and *PRT* prints the results of the Sort process.

The reason for the Sort is that the root records were scattered randomly on the root disks, whereas it was more useful to see the errors ordered by, say, account number within error type. Since the number of errors should gradually diminish to zero as program bugs in the access methods were fixed, the overhead of the Sort process would diminish over time also.

This program as shown above took 2 hours to run, even though we were using a test database, with a small subset of the data, so we absolutely had to speed it up!

My first realization was that the *CF* component was heavily I/O-bound, as it was spending most of its running time doing direct accesses to disk records, which usually included a seek, disk latency and then a read of a record into storage. I figured that, if we could run a large number of these processes concurrently, the I/O times of the different processes would tend to overlap. However, if we had too many parallel processes, they would start contending for resources, i.e. channels and arms. I therefore decided rather arbitrarily to have 18 of them running concurrently.

I also thought that, since the roots were scattered across multiple packs, we might as well assign each pack its own reader and let them run in parallel also. And, if I was going to do that, why not use the full track reader I described earlier in this chapter? Its output is data records, in the right order (although this wasn't even strictly necessary for this application), so the next process downstream wouldn't see any difference.

Lastly, I needed something to tie together these two kinds of process: I needed a process which would assign incoming root IPs to one of the CF processes, in a balanced manner. I could have just done this using a round-robin technique, but I wanted to try something a little "smarter": could I select the CF process which had the least work to do, and thus keep the load across all the CF processes in balance? I reasoned that the most lightly loaded process should have the smallest build-up in its input connection, so if I always sent a root IP to the CF process with the fewest IPs in its input connection, this would have the desired effect. I therefore wrote a load-balancing component which checked its output connections looking for the one with the smallest number of IPs. I feel this approach is quite general and could be used in many multi-server situations.

Chap. XXI: Performance Considerations

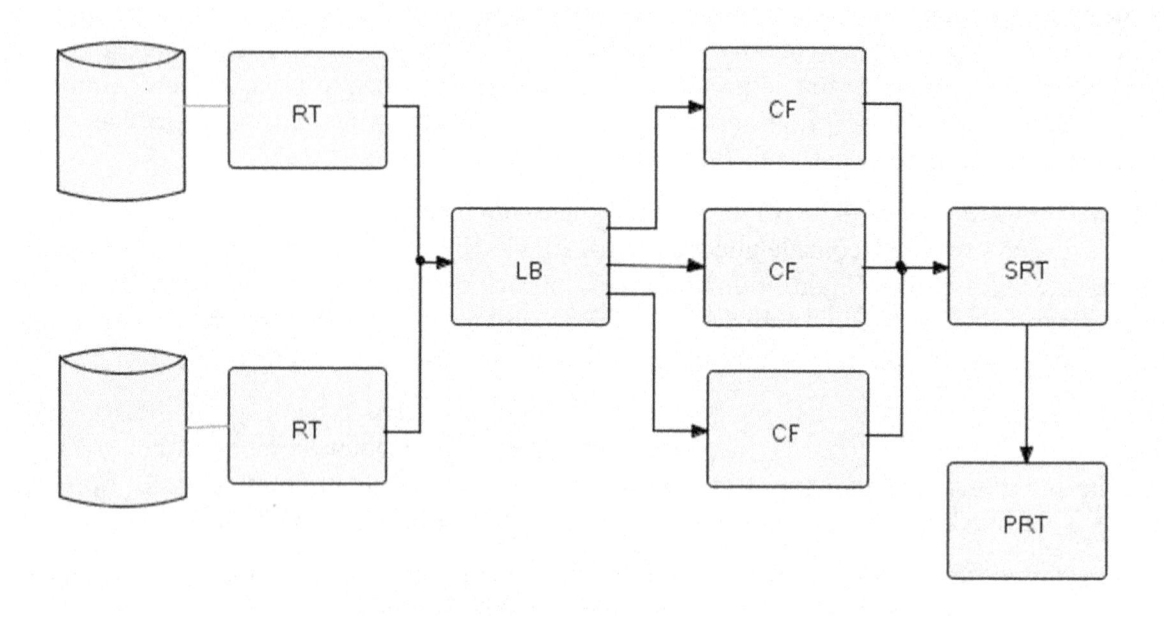

Figure 21.2

where *RT* is the full track reader, *LB* is the Load Balancing process, and the other processes are as before.

Figure 21.2 shows the final structure.

- Final result: elapsed time down from 2 hours to 18 minutes.
- Programming cost: one new generalized component (*LB*) and a change to the network. We might want to count *RT*, depending on whether we feel this was written for this purpose, or independently of it (it sort of happened along at the right time!). Furthermore, all these generalized components can be used in future applications.

The FBP diagramming tool, DrawFBP, supports the multiplexing function shown above using a "compressed" notation, which also lets the designer fill in the multiplexing factor. This notation is shown in Figure 21.3.

Chap. XXI: Performance Considerations

Here is how part of such a network might be written in JavaFBP. As before, we omit the package name and imports. The `main` method is shown here, using a slightly different notation. Because we are using "generated" process and port names, we have to use the long connect notation (see the Appendix).

For illustrative purposes, I have shown the multiplexing factor as dependent on the number of processors on the machine – however, someone will have to do some experiments to determine if this is a useful strategy!

```java
public class TestLoadBalancer {
  public static void main(final String[] args) {
    try {
      new Network() {

        @Override
        protected void define() {
          Runtime runtime = Runtime.getRuntime();
          int nrOfProcessors = runtime.availableProcessors();
          int multiplex_factor = nrOfProcessors * 10;
          component("generate", Generate.class);
          component("sort", Sort.class);
          component("display", WriteToConsole.class);
          component("lbal", LoadBalance.class);
          connect("generate.OUT", "lbal.IN");
          initialize("5000 ", component("generate"), port("COUNT"));
          for (int i = 0; i < multiplex_factor; i++) {
            connect(component("lbal"), port("OUT", i),
                    component("passthru" + i, Passthru.class), port("IN"));
            connect(component("passthru" + i), port("OUT"), "sort.IN");
          }
          connect("sort.OUT", "display.IN");
        }
      }.go();
    } catch (Exception e) {
      System.err.println("Error:");
      e.printStackTrace();
    }
  }
}
```

Figure 21.4

Chap. XXI: Performance Considerations

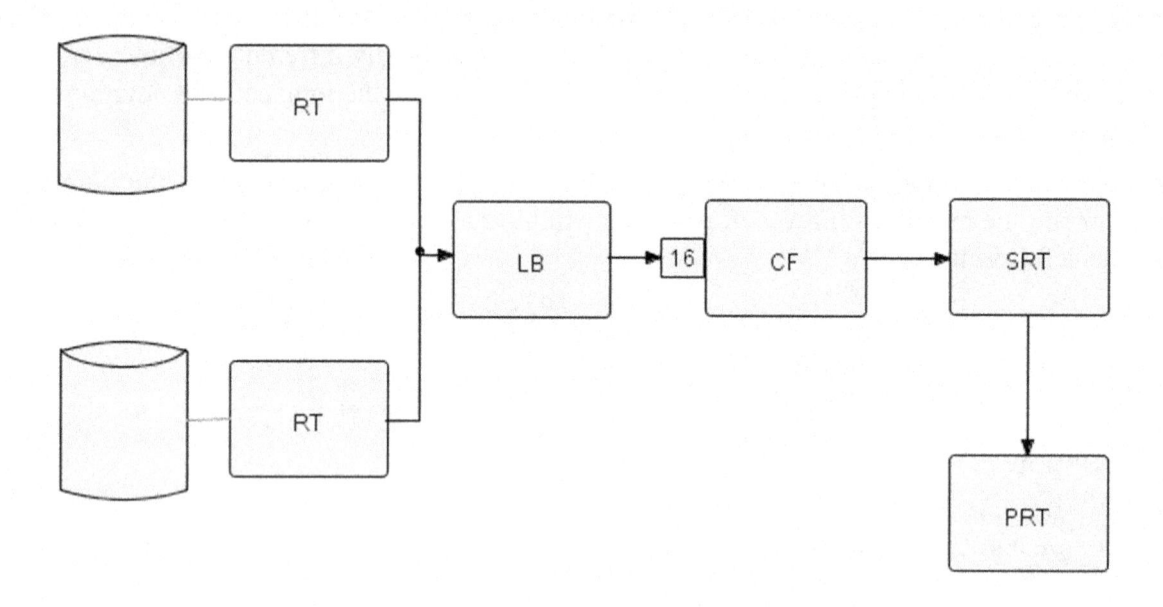

Figure 21.3

Discussion of multiplexing leads me to the question of performance on multicore machines. The earliest FBP implementations (AMPS, DFDM and THREADS) all used what are now called "green threads" or "fibres", also called non-preemptive implementations. Here, the thread of control (which I've been calling a "process") only gives up control at a `send` or `receive` or wait on external event (or `sleep`). Typically such implementations are very fast, but they have two basic flaws: a) they cannot take advantage of multiple cores, and b) they cannot multithread with preexisting code that was not written using them. Some languages support asynchronous I/O, so this can be used in a green thread environment, but larger packages, such as database access, can hang the whole application.

JavaFBP and C#FBP, on the other hand, use native (preemptive) threads, so do not suffer from the problems of non-preemptive implementations. Not only that, but, being threads-based, they allow you to multiplex CPU-intensive components as well as I/O-bound components, while with fibre-based implementations there is no advantage to multiplexing CPU-intensive components.

In spite of all the recent improvements to Java performance, a number of people worry that Java threads are not "fast enough", so there is a continuing interest in languages which support green threads, such as Python Stackless. Java no longer supports "green" threads, often called "fibres", and in fact Java multithreading is improving steadily, plus the fact that most fibre implementations do not support multiple cores. However, Sriram Srinivasan's Kilim, described

Chap. XXI: Performance Considerations

below in Chapter 27 (page 281), combines Java threads and fibre-like objects (which he calls Tasks), resulting in an extremely fast system, due in part to the fact that it can take advantage of multiple cores, so a suspended fibre does not suspend the whole application.

Comparing thread systems vs. systems using "green threads" only, an article in Wikipedia (*http://en.wikipedia.org/w/index.php?title=Green_threads&oldid=337440392*) says:

> Benchmarks on computers running the Linux kernel have shown that:
>
> - green threads outperform Linux native threads on thread activation and synchronization.
>
> - Linux native threads have much better performance on I/O and context switching operations.

The full article, by Sung, Kim, Park, Chang and Shin, of the School of Computer Science and Engineering, Seoul National University, Seoul, can be found at *http://citeseerx.ist.psu.edu/viewdoc/download?doi=10.1.1.8.9238&rep=rep1&type=pdf*.

On the other hand, Sriram Srinivasan states that there are some situations where you need tens of thousands of schedulable tasks, so a hybrid system makes a lot of sense in this environment (although Sven Steinseifer has successfully conducted tests with thousands of Java threads). However, basing FBP on a thread architecture seems quite adequate for many, if not most, of the applications I describe in this book.

Various people have started using JavaFBP and C#FBP on multi-core machines. One concern that came up recently (Autumn 2009) was that JavaFBP (and C#FBP) did not seem to be as responsive, on a multiprocessor machine, to varying the capacity of connections as on a uniprocessor or on fibre-based systems. However, later studies on a 2-processor machine indicated that our tests simply did not have enough threads running concurrently, so the underlying operating system was trying to balance the load on the processors, and working against the natural performance tuning abilities of FBP. Using a much larger number of threads, the connection capacity turned out to have the desired effect.

The test was run on my my desktop machine (2 Intel® Pentium® 4s) (December 1, 2009), and involved 50 `Generate` processes, generating a total of a million IPs, and feeding 50 `Discard` processes:

Chap. XXI: Performance Considerations

Connection size:	10	100
Run times (secs.):	59.531	54.937
	58.109	52.359
	58.500	50.766
	60.172	51.094
Average run time:	59.078	52.289

Figure 21.5

which seems to indicate fairly conclusively that, in this case, connection capacity does have a significant effect on run time.

However, for interest, I recently ran the exact same code on a recently purchased desktop machine (with 4 AMD Phenom™ II X4 925 processors) (April 2010), and here are the corresponding times:

Connection size:	10	100
Run times (secs.):	12.121	12.371
	12.652	12.308
	12.012	12.526
	12.761	12.340
Average run time:	12.387	12.386

Figure 21.6

In the case of the smaller connection size, the average works out about the same, but the *range* of the run times is a bit wider than in the case of the larger connection size.

I then added a *PASSTHRU* process to each path of the network, and found to my surprise that, running these networks on the 4-processor machine, that there was no significant improvement once the connection capacity was increased past 4 or 5. There was, of course, a big difference between a capacity of 1 and a capacity of 5, but not much improvement after that! At the time I did not have enough multiprocessing experience to explain this result, but Vladimir Sibirov has recently pointed out that it just means the downstream processes are running fast enough to prevent queues from building up. Thanks, Vladimir! By the way, these tests keep all 4 processors over 90% busy.

Chap. XXI: Performance Considerations

We talked before about "non-loopers" vs. "loopers": the operators that Mike Beckerle and his group base their work on are more similar to what we would call non-loopers. In a personal communication, he states:

> We eventually moved away from loop-oriented APIs entirely. Even our external sort operator was written as an event-driven action-routine-based pattern. It just proved to be the simpler pattern for people to learn and use versus writing a loop. Otherwise people were confused about when to use a loop and when to use the event-oriented pattern. The event oriented pattern enables important optimizations which improve performance tremendously and allow use of very small fine-grained operators/components, but they also can be implemented by having the execution framework just surround them with a loop. So the framework gets to choose how to realize them.

Given this orientation, they can let the scheduling software decide how to schedule their operators, and how to utilize the machine processors. In the existing JavaFBP and C#FBP implementations, loopers and non-loopers put different constraints on storage use, but Mike's approach is thought-provoking, and, in conjunction with some of the advanced ideas in Ohua (alluded to above), may in fact afford a way to merge the two concepts in the long run.

Interestingly, when explaining FBP concepts, our group found it *less* confusing for the beginner to treat all components as loopers, and leave non-loopers to a later stage in the exposition. This can be contrasted with Mike's contention that non-loopers give them more flexibility.

From Mike's point of view, non-looper style operators have another big advantage: in many cases you can run a number of them in the same thread, using direct transfer, rather than fixed-capacity connections. How can you have FBP-style thinking without multiple fibres or threads? We'll let Mike tell us:

> To me there is a conceptual separation in FBP between the way you use an operator, and the way you write one. You connect them together on flow-based diagrams, without concern for how they are implemented.
>
> You write them hopefully using a very convenient API that makes writing the operator you want very easy, and key point, does not care about how any other operator is implemented. So when I say one operator calls another, I don't mean the operator author takes any special action in their code. Rather, the operator author does whatever they do for data to be transmitted. Depending on the API this might be some sort of send/transmit call, or it might just be what happens when you return from the action method.
>
> The power of the model is because you must assume asynchrony, you can't use side-

Chap. XXI: Performance Considerations

effects to communication via hidden "backchannels" because you really don't know when things are happening. This freedom from non-explicit communications gives all sorts of implementation freedom, including the ability to implement in a totally synchronous way so as to lower overhead.

That is, if the API for writing the operator allows it.

The beauty is, because the model is asynchronous, all sort of implementation freedom ... is available.

One possible implementation is to let the operators communicate by direct transfer of data, rather than via FBP-like connections – this can be thought of as a "zero-capacity" connection – running under a single thread. One way this can be implemented is to call the operators in sequence – while this places restrictions on what they can do (e.g. you cannot rearrange the sequence of outgoing packets), it allows extremely fast context-switching. In turn, this gives much finer granularity. But, of course, for anything more complex you can always fall back on the full power of FBP. Similarly, Mike stresses that he would use larger-grain processes running on separate threads for anything to do with I/O.

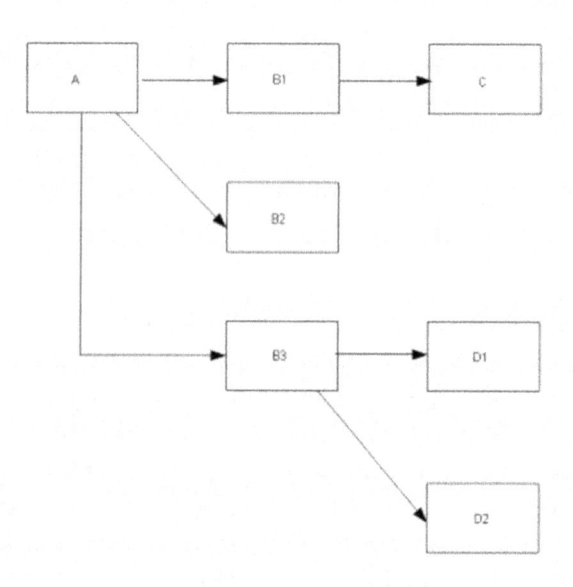

Figure 21.7

Two common patterns that they describe are the following (of course we have run into them many times already in this book):

Chap. XXI: Performance Considerations

- 1 : 1 – i.e. one input port and one output port (i.e. simple "transforms")
- 1 : 0-n – i.e. it has one input port and 0 to n output ports ("fan-outs")

You can string together a bunch of the above type of transforms, and the result is like the "string of pearls" topology mentioned above. When you add some fan-outs, you get a 2-dimensional pattern, which the logic will walk in depth-first sequence.

Figure 21.7 shows a picture of a sample network of such small-scale transforms and fan-outs, where *A* and *B3* are fan-outs, *B1* is a transform, and *C*, *B2*, *D1* and *D2* are "leaf" nodes which actually feed output ports of the higher-level process.

Mike and Sebastian's description of what we are calling "zero-capacity" connections prompted me to to try implementing the above under a single process in JavaFBP – I am tentatively calling them "actors" (Mike's suggestion). Using 100 transforms in a "string of pearls" pattern, the prototype clocked in on my 2-processor machine at a respectable 1.7 microseconds per API call (basically a `create` and a `send` for each actor, times the number of IPs, where `send` is basically a "store" operation)! This test however, only has 3 processes altogether, so I don't expect to see much speed-up when adding processors. In fact, running it on the newer desktop (4 AMD processors), the average time per API call was 0.6 microseconds – presumably due to the faster processing time of the processors (it basically only used one processor).

The driver component can be found on SourceForge, called (not very originally) `ActorDriver`. For a sample actor network, see *http://www.jpaulmorrison.com/fbp/jsyntax.htm#actors*.

Parallelism issues

On this topic, Mike Beckerle and his group have adopted a very different policy towards capacity of connections, and whether a process should run as long as possible, etc. Here is what Mike says about this:

> This is related to the deadlock-avoidance stuff [described in the chapter on Deadlocks], but the general principle assumes we have many more component/operator instances than physical CPU cores to run them on, or can elaborate the graph in such a way that this holds. In this case, which operators should get to occupy the CPUs? The answer to this is surprisingly simple. Any enabled operator which is closer to the "end" of the graph should take priority over anything "upstream" of it. In addition, when there is parallelism, as in a single FBP operator creates 2 or more instances at run time, statically assign them different priorities. That is, do not be "fair". The point of this unfair, but output-favored scheduling is that it minimizes data held in the graph, which minimizes memory footprint, while still keeping all CPU cores busy. The unfairness improves data locality. Why switch to another component just to be fair, if the data for one that is running is sitting in the

Chap. XXI: Performance Considerations

closest fastest cache already? Note that this strategy optimizes throughput, not overall latency. Some packets can enter such a flow and stay there a long time, while others zip right through, but overall the work done and memory occupied is minimized.

The issue arises of how many operators are enough, given modern computer systems with many CPUs and/or CPU cores and potentially clusters of these computers. FBP practitioners generally begin by trying to closely match FBP operator instances to the number of CPU cores. Mike's experience with these systems suggests something more aggressive – quoting him:

> To keep systems busy with useful work we depend on FBP principles which make the scheduling granularity large by buffering the flow arcs. We also used a technique called overpartitioning which insures you have excess work available. E.g. if one has 16 CPUs spread over 4 computers we would probably use 32 or 64 partitions not 16. Each operator that can operate in parallel will then get 32 or 64 instances. A flow can easily have hundreds of operator instances in such a realization. So the 16 CPUs would pretty much always have lots of work even if some operator is performing I/O or some reluctant buffer was misbehaving slightly somewhere.

In much of this book, we have talked as though the number of processes depends simply on the logic of the application – except, of course, for techniques like multiplexing, described above. Another possibility, implied in the foregoing, is to decide on the partitioning based roughly on the number of processors available, multiplied by some factor. Both of these approaches seem valuable. Here is a quote about Ohua from a note by Sebastian Ertel:

> ...the Ohua system allows to gather operators on one thread. The algorithm takes a flow graph and splits it up. The final flow graph pieces are called "islands". An island in the end is just a part of the flow graph which can be one or more consecutive operators. As soon as an island is assigned its own operator scheduler Ohua refers to it as a "section". Every section gets executed on a thread from a global thread-pool. The result is a section graph on top of a flow graph. ☺

Mike and his coworkers have clearly built up an impressive amount of operational experience with their technology, and I am hoping that, as time goes on, they will be able to share this experience with the FBP community as a whole.

Chap. XXII: Defining Networks

FBP applications basically start off life as pictures or hierarchies of pictures, which have to be made "machinable" for execution. During most of our several decades of experience with FBP, we never had advanced picture-drawing tools, so we tended to draw networks using pencil and paper, and then convert them by hand into executable networks. Although we have experimented with different notations over the years, the information which needs to be captured has remained fairly constant. It is certainly true that FBP lends itself to visual programming techniques, so nowadays the following notations should also be able to be generated by software.

The diagrams typically used for Structured Analysis represent processes and their connections. To turn such a diagram into an FBP diagram which can actually be executed, you will have to add the following data:

- port names (or numbers)
- parametrization
- automatic ports

For ease of understanding, we often added the following to our hand-drawn Structured Analysis diagrams:

- stream descriptions
- process descriptions (e.g. "merge masters and details", as opposed to just "merge")
- icons for external objects, users, etc.

The same is true for FBP diagrams. When we mostly used pencil and paper, we never really worried too much about the exact diagramming conventions to be used – now, however, we have

Chap. XXII: Defining Networks

high resolution screens, supported by powerful graphical software, so we can start to take advantage of the cycles available on everybody's desks.

A few years ago I built a diagramming tool using C, which was used to document a number of complex production programs. A few years later, I built a new and improved version using Java Swing, which I called DrawFBP (*http://www.jpaulmorrison.com/fbp/index.shtml#DrawFBP*). These diagramming tools allow the user to build up a complex network, using the "stepwise decomposition" concept of Structured Analysis.

With DrawFBP, a diagram block can be associated with a Java component, or with a subnet, in which case DrawFBP shows the block with a double boundary. Double-clicking on the latter type of block brings up the subnet in another frame, while double-clicking on a component displays the Java code (thanks to Adler Perotte for this suggestion!). Conversely, a user can draw a network, then draw an outline around part of it, and "excise" it, turning it into a subnet, and replacing it with a single block which names the subnet. DrawFBP can also generate a runnable JavaFBP network, provided it is given all the necessary information (component and port names, etc.) – it will prompt the user for the missing information.

The potential for adding new capabilities to such a tool is virtually limitless. As components have metadata describing their ports, we could pick up an icon for, say, a Collate component, and place it on the diagram, complete with "sticky" ports ready to be connected to its neighbours, sort of like the "valence" hooks that are sometimes shown on diagrams of atoms. However, it is hard to make this function sufficiently general – so instead, when a component or subnet is selected, DrawFBP checks the ports used in the diagram against the port requirements specified in the component or subnet attributes.

Similarly I decided not to use specialized icons for different components in DrawFBP: my feeling is that there will eventually be large numbers of components being contributed by different vendors, and the main thing users want to know is what the component is used for – not which component is being used (although that information should be available if needed).

We have drawn a number of pictures in what has gone before, but we have yet to talk about how we get these into the machine to be executed. We will just describe at a high level some of the approaches that have been used up until now. This section is intended to show how our thinking evolved over the years.

The very first FBP software, AMPS, was written in IBM S/360 Assembler language, and networks were also expressed using Assembler macros (think of them as inline methods – or a special-purpose language). Each process was specified using a single macro statement, which also listed the named connections between that process and the other ones. In what follows, I will use a simple network and show how it was specified to the system in the various FBP dialects. Let us take as our sample network the one shown in Figure 22.1.

Chap. XXII: Defining Networks

In AMPS and DFDM ports were specified numerically, so I have marked the ports as numbers in this diagram. (In DFDM input and output ports were numbered separately, while in AMPS one set of numbers covered both – this diagram follows the DFDM convention).

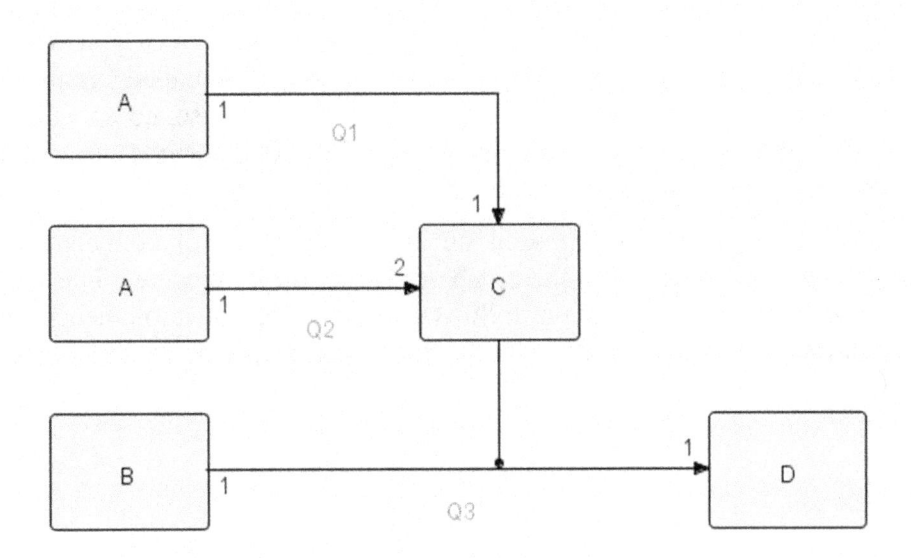

Figure 22.1

In AMPS, we named the connections as shown in the diagram. The diagram was then coded up using one macro call per process, with the connections listed sequentially. Parameters could also be specified in the network, and were added using an optional parameter on the process macro. As each macro describes a separate process, there is no need to distinguish between different uses of the same component.

Notice a concept common to all the varieties of FBP: when more than one output port is connected to one input port, *it is treated as one connection (queue)*. Connections can be many-to-one, but not one-to-many.

Parameters in AMPS were more general than DFDM's: an AMPS parameter could be a data structure of any form, while DFDM parameters were always variable length character strings – DFDM's were consistent with the format of parameters passed to a job step by the MVS operating system, supporting the idea of stepwise decomposition.

DFDM had two different notations: *interpreted*, which was used to build the network dynamically at run-time, and *compiled*, where the control blocks for the network were built as a

Chap. XXII: Defining Networks

single Assembler program, which, when compiled and link-edited, resulted in a ready-to-run network control block structure. The interpreted notation allowed a program to be modified and tested many times during a session. Test components could also be added easily to monitor the contents of connections or to create test data. The compiled format did not have the interpretation overhead, but took a little longer to generate, so was more appropriate when a network was put into production or you wanted to study a program's performance. Once you were ready to go from interpreted to compiled format, you used a utility program (called "Expand") to do the conversion. The other main difference was that, in the interpreted case, components were loaded dynamically at run-time, while in the compiled case all the components were linked together, along with the network, into a single executable block of code.

Both of these DFDM notations were based on specifying a list of connections, rather than processes. These connections specified the processes which they connected, but were themselves unnamed. This is the approach we have followed in all successor implementations (including JavaFBP and C#FBP). So the connection list for the above diagram would look something like the following:

```
A -> C -> D,
A.X -> 2 C,
B -> D;
```

Figure 22.2

where we have distinguished the second occurrence of A with the qualifier X (any character string would have done). This suggestion came from Wayne Stevens.

The corresponding compiled specification would then be as shown in Figure 22.3. As you can see, both notations use the same qualifier notation.

```
X       NETWORK
        CONNECT A,C
        CONNECT C,D
        CONNECT A.X,(2,C)
        CONNECT B,D
        NETEND
        END
```

Figure 22.3

One other major difference between the interpreted and compiled notations of DFDM is that the interpreted notation is hierarchical, whereas the compiled is "flat" (it is "flattened" when it is expanded, so that the whole network becomes a single module). In the interpreted notation, you could define a subnet, call it G, with "sticky" connections, e.g.

Chap. XXII: Defining Networks

```
G:   -> A -> 2 B ->, I -> B
```

Figure 22.4

would mean that *G* has one input port and one output port which will be connected when *G* is used. Arrows with an open end are the external interfaces of the subnet, in this example, the arrow feeding *A* and the arrow coming from *B*. *G*'s picture is shown in Figure 22.6.

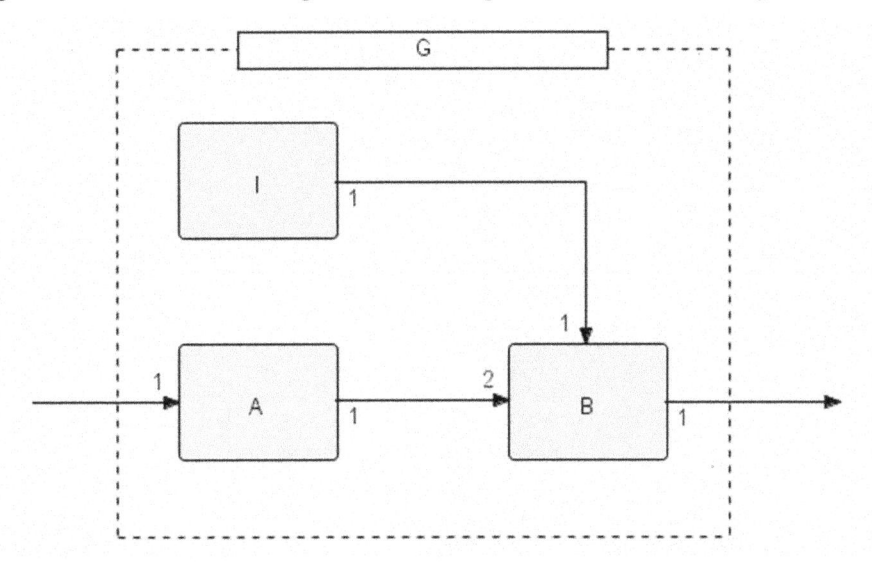

Figure 22.5

G has two external ports: one input and one output. These are the arrows which cross the "boundary" of *G* (shown as a dotted line).

G can therefore be used as an ordinary filter in a network, and, like all components, can be used more than once in a network.

Here is a simple network using *G* (twice):

Chap. XXII: Defining Networks

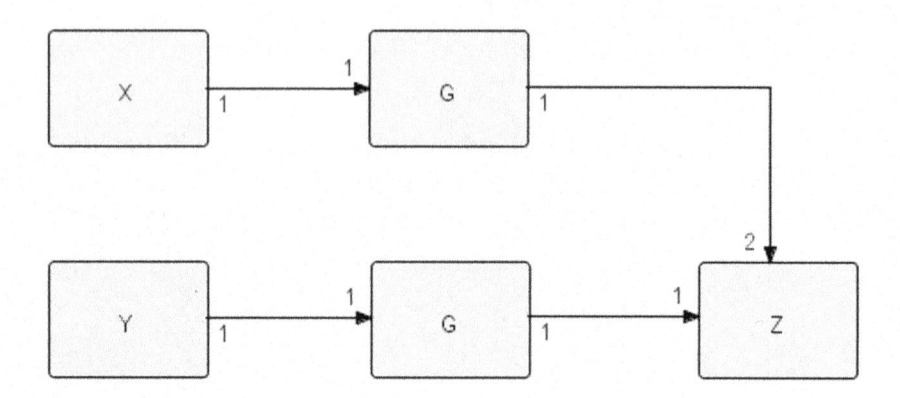

Figure 22.6

This might be coded as follows in the interpreted notation:

```
X -> G -> 2 Z,
Y -> G.2 -> Z
```

Figure 22.7

Note that composite components can be qualified just like elementary components – at this level, the network doesn't know that *G* even is a composite.

In the case of JavaFBP and C#FBP, the network is defined procedurally. Here are two sample Java statements from a JavaFBP network definition:

```
connect(component("Read Details",Read.class),port("OUT"),
     component("Collate"),port("IN",1));    // array port

connect(component("Collate"),port("OUT"),
     component("Process Merged Stream",Proc.class),port("IN"));
```

Figure 22.8

This takes advantage of the power of Java to use the same method name with different sets of parameters: the `component()` method can either specify the class associated with a process name, or just reference the name alone. Similarly, the `port()` method call can either specify a simple port, or can specify a specific element of an array port. At the suggestion of David Bennett of

- 232 -

Chap. XXII: Defining Networks

Powerflex Corporation in Australia, who was working on a C# version (not quite the same as C#FBP), we later introduced a "shorthand", where the process name and port name (and even port array element, if constant) are combined into a single string, e.g.

```
connect("Read Details.OUT", "Collate.IN[1]");

connect("Collate.OUT"), "Process Merged Stream.IN");
```

Figure 22.9

In this case, the `component()` method must be called separately. Of course the older notation is still supported, and may in fact even be required, e.g. when the port array element number is variable. This of course requires that, at a minimum, the period and square brackets not be allowed in process names.

The `connect()` method can also specify a connection capacity. As Java and C# allow methods to specify different parameters, we can simply specify an `int` value as the last parameter on either of the formats described above.

The C#FBP version of both these notations is almost identical, except that the method names start with upper case, not lower case, and the notation for classes is different (`typeof x` instead of `x.class`). Fuller descriptions can be found on my web site at *http://www.jpaulmorrison.com/fbp/jsyntax.htm* for the Java implementation, and *http://www.jpaulmorrison.com/fbp/csyntax.htm*, for the C# implementation.

An enhancement to Release 2.5 of JavaFBP is a "count" facility that supports monitoring of the number of IPs received at an input port. This is specified by an optional boolean value on the `connect()` method call. If this is specified, IPs are counted as they are received at that input port, and the counts for all such "monitored" connections are maintained in a shared location, where an asynchronous process can interrogate them at regular intervals or on receipt of a signal. Either or both of capacity and the "count" indicator can be specified on any `connect()` method call. If this function proves out, it will also be incorporated in Release 2.4 of C#FBP.

Here is an example of a `connect()` with both a capacity (of 20) and counting specified:

```
boolean MONITOR = true;

connect("Collate.OUT"), "Process Merged Stream.IN", 20, MONITOR);
```

Figure 22.10

Chap. XXII: Defining Networks

Although a network diagram on your screen can be converted fairly easily into such a specification, procedural specifications are not easy to grasp directly – and, as they are really equivalent to a list of connections, it might be argued that a list format is preferable. Another argument in favour of lists is that the programmer might be tempted to insert other code into the network specification. Of course, the reverse argument is that this may in fact be necessary, as long as the programmer keeps in mind the exact timing of events during program invocation, and he or she should have the option to do so if it is required.

If we are going to stay with lists, a number of my correspondents have suggested that the network could be defined using XML. Christopher Shreve suggests something like:

```
<connection srcName="FileReader" srcPort="OUT" dstName="ReadLine"
    dstPort="SOURCE"/>
```

Figure 22.11

He says that people could actually code this directly, without needing an IDE.

The diagramming tool DrawFBP, mentioned several times already, in fact records its network definitions in XML, in a somewhat similar format, e.g.

```
<connection> <fromx>96</fromx> <fromy>62</fromy> <tox>96</tox> <toy>88</toy>
<fromid>5</fromid> <toid>1</toid> <id>10</id>
<downstreamport>COUNT</downstreamport></connection>
```

Figure 22.12

This format contains enough information to completely rebuild the diagram (`fromx`, `fromy`, `tox` and `toy`), but it also captures the connectivity of the diagram (`fromid` and `toid` refer to the id's of other blocks in the diagram), so in theory it could also be used as the network definition by an appropriate execution engine.

I have gone into some detail on the various approaches to notations because, for many jobs, the network notation is all the code a programmer ever has to write. Whether we name the connections or the processes, all we are really doing is specifying a list of connections. As such, sequence really doesn't matter. Such a list also has a natural relationship with pictures, which are much more manageable for many people.

For debugging conventional languages, we are just starting to get packages which allow the developer to walk through a program interactively – it would be great to have a graphical aid to debugging FBP networks which would allow you to monitor the data passing across a connection, or track a single IP as it travels through the whole network and observe its transformations. Hopefully we will see such tools in the near future.

Chap. XXIII: Related Compiler Theory Concepts

References to *TR1* in the text refer to an application component which is used in examples earlier in the book – see Chapter 10 (page 97). *TR1* "extends" detail records by multiplying a quantity in a detail record by a unit price obtained from a master record in another file. Processes "upstream" of *TR1* have merged masters and details, so *TR1* is fed a single merged stream containing masters and details, and with related records delimited by special IPs called "brackets".

It has been noted by several writers that there seems to be a good match between compiler theory and the theory of sequential processes. FBP processes can be regarded as "parsers" of their input streams.

The component labelled *TR1* in the example in Chapter 10 can be considered as a parser, while the structure of its input stream can be specified using a syntactic form called a regular expression. This allows a number of the concepts of modern compiler theory to be applied to it. Let us express the input stream of component *TR1* in that application as a "regular expression", as follows:

```
{ ( m d* ) }*
```

which can be read as:

  zero or more groups of:
- one open bracket, followed by
- one master IP (*m*), followed by
- zero or more details (*d*), followed by
- one close bracket

In what follows, I will use brackets to represent bracket IPs, and curly braces will have syntactic

Chap. XXIII: Related Compiler Theory Concepts

meanings. To simplify things, I will treat masters as always present, rather than optional.

Each of *TR1*'s output streams consists of repeating strings of identical IPs. Representing modified masters as m', extended details as d' and summaries as s, we get the following "regular expressions" for the three output streams:

```
m'*
d'*
s*
```

Each of these output streams has a well-defined relationship with the input stream, and it would be very nice if some notation could be developed to show this relationship clearly and concisely. In fact, this would constitute a complete description of what *TR1* does: a component's function is completely described by its input and output streams, and the relationships between them.

In Aho and Ullman's 1972 book they show that a regular expression can be parsed by a deterministic one-way finite automaton with one tape, usually referred to simply as a "finite automaton". This tape contains "frames", usually containing characters, but in what follows we shall think of the frames as containing entire IPs. As each frame is scanned, the automaton may or may not change state, and may or may not perform an "action", such as reading or writing a frame. Whether or not there is an action, the tape continues moving.

A convenient way to represent the various state changes is by means of a "Transition Graph", where each node represents a state, and each arc represents a transition from one state to another (or from a state to itself), and is marked with the name of the IP being scanned off, as follows:

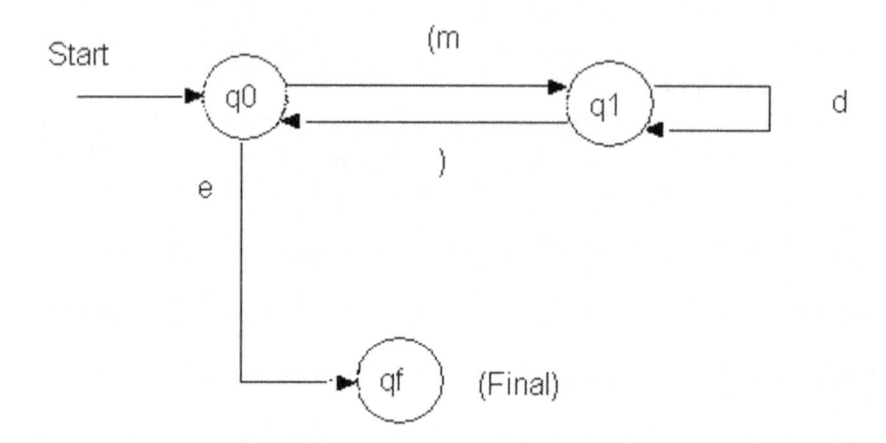

Figure 23.1

In these diagrams, e is used to indicate the "end of data" condition; m, d, $($ and $)$ represent

Chap. XXIII: Related Compiler Theory Concepts

masters, details, open and close brackets, respectively. Since an open bracket is always followed by a master in this example, I have shown them combined on a single transition arc.

An alternative to the transition graph is the "State Table". This uses a tabular format, which is often more convenient. The table shown in Figure 23.2 is equivalent to Figure 23.1.

State	Input	New State
q0	(m	q1
q0	e	qf
q1	d	q1
q1	)	q0
qf		Final State

Figure 23.2

Aho and Ullman next show that any regular expression may be described by a "right linear grammar", expressed as a series of productions, each of which describes a pattern in terms of the sub-patterns or final symbols which make it up.

Productions can be understood in a generative sense – i.e. all legal streams can be generated by successively taking choices from the set of productions, starting with S. Alternatively, productions can be used to describe relationships between patterns being scanned off by a parser.

A grammar is called "right linear" if patterns on the right-hand side may only occur at the end of a production. Here is a right linear grammar which is equivalent to the "regular expression" given above, using the notation of productions, but using lower-case letters to represent IP types, as in the state diagram above. Ø means a null stream.

```
S -> Ø
S -> (mR
R -> )S
R -> dR
```

Figure 23.3

where the two lines starting with S indicate two patterns which both constitute valid S's, and similarly for the two lines starting with R.

Since lower-case letters in the productions represent objects that cannot be parsed further (i.e. IPs), upper-case letters may be thought of as representing expectations or hypotheses. Thus R in the above productions represents "that part of a stream which can follow a master or detail". Thus, when a master is detected, the automaton's expectation of what may follow changes from

Chap. XXIII: Related Compiler Theory Concepts

what it was at the beginning of the stream, and, when a close bracket is detected, it changes back. This exactly mirrors the state changes of the finite automaton shown above.

While the right linear grammar shown above adequately represents the automaton traversing the stream one IP at a time, it cannot "see" patterns which consist of more than one IP, and therefore cannot express one's intuitive feeling for the hierarchic structure of the IP stream. For this we must go to a more powerful class of grammar, called the context-free grammars.

The set of "context-free grammars" (CFGs) is a superset of the set of right linear grammars, in that a pattern symbol is allowed to occur anywhere on the right-hand side of a production. Since CFGs are more general than right linear grammars, they require a more complex type of automaton to process them: the "pushdown automaton" (PDA), which has, in addition to its input tape, memory in the form of a "pushdown stack". This may be thought of as containing subgoals or hypotheses established during stream processing, to be verified or discarded.

The following set of productions of a context-free grammar is also equivalent to the regular expression given above:

```
S -> ø
S -> AS
A -> (mT
T -> )
T -> dT
```

Figure 23.4

Here the first two productions together can be read as follows: a stream consists of zero or more *A* patterns (or substreams).

We can also express this in "state table" format, adding *stack state (S)*.

Q	S	Input	Action	Q'	S'
q0	–	(m	push A	q0	A
q0	A	)	pop A	q0	–
q0	A	d	pop A/ push A	q0	A
q0	–	e		qf	–
qf				Final State	

Figure 23.5

Chap. XXIII: Related Compiler Theory Concepts

A pushdown automaton will have "stack states" in addition to "automaton states": in this example the automaton state is trivial, as there is really only a "normal" state ($q0$) and a "final" state (qf), to enable the automaton to stop.

In the above diagram, Q means "automaton state" and S is the "stack state" (– means empty, and x means that there is an x at the top of the stack). It will be noticed that "push" and "pop" change the "stack state" in the same pattern we saw in connection with the "automaton state" in the Transition Graph shown above. Q' and S' mean the new states of the automaton and the stack respectively.

The actions shown as

```
push x
pop x
```

are to be read as "push IP x onto stack," and "pop IP x from stack," respectively.

You will recognize that this use of the stack exactly parallels the use of a stack in FBP to hold IPs being worked on, discussed in an earlier chapter (Chapter 9 – page 90).

In FBP we restrict the use of the stack as follows: while an IP is in the stack, it is not available for use by the component's logic. It must therefore be "popped" off the stack to make it available for processing. At the end of processing, it must be explicitly disposed of before the automaton leaves that state, either by being returned to the stack, or by being sent or dropped. This is the reason for the pop/push combination – if we weren't using an FBP implementation, we could leave it out altogether, as it leaves the stack state unchanged, but in FBP it is required in order to make A available for processing.

It can be seen from the above that the only function of the state Q is to determine when the automaton has reached a final state – the rest of the time the automaton is in its normal state. The two states of the stack correspond one-to-one with the states $q0$ and $q1$ in the non-pushdown automaton, so that the stack has a dual function: that of storage for IPs being worked on, and control. This exactly mirrors the way FBP uses a stack for holding control IPs. The process of stacking a subgoal which represents a substream corresponds to the FBP concept of stacking an IP to denote the entire substream.

Where do we go from here? There has been quite a lot of work on describing applications using PDAs, but I am not aware of work tying them together with data streams (I would appreciate hearing about such work). This seems to me a fruitful direction for more research, and may yield new ways of looking at applications, or even new hardware designs.

Chap. XXIV: Streams and Recursive Function Definitions

In what follows, Collate refers to a general, "black box", reusable component that merges 2 or more streams on the basis of parameters describing the location of control fields in its incoming IPs, and optionally inserts grouping IPs called "brackets" into its output stream. It is described in some detail in Chapter 8 (page 77).

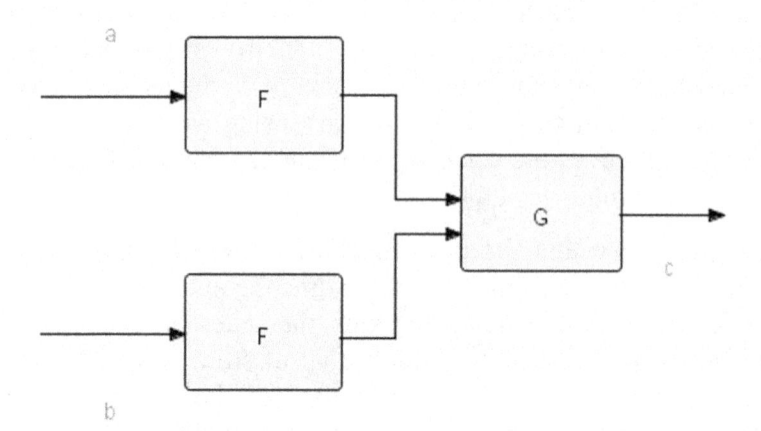

Figure 24.1

It is easy to see that an FBP component can be regarded as a function transforming its input stream into its output stream. These functions can then be combined to make complex expressions just as, say, addition, multiplication, etc. can be combined in an algebraic expression. A number of languages have used this as a base for notations. Figure 24.1 shows a simple

Chap. XXIV: Streams and Recursive Function Definitions

example.

If we label streams as shown with lower case letters, then the above diagram can be represented succinctly as follows:

```
c = G(F(a),F(b))
```

Figure 24.2

I deliberately used *F* twice to underline the fact that the same function can be used many times in the same expression. Of course, this relies on the function having no side effects – this is one of the desirable characteristics of functional languages (and one of the qualities which are desirable when designing FBP components). We will return to this point later on.

Now we have seen that streams are made up of patterns of IPs, which in turn have fields or data items. Is it possible to carry functional notation to the point where we can actually build systems processing real data? I believe it is, but in a way that will not be as "mathematical" as most treatments of recursive programming. In the rest of this chapter, I will develop the concepts of recursive stream definitions. But first, for those of you whose math is a bit rusty, we should talk about what exactly are recursive definitions. The rest of you can skip ahead!

Recursive techniques are often taught using the formula for factorials as an example. A factorial is the product of all the integers greater than zero up to and including the number whose factorial you want to calculate. Although factorials can be (and often are) calculated iteratively, the classic expression for calculating factorials is the following recursive calculation:

```
factorial(x):
  if x = 1
      return 1
  else
      return x * factorial (x - 1)
  endif
```

Figure 24.3

The term "recursive" means that "factorial" is actually defined in terms of itself, but used on a "smaller" part of the problem. Since we use factorial on *x-1*, and the first test is always to see if we have reached 1, we are actually getting one step closer to our goal each time around the definition. If you want to visualize how this might execute, think of a stack holding the environment for each invocation of factorial. Each time we start a factorial calculation, we push the information we will need onto the stack, so the stack gets deeper and deeper. When we eventually get a true condition on the first test, we can calculate a factorial (1) without pushing a

Chap. XXIV: Streams and Recursive Function Definitions

new environment on the stack. Now we can finish all the factorial calculations (in reverse sequence), so that eventually we arrive back at the top of the stack and we're finished. Speakers of German will be familiar with a similar phenomenon which occurs in that language, where several "contexts" may be "stored" until the end of the sentence, at which time each context is terminated with the production of an infinitive or past participle.

The advantage of the recursive definition is that it has no local storage variables. We therefore suspect that this characteristic may have a bearing on some of the problems we identified earlier in this book with the "pigeon-hole" concept of storage. Functions also ideally have no side-effects, so they can easily be reused. If we combine these concepts with some other concepts which have appeared in the literature, we can actually describe (a small piece of) business processing in a way which is free from a number of the problems which bedevil the more conventional approaches. I also believe that if you look back at Chapter 18 (page 178), you will find that there are similarities between that notation and what will be pursued more rigorously in this chapter. Admittedly this will be a tiny example, but my hope is that someone will be sufficiently intrigued that they will carry it further.

Recursive functions are attractive to mathematicians because they have no side-effects, and therefore are easier to analyze and understand. In W.B. Ackerman's paper (1979) he states: "the language properties that a data flow computer requires are beneficial in their own right, and are very similar to some of the properties that are known to facilitate understandable and maintainable software, ..." Some of these beneficial properties are as follows:

- locality of effect
- freedom from side effects
- "call by value"

Ackerman defines an applicative language as one which does all of its processing by means of operators applied to values. The earliest known applicative language was LISP.

By now you should be familiar with the use of the term "stream" in FBP to describe the set of IPs passing across a particular connection. The stream does not all exist at the same time, but is continuously being generated at one end and consumed at the other. However, it has a "real" existence, and it can be manipulated in various ways. W.H. Burge (1975) showed how stream expressions can be developed using a recursive, applicative style of programming. D.P. Friedman and D.S. Wise contributed a number of papers relating applicative programming to streams by adding the concept of "lazy evaluation" (1976) to Burge's work. This style has the desired freedom from side effects and has another useful characteristic: the equals sign is *really* a definition statement, and can be used for proving the validity of programs as well as for doing the actual data processing. Such a language is called "definitional".

Quoting W.B. Ackerman (1979) again: "Such languages are well suited to program verification

Chap. XXIV: Streams and Recursive Function Definitions

because the assertions one makes in proving correctness are exactly the same as the definitions appearing in the program itself." One can put a restriction on assignment statements to the effect that the definition should not assign a value to a given symbol more than once in a single scope.

Thus a statement like

```
J:=J+1
```

Figure 24.4

is ruled out because *J* would have to be given an initial value within the scope, resulting in two assignments within that scope. Also, viewed as a definition, it is obviously a contradiction! A number of writers on programming have described their feelings of shock on their first encounter with this kind of statement, only to become so used to it over the years that they eventually don't notice anything strange about it!

We shall now talk a little bit about the possibility of writing programs in a way that avoids the problem of rebinding variables within a scope, following (Burge 1975) and (Friedman and Wise 1976) in the area of stream functions.

Typically, like the definition of factorial shown above, the desired output is defined in terms of two functions:

- a function of the first item in the stream
- a function relating this item to the rest of the stream
- and a termination rule specifying a value to be returned when the function bottoms out.

The following example resembles the definition of factorial shown above, but moves closer to business applications. Even though it may not much resemble the type of business applications that you are accustomed to, you will have to admit that it is very compact! Suppose we want to count all the IPs in a stream. Then, analogously to the factorial calculation above, we could write a "counter" function F as follows:

```
F(S) = if  S is null,
    then  0,
    else  1 + F(rest(S))
```

Figure 24.5

where the result is specified directly by a value, e.g. *0*, or *1 + F(rest(S))*.

With respect to the rest of this notation, functions are expressed using the conventional bracket notation, and sublists will be specified by means of curly braces. For instance, *{w,x,y,z}* is a

Chap. XXIV: Streams and Recursive Function Definitions

sublist consisting of *w*, *x*, *y* and *z*. *null* tests for a stream with no IPs in it, i.e. {}; *first(S)* is the first IP of a stream, i.e. *w* in the above example, and *rest(S)* is a list comprising all the rest of the IPs in the stream, i.e. *{x,y,z}*. Notice that, while *rest* returns a list, *first* only returns a single IP.

In this first example, *F* is called recursively to return a value based on processing a stream *S*. At each invocation of *F*, its environment (the part of the stream that it can see) is pushed down on a run-time stack. When an invocation of *F* finds itself looking at an empty stream, the null test returns true, *F* bottoms out, and the stacked environments are progressively popped up, until the original one is reached, at which point the process stops. Notice that there is a family resemblance between recursive definitions which only "recurse" at the righthand end, and right linear grammars (described in the previous chapter). This kind of recursive definition can also have special processing applied to it which maintains the stack at a constant depth.

Now so far we haven't actually used the data in the stream IPs. Suppose therefore that we want to sum all the quantity fields in a stream of IPs. We will introduce the convention *a:x* to mean "field *a* of *x*". This notation and the "mini-constructor" notation described below are based on the Vienna Definition Language, developed some years ago by the IBM Laboratory in Vienna. The desired calculation can now be expressed recursively as follows:

```
F(S) = if    S is null,
       then  0,
       else  q:first(S) + F(rest(S))
```

Figure 24.6

where *q* is the quantity field of an IP.

So far, we have only generated a single quantity from our stream. To do anything more complicated, we will need to be able to generate IPs and string them into streams. To do the former, we will need something which can build an IP given a set of values for its fields. We will use a special function for this which I will call the "mini-constructor" (μ). This takes as its argument a list of selector symbols and values, and returns as a result an IP with those values inserted into the fields designated by the selectors. A selector and its value are separated by commas, while selector/value pairs are separated by semi-colons. The mini-constructor is a concise way of specifying how new IPs are to be built.

To combine IPs into a stream, we use a variant of the well-known list-processing function *cons*, which was first used in functional languages to join two lists together. The following equivalence holds:

Chap. XXIV: Streams and Recursive Function Definitions

```
a = cons(first(a),rest(a))
```

Figure 24.7

Friedman and Wise (1976) have extended this concept by removing the requirement that both of the arguments of *cons* be available at the same instant of time. Their "lazy cons" function does not actually build a stream until both of its arguments are realized – before that it simply records a "promise" to do this. This allows us to imagine a stream being dynamically realized from the front, but with an unrealized back end. The end of the stream stays unrealized until the very end of the process, while the beginning is an ever-lengthening sequence of items.

Suppose we want to create a stream of extended details (where the quantity field has been extended by the unit price for the product): if the unit price were repeated in every IP, there would be no problem, as all the information that a particular call to the function requires is immediately available. Assigning selectors *p, s, d, q, u, e* to product number, salesman number, district number, quantity, unit price and extended price, respectively, we would then be able to define the extended details stream as follows:

```
F(S) = if S is null,
          then null
          else cons (E(first(S)), F(rest(S)))

E(x) = μ(p,p:x; s,s:x; d,d:x; u,u:x; e,q:x*u:x)
```

Figure 24.8

where *E* is a function which creates a single IP. The expression after the last semi-colon in the definition of *E(x)* would read in English: "set the extended price field of this IP to unit price multiplied by quantity". This would be fine except for the fact that unfortunately the unit price is not in the same IP as quantity!

In fact, in the case of the merged stream being processed by TR1, the unit price for a given product is held in only one IP per substream – namely the master IP for that product. We could define a function "PM" ("previous master"), but that would violate the rule that a function can only "see" an IP optionally followed by its successors. Instead, let us broaden the concept of *first* and *rest* to work with lists of lists (just as LISP and the other functional languages do).

This concept of lists of lists allows us in turn to take advantage of the fact that a stream can automatically be structured into substreams by a Collate type of component. Thus, suppose the output of a Collate run is as follows:

Chap. XXIV: Streams and Recursive Function Definitions

```
((m1,d11,d12),(m2,d21),(m3,d31,d32,d33))
```

Figure 24.9

where brackets represent bracket IPs. Then to convert this logically into a structure of lists and sublists, merely replace the open and close bracket IPs with curly brackets, i.e.

```
S:= {{m1,d11,d12},{m2,d21},{m3,d31,d32,d33}}
```

Figure 24.10

Now *first* and *rest* at the list level will return sublists, i.e.

```
first(S):= {m1,d11,d12}
```

Figure 24.11

and

```
rest(S):= {{m2,d21},{m3,d31,d32,d33}}
```

Figure 24.12

Note that, analogously to what we saw above with simple lists, *first* reduces the "nesting level" of a list by one level, while *rest* leaves it unchanged. The processing for extended details can now be shown succinctly as follows:

```
F(S) = if S is null,
       then null
       else cons(G(first(S)), F(rest(S)))
G(x) = G'(first(x),rest(x))
G'(x,y) = if y is null,
       then null
       else cons (E(x,first(y)), G'(x,rest(y)))
E(x,y) = μ(p,p:y; s,s:y; d,d:y; e,q:y*u:x)
```

Figure 24.13

Here the one-argument function G is defined in terms of a two-argument function G', whose first argument is always a master IP, and E now takes two arguments instead of only one.

- 246 -

Chap. XXIV: Streams and Recursive Function Definitions

In the above it can be seen that we will generate one output IP for each incoming detail (all IPs within a lowest level substream are details except the first one, which is the master). We can also see that x in G' acts as a place-holder for the master IP – it remains unchanged throughout the whole evaluation of function G.

Please note that, just because this particular application can be expressed in functional notation, it should not be assumed that FBP and functional notation are exactly equivalent – one obvious difference is that FBP allows cycles in its graphs. An FBP network is just that: a *net*, whereas the ideal graph for functional notation is essentially a "convergent" graph, where a number of functions are combined to produce one output. In the case of TR1, described above, the requirement for several output streams seems as though it would result in quite a bit of duplicate code.

Although we have been able to show some of these calculations in recursive form above, it appears that, in this particular case, the same information content can be expressed almost as succinctly using a quite simple notation which does not require any mathematical expertise at all, as suggested in Chapter 18. We are not going to have to persuade application developers to get their heads around recursive logic!

We have alluded above to the need to minimize the gap between the business requirement and the means of expressing it. What is the absolutely most concise way of expressing the requirement "build a stream of IPs containing extended quantities calculated as follows: ..." to a machine? In a 1990 article, K. Kahn and V. Saraswat suggest that it may not even have to be text as we know it – they propose that it may be possible to express both definitions and execution using a visual notation with almost no text at all, except for strings and comments. They point out that a major use of names is to make connections, something they are not particularly well suited for!

Part of my motivation in this chapter (and in this book as a whole) is to try to shake up some preconceptions about how programming has to be done! We cannot predict where the next breakthrough will be made, so it is important that we remain as open as possible to new ideas and new ways of doing things. The above few chapters also suggest some desirable characteristics that these new ways should have, so we can measure whether we are moving in the right direction or away from it. As I shall suggest in the last chapter of this book, everyone should have their minds stretched regularly, and this kind of exercise is nowhere more important than in the computer business!

Chap. XXV: Comparison between FBP and Object-Oriented Programming

Object-Oriented Programming (abbreviated in what follows to OO) has captured the imagination of a sizable, and influential, segment of the computer world, and understandably so, since it promises solutions to many of the problems which confront our industry. Not only does it have proven successes in the area of user interfaces, but it offers the very inviting prospect of libraries of reusable programming components which can be bought and sold on the open market. On the other hand, its very success has resulted in its being broadened until the term OO now covers a wide spectrum of different technologies with a few basic concepts in common. The literature on the subject is confusing to the uninitiated, and the more one reads about the subject, the more different variations one encounters, all rallying behind the Object-Oriented banner. Given all the excitement, I have spent some time trying to understand what is being offered and what it can do for us. This chapter is the result of this work, and I hope that some readers will find it helpful. Naturally, one of the effects of the diversity of different views about what OO is is that almost any comment I may make about it can be countered by someone who has a different view, but I base these observations mostly on the most widespread dialects of OO, so I believe they have some validity.

Before I go any further, I would like to say that I believe FBP shares many characteristics with OO, but at this point in time I hesitate to call it object-oriented, as there are certain fundamental differences of approach. However, after reading this chapter, some of my readers may conclude that any differences are basically surface differences, and that FBP is an object-oriented technology. Interestingly, Rob Strom, who developed NIL (Strom and Yemini 1983), described in the next chapter, which has strong similarities with FBP, told me that initially his group thought it important to disassociate themselves from OO, but later they came to feel that OO is now so

Chap. XXV: Comparison between FBP and Object-Oriented Programming

broad and there were so many similarities between NIL and OO that they are now actively working with the OO community.

OO is also another perfect example of the gap between business and academia that I talked about earlier: a lot of the interesting research work on OO is hard to apply to business needs, while business badly needs technologies which can ease the burden of developing and maintaining application code. When academics start using payroll applications for their examples, rather than rotating squares and rectangles, we will know that we have turned a corner!

To lay a foundation for discussing the differences and similarities between FBP and OO, we need to talk about a few of the basic concepts of OO for those not familiar with its concepts. The basis of all OO systems is the "object", which can be described as a semi-autonomous unit comprising both information and behaviour. OO objects are usually selected to reflect objects in the real world, and this relationship is a major source of the appeal of OO to application developers (as I mentioned above, it is also a characteristic of simulation languages, and also of IPs in FBP). Of course, since real world objects vary widely in size and complexity, it becomes far from trivial to decide what the objects in your universe of discourse are going to be. Just as it is in conventional programming, it is extremely important to do a good job of modelling your data before you start an OO design. The approach of Object-Oriented Analysis is somewhat different from that of conventional data modelling, but many workers in the field claim that proper modelling is even more important with OO as an error at this stage can adversely affect your whole design. This is also true of course for FBP.

One very powerful but non-obvious similarity between FBP and most OO implementations is that they both use "handles" to refer to objects (except in the case of primitive data types). Objects typically belong to "classes", which determine what attributes they have. When I request a new instance of a class, I get a set of instance variables "out there", and a handle to let me refer to it, just as we have seen happens when we create a new IP in FBP. We can then do things with this object handle, e.g. send messages to it or use it as a parameter in a message to another object. OO implementations also look after "garbage collection" of the object if its handle is no longer in use – this function could easily be added to FBP, but as I said earlier we're not sure whether it's desirable.

These object handles are what allows objects to talk to each other. Once we have selected classes of objects which will represent the real world objects of interest to our application, the next requirement is that these objects be able to communicate – in short, that their behaviour be cooperative. For this function, one of the earliest OO languages, Smalltalk, decided to use the term "message sending": Smalltalk objects are said to send messages to each other, resulting in activity on the part of the receiver, which may in turn send messages on to other objects. This also is a good fit with how we think of the real world, and may have contributed to Smalltalk's early popularity! Unfortunately, this Smalltalk terminology is misleading if it suggests any kind of asynchronous message flow, as Smalltalk's "message sending" is purely synchronous: the

Chap. XXV: Comparison between FBP and Object-Oriented Programming

sender has to wait until the receiver comes back with a reply. In today's terminology of parallel processes, the sender is "blocked" until the reply is received. This mechanism is essentially equivalent to a subroutine call, and this is in fact how it is implemented (with a subtle difference which we will discuss in the next paragraph). Smalltalk does support asynchronism by means of its fork and semaphore facilities, but its basic paradigm (and that of all of the more commonly used OO language) is synchronous and, as we have seen above, this restricts the developer in certain fundamental ways. In other OO languages, this technique is referred to as "method invocation", which is a more accurate description of what is really going on.

Method invocation is essentially an indirect subroutine call. The caller specifies an operation, and it is the class to which the receiver belongs (to use Smalltalk's terminology) which determines the actual piece of code which is executed. The method is part of a class and its address is not directly known to its caller. The caller specifies the function desired by naming an object (or the class itself) and the desired function, e.g. it might tell an object of class "rectangle" "rotate 90 degrees". The underlying software then uses the class information of the object to locate the actual code which is to be executed.

Although this seems very straight-forward in the classical OO examples, in practice I often found it really frustrating to me as a user, because it is inherently asymmetrical. Many of these requests involve more than one object, so you have to pick one as a receiver, and pass the others (or their handles) as parameters. This means that I, as the user, was never quite sure which object should be the receiver, and sometimes a series of similar functions would flip back and forth bewilderingly. For example, when displaying a series of data objects, I had to use several different messages, some of which were sent to the medium object with the data object as parameter, and some of which were the other way around. Another example: because of this problem, Smalltalk has problems with such simple commutative operations as + and *. Smalltalk V/PM has actually implemented a facility where, if an operation fails, the system reverses it and tries again. This function is only available to primitive operations, and is not even used there consistently. You also have to be careful not to write methods which go into a closed loop! Although some OO dialects, like CLOS, select the method based on the classes of more than one participating object, I would expect that allowing method selection to be based on several classes not only would result in even larger numbers of methods, but could result in significant management problems.

The indirect call characteristic of OO systems does provide a degree of configurability, since it is true that the caller does not have to know the name of the subroutine which will actually be executed. In addition, since different classes can support the same function identifier (sometimes called the "selector") in different ways, you get an additional useful characteristic which used to be called "genericity", but now more commonly "polymorphism". Some writers consider this the basic characteristic of OO systems (many others don't, though). However, the requester of a function does have to be able to locate the object that it wants to send the message to and also has

Chap. XXV: Comparison between FBP and Object-Oriented Programming

to specify the name of the desired function, e.g. "print" or "rotate", so we still have a configurability problem, once removed, unless the process of identifying the recipient object can be completely externalized from the requester's code. Remember, to achieve full configurability we need to be able to hook together components into different patterns without modifying them in any way, which also means having an independent specification of how things are connected. This can only be done today by having "high-level" methods which specify how things are hooked together. I find it interesting that, in most of the literature, the orientation of OO is very much towards building new classes, rather than towards reuse. Applications are developed mainly by cloning old methods, with its attendant problems, rather than by using black box code. The very idea of allowing a developer to modify the behaviour of an existing class, even if only for his or her own purposes, runs counter to the reuse concepts described earlier in this book.

Two last comments about polymorphism: my (limited) experience is that application developers don't use it very much, and its main triumphs seem to be in the GUI area. When asked to give examples of polymorphism, writers on OO always seem to pick "display" and "destroy". It may be that, in business, you don't often use the same messages for different classes. For instance, at the numeric value level, subtracting a number of days from a date is quite different from subtracting a date from another date, or a date from days (you can't), so the user has to be very aware of the types of the operands. To me this means that it doesn't buy you much to be able to call them all "-". In fact, in Smalltalk you often see message names like "subtractDaysFromDate", to tell the user what types the message expects (there is no type checking at compile time, so this is particularly important). The fact that, in Java or C#, the three "subtracts" mentioned above *can* all use the same method name might in fact be more confusing than helpful! Now, if you don't make much use of polymorphism, all you have left is the indirect call mechanism, which should be part of any programmer's toolkit anyway!

The following three attributes seem to be present in all OO systems to a greater or lesser extent, but they are given different weights by different writers: polymorphism, encapsulation and inheritance. We have already talked about polymorphism in OO. Polymorphism is also implicit in FBP as the same IP can be sent to different processes to achieve different results (and usually is), or components can be designed to accept a narrower or wider range of possible input formats as determined by reuse considerations. For instance, a Collate could accept only two input streams, or *n* input streams. It could accept just one input IP format, or many, determined by descriptors as we described above.

Inheritance is claimed by some to be the major characteristic of OO, and it is certainly an important concept, but my personal view and that of other people I have talked to is that its use should not be pushed to extremes. As long as inheritance is used to reflect the fact that things in real life can usually be grouped into classes which are subsets and supersets of other classes, it works quite well, and would in fact fit in quite well with the IP type concept that is implemented by descriptors in FBP. For instance, a file might contain records representing vehicles, which you

Chap. XXV: Comparison between FBP and Object-Oriented Programming

would then "specialize" into Volkswagens, Pontiacs, etc., based on a code within the common part of the records. Some processing would then be valid for all vehicles, other processing just for Pontiacs. If a message cannot be answered by a Pontiac, it is passed up to the "vehicle" level. Generally, as you move down the class hierarchy, you add more attributes – so start off with the set of attributes common to all vehicles. When you discover that a file record represents a Pontiac, you now know how to read the remaining attributes. This concept could in fact be added quite naturally to the descriptor mechanism of FBP.

The major difficulty with classification, however, is that, as soon as you try to become more analytical about what a class really is, things start to get more confusing. What seems clean and intuitive when applied to oak and fir trees becomes less clear when you look at it more closely. In fact, the OO concept of "class" seems to involve several different concepts which are combined in different combinations in different OO implementations. For those interested in this topic, there is an interesting recent article by W. Lalonde and J. Pugh (1991) which attempts to separate out the different ideas underlying the idea of "class". To give you some flavour of this debate, consider the difference between a square and a rectangle from an OO point of view. There was a recent interesting exchange of letters on this topic in Communications of the ACM, triggered by a letter from J. Winkler in the Aug '92 issue: in a hierarchy of geometrical shapes, a square is usually defined as a rectangle with all four sides equal. From one point of view, it is therefore a subclass of rectangle. However, subclasses usually have more instance variables (attributes) than their superclasses, while a square can be completely specified using only one measurement, instead of two. As if that weren't bad enough, OO rectangles can accept messages asking them to change individual dimensions, e.g. "set height to:". If you change a rectangle's height to be the same as its width, does it change to being a square, or must you create a new intermediate class – that of "square rectangles"? The point is that this is an example of specialization by the addition of constraints. There needs to be some general mechanism to specify constraints on objects, and we also have to decide whether to use the constraint, e.g. by allowing one dimension to change the other, or just use it to detect errors on the part of the client, e.g. "violates constraint – please check dimensions". The heading on Winkler's letter is "Objectivism: 'Class' Considered Harmful" (Winkler 1992)!

While human beings naturally try to classify the world to make it easier to grasp, the real world may resist being so classified. As a non-zoologist, I had imagined that all mammals had been neatly categorized long ago, so I was amused recently to run into this description of the difficulty zoologists encounter in trying to classify the hyrax (Krishtalka 1989): "They resemble a cross between a rhinoceros and a rodent. ...the hind limbs have three toes (rhinos), one of which ends in a long claw (rodents), the other two in hooflike nails (rhinos)...." The list goes on for a bit, then Krishtalka writes: "Such a smorgasbord of physical traits earned a dyspeptic taxonomy.... Recent opinion is divided between a horse-rhino-hyrax evolutionary connection and a sea cow-elephant-hyrax linkage." The latter seems to have won out, with hyraxes being closely related to, but forming an outgroup to, an assemblage of elephants, sirenians, and some extinct orders – see the

Chap. XXV: Comparison between FBP and Object-Oriented Programming

Wikipedia article (*http://en.wikipedia.org/w/index.php?title=Hyrax&oldid=337804597*). While this kind of confusion can actually be amusing, our tendency to make snap classifications and then act as if they were the whole truth may actually be harmful, either to ourselves or to others: while everyone today with a reasonable education knows that whales are mammals, not fish, the old mental association may be what allows officials to refer to "harvesting" whales. We can certainly talk about "harvesting" herring, but we don't talk this way about tigers, cattle, butterflies or people, so why whales? If you are interested in this area of linguistics, you should take a look at the work of the linguist B.L. Whorf (1956), alluded to elsewhere in this book, on how the words we use affect our actions.

As we move into the world of business programming, we run into situations where class hierarchies may seem very natural at first sight, but in fact are really not appropriate. For instance, it might seem natural to assign a bank account object to one of a set of account type classes: SAVING, CHEQUING or COMMERCIAL. This way, a deposit could be sent to an account and automatically cause the right piece of code to be invoked as a method. While this seems quite attractive at first, in fact, at best this would result in a number of very similar methods which would have to be separately managed and maintained. At worst, it could make it very difficult to develop new, hybrid offerings, such as a chequing account which offers daily interest. Banks have found that it is better to make this kind of processing "feature-oriented" – one should decide what are the atomic features of an account, such as interest-bearing or not, bankbook vs. statement, cheques to be returned or not, and then implement them under switch control to produce the various types of account processing. Hendler gives a somewhat similar example (1986), using professions. He points out that while professions are often used as examples of classes, they may not be mutually exclusive – a person might be both a professor and a doctor – so a person may carry attributes which relate to both of these professions. Mixed classes provide a possible solution, but this technique has problems as well. In FBP, the "tree" technique seems a natural way to implement this kind of thing (see Chapter 12, on Trees – page 120), as the data associated with each profession can be held in separate IPs attached to the IP for the person.

In spite of what I have said above, I do believe that one of the most important contributions OO has made towards changing the way application design is done is that it has moved data to the foreground. Programmers coming to FBP from conventional programming have to undergo precisely the same paradigm shift: from concentrating on process to concentrating on data. Typically, in FBP, as we have seen in the foregoing chapters, we design the IPs and IP streams first and then decide what processes are needed to convert between the different data streams. In OO you have to decide on the object classes, and then decide what messages each class should be able to respond to.

For many OO enthusiasts it is this concept of "encapsulation" which is the central concept of OO. In fact, this is not a new concept at all (one of Dijkstra's famous remarks was that programs

Chap. XXV: Comparison between FBP and Object-Oriented Programming

should be "like pearls"), and Parnas wrote one of the seminal articles on encapsulation in the early '70s (Parnas 1972). Encapsulation simply means the idea of having the vulnerable insides of something protected by a protective outer coating, sort of like a soft-centred candy (or a turtle). This is obviously a good design principle, and the reader will notice that FBP components in fact have this characteristic, as they are free to decide what IPs they will accept for processing, and can do more or less validation of their input data, depending on how reliable their designers judge their data to be. Encapsulation can also be implemented at the network level, by having outer processes protect inner ones, or by inserting transformer processes into the network. This is a better solution than building the validation into every component, as the processing component can just provide the basic function, and the designer can request more or less validation by adding or removing editing processes. In OO, an object is encapsulated together with all of its methods, which involves predicting all the services that an object may ever be requested to perform. This, however, is very hard to do, and may result in a never-ending stream of requests for enhancements as new requirements come up. How can one predict all the functions that, say, steel might be used for? Remember Wayne Stevens' story about an airline attendant using a hearing set to tie back a curtain (recounted elsewhere in the book)!

In FBP, we always encapsulate processes and can also encapsulate IPs if desired – the former occurs automatically as nobody has access to the internals of a process except the supplier: users can only know its inputs, outputs, parametrization and some behavioral aspects, such as what it does when it sees a closed output port. As far as protecting IPs is concerned, a number of techniques are available, as required by the designer, and it is quite possible to have IPs whose structure is never seen by application code. However, FBP does not insist that we predict all the processes that will ever handle a particular IP type. Rather, the emphasis is on deciding which IP types a given process will accept or generate. Instead of having to predict all the uses that steel might be put to, we only have to decide which materials we can build a bridge out of. The latter seems a much more manageable problem!

Because Smalltalk's "message sending" terminology sounds like data flow, it is often thought that OO should be relevant to distributed systems design, but in fact, as Gelernter and Carriero point out in an article analyzing the differences between their Linda system (described in the next chapter) and OO (Carriero and Gelernter 1989), it is actually irrelevant to it. In fact, as they say, a truly distributed message passing system has to be built on top of an OO system, just as it does on top of a conventional subroutine-based approach. Here is a quote from a paper by another of the gurus of this area, Barbara Liskov, and her coworkers: "We conclude that the combination of synchronous communication with static process structure imposes complex and indirect solutions, and therefore that it is poorly suited for applications such as distributed programs in which concurrency is important" (Liskov et al. 1986). It is interesting that "basic" FBP occupies the "asynchronous, static" quadrant of Figure 2-1 of this article, while the addition of dynamic subnets moves FBP into the "asynchronous, dynamic" quadrant, which the authors of this article say is unoccupied to the best of their knowledge. Interestingly, they go on to say, "Although such languages may exist, this combination appears to provide an embarrassment of riches not needed for expressive power." Our experience, on the contrary, is that adding a dynamic capability to asynchronous communication can be extremely productive!

Most OO implementations are synchronous, so the basic primitive is the indirect call through the class. As I said elsewhere in this book, our experience with FBP tells us that the subroutine call is not the best foundation on which to build business applications. A "call" can in fact be simulated very nicely by issuing an FBP "send" followed by a "receive". This will have the effect of suspending the requester on the "receive" until the downstream process returns an answer, just as a "call" suspends the caller. Gelernter and Carriero make the same point and go still further in the above-mentioned article:

> "In our experience, processes in a parallel program usually don't care what happens to their data, and when they don't, it is more efficient and *conceptually more apt* [my italics] to use an asynchronous operation like Linda's "out" than a synchronous procedure call.... It's trivial, in Linda, [or FBP] to implement a synchronous remote-procedure-call-like operation in terms of "out" and "in" [FBP "send" and "receive"]. There is no reason we know of, however, to base an entire parallel language on this one easily programmed but not crucially important special case."

A call which spans multiple machines is sometimes called Remote Procedure Call (RPC), and a number of the people working on distributed systems have pointed out the inappropriateness (as well as poor performance) of this algorithm when building complex distributed systems. K. Kahn and M. Miller (1988) point out the problems of basing a design for distributed systems on RPC. They also stress the desirability of having a single paradigm which scales up from tightly coordinated processes within a single processor to largely independent cooperating processes, perhaps on different machines.

FBP and Linda (we will talk about Linda in more detail in the next chapter) are fundamentally asynchronous, whereas conventional OO is synchronous. The real difference here is that, although the methods of an object are the only routines which can have access to the object's internal data, *when* these methods are to be executed is determined by other objects, whose methods in turn are driven by other objects, and so on. While such synchronous objects show autonomy of data and behaviour, they do not have autonomy of control. As such, I feel that synchronous OO objects are more similar to FBP IPs than they are to FBP processes. In a OO application (unless it uses multithreading – which is complex), there is actually only one process. This can lead to counter-intuitive solutions. For example, in a recent book about C++ (Swan 1991), in an example involving a simulation of people using elevators, the class Building (which is really running the whole simulation) apparently has to be treated as a subclass of the class Action. The problem, of course, is that there is only one process, external to all the objects, which is basically "Run the simulation".

Chap. XXV: Comparison between FBP and Object-Oriented Programming

If you cast your mind back to the Telegram problem described in Chapter 8 (this is the problem where text is read in from a file and must be written out in records of a different size, without breaking individual words), you will remember that the conventional programming solution required several of the routines to be invoked repeatedly using handles to maintain continuity. This solution maps very nicely onto an OO "collaboration diagram" which changes subroutine calls into "message sends" and "replies" between objects (remember the caveat about what "message sending" actually means). Here is basically Figure 8.7, recast into OO terms (I have created 4 "stream" objects: 2 word streams and 2 I/O streams):

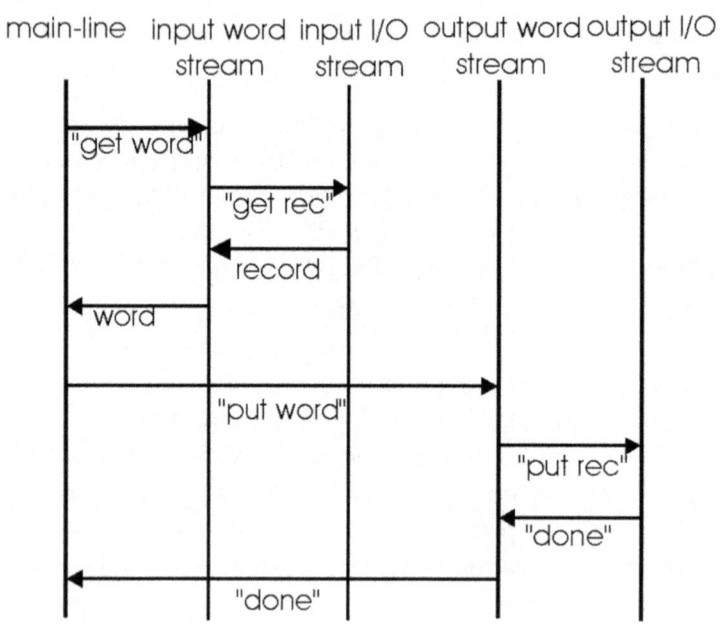

Figure 25.1

While this solves the problem of subroutines which have to maintain continuity between successive invocations (the infrastructure maintains the continuity), this is still a purely synchronous solution. Now let's show an FBP solution to this problem (from Figure 8.2):

Chap. XXV: Comparison between FBP and Object-Oriented Programming

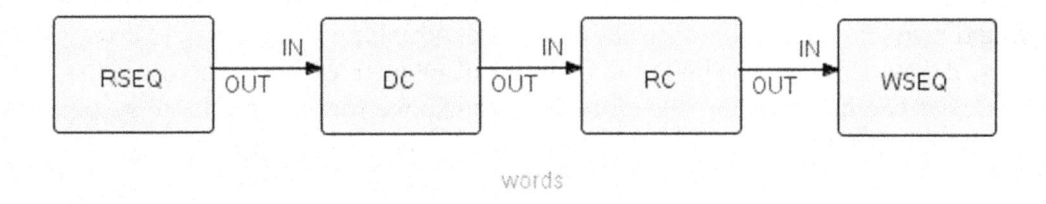

Figure 25.2

In this diagram, RSEQ means "Read Sequential", WSEQ means "Write Sequential", DC is "DeCompose" and RC is "ReCompose".

Not only is this much easier to grasp intuitively, but it uses reusable components; also it is very obvious how the function can be extended if the designer ever needs to.

I have tried to show in the earlier chapters that asynchronism is liberating, and I hope I have managed to convey some feeling for its power. In fact, many of the leading thinkers in OO also realize the need to add asynchronism to OO to relax the tight constraints imposed by the von Neumann machine. Many of today's advanced machine designs in fact require these asynchronous design concepts (for a survey, see a recent (1990) article by Gul Agha). Agha uses the term Concurrent OOP (COOP) to describe his approach, which combines the concept of "actors" with OO. Another term you may run into is "active objects", which *act*, as opposed to "passive objects", which *are acted on*. In modern user interfaces we already see functions which behave much like active objects, e.g. printers (for printing objects), shredders (for destroying objects), and so on. You just drag and drop the icon (small graphical symbol) of an object, e.g. a file, onto a shredder icon – this is like pressing the start button on a trash compactor. Before it starts, however, the shredder politely asks you if you really want to do this. This is another characteristic of this kind of object: they can independently gather information for themselves. Once the shredder or printer has started, the user is then free to attend to other things.

Another researcher who feels that basic OO has to be broadened by the addition of asynchronism is de Champeaux at Hewlett-Packard. He is looking at the use of a trigger-based model for inter-object communication. Here is a quote from an article about OO research directions that appeared in the Communications of the ACM: "This model [where the sender is suspended until the receiver sends the result back] is not rich enough to describe all the causal connections between objects an analyst needs to model." (Wirfs-Brock and Johnson 1990) Interestingly, de Champeaux's work suggests that a richer interaction model than (data-less) triggers is necessary. One of the forms he is looking at is "send-no-wait" (where data and the trigger are

Chap. XXV: Comparison between FBP and Object-Oriented Programming

simultaneously transmitted). One of the chapters in a recent book (Kim and Lochovsky 1989), is called "Concurrent Object-Oriented Programming Languages", written by C. Tomlinson and M. Scheevel, and provides an excellent survey of this new thinking about ways to combine OO with concurrency. Again, Brad Cox, who is the inventor of Objective-C and one of the acknowledged gurus of OO, has come to feel that OO alone is not adequate for building large systems. He came to the conclusion that FBP concepts should be implemented on top of Objective-C, and then could be used as building blocks for applications. Using a hardware analogy, he refers to Objective-C as "gate-level", and FBP as "chip-level". He had in fact already started experimenting with processes and data flows independently when he found out about our work and contacted me. He has advanced the idea that the time is ripe for a "Software Industrial Revolution", much like the previous Industrial Revolution which has so totally transformed the world we live in over the past couple of centuries. Like Brad, I believe many of the tools for this revolution are already in place, but many writers have remarked on the enormous inertia of the software industry – this has always struck me as ironic, given the incredible rate of change in the rest of the computer industry.

Let us try to show with an example some other differences between synchronous OO and FBP. It is quite hard to find an example which lets one compare the two technologies fairly, as the synchronous orientation of most OO work means that their examples tend to be synchronous as well. However, given that batch programs are not going to go away (in fact, there are good theoretical reasons why they never will), I will use as an example Brad Cox's example of calculating the total weight of a collection of objects in a container: say, pens and pencils in a pencil holder. While being totally procedural, it is an example of the "small batch" logic which is also handled very well by FBP.

The basic design mechanism in this kind of procedure is the collaboration diagram, of which we gave an example above. At any point in time we will have three objects: a requester, a container and an object within it. The interaction is then as shown in Figure 25.3.

I can still remember my feeling of dismay at seeing the right-to-left, returning flows in the above diagram – these mark this diagram as being call logic, rather than flow logic. Every pair of lines represents a client-server relationship – OO people call this "delegation", but it is not delegation as humans practise it. Rather it is like standing over someone, and saying, "Now type this line; now type this line". In fact, client-server relationships make much more sense when the relationship is asynchronous, allowing the client to go about his/her business while the server is doing its thing. Human beings don't see any point in delegating work to others unless it frees them up to do something else. This kind of interaction is also not "cooperative" as FBP understands the word. In FBP all the processes are at the same level – there is no boss.

Chap. XXV: Comparison between FBP and Object-Oriented Programming

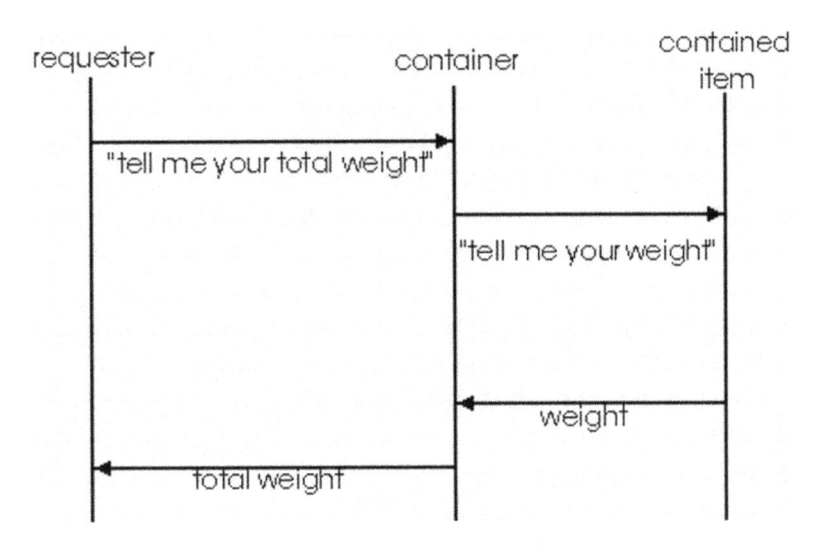

Figure 25.3

In the above diagram, while there may well be situations where either object can drive the other, one of the objects still has to be the driver (as long as one stays with passive objects only). There is very definitely a boss, and it is the object at the far left.

The logic for the "compute total weight" method of the Container object is a loop which steps through its contained items. It could be described by the following pseudocode:

```
set total weight to tare weight (empty weight)
get first contained item a
do as long as get is successful
        send message to a to get its weight
        add result to total weight
        get next contained item a
enddo
return total weight
```

Figure 25.4

This method needs functions to "get first" item and "get next" item within the container. These functions would return an item's handle, plus an indication of whether the request was successful. Once an object has been located, the container can send messages to it.

Although the same general logic can step through a variety of different collection structures (you basically need different method subroutines for each collection type), there is a basic assumption in the above logic, namely that all the items in the collection are available at the same time. As

Chap. XXV: Comparison between FBP and Object-Oriented Programming

we have seen in previous chapters, this is not really necessary (since only one item is handled at a time), and may not even be possible. In addition, our experience with FBP tells us that this function should really be designed as a reusable component which is usable as is, in object code form, without needing any modification or recompiling. Most programming systems tend to present their ideas from the standpoint of someone writing new code, whereas FBP experience tells us that people don't want to write new code if they can get something off the shelf which does the desired job. Key to this (and also to being able to distribute such systems, now or later) is the requirement to avoid calls – as we pointed out above, the subroutine call mechanism forces tight coupling, whereas we want the data being generated by a procedure to go *onwards*, not *back*. The only way I know of to achieve all these goals is to design the function as a stand-alone function which uses ports to communicate with its neighbours. This results in a component with the following shape (you will recognize this as a "reference" type of component):

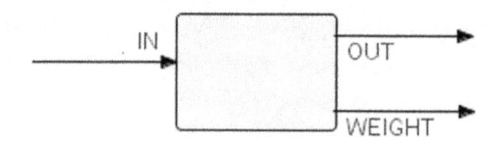

Figure 25.5

This component accepts a stream or multiple substreams of IPs and generates one IP containing the total weight (or one per substream). Since the container has weight (its tare weight), let's provide it as the first IP of the (sub)stream. The logic of the above process can then be represented by the following:

```
        create IP to contain total weight
        receive from port IN using handle a
        set total weight (in weight IP) to (tare) weight of a
        send a to port OUT if connected
                else drop a
        receive from port IN using handle a
        do as long as receive is successful
                add a's weight to total weight
                send a to port OUT if connected
                        else drop a
                receive from port IN using handle a
        enddo
        send weight IP to WEIGHT port
```

Figure 25.6

- 260 -

Chap. XXV: Comparison between FBP and Object-Oriented Programming

Not surprisingly, it has the same general structure as the method pseudocode shown above, but there are certain key differences. The logic shown above can process any data stream for which "*a*'s weight" is defined for each IP in the stream. Incoming IPs are passed on to OUT (if it is connected), and the weight goes in an IP of its own to the port called WEIGHT. Remember Gelernter and Carriero's remark that "processes in a parallel program usually don't care what happens to their data." Since "receive" and "send" can be suspended until data or queue slots, respectively, are available, this routine works even though not all IPs are in storage at the same time. We now have a portable component which can compute the total weight of any stream of IPs for which "weight" is defined.

In addition, in OO, this function has to be a method contained in any collection class for which you might need to perform this function, whereas in FBP, once this function has been built, we can use it (just by referencing it in a network) on any data stream which conforms to certain conventions, without having to modify the definitions of any of the classes involved. As we said above, "*a*'s weight" has to be defined for each IP in the stream. However, we can even parametrize the attribute name, so we can use the same object code to get a "total *x*" from all data streams for which "*x*" is defined. Instead of having a myriad small, special purpose, methods for every different class in the system, we arrive at robust, flexible, functions which are highly portable, e.g. (in this case) a function to determine the "total *x*" for any *x* which is defined for the IPs in the stream. In fact, we could even generalize this function still more: you could use a very similar structure to get the maximum or minimum weight of all the contained items. Of course, in this case "tare weight" would not be too relevant, but whether we are adding the contained item weights together or taking their maximum could also be provided as a parameter to our component.

To recast this function in OO terms, we would need to provide some kind of configurability. Assuming that we follow OO and make the `send` and `receive` functions "messages" to objects, then the objects `send` and `receive` talk to could actually belong to any of the following object types: other processes, streams, connections or ports. The only one of these which would not reduce the component's portability would be ports, unless the names of the other objects were passed in as parameters to the process. However, the latter alternative would clutter up the component's parameters with connection information. Port names would be the way a process identifies its "own" ports, and could be instantiated by a function very like THREADS's "define ports" service, which would accept port names and return an object handle. The "compute total weight" process logic can then send messages to its ports, to do receiving or sending, using normal OO syntax. We will of course need some kind of scheduler or "connection" engine to connect our processes together using these ports together with a list of connections, to give us our desired configurable modularity, but this is outside the component logic.

The last thing we need to decide before we can recast our component in OO terms is how to determine the "x" of a given IP. There is no problem conceptually with making this a normal OO

Chap. XXV: Comparison between FBP and Object-Oriented Programming

"message", as "get first" and "get next" will have returned a handle to an IP, which we can then send messages to. However, how should we name the function of obtaining "x" for the subject IP? Based on FBP experience, I suggest that the simplest technique is to have a generic "get" and "set" function which accepts the field name as a parameter (or even multiple field names to reduce the overhead). OO purists may feel that it is better to have multiple "get" and "set" methods – one of each per field – but this leads to a very large number of almost identical method subroutines.

Whether we implement attributes as OO methods or by using subroutines hung off the descriptor, we can do other things than just retrieve real data. We could also use these techniques to make sure related field values are kept in step (data integrity), or to support "virtual fields" (fields which are computed as they are needed). Thus a request for the number of children of Joe could scan Joe's attached IPs (where Joe is a "tree" structure) and return the result. The requester need not know whether the field is real or virtual. Such a mechanism would let the data designer either go for computation speed at the expense of having to maintain duplicate data, or, on the other hand, go for highly consistent data at some cost in performance. Another capability is what is sometimes referred to by the name "daemons": this involves the ability to automatically trigger events when a field value changes or passes some maximum or minimum. When combined with asynchronism, this could be a very powerful structuring tool for building business applications.

One important topic I want to address is the issue of granularity. All discussions of both OO and FBP eventually come up against this topic: how "big" should FBP processes and OO classes be? The lower end of FBP granularity is determined by the fact that IPs normally have multiple fields and often represent objects in the outside world. You could chop a business IP up into one IP per field, but then you would have to pay a lot of overhead to recombine it to write it on a file, database, screen or report.

As I talked to people about OO, however, I came to realize that there is one area which OO does address which is a problem which has been worrying me for several years: the need to be able to prevent illegal operations on data fields, e.g. to stop currency values from being multiplied together, or dates from being added (this was referred to as a problem above). However, this ability can only be taken advantage of if one uses classes, rather than numeric primitives – and even OO languages do not *force* the coder to do this. As we said before, the vast majority of HLLs are based on mathematical ideas of data, and treat numeric fields as dimensionless. They thus cannot provide intelligent handling of most of the numeric values one runs into in business applications – these are either dimensioned numeric quantities (like money or weight) or are complex values (e.g. dates). In HLLs, all these types of data are compressed into a single numeric format. In OO all accesses to data values are (or should be) via methods, so we are not forced to throw away our knowledge about what fields really represent.

If all of the above seems unduly negative, it is mainly that I feel a need to put OO into a proper perspective. OO is a simple technique, whose main importance is that it has started a sea-change

Chap. XXV: Comparison between FBP and Object-Oriented Programming

in the way programmers think. However, if we stop at this point, eventually frustration on the part of programmers is going to win out over the initial excitement. While I recognize that learning and using OO is an important learning experience, in its present form, without configurable modularity, the result will only be marginally more maintainable code. Configurable modularity can be added to OO, as can multithreading, just as they can be to conventional programming, and it is exactly the combination of these which starts to open up interesting possibilities.

In an FBP environment, it is possible and, I believe, could be interesting to be able to mix processes running different languages, some OO and some non-OO. For instance, one process might be running a pure OO language, another one an HLL, another C/C++, and so on. Such a mixture would require that IP layouts become a public interface between processes, but note that this public interface should preferably be IPs associated with their descriptions. We now have a natural role for IP descriptors: to allow us to retain the IP attributes' domain information, which could be exploited by OO, across processes which do not use this information (e.g. ones written in existing HLLs). OO processes could in fact be protected by interface processes which turn IPs into some format acceptable to the OO language chosen. XML seems to have become a de facto standard, in spite of its shortcomings, but maybe the combination of FBP and OO will suggest other possibilities. Such a combination of processes could even be packaged as a composite component, giving what seems to me to be the best of all worlds!

Wayne Stevens suggested a few years ago that objects might split very naturally into "process-like" and "data-like" objects, where, essentially, process-like objects would correspond to FBP processes, and data-like objects to IPs. In the phrasing I used above, data-like objects are passive, while process-like objects are active. Process-like (active) objects are able to act without necessarily always having to be triggered by an event external to them. In traditional OO systems, all objects are passive, and the whole assemblage is triggered by one (non-object) trigger that starts the whole thing running. This approach is obviously going to suffer from the same difficulties as traditional hierarchic non-FBP programs. If, instead, some of the set of objects can be active, we can start to capitalize on our experience with FBP. Having process (active) objects and data (passive) objects looks like a very good way to combine the strengths of these two complementary technologies. In fact, with the appropriate infrastructure, different objects can be coded in different languages. Since, as we have shown above, one of the basic reuse mechanisms in FBP is the external definition of connections, we could also add a "driver" and "network" object: this would be an active object using the network definition as reference data.

A number of writers in the OO field have started to explore the possibilities of active objects. In Chapter 1 of a collection of essays compiled by Kim and Lochovsky (1989), O. Nierstrasz makes the point that systems which mix active and passive objects would not be uniform, and this seems a valid point. However, one possible solution is offered by a system called Emerald (Black et al.

Chap. XXV: Comparison between FBP and Object-Oriented Programming

1986), which was designed for implementing highly distributed systems, and which maintains uniformity across all its objects by allowing every object to have a single process in addition to methods. Not all objects may activate their processes, but the potential exists for them to do so. This suggests a very workable generic structure for all the objects in a combined FBP/OO hybrid.

OO research and development seems to have entered a stage of accelerated growth, and it is very exciting to me that some of the newer work bears an uncanny resemblance to FBP! A dichotomy seems to be developing between the synchronous and asynchronous OO approaches, just like the one we have seen in non-OO. A number of OO researchers believe it is the asynchronous approaches which will turn out to have the most to contribute to the programming art in the long run. More and more of these people are discovering the power of active processes to broaden OO and make it better match the real world. Tsichritzis et al. (1987) have used the concept of active objects in knowledge processing – they call their objects KNOs (KNowledge Objects). KNOs can also have a complex structure, analogously to FBP composite components. Still more recently, Nierstrasz, Gibbs and Tsichritzis have collaborated on another paper on Component-Oriented Software Development (1992) which approaches FBP even more closely, but is still based solidly on traditional OO concepts. While their terminology is different from that of FBP, many close correspondences between the two can be established. They use the term "script" to mean "a set of software components with compatible input and output ports connected". While scripts can be data flow or object-oriented, the data flow version corresponds closely with FBP networks. "Scripting" means the construction of scripts, so the term "visual scripting" is defined as "the interactive construction of applications from prepackaged, plug-compatible software components by direct manipulation and graphical editing". In their article they talk about reusable components, ports, SACs (scripts as components) and visual scripting – all ideas that have direct counterparts in FBP. The same article goes on to describe an application of these concepts to multimedia called the "visual museum". "Media objects" (which are active objects, i.e. processes) work on "media values", which are

> "...temporal sequences.... Media objects produce, consume and transform media values.... Media objects, in turn, are grouped into multimedia objects by specifying the flow of values from one object to another – we call this flow composition.... flow composition actually produces applications...".

Another remark in the same paper that I found interesting was,

> "One benefit of flow-based composition is that new functionality can be added, or removed, by simple modifications to the script".

In the conclusion of their article they stress a number of the points I have made elsewhere in this book: the difficulty of generalizing to create good reusable components, and the economic and project planning impediments to producing such components. This equation of objects =

processes seems to be gaining acceptance: the article describing A'UM (Yoshida and Chikayama 1988) matter-of-factly describes the system as consisting of "streams" and "objects" (for more on this interesting system see the next chapter). They then go on to say that of course streams can be objects also – however, in this case, the object is stretched out in time, which will be awkward to implement in most existing OO languages, to say the least.

From an FBP point of view, the concept which I feel is missing from traditional OO (not from the work on active objects) is the concept of "transformer" processes (many of the media objects described in the above-mentioned paper are explicit transformers). As Nan Shu (1985) has pointed out, much of business programming has to do with transforming data from one format to another. The paradigm of passing a stream of data packets through a transforming process seems to fit very naturally with this image, but this does not seem to fit well with traditional OO. Rich Hickey makes a related point in his keynote speech at JVM Languages Summit 2009, called "Are We There Yet?": *http://www.infoq.com/presentations/Are-We-There-Yet-Rich-Hickey*, in which he stressed that business applications usually work with long-running *processes*, rather than side-effects-free subroutines. Since the traditional OO paradigm specifies that only the methods of a class should know an object's internal state (which is presumably held in some canonical form), this would seem to imply that transformations are only of interest at the boundaries of an application (when one is bringing in or outputting "foreign" files, reports or screen data). In practice, as businesses build bridges between more and more of their applications, we will spend quite a lot of time converting data between different formats. Some of these applications will be vendor-provided, so the users will have even less control over their data formats. If these applications are OO, how will their classes be merged with the corresponding classes of the users? Data conversions will also be required for many of the common data transportation techniques – this will become more and more important as we move towards distributed systems. Thus, you might decide to convert binary data into character format to simplify transportation between PCs and hosts. Descriptor-driven transformers in an FBP environment will provide a simpler paradigm and will help to make all this run smoothly. Interestingly, in the paper I was talking about above, the authors also feel that multi-media applications will require a wide range of transformations of media values into different forms, depending on the various uses they need to be put to.

I found it significant that many of the media objects in the paper on Component-Oriented Software Development have names which are verbs, rather than nouns, e.g. render, interpret, provide (in FBP, processes are usually verbs, while IPs are nouns, e.g. customer, account, department). Traditional OO essentially works with nouns, with the verbs relegated to the methods – this has the effect that, for instance, to record the fact that a student has taken a course, you express this by having the student send messages to the course, or the course to the student. From an FBP viewpoint, it seems more natural to handle this with a process which transforms the student in well-defined ways. So an OO approach which is perhaps closer to FBP's way of thinking would be to send both student and course to a separate "attacher" object, which has the

Chap. XXV: Comparison between FBP and Object-Oriented Programming

ability to associate students and courses. This object would be an active version of the general category of object called "dictionaries" in OO languages. These are two different, not necessarily incompatible, viewpoints.

The many arguments in favour of the asynchronous process approach to applications design lead me to believe that, if OO starts to be used for business production programming, it will be the concept of active objects (process objects) which will turn out to be more productive for OO than the original indirect call mechanism. To me active objects seem to be a natural evolution of OO in a direction which will eventually converge with FBP. If one can say that conventional OO (static objects) provide autonomy of data and autonomy of logic, then active objects also provide autonomy of control. Without the last, I believe it is not possible to build the systems we need in the future.

After I wrote the above, I came across the following comment by C. Ellis and S. Gibbs in Kim and Lochovsky (1989):

> "In the future, as we move beyond object-oriented programming, it is likely that one of the useful enduring concepts is that of 'active objects'."

I agree absolutely! Over the next few years I believe that we will see more and more OO proponents talking about the advantages of active objects. I applaud this as it will expose FBP to a wider audience, but it may leave the programming public with the erroneous impression that FBP is a rather complex extension of the basic OO set of concepts. In reality, as I have shown in the foregoing pages, FBP can in fact be implemented with quite simple software and yet yield great gains in productivity, while OO can only do this if it incorporates advanced concepts which seem to be converging with FBP. To quote Ellis and Gibbs again on this matter:

> "Although we foresee that object-oriented programming, as we know it today, is close to its deathbed, *we foresee tremendous possibilities in the future of active object systems* [my italics].... Vive l'objet actif."

The celebration may perhaps be premature, but, if you have read this far, you will have some idea why so many of us feel so excited about these concepts!

Before leaving this topic, I would like to make a last point which I consider vitally important: any evaluation of a programming technology must be done in the context of building and maintaining real business applications. There are only three reasons I am aware of for adopting a new technology: performance, productivity and maintainability. Even if a new technology allows us to get applications working faster or sooner, if it does not result in significant gains in maintainability, it may not be worth the effort. As I said earlier, we have to try out potential tools on the day-to-day concerns of business programmers, rather than on artificial, theoretical puzzles, no matter how intellectually stimulating they may be! When we have an OO application which

Chap. XXV: Comparison between FBP and Object-Oriented Programming

processes every one of over 5,000,000 accounts 5 days a week at a bank, is easy to maintain and does not use prohibitive amounts of resources, we will truly be able to say that OO has come of age!

Although most of the above was written 15 years ago, it seems to have stood the test of time! Recently (November, 2009), Henri Frilund wrote me a note from Finland stating in part:

> This is the reason people are now looking into things like FBP and Erlang [Erlang was designed by Joe Armstrong for Ericsson, explicitly with concurrency in mind – more about it later]. Synchronous OOP applications won't scale to multi-core systems! And the cores are multiplying as we speak..recently I heard that NVIDIA [*http://www.nvidia.com/content/global/global.php*] is planning to create a 3D accelerator with 512 cores. Object networks that are glued together with synchronous message passing don't scale and that is a real problem. The way I and my colleague see it is the future will be asynchronous in one way or other and FBP seems an excellent paradigm for writing asynchronous systems.
>
> It's amazing that it was known 15 years ago that synchronous OOP solutions won't distribute or scale and yet here we are, trying to put the square peg into a round hole. In fact a large part of the J2EE infrastructure (where the big money also is), is about trying to make OOP solutions distributed and scalable.
>
> All in all I think the chapter is very much relevant and the only things that might disturb a new reader are the old references [many of which have been removed in the latest edition!], but then again I'm not sure if critical assessment of OOP has been done at all in the past 15 years..

Thanks, Henri!

Chap. XXVI: Related Concepts and Forerunners

This chapter lists various projects that have similarities to FBP – as of 1994, when the first edition of this book was written. For the current edition, I will be pruning the list drastically, to try to reflect systems that are still active and/or being heavily cited in the literature. In the following chapter, I will be talking about systems that seem to share concepts with FBP (whether or not their documenters give credit to FBP or not!).

My main problem with trying to give a good overview is that new software is appearing faster than I can keep pace with it! Every time I open a magazine or click on a web site I see work that has resonances with FBP, which I therefore resolve to read. Then I have to follow up *their* bibliography, which results in more to read, and so on!

In this chapter and the next one, I will summarize what I regard as the salient features of each item, although I may have misunderstood their thrust. In most cases I have had no contact with the authors, and I will inevitably tend to look at their work through FBP-coloured glasses. Please contact me to exchange ideas or to throw brickbats!

FBP seems to me to stand on three main "legs":

1. asynchronous processes
2. data packets (IPs) with a lifetime of their own
3. external definition of connections

You will find one or two of these in many systems, but it is the combination of all three which makes FBP unique. And even when you find all three of these items present in a system, you will often find that they have been used to address a particular area or problem, such as distributed systems. I believe many of their developers have not yet understood the potential of this

Chap. XXVI: Related Concepts and Forerunners

combination for improving *all* application development.

The first system listed below is not even an application development system, but a simulation system. In the preceding chapters we have often remarked that FBP allows simulations to be "grown" into full-scale applications, and the developers of GPSS saw this as a very intriguing possibility.

GPSS (General Purpose Simulation System)

This is a simulation system developed by Geoffrey Gordon and his team at IBM in the early 60s. I am including it because it actually shares all three characteristics listed above (the data packets were called "transactions"), and it was a very successful system for simulations. I also include it because it profoundly influenced my thinking about how to do application development. Gordon had hopes of extending it to run as an operating system control program, and did quite a bit of work in this area. Many people have also dreamed that it should eventually be possible to "grow" an application from its simulation, and in fact the GPSS had some success with this as far back as 1963 (nearly 50 years ago!). With FBP of course this process is now very straight-forward.

MASCOT (A Modular Approach to Software Construction, Operation and Test) (K. Jackson and H. Simpson 1975)

This system, built by Ken Jackson and his team at the Royal Radar Establishment in England, shares all three of the above characteristics also. This is listed chiefly because of its timing. Jackson's motivations for developing MASCOT were similar to ours, plus a desire to make interrupt-driven software resemble the remainder of the computer load, as a lot of their signals work involves handling asynchronous interrupts. In MASCOT an IP is called a "message", as in much of the work listed below, and a connection a "channel". The basic MASCOT unit of software is a subnet, called a "subsystem", and is drawn graphically, and then converted into a textual representation. MASCOT's services are somewhat lower level than FBP's, but its channel management is very similar overall. Here's a quote on how well the developers feel they met their objectives:

> " ... the overall philosophy of MASCOT operation ... is to process data when it is available, to explicitly wait when no data is available and to pass on a stimulus to adjacent data users when data of interest is passed on.... Further, the use of the control queue within the interrupt handling software enables the expression of interrupt handling software to be unusually straightforward. The elimination of polling and searching within the kernel is complete... "Conclusion "MASCOT provides a very basic yet sound machine-independent kernel to produce a suitable environment for real-time programming.... Finally MASCOT looks to be a promising base upon which to build the high integrity systems which are the subject of current research."

What I find interesting here is the early application of FBP-like concepts to signal processing.

Chap. XXVI: Related Concepts and Forerunners

Today there is a a whole discipline of Digital Signal Processing (DSP), which appears to be an excellent match with FBP concepts.

CHIEF

This seems a classic case of parallel development, as this work must have been going on at about the same time as ours was going on in Canada, but was totally independent of it. J. Boukens and F. Deckers, working for the Shell Company in Holland, came up with a system which shows a number of really remarkable similarities to FBP. In fact, the main difference is that their diagrams are vertical, whereas FBP's are horizontal! Another difference is that they allow multiple consumers for a connection (causing the records to be automatically copied), while in FBP we do not allow this. On the other hand, FBP dialects usually have an off-the-shelf Replicate component, which has the same effect. CHIEF's ports are numbered, as in AMPS and DFDM. To convert one of their diagrams into machinable text, they list the connections (called buffers), naming their producers and consumers. A list of such specifications is called a "cooperation". To program individual processes they developed their own interpretive language, whose execution was integrated with the multithreading driver. There is also a discussion of deadlocks.

When reading their paper, and especially the discussion after their presentation, I felt very strongly their excitement over these concepts, and perhaps some frustration that others weren't feeling this excitement too...

Morenoff and McLean

Actually, speaking of parallel evolution, after I had been working on these concepts for a few years, I came across two papers dating back quite a few years: one was written back in 1967 by two people at the Rome Air Development Center, E. Morenoff and J.B. McLean, entitled *"Inter-program Communications, Program String Structures and Buffer Files" (1967)*, describing a program interconnect structure based on the control of data flow via intermediate queues. For a single processor, queues could be maintained in main memory. For a distributed processor structure, queues could be held on disk.

PORTS

A few years later (1971) R.B. Balzer published a paper on what he called *PORTS*, describing work done at RAND where modules could be shielded from other modules by utilizing software commands such as "connect", "disconnect", "send" and "receive". It is interesting that this paper was at one time one of the most cited papers in the field, but, according to private communications with the author, little came of it.

Chap. XXVI: Related Concepts and Forerunners

NIL → Hermes

This system, developed by Rob Strom and his team (1983) at the IBM Research Center at Yorktown Heights, has some very strong similarities to FBP, except that it is a programming language, rather than a coordination language. The original motivation for NIL seems to have been for programming communication software – you will perhaps have noticed that the multiple layers of communications software can be implemented as pairs of complementary processes. They also wanted good inter-process protection, which, as we have seen above, means minimizing side-effects. Like FBP, NIL also allows applications to be built up out of communicating sequential processes; only one process can own a data object at a time; "send" is "destructive" (the sent object can no longer be accessed by the sender); and so on. Strom makes the point that the ability to have processes on the same machine run in a single address space makes the cost of a message exchange very low, comparable to the cost of a subroutine call, and also makes it possible to have larger numbers of smaller-grained processes.

While it does not have an explicit coordination language, NIL is so powerful that this kind of language can easily be added – a parent process has enough facilities available that it could build a running program based on a file which specifies the connections between processes. NIL was deliberately designed to allow dynamic modification of networks, where processes can be created dynamically, and also ports of the created process can be dynamically connected to ports of other processes, both at process creation time and during subsequent execution of the process. The way it does this is by making ports objects, so that the process of connecting ports happens at run-time, under control of what are called "capabilities".

Just as in FBP, the only way processes can affect each other is via the communication channels. Strom and Yemini (in a recent paper on NIL) point out that this fact, plus an extension to strong typing in the NIL language called "typestate checking", provides a high degree of security. Since NIL has its own compiler, it can enforce typestate checking, and thus eliminate the risk of moving data to an address defined by an uninitialized pointer. DFDM, on the other hand, was explicitly designed to interface with existing languages: S/370 Assembler, PL/I and COBOL, and THREADS is C-based, so this risk is present with these implementations, but it can be minimized by good programming techniques and inspections. DFDM and THREADS also adopt the strategy of invalidating a pointer to an IP after that IP has been disposed of – this ensures that an erroneous attempt to access that IP afterwards will cause an immediate crash. Like the NIL group, we also found that this kind of environment provides very good isolation between processes. I believe there were very few cases where one process damaged another one's code or data.

Strom's group has since developed a follow-on to NIL, called *Hermes* (Strom et al. 1991) because Hermes was the "process-server of the gods"! Strom's team has also been doing interesting work on what they call "Optimistic Recovery" – recovery strategies based on the idea that failures are rarer than successes, so one should go ahead with logic on the assumption that things will work and only undo it if there is a failure. Their infrastructure would keep the required information so programmers really don't have to think about recovery. There is a "post mortem" on Hermes at *http://www.cs.ubc.ca/local/reading/proceedings/spe91-95/spe/vol25/ issue4/spe950wk.pdf.*

Parallel Logic Programming

There is an ever-growing series of parallel logic programming systems like *Parlog*, *Vulcan*, and a number of projects proceeding under the aegis of ICOT in Japan. Prolog itself can be combined with FBP to give some very interesting capabilities, so it is not surprising that some of these projects are starting to look a lot like FBP: for example, I find *A'UM* by K. Yoshida and T. Chikayama (1988) very interesting. Incidentally this article has an excellent bibliography. The subtitle of this article is itself quite evocative: A Stream-Based Concurrent Object-Oriented Language – all the good words in a single title!

This same article started me thinking again about "streams". In A'UM and some of the other systems related to it, a distinction is made between "streams" and "channels". If I understand it right, in A'UM, a "stream" runs from one source to one destination, whereas a "channel" may contain more than one stream, coming from different sources: the items in each stream must stay in sequence relative to each other, but the streams in a channel are not constrained relative to each other. In A'UM only one reader is allowed for a channel, while in Tribble's paper on channels (Tribble et al. 1987), he allows multiple readers for a channel. The authors of A'UM feel that not allowing multiple readers makes their semantics sounder and the implementation simpler. Our experience tends to support this view.

In FBP we define a stream as the set of data IPs passing across one connection, but we also allow multiple sources (but only one destination). It may well be that the distinction between stream and channel is more rigorous than the FBP concept, and I look forward to seeing how these concepts evolve. We also pragmatically allow a stream which is accepted by one process to be passed on to the next, e.g. a stream of detail records might flow from a Reader, through an Edit, and on to a Process component. Some writers might prefer to call these multiple streams which just happen to contain the same data. I admit in hindsight that our concept of streams is a little fuzzy at the edges, but I feel it has never caused confusion in practice, and has been implemented in all of the FBP dialects. Multiple destinations, on the other hand, have never been implemented in any of our implementations, partly because it is not clear whether the data should be replicated or should be assigned randomly to the receivers, like Linda's piranhas (see below) – in any case, both solutions can be realized very easily by means of generalized components.

Hewitt's *Actors* take processes down to the finest possible granularity: "Hewitt declared", to quote Robin Milner (1993), "that a value, an operator on values, and a process should all be the same kind of thing: an actor." This approach has considerable theoretical attractiveness, but in

Chap. XXVI: Related Concepts and Forerunners

my view, to be practical, it basically has to be implemented as hardware, rather than software. There are also of course a number of projects growing out of Hewitt's Actors, which also seem to be on a converging path with all the other work (albeit at the more granular end of the scale), e.g. Agha's COOP (1990).

BSP

In Chapter 1, I said I would describe L.G. Valiant's work (1990) in a little more detail, so this is as good a time as any! BSP stands for "bulk-synchronous parallel", and it is of considerable interest because the author proposes it as a new "bridging model", to replace the current, von Neumann bridging model. He stresses that he is proposing it neither as a hardware nor a programming model, but to "insulate software and hardware development from each other, and make possible both general purpose machines and transportable software." The BSP model is defined as comprising the following three attributes:

1. A number of components,.....
2. A router which delivers messages point to point between pairs of components,
3. Facilities for synchronizing all or a subset of components at regular intervals of L time units, where L is the periodicity parameter. A computation consists of a sequence of supersteps. .... After each period of L time units, a global check is made to determine whether the superstep has been completed by all the components. If it has, the machine proceeds to the next superstep. Otherwise, the next period of L units is allocated to the unfinished superstep.

Now look back at Chapter 19 (page 185), and you can see that Valiant's third attribute is very similar to FBP's use of subnets in checkpointing, except that he checks for completion on a regular basis – in FBP implementations, we usually count the processes, and then wait until that number have terminated. Otherwise it is very similar.

Valiant describes a variety of implementations, plus their appropriate performance measures, such as packet switching networks, a hypercube-connected computer and optical crossbars. Here is an interesting comment in his conclusion: "... if the relative investment in communication hardware were suitably increased, machines with a new level of programmability would be obtained." Note the juxtaposition: not just improved performance, but improved programmability.

UNIX™ and its descendants

There is another group of related approaches, based on the very popular UNIX system. In these systems, the connectivity seems to be less rich, but the data passing between the processes is more like IPs or file records than messages. UNIX supports the concept of "pipelining", where the output of one process becomes the input of another, and so on repeatedly. This is definitely a form of configurable modularity, and I found a lot of their experience using this technique relates closely to things we discovered using FBP.

You will find the word "pipe" used quite often for what we call "connection" in FBP. In UNIX the | operator represents what it calls a "pipe". Processes can be assembled into working systems by connecting them together using this operator. For instance, suppose a user enters:

```
ls | pr -2 | lpr
```

The effect is for *ls*, *pr* and *lpr* to be assembled on the fly in such a way that the "standard output" of *ls* feeds the "standard input" of *pr*, and so on. So this command means "list the files in the current directory; format the result 2-up and send the results to a line printer". UNIX's equivalents to ports are the file descriptors 0 (standard input) and 1 (standard output), which are automatically opened whenever a process gets control. What flows between the UNIX processes is streams of characters, rather than structured IPs, so the metaphor is not as powerful as FBP's, nor does UNIX pipelining support complex networks. On the other hand UNIX's character string orientation makes it a very suitable for text manipulation, and a large number of the well-known UNIX components address this application area.

CMS/TSO (or Hartmann) Pipelines

This system was developed by John Hartmann of IBM Denmark for the CMS environment. It is also consciously modelled on UNIX, but since it is specialized for the CMS environment, it is record-oriented, rather than byte-oriented. It supports more complex topologies than UNIX does by means of a notation for ending one pipeline and starting a new one attached to a previous "stage" in the pipeline definition (using a label notation). I therefore see it as a halfway house between UNIX and FBP). A program may also dynamically redefine the pipeline topology by replacing itself or one of its neighbours with a newly defined pipeline.

Here is an example of a CMS Pipelines pipeline:

```
pipe < logged users | split , | take 5 | console
```

This is a CMS command to set up a pipeline which reads the file called LOGGED USERS, splits each record into multiple records, using the comma as the delimiter, selects the first 5, and displays them at the console.

Pipelines components are written in REXX, using a SUBCOM environment for the "pipe" services.

Chap. XXVI: Related Concepts and Forerunners

CSP (Communicating Sequential Processes)

This seminal work by Tony Hoare (1978) has been the basis for a large amount of work by other writers, and is probably one of the most heavily cited in the literature. Here, the external specification indicates which processes are running concurrently (using the || operator to indicate parallel execution), not how they are connected. The actual connectivity is implied by the send and receive commands, which must explicitly name the process being communicated with. Connections are assumed to have zero capacity.

As an example of the CSP coordination notation, here is Hoare's notation, given in his article, for what I have referred to above as the Telegram problem, as follows:

```
[west::DISASSEMBLE||X::COPY||east::ASSEMBLE]
```

Here "west", "X" and "east" are process names, while the capitalized names stand for program sections (analogous to FBP components).

The problem is that DISASSEMBLE has to know the name "X", COPY has to know the names "west" and "east", etc. Hoare's orientation seems to be towards 'write new', rather than reuse. He does mention port names as a possible solution to this problem, but doesn't stress the fundamental paradigm shift involved in changing from 'write new' to reuse, nor the importance of finding a good notation for combining black box components.

Interestingly, he also makes the same point that Carriero and Gelernter made about a subroutine being a special case of a coroutine.

You will notice the frequent occurrence of processes, connections and sometimes ports, with different names being used from system to system. Also configurable modularity at any more complex level than that of UNIX requires some agreement of names (or numbers) between the outsides and insides of processes. NIL avoids this by making ports local to a process, but allowing a parent process to pass information about connections to the child process in the form of parameters.

Linda

Now let's move off in a different direction: Carriero and Gelernter, whom I have mentioned above, have developed and written extensively about a very interesting system called *Linda* (1989), which has stirred up a lot of interest in academic circles. Instead of IPs, Linda uses "tuples", ordered lists of values. "Tuples" are created in "tuple space", just as FBP IPs are created in space managed by FBP, not by the components. Unlike FBP's IPs, however, a tuple just floats in tuple space until retrieved by a process which knows its identification (or part of it). Professor Gelernter uses a neat analogy in a recent Scientific American article to explain his concept of a "tuple". Imagine two spacemen working in space building a space station: one of the workers has finished working with a wrench and wishes it to be available for other workers – he or she can put it "down" (so that it follows its own orbit in space), and the other worker can then pick it up whenever convenient. In the same way, tuples or FBP IPs have an independent existence and follow their own orbit from one worker (process) to another.

How does the spaceman actually pick up the wrench? Here is chiefly where Linda diverges from FBP: in Linda, access is done by pattern matching. A process may need a tuple with value X in field Y – it just has to request a tuple matching those specifications, and it will eventually receive an appropriate tuple. Receiving a tuple can be destructive or non-destructive ("consume" or "read"). If more than one tuple matches the specification, the system picks one at random. If there are none, the requesting process is suspended. Values are not communicated back from the receive to the tuple.

One other important feature of Linda is that of "active" tuples – these are tuples which execute code at the moment of creation, and then turn into ordinary "passive" tuples. You can do distributed logic such as matrix operations this way, where each tuple does a calculation when it is created and then becomes a passive matrix element. Perhaps the nearest to this in FBP is something like the Subnet Manager, which takes a passive chunk of code and turns it into a process.

Another Linda image which is evocative is the "school of piranhas". Here a number of processes lie in wait for a tuple, and when it appears in the tuple space any one of them can grab it. This is an effective technique of load balancing. In Chapter 21 (page 210), I described a performance improvement technique where we had 18 occurrences of a process executing the same disk traversal logic. In this case, we had to provide connections from the client to the 18 servers, so we had to have a "load balancing" process in between – the piranha technique would do this without the need for the extra process.

To summarize the essential difference between Linda and FBP, Linda is a *bus* while FBP is a *tram* – Linda has more degrees of freedom but I believe is more expensive in terms of resources. If one Linda process generates a series of tuples with an extra field containing numbers in ascending sequence, you could have another process request them in sequence. So Linda can simulate FBP. Conversely, FBP can just as easily simulate Linda's associative style of retrieval by having one or more processes manage an associative store. It seems to me that Linda and FBP are so closely related that systems of the future may combine both approaches. After all, there may be areas of an application where tracks are more appropriate, and others where you want more degrees of freedom – sort of like containers moving from rail to ship and back to rail. Here is a final quote from Gelernter and Carriero (1992):

> "In general we see computation and programming languages as areas in which further progress will be slow, incremental and, in many cases, of marginal importance to working programmers. Coordination languages are a field of potentially great significance. A growing number of groups will play major roles in this work."

Chap. XXVI: Related Concepts and Forerunners

I couldn't agree more!

Advanced Hardware Designs

Another characteristic of the three "legs" of FBP listed above is that they could actually describe a network of independent processors, all interacting to do a job of work. This approach to building super-powerful machines is getting a lot of attention lately, as it is generally recognized that the single processor is running out of steam. Although we can probably make individual processors smaller and faster (after all, a bit is simply a choice between two states, for instance two states of a molecule), you start to run into limitations such as the speed of light or the potential damage which can be caused by a single cosmic ray! A lot of work is going on on linking multiple processors together to achieve enormous amounts of computing power without any one processor having to be incredibly fast. Suppose we put 1000 processors together, each running at 20 MIPS (millions of instructions per second) – this would provide 20,000,000,000 instructions per second. Since such a machine is normally thought of as being oriented towards scientific calculations, so that the instructions would tend to be floating-point operations, this machine would be a 20 gigaflop machine. Multiply either of these factors by 50 (or one by 5 and one by 10), and you are into the "teraflop" per second range (1,000,000,000,000 floating point operations per second). In comparison, Intel® Pentium® 4s have been rated at almost 10,000 MIPS (*http://en.wikipedia.org/w/index.php?title=Instructions_per_second&oldid=353915299*), so it would only take 100 working together to get up in the teraflop range.

The two main approaches here are *multiprocessors* and *multicomputers*. I am indebted to my son, Joseph Morrison, for some of the following comments. A number of writers seem to favour *multiprocessors* (with shared memory) because they do not require us to radically change our approach to programming. The programming technique I have described in the foregoing pages seems to be a good match with this approach, as it can be mapped onto a multiprocessor in a straightforward manner: IPs are allocated from the shared memory, and FBP processes are spread across the available processors to obtain parallelism. All commercial multiprocessors provide concurrency control mechanisms such as semaphores; these can be used to manage the concurrent accesses to the IPs. Examples of this type of machine are the *KSR 1, CEDAR, DASH, T*, Alewife* – this list is from (Bell 1992).

FBP networks also have a natural mapping to *multicomputers*. Here parallelism is obtained by having a network of connected processors, each with its own memory. The data must be transmitted from one processor to another, as required, so communication speed and bandwidth become important considerations. Examples of this type of machine are the *Intel Paragon, CM5, Mercury, nCube 2* and *Teradata/NCR/AT&T* systems. A number of different network topologies have been investigated – examples are meshes, tree structures, hypercubes, and ring structures.

FBP could be mapped onto multicomputer systems by again evenly distributing the processes among the processors. An IP would be created in the local memory of the processor on which the creating process resides. If an IP had to be transferred to another processor, the entire IP could be copied over the communication network. Although this sounds inefficient, communication costs can be minimized by having "neighbour" processes reside in directly connected processors, or even in some cases time-share the same processor, where the economics justify it. There is a considerable body of work on different strategies for handling communication between processors, and for doing the routing when paths are tied up or damaged, and I was struck by how similar some of the problems they have to solve are to those we had to solve for FBP. I found the article by P. Gaughan and S. Yalamanchili (1993) a good survey, as well as providing some interesting solutions and simulation results. Of course, I am not a hardware person, but it does seem that some of the techniques described would support FBP quite nicely.

Most of the academic work with multiprocessor configurations seems to be oriented towards determining what parallelism can be obtained from a COBOL or FORTRAN program. However, MIT has a dataflow computer called *Monsoon*, which "demonstrates scalability and implicit parallelism using a dataflow language" (Bell 1992), to be followed by one called *T** which will be "multithreaded to absorb network latency". Researchers at Berkeley are using a 64-node CM5 to explore various programming models and languages including dataflow. There is an enormous amount of research going on in the areas of multiprocessors and multicomputers. This is a whole area of specialization within computing research, and one which I expect I will never get to know very much about! However, a lot of people who do have some understanding of this area see a good match with FBP. Applications designed using FBP should map very naturally onto a system of communicating processors. If you have more processors than processes, this mapping should be pretty easy; if fewer, then some processors are going to have to time-share, just as the present implementations of FBP do today. Here is a quote from an article (Cann 1992) comparing FORTRAN with functional languages for programming tomorrow's massively parallel machines (remember that we related FBP to functional languages in an earlier chapter):

> "Tomorrow's parallel machines will not only provide massive parallelism, but will present programmers with a combinatorial explosion of concerns and details. The imperative programming model will continue to hinder the exploitation of parallelism. In summary, the functional paradigm yields several important benefits. First, programs are more concise and easier to write and maintain. Second, programs are conducive to analysis, being mathematically sound and free of side effects and aliasing. Third, programs exhibit implicit parallelism and favour automatic parallelization. Fourth, programs can run as fast as, if not faster than, conventional languages."

One last point about the data flowing between these computing engines: a lot of the mathematically oriented work with big computers (and most of this work is mathematically oriented) seems to assume that what should travel between the processors is either values, like integers or strings, or messages. I actually started out with simple values in my early work, in 1967, but became convinced over the years that you should send whole "things" (entities, records or IPs), which stay together as they travel, rather than low-level datatypes (e.g. integers or strings) which are not in the application domain. Our experience is that, if you decompose a record into individual values, it may be so expensive to recombine them that it's not worth it.

IBM Messaging and Queuing (MQSeries).

At the beginning, I mentioned the growing use of these concepts for programming distributed systems. I would like to mention the recent IBM announcement of MQSeries. Similar efforts by other companies are listed in a recent article (Moad 1993). IBM plans to bring out a set of products which will allow asynchronous communication between a large set of IBM and non-IBM platforms. There will be a standard interface based on the concept of queues, which will relieve programmers from the complexities of making different applications communicate between different vendors' hardware and software. Instead of having to use one set of macros for IBM's basic telecommunications software, different commands for CICS, still another set for IMS, all applications will use the same simple set of MQI (Messaging and Queueing Interface) calls. This concept seems to me to be completely compatible with the application structuring ideas presented in this book. In Chapter 15 (page 140), we talked about the ability to cleave networks across systems – the combination of FBP and MQSeries or similar software should provide a very powerful way of splitting an application across multiple systems or locations, or of moving functions from one node to another as desired. As I said in that chapter, cleaving applications between different computers introduces new problems of synchronization, but they will definitely be solved! It doesn't make sense to try to pretend that a distributed system is one big, synchronous application. If you request data from a remote location, you want to be able to do other things while the data is working its way through the system. Systems are getting just too big. Also, many of the systems which are being connected "speak different languages", so we are seeing the development of standards which will allow them to interpret each others' data formats. I predict that those problems which will inevitably arise will be solved, but not necessarily by means of one general solution for every problem.

Summary

As you read this chapter, I hope you have got some impression of how ideas spring up independently in different places and times, how they flower in unexpected places, how they cross-pollinate and give rise to interesting new hybrids. You have to be a botanist to keep track of it all! There are many other concepts and languages, other than the few I have mentioned here, which have points in common with FBP, and which have certainly been influential in the field of

Chap. XXVI: Related Concepts and Forerunners

computing, but there is not room in this book to do them justice. They have cross-fertilized each other and in many cases only industry archivists know which led to which. Examples which spring to mind are: SIMULA, MODULA-2 (and now MODULA-3), Concurrent Pascal, Ada, Lucid, Occam, ...

Back in 1994, I wrote that it would be wonderful if any readers who are expert in these different languages could share their knowledge and insights with the rest of us. I have occasionally dreamed of collecting all the developers and theoreticians of concurrent, stream-oriented, modular systems together in a huge symposium, and seeing if we can't get some synergy going. I have found that there is something about data-orientation which seems to allow practitioners of different disciplines to communicate (just as Information Packets do for different languages!). I sincerely hope that we won't waste our energy in internecine wars, as has happened in some disciplines, but that we will all be able to work together towards a shared goal. There are far more similarities than differences in our work, and if we can get a real dialogue going, who knows what we might achieve together!

As of 2010, this kind of symposium hasn't happened yet, but things are exploding in all sorts of different directions, as described in the next chapter, so hopefully, this will happen one day soon! Perhaps one of my readers, with better organizing skills than mine, will devote some time and energy to making it happen!

Chap. XXVII: The FBP Explosion

On *http://digg.com/programming/Tired_of_coding_try_FBP_Flow_Based_Programming*:

> About 30 years ago, one Hacker hidden in his cubicle created something nobody would have predicted, way ahead of his time. You'll laugh, you'll cry, you'll laugh some more, now go RTFA! [sic] (Digg Dec. 2, 2008 by Felipe Valdés, and frequently copied since then)

In recent years we have had a veritable explosion of products and systems, some consciously following Flow-Based Programming's concepts and some following on parallel tracks. There is an exploding interest in FBP propelled by a number of factors: the most important being that, as we move to more and more processors in our machines, everybody seems to be preaching the need for multithreading, but all the experts stress that programming this way is dauntingly difficult, so there is a frantic search for better ways to do this! Herb Sutter described this in his famous 2005 article, "The Free Lunch Is Over" (*http://www.gotw.ca/publications/concurrency-ddj.htm*). FBP, which has been around for around 40 years (as of 2010), on the other hand, gives the programmer a simple mental model while supporting multithreading in a very natural way. It is especially appropriate where large amounts of data and/or multiple processors and computing nodes are involved.

I don't want to appear to claim that all the systems mentioned in this chapter arose from my work, as I believe in the concept of "steam-engine time": when it's time for steam-engines to be invented, they will pop up in several different places at the same time. Wayne Stevens used to say that, after someone invented the hula hoop, people would start to manufacture hula hoops all over the place... Also, to add to the confusion, "Flow-Based Programming" has started to be used generically – like "Bandaid" or "Xerox" – so that there are now people using the term who

Chap. XXVII: The FBP Explosion

may never have read my book. We could call this the genericization of FBP! As of Feb. 2011, Googling "Flow-Based Programming" (with quotes to get an exact match) resulted in over 17,000 hits!

A striking example of what I call "steam-engine time" shows up in the parallels between my history and that of the late British computer scientist, Robin Milner. I had of course heard of him, but didn't know until recently that, like me, he attended Eton (it turns out that we were both scholarship boys) and King's College (we seem to have overlapped at both places); we both entered the (rather new) field of computing at about the same time, and both wound up working on computing parallelism later. After university, Robin pursued an academic career path, and became very well-known in that arena, while I laboured in the salt-mines of the business world! We both started working on concurrency in the '70s. Robin's "Calculus of Communicating Systems" (CCS – *http://en.wikipedia.org/w/index.php?title=Calculus_of_communicating_systems&oldid=355294057*) was intended to model networks of processes which communicate across predefined connections, but was more abstract than FBP. CCS treats connections (bounded buffers) as just a type of process (as actually suggested in Chapter 15 above), so communication between processes can be treated as instantaneous. However, in FBP we have found it practical to bury connections in the infrastructure.

Robin later developed his "π-calculus" (*http://en.wikipedia.org/w/index.php?title=Pi_calculus&oldid=355292413*) to describe concurrent networks whose configuration may change during the computation. In a private communication with me (April 2010), Professor Michael Fourman of Edinburgh University says of FBP: "... the resonance with Robin's ideas for his calculus of communicating systems is striking."

I now realize that Robin's work should really have been included in the previous chapter, but I just wasn't aware of it when I wrote my book. So here are two people with somewhat parallel (non-computing) backgrounds, who started working on similar concepts at about the same time – completely independently, and on different continents! Maybe, as I said before, computing was in the air at King's! In fact, many of the projects described in this chapter and the previous one developed independently of each other – which suggests that we have collectively stumbled on a fundamental truth!

I would like to take the opportunity to stress that, although I did not have the privilege of meeting, or communicating with, Robin, my "hobby" (FBP) *has* allowed me to meet (by email, if not in person) some extremely brilliant – and nice – individuals over the years! You are too many to list here, but if your name doesn't appear somewhere in the pages of this book, please don't feel that that means I appreciate your contributions, help and support, any less!

My first inkling that the FBP was starting to spread "virally", as they say nowadays, came when Google came across an item in the Donegal News, dated Friday, Jan. 26, 2007, describing the "BT [British Telecom] Young Scientist of the Year 2007" – a prestigious competition which was

Chap. XXVII: The FBP Explosion

then in its 43rd year. It said, in part: "A number of other students and their projects were highly commended for the work they had entered into the competition.... They were: Stephen Dolan from Choláiste Cholmcille, Ballyshannon, Ireland, for his project 'Streams: Flow-Based Programming in Python' ....". I expect great things from Stephen and his generation!

Since then, things have been picking up speed, I am now being contacted by people from all over the world (from Malaysia to Israel to Finland), and, what is even more suggestive in our electronic age, FBP is being mentioned on blogs more and more frequently. People seem to be discovering it for themselves, or by word of mouth, and it is definitely beginning to look as if, as Adler Perotte (currently at Princeton University) told me, "Flow-Based Programming is the way of the future." The strange thing is that I really have no idea how many companies or individuals are currently using JavaFBP or C#FBP, because, as these implementations are freely available as Open Source, their users are under no obligation to notify me when they are using them – and, in fact, companies often impose confidentiality restrictions on the uses they put them to, which means that developers can't talk to me even if they want to!

Conversely, the people I do hear from are either academics who are trying to extend the ideas for a thesis, or businesses who have built their own versions and are soliciting feedback on where I feel their product should be improved. A number of people seem to have built their own versions (in various languages), but, although some of them use the term "Flow-Based Programming", it is often not clear how they differ from the basic FBP architecture. The people I really love hearing from (and very seldom do) are people actually using one of the FBP implementations who have ideas about how it should be improved – for everybody's benefit!

So this chapter will be a mixture of things that claim to be "Flow-Based Programming" but may not be, and things that do not use the term, but seem closely related! There is so much going on that I can only provide thumbnail sketches. Also, if your favorite project does not show up in this chapter, apologies! Please feel free to let me know about the oversight. Much of the following material is put together from web sites (including, naturally, Wikipedia), blogs, and personal communications, so will not be listed in the Bibliography.

In a private communication, Richard Harter told me:

> I feel there should be an explicit distinction between static flow structures and dynamic flow structures. In languages like Hermes, Erlang, Axum, and Go, processes (components) are created on the fly during execution. Now this means that you can't describe the structure with a picture (visual programming) because the structure can be continually changing. OTOH [on the other hand] in business programming etc. you have a fixed flow structure that you are modeling and visual representation works. This seems to me to be a major bifurcation.

Chap. XXVII: The FBP Explosion

Mike Beckerle sent me the following list of "flow" types:

- static (draw the flow),
- quasi-static (draw the logical flow – static "realized" flow is an expansion e.g., parallel version),
- flow-generators (e.g., SQL language compiled into a flow which is different each time), and
- really dynamic (flow is evolving as it executes.)

Only the last one is questionable as to whether it is "really FBP" or not. The prior three are all clearly useful and there are real commercial systems using all of them.

Ingo Lütkebohle has recently (March 2010) made a stab at elucidating the different attributes shared in differing degrees by various FBP-like implementations – here is his list:

- Activation model: data-driven, demand-driven, independent threads
- Parallelity [sic] (per node): Single, bounded, unbounded.
- Granularity: instruction-level, "sync/async", clustered, unspecified
- Data exchange: FIFO queues, synchronous queues, bounded buffers
- Concurrency (overall): Single-threaded, shared thread pool, thread per node.
- Scheduling: static, dynamic

For example, FTS (see below) is data-driven, has single parallelity, "sync/async" granularity, FIFO queues, engines for either single-threaded or thread-per-node execution and dynamic scheduling. For the full discussion, see *http://groups.google.com/group/flow-based-programming/browse_thread/thread/da7d1064f76a2a84*.

By the way, I do realize that some of the descriptions given below are pretty sketchy. I can only suggest that the interested reader follow the links provided, and do his or her own research!

AMQP (Advanced Message Queue Protocol). Joe Armstrong (mentioned above) just pointed me at this (Mar. 2010) – he says it's exploding, so that fits right in with the name of this chapter! Here is what he says:

> AMQP provides (in a nutshell) reliable asynchronous messaging to named queues. Applications can *only* interact by reading and writing from named (= addressable) queues.

- 284 -

Chap. XXVII: The FBP Explosion

The queues are persistent (= fault tolerant) – once something is put in a queue it stays there forever, or until it is explicitly removed.

Sounds familiar? – Yup, it provides the basic infrastructure to build a FBP system.

Read more here: *http://www.hpts.ws/session5/das.pdf*

Now the fun bit: NASA has built a cloud infrastructure (called "Nebula") – one picture says it all: *http://nebula.nasa.gov/services/* .

Nebula interposes a AMQP layer directly on top of the hardware (or virtualised hardware), actually it's called the RabbitMQ message layer (RabbitMQ is an Erlang implementation of AMQP). ☺

Having seen this picture – I thought – "yes of course" that's how to build clouds. This is the layer underneath the databases, and the "eventually-consistent" stores. ☺

It's all about sending messages to named queues – add persistence and you have everything you need.

So we take the hardware – and add a message-passing middleware layer directly on top. This provides persistence, asynchronous named queues (the bit missing from TCP).

Then everything falls into place.

As far as I can see all that is needed is a set of abstractions to glue together processing elements with the named queues.

The Rabbit MQ reference page: *http://www.rabbitmq.com/how.html* lists many applications built on a messaging infrastructure.

Many of these seem to have strong architectural similarities to [FBP].

A Selection of Commercial and Open Source Products

(Quotes are from their documentation)

Chap. XXVII: The FBP Explosion

Kettle by Pentaho – see *http://kettle.pentaho.org/*

Quoting from their web site:

> PDI [Pentaho Data Integration] is easy to use. Every process is created with a graphical tool where you specify what to do without writing code to indicate how to do it; because of this, you could say that PDI is *metadata oriented*.
>
> PDI can be used as a standalone application, or it can be used as part of the larger Pentaho Suite. As an ETL tool, it is the most popular open source tool available. PDI supports a vast array of input and output formats, including text files, data sheets, and commercial and free database engines. Moreover, the transformation capabilities of PDI allow you to manipulate data with very few limitations.

Proto Software – see *http://www.protosw.com/*

Their web site tells us that there are two basic types of data in Proto:

- Single values like dates, numbers, text values, etc.
- Tables of data that store rows and columns of data (single values and other tables)

Quoting from their web site:

> Both of these types of data flow across one-way connections from one Component to another. Though the data is not actually copied at every step, each Component can behave as though it has a full copy of the data.

Proto allows the user to build and modify graphically what they call "dashboards" to specify the flow of data between components.

Talend – see *http://www.talend.com/index.php*

Says they are the "recognized market leader in open source data integration".

> Talend Open Studio's Job Designer provides both a graphical and a functional view of the actual integration processes using a graphical palette of open source components and connectors. Integration processes are built by simply dragging and dropping these open source components and connectors onto the workspace, drawing connections and relationships between them, and setting their properties.

Signify by Trelliswerk – see *http://www.trelliswerk.com/*

> Signify is a Microsoft .NET library for structuring parallel computations that respond to live data sources using continuous queries over objects called signals. Packaging of signals into reusable software components that work with heterogeneous

information flows requires techniques that are traditionally available only to embedded systems, control engineering or academic specialists.

Omnimark – see *http://www.stilo.com/ProductsServices/OmniMark/tabid/57/Default.aspx*

In *http://developers.omnimark.com/OmniMark_Design_Principles(letter-size).pdf* they say:

> The streaming paradigm is an approach to programming that concentrates on describing the process to be applied to a piece of data, and on processing data directly as it streams from one location to another.

InforSense – see *http://www.inforsense.com/*

> The drag and drop environment enables analysts to easily build visual analytical applications by combining data from data warehouses, marts, Excel and web services, applying predictive and statistical modelling techniques and deploying to end users via VisualSense interactive web pages.

Pipeline Pilot by accelrys – see *http://accelrys.com/products/scitegic/*

> Pipeline Pilot solutions are based around a powerful client-server platform that lets you construct workflows by graphically combining components for data retrieval, filtering, analysis, and reporting.

Konstanz Information Miner – see *http://www.knime.org/*

> ... a modular data exploration platform that enables the user to visually create data flows (often referred to as pipelines), selectively execute some or all analysis steps, and later investigate the results through interactive views on data and models.

IBM InfoSphere DataStage – see *http://en.wikipedia.org/w/index.php?title=IBM_InfoSphere_DataStage&oldid=339636024*

IBM InfoSphere DataStage is an ETL tool and part of the IBM Information Platforms Solutions suite and IBM InfoSphere. It uses a graphical notation to construct data integration solutions and is available in various versions such as the Server Edition and the Enterprise Edition.

In April 2001 IBM acquired Informix and took just the database business leaving the data integration tools to be spun off as an independent software company called Ascential Software. In November 2001, Ascential Software Corp. of Westboro, Mass. acquired privately held Torrent Systems Inc. of Cambridge, Mass. for $46 million in cash. Ascential announced a commitment to integrate Orchestrate's parallel processing capabilities [Torrent Systems' Orchestrate is an FBP system, as Mike Beckerle stated earlier] directly into the DataStageXE platform. In March 2005

Chap. XXVII: The FBP Explosion

IBM acquired Ascential Software and made DataStage part of the WebSphere family as WebSphere DataStage.

IBM BatchPipes – *see http://www-01.ibm.com/common/ssi/rep_ca/3/897/ENUS200-093/ENUS200-093.PDF.*

DataRush by Pervasive Software – see *http://www.pervasivedatarush.com/Pages/default.aspx*

The article in the Java Developer's Journal by Jim Falgout and Matt Walker – "It's a Multi-Core World: Let the Data Flow" (*http://java.sys-con.com/read/419717.htm*) – gives a historic survey of Data Flow programming approaches, and lists good areas in which to apply Data Flow. At the end it goes into some detail on their product, and describes results of a benchmark using it.

expecco – see *http://www.exept.de/en/products/expecco*

From a talk by Claus Gittinger, eXept, Software AG, April 2010, at CHOOSE (Swiss Group for Object-Oriented Systems and Environments):

> ...an IDE for visual Flow-Based Programming called Expecco which is rooted in Smalltalk/X. ... Expecco is attacking the market for IDEs used to create automated end-to-end tests... test engineers create appropriate atomic building blocks targeting their specific context. ... test designers visually compose and connect those building blocks towards complex but reusable, readable and tweakable end-to-end tests.

Quote from the expecco web site:

> ...we offer a solution to easily create the most complex test scenarios. The basic idea of the model is based on UML activity diagrams. Test runs are compositions of networked blocks. The strengths of expecco lie in functional system-, acceptance and integration tests (black box).

expressor – see *http://www.expressor-software.com/* : A data flow-based ETL tool. Jerry Callen, one of the original Torrent Orchestrate team members, and long time FBP advocate, is currently at Expressor.

- **expressor illustrator**: a Windows desktop-based visual integration flow design application targeted at developers who are responsible for designing and testing a data integration application.
- **expressor processor:** The expressor processor is a high-performance parallel data processing engine that runs a deployed data integration application. To support increased throughput, the engine supports parallel processing on a wide range of hardware and

Chap. XXVII: The FBP Explosion

software platforms.

Note that expressor uses the term "operator" where FBP uses "process" or "component".

Pypes by Eric Gaumer – see *http://www.pypes.org/*. An FBP-like system built using Stackless Python (*http://en.wikipedia.org/w/index.php?title=Stackless_Python&oldid=329729671*), so uses "green" threads. Cute logo, by the way!

Python seems to be quite a popular language for implementing FBP. Matt Harrison – *http://wiki.python.org/moin/FlowBasedProgramming* – has come up with the following list (in addition to Pypes):

- **PyF** – see *http://pyfproject.org/en/welcome*.
- **Papy** – see *http://code.google.com/p/papy/*.
- **zFlow** – see *http://www.thensys.com/?page_id=21*.
- **Kamaelia** (described in detail below)
- **"simple pype"** by Arvind Narayanan – see *http://arvindn.livejournal.com/68137.html*.

Zatori by Marcel Lüthi (*http://mlsystems.ch*). Also Python-based. When we last corresponded, Marcel was using Twisted (*http://twistedmatrix.com/trac/*), which he chose because he felt its threading model is superior to the basic Python one, based on its Global Interpreter Lock (GIL) – see also *http://www.linuxjournal.com/node/7871/print*.

I should also include:

FilterPype by FlightDataServices – see *http://pypi.python.org/pypi/FilterPype/0.2.9*.

A "process-flow pipes-and-filters Python framework". Some of its features:

- Advanced algorithms broken down into simple data filter coroutines
- Pipelines constructed from filters in the new FilterPype mini-language
- Domain experts assemble pipelines with no Python knowledge required

Apache Pig – see *http://hadoop.apache.org/pig/*

Pig is a platform for analyzing large data sets that consists of a high-level language for expressing data analysis programs, coupled with infrastructure for evaluating these programs. The salient property of Pig programs is that their structure is amenable to substantial parallelization, which in turns enables them to handle very large data sets. Apparently they don't use "flow-based" as a specific term, preferring "data flow programming" as the term of art.

Ab Initio – see *http://www.abinitio.com*

This is a company also formed in the mid 1990s and has the parallel-partitioned commercial data processing FBP stuff at its core. Their system seems to be very successful, and comprises:

- Co>Operating System [sic] (the foundation for all Ab Initio applications)
- Component Library (Reusable Building Blocks)
- Graphical Development Environment

IXP – Clemens Ott – see *http://www.ixp.com/code_does_not_matter.jsp*

Kilim by Sriram Srinivasan (*http://www.malhar.net/sriram/kilim/*) is philosophically very close to FBP, but combines fibres with Java threads to provide very fast context switching. By default, there is a single scheduler that creates as many threads as the number of processors, but one can configure multiple schedulers that manage independent thread pools. Sriram rewrote the enormously popular Berkeley DB library, replacing its threads with Kilim tasks, and supplying a transaction-savvy scheduler, resulting in almost a 2x speed-up on their hand-optimized production code. These benchmarks and the architecture are described in his PhD thesis: *http://www.malhar.net/sriram/sriram-diss-final-jan28.pdf*.

Kilim also addresses the need for a type system that tracks ownership and containment.

There is a video on YouTube – *http://www.youtube.com/watch?v=37NaHRE0Sqw* – in which Sriram describes studies showing Kilim "was able to compete favourably with Erlang on tasking, messaging and scalability" (*http://www.malhar.net/sriram/kilim/kilim_ecoop08.pdf*). (Erlang is generally considered to be the fastest multithreaded implementation around.)

Kilim requires methods which are suspendable to be tagged with an exception indicating this – although at first glance this looks cumbersome, especially since methods that call a suspendable method have to be tagged as well, it turns out that it is actually beneficial to have to indicate this characteristic. And the exception-handling mechanism of Java handles checking for these relationships automatically.

Kamaelia – see *http://www.kamaelia.org/Home*

Kamaelia is a Python library by BBC Research for concurrent programming using a simple pattern of components that send and receive data from each other.

Chap. XXVII: The FBP Explosion

From *http://linux.wareseeker.com/Programming/kamaelia-0.5.0.zip/329299*:

> A networked UNIX pipe for the 21st century – a way of making general concurrency easy to work with, and fun. A framework providing the nuts and bolts for building components. A library of components built using that framework. Components are implemented at the lowest level as python generators, and communicate by message passing. Components are composed into systems in a manner similar to Unix pipelines, but with some twists that are relevant to modern computer systems rather than just file-like systems... Kamaelia is trying to make concurrency natural and easy to work with, because we are trying to solve some specific challenges regarding putting (some or all of) the BBC Archive online.

Dendrite (*http://www.digitalmars.com/webnews/newsgroups.php?art_group=digitalmars.D.announce&article_id=17948* – retrieved 2010-04-13)

Described as a D-based FBP system. Interestingly the author uses the term FBP to refer to it, as in: "FBP allows a developer to write simple, cooperative components that exchange messages via mailboxes to create pluggable, concurrent, modular applications", but says Dendrite "was inspired by various FBP systems including the Unix command shell and the Python-based Axon system written by Michael Sparks of BBC Research." Axon is the core of Kamaelia (above). D is presumably the D programming language (see *http://en.wikipedia.org/w/index.php?title=D_%28programming_language%29&oldid=354073485*). A perfect example of the genericizing of FBP!

Aluminium 0.4 (note the British/Canadian spelling)

From *http://linux.wareseeker.com/Programming/aluminium-0.4.zip/291164c346*

> Aluminium 0.4 is known as a useful visual data-flow(-ish) programming language, designed for small web applications. It turned out as a visual data-flow based programming language. Aluminium was started as an effort to find a different way of creating web applications.

Urbi – see *http://www.gostai.com/downloads/urbi-sdk-2.0/doc/urbi-sdk.htmldir/urbi-sdk.html#urbi-sdkpa2.html*

Quote:

> urbiscript is a programming language primarily designed for robotics. It's a dynamic, prototype-based, object-oriented scripting language. It supports and emphasizes parallel and event-based programming, which are very popular paradigms in robotics, by providing core primitives and language constructs.

Chap. XXVII: The FBP Explosion

RobotFlow is another robotics toolkit – see *http://robotflow.sourceforge.net/*

Quote:

> RobotFlow is a mobile robotics tookit based on the *FlowDesigner project*. FlowDesigner is a data-flow oriented architecture, similar to Simulink (Matlab) or Labview that is free (LGPL) and versatile. The visual programming interface provided in the FlowDesigner project will help people to better visualize & understand what is really happening in the robot's control loops, sensors, actuators, by using graphical probes and debugging in real-time.

Cascading – see *http://www.cascading.org/*

Quote:

> Cascading is a feature rich API for defining and executing complex, scale-free, and fault tolerant data processing workflows on a Hadoop (*http://hadoop.apache.org/core/*) cluster.
>
> The processing API lets the developer quickly assemble complex distributed processes without having to "think" in MapReduce. And to efficiently schedule them based on their dependencies and other available meta-data.

Anic (*http://code.google.com/p/anic/*) - pointed out by David Bennett of Powerflex Corporation

> *"Faster than C, safer than Java, simpler than *sh"*

David says it's "Flow-Based Programming, but in a very different guise".

ETL, RDBMSs, and MapReduce

These three areas all have to do with processing large (even huge) amounts of data, and appear to be good matches with FBP. There is an excellent article by Mike Beckerle, which is quoted from further on in this chapter, in the Oco Inc. blog called "BI in the Cloud" – see *http://blog.oco-inc.com/business-intelligence/bi-in-the-cloud/bid/28462/MapReduce-Redux* .

To start with, however, I will give short descriptions of these three areas, partially based on the relevant Wikipedia articles:

Chap. XXVII: The FBP Explosion

ETL (Extract/Transform/Load) – see *http://en.wikipedia.org/w/index.php?title=Extract,_transform,_load&oldid=337872788*

ETL has to do with massaging large amounts of data, usually in batch mode. Its name comes from the fact that it is typically a three-stage process (the following is partially taken from Wikipedia):

- The *extract* process involves extracting the data from the source systems. Most data warehousing projects consolidate data from different source systems. Each separate system may also use a different data organization/format.

- The *transform* stage applies a series of rules or functions to the extracted data from the source to derive the data for loading into the end target.

- The *load* phase loads the data into the end target, usually the data warehouse.

From everything you have read in this book, you can see that ETL is a natural fit with FBP. Here is what Eric Gaumer says about ETL:

> "It seems like organizations are continually moving data around and that is where Flow-Based Programming really shines (in my opinion). I looked at some research on ETL tools a while back and studies showed that nearly 70% of organizations surveyed rolled their own ETL solution. Many felt they could build an optimal system that was more specific to their needs. I haven't seen a commercial ETL system that boosts flow-based design principles. Many require a lot of configuration to support custom components."

Eric also stresses elsewhere that Search Engines are "hot" these days, and are a different domain from ETL. I include some of his remarks below.

In the interests of completeness, I will repeat the reference to the 2009 paper by Sebastian Ertel, Mike Beckerle, and Christof Fetzer, with the title, "ETL data streaming with EAI-style transactional data delivery guarantees, and transparent checkpoint/restart capability" – *http://ohua.sourceforge.net/ohua-paper.pdf*.

Relational Database Management Systems (RDBMSs) – see *http://en.wikipedia.org/w/index.php?title=Relational_database_management_system&oldid=337588084*

From Wikipedia:

> A relational database management system (RDBMS) is a database management

Chap. XXVII: The FBP Explosion

system (DBMS) that is based on the relational model as introduced by E. F. Codd. Most popular commercial and open source databases currently in use are based on the relational model.

A short definition of an RDBMS may be a DBMS in which data is stored in the form of tables and the relationship among the data is also stored in the form of tables.

MapReduce – see *http://en.wikipedia.org/w/index.php?title=MapReduce&oldid=338853483*

From Wikipedia:

> MapReduce is a framework for processing huge datasets on certain kinds of distributable problems using a large number of computers (nodes), collectively referred to as a cluster.
>
> "Map" step: The master node takes the input, chops it up into smaller sub-problems, and distributes those to worker nodes. A worker node may do this again in turn, leading to a multi-level tree structure. The worker node processes that smaller problem, and passes the answer back to its master node.
>
> "Reduce" step: The master node then takes the answers to all the sub-problems and combines them in a way to get the output – the answer to the problem it was originally trying to solve.
>
> ... Provided each mapping operation is independent of the other, all maps can be performed in parallel – though in practice it is limited by the data source and/or the number of CPUs near that data. Similarly, a set of 'reducers' can perform the reduction phase – all that is required is that all outputs of the map operation which share the same key are presented to the same reducer, at the same time. ...

Here are some quotes from the above-mentioned article ("BI in the Cloud") by Mike Beckerle about these three areas and their relationship to FBP:

> Scalable computing via parallel processing is big business these days. There's heavy data lifting at the transaction processing level, at the data analysis level, for web search indexing, for enterprise search indexing, scientific computing, data mining for target marketing, affinity advertising. There are many places where data processing of really large amounts of data has commercial benefits, and that means parallel processing adds lots of value.
>
> At the smaller end of the parallel processing scale there's actually a crisis of sorts –

Chap. XXVII: The FBP Explosion

we need parallelism to use up all these multi-core CPUs that the chip makers can now create easily, yet there is no mainstream accepted programming idiom that creates the multi-threaded programs yet is easy to use.

MapReduce was designed initially for the other end of the spectrum – huge data, Internet-scale data. Much bigger than enterprise data for even the largest enterprise. This is where clearly you want to use lots of computers all at once. Advocates will tell you it's also great for that downward scale to multi-core CPU thing – and I concur. But that wasn't the first intention for it.

The other big scalable computing systems of commercial import are the relational database engines, and the ETL tools that transform data, and sometimes also support data mining. In common to both of these: commercial data, commercial data types, lots of structured data in the mix, of course with gradually improving capabilities to handle unstructured data. Databases are of course data storage tools, where ETL systems are algorithmic systems. For example, in a database when you talk about how to break up data into partitions you are talking about how it is stored. In the ETL world, partitioning data is about how it is moving, and incidentally it can be stored that way also. This latter is very close to the way MapReduce folks talk about data even though I don't think ETL folks and MapReduce folks drink in the same bars.

What all three of these kinds of systems, MapReduce included, have in common is that they are all about scalable Flow-Based Programming ... to some degree. Not everyone agrees on this term Flow-Based Programming, preferring dataflow, or streaming, or flow-graph or some other term. RDBMS systems have their query graphs at their query processing cores – they transform SQL into these. A query graph is an FBP. ETL tools let you draw these graphs (and script them also sometimes). They allow the graphs to have multiple outputs, unlike a query graph, but otherwise are fairly similar. If you use the Apache Pig ... system to create MapReduce programs, it cascades the map-reduce operations together into a flow graph. This was created because so many map-reduce applications found themselves wanting to connect one MapReduce back to back into another that someone wisely observed that this flow composition was FBP and that was really part of the idiom.

The primary source of parallelism in all the above is called partitioning. Basically it is the principle that if you have a large piece of data, or large collection of data items, you can divide-and-conquer it, and then put the pieces back together (if necessary). The divided processing is the "map" part, the putting back together is the "reduce" part. You might map and map and map and then reduce, or alternate. Do this kind of thing over and over as you process the data, flowing the output of one such operation to the input of another.

So here's one major point of total agreement: There's an agreement across many different areas of computerdom that Flow-Based Programming is a very good way to go if you want parallelism. I think people would also say the idiom is pretty easy to learn, adequately expressive for many problems, and so forth.

That's very important common ground. If you are a software developer and can say you've done object-oriented programming and you've used threads or actor libraries or some such, you may feel relatively accomplished at your trade. If you are not directly familiar with this FBP idiom it is something you should learn about, because you will likely find it very valuable, and it will change the way you think about solving problems.

Mike's article continues on about the three areas listed above, and his article is definitely worth reading.

It concludes as follows:

So the conclusion should not be surprising: it's "horses for courses" [Wiktionary: The phrase stems from the fact that a racehorse performs best on a racecourse specifically suited to it] – none of these technologies is superior to the other. They all share Flow-Based Programming principles – the jury is back, Flow-Based Programming is a GOOD IDEA whose time has come and it is being used all over the place. Beyond that, what kind of processing are you doing? What kind of data is at its core, and at what scale?

Search Engines

Here is what Eric Gaumer has to say about Search Engines:

"Enterprise search (typically) requires heavy data processing semantics which Flow-Based Programming helps simplify. This process often involves, ontological mapping (taxonomies), information extraction, classification, and general data normalization and cleanup (i.e., tokenization, language detection, synonym expansion, stopword removal, etc.). All of this has to happen on extremely large volumes of data (initially) and then in near real-time on a transactional basis.

In these types of applications, data is the primary focus. FBP provides a component

Chap. XXVII: The FBP Explosion

oriented model making it easy to add new business logic on the stream of data."

Sawzall – Interpreting the Data: Parallel Analysis with Sawzall – *http://research.google.com/archive/sawzall-sciprog.pdf*

Joe Armstrong, of Erlang fame, calls this "FBP on a grand scale."

Wikipedia – *http://en.wikipedia.org/w/index.php?title=Sawzall_(programming_language)&oldid=327688434* – describes Sawzall as follows:

> Sawzall is an interpreted, procedural, domain-specific programming language, used specifically by Google, to handle huge quantities of data. Sawzall is built upon existing infrastructure at Google: Protocol Buffers, the Google File System, the Workqueue, and MapReduce.

And an intriguing recent addition to the list:

Eon: a language and runtime system for perpetual systems – see *http://portal.acm.org/citation.cfm?id=1322279*.

To quote from the abstract:

> To our knowledge, Eon is the first *energy-aware* programming language. Eon is a declarative coordination language that lets programmers compose programs from components written in C or nesC [a language from the UC Berkeley WEBS project, described on *http://nescc.sourceforge.net/* as a "programming language for deeply networked systems"] . Paths through the program ('flows') may be annotated with different energy states. Eon's automatic energy management then dynamically adapts these states to current and predicted energy levels. It chooses flows to execute and adjusts their rates of execution, maximizing the quality of service under available energy constraints.

This came up because they reference my book – presumably the "flows" between components are similar to those of FBP. The idea of using FBP to support perpetual systems is reminiscent of Wayne Stevens' description of how to repair a dam, described in Chapter 7 (page 71).

Related approaches based on the "event" concept:

Event-Driven or Event-Based Programming – *http://en.wikipedia.org/w/index.php?title=Event-driven_programming&oldid=339537662*

Chap. XXVII: The FBP Explosion

Wikipedia says:

> In computer programming, event-driven programming or event-based programming is a programming paradigm in which the flow of the program is determined by events — i.e., sensor outputs or user actions (mouse clicks, key presses) or messages from other programs or threads.

Wikipedia describes an "event" (*http://en.wikipedia.org/w/index.php?title=Event_%28computing%29&oldid=339529751*) as

> ... an action that is usually initiated outside the scope of a program and that is handled by a piece of code inside the program.

Now an important attribute of an event is the *time* at which it happened, so FBP can handle event-driven processing as long as an IP is generated for the event. If you insert an accurate timestamp in the IP, then the timing information can be preserved throughout the rest of the processing.

The quote goes on to say that in EDP the event is often handled by means of a callback – often referred to as "Inversion of Control", or somewhat facetiously the "Hollywood Principle" (don't call us, we'll call you). This sounds reminiscent of the "Jackson Inversion" discussed in Chapter 3 (page 20).

In my opinion, it doesn't seem necessary to give a different label to this type of processing – as with so many other dichotomies (such as batch vs. online), I feel this one becomes unnecessary once you get all the participants under the FBP umbrella!

Someone who sees a difference is Ingo Lütkebohle at the University of Bielefeld in Germany – there are some of his comments below about the differences he sees, and how FBP and EDP might tie together.

Functional Reactive programming (FRP)

Here is a quote from David Harel, referred to above, quoted in
http://www.codeproject.com/KB/cpp/UML_StateChart_StatWizard.aspx :

> A reactive system is characterized by being, to a large extent, event-driven, continuously having to react to external and internal stimuli. Examples include telephones, automobiles, communication networks, computer Operating Systems, and missiles. The problem is rooted in the difficulty of describing reactive behaviour in ways that are clear and realistic, and at the same time formal and rigorous, sufficiently so to be amenable to detailed computerized simulation.

Chap. XXVII: The FBP Explosion

To address this, Harel designed what are called "Harel StateCharts" – quoting from the above-mentioned web site again:

> Harel StateCharts are gaining widespread usage since a variant has become part of the Unified Modeling Language. The diagram type allows the modeling of superstates, concurrent states, and activities as part of a state.

As we have seen above, statecharts are fully compatible with FBP.

FTS Event-Flow Toolkit – see *http://www.ohloh.net/p/fts*

Quotes from three personal communications with Ingo Lütkebohle, coauthor of FTS with Sebastian Wrede (EBS means "Event-Based System"):

Portions of note #1:

> What characterizes Event-Based-Systems is, not surprisingly, the notion of an event, which, importantly, is separate from just data produced.
>
> For example, a temperature sensor might output one measurement per second, but the Event is not the measurement, but rather is the fact of a measurement satisfying some condition like "freezing: temperature lower than zero degrees Celsius".
>
> Of course, and that is where it becomes murky, one needs communication and usually communication state changes cause events at a lower level (e.g., "new data available"), so it is easy to confuse production of new data with an Event, but that is really not the intention of EBS.
>
> This has the consequence that the same data might be an event for one consumer and not be an event for another consumer. You always have to look at the particular event conditions.
>
> Anyway, I am probably not alone in saying that this level of debate of what is and isn't an event is not really all that useful when talking what you want to get *out* of a system: It is more an of architectural and tool-vendor view. Therefore, in my own writing I have started to use the term "reactive system" when I don't care about the particular realization. I believe the term is due to work in the early eighties by Harel and Pnueli.
>
> Anyway, back to the original, problematic, definition: FBP and similar formalisms can easily *realize* event-based systems through filtering nodes -- after the filter, a

Chap. XXVII: The FBP Explosion

message is equivalent to an event notification. That is also what we're doing.

However, when you're *modeling* your system at the level of connected nodes and express events through filters, I would argue that you're not really working on the event-based systems level. On the EBS level, you should be able to *declaratively* say "do A when condition B is satisfied" and not care how that is realized -- more complicated conditions might easily map to graphs with much more than just one filter, for example.

I took some time in coming to this view and the original statement was written before it. Furthermore, while the event-based systems community would probably agree that such a declarative model is typical or even essential, they might not consider it *the* characterizing factor, as I do.

At the end, the consequence of all this is that in an EBS, the *filters* specify which components are connected (not on the communication level, but on the information level). This is what I meant in my statement as the idea taken from EBS and I believe this is a different meaning of "connection" as the one in FBP. The problem seems to be that there are two different meanings of connection implied. I really should look for a better word to use and I will have to do that soon, as I'm currently writing up my thesis and the chapter on all this is coming up ☺

Portions of note #2:

It would appear to me that FBP is somewhere in the middle [between von Neumann machines and what he calls "data flow"] and this also seems to be a sweet spot hit by some of the dataflow software languages mentioned in the paper above [*http://www.citeulike.org/group/60/article/86951*].

... all EBSs I know of are based on asynchronous communication. Usually message-passing or queueing.

So, coming back to what might be a distinction between FBP and EBSs is this: EBS presupposes a dynamic means of connecting independent components by means of declarative event conditions. In this context, "independent" component usually means in its own process, or even distributed between machines. Also, the declarative event conditions usually support a powerful expression language which often includes temporal constraints. Last, but not least, many of these "connections" might be fairly short-lived, with conditions changing in response to system activity.

Chap. XXVII: The FBP Explosion

In this view, EBSs are at the inter-component level.

When you take some of these ideas to the intra-component level, something very close (or even the same) as FBP emerges -- and that is what we have done in the FTS toolkit. Actually, and this may be behind your question, we probably could have built this using your FBP library. I have to admit that, at the time, we simply didn't know about it...

... but we made a couple of different decisions regarding the Node/Engine interface that are inspired by functional reactive programming ... Still, I think that our toolkit [is based on] basically many of the same ideas, just in a slightly different way. ...

I think the main difference is that EBSs are meant to be independent components.

Note #3 (which Ingo felt was important to add):

... most event-based systems are (conceptually) talking about an "event cloud" where events are filtered from, based on subscriptions. Some systems establish dedicated communications channels upon subscription (mostly to optimize things), whereas others look at every event as a new one.

Thanks, Ingo!

By the way, the article cited above has a large number of references, both to data flow systems mentioned in this book, and to others that I don't have space to touch on. A complete list would be impossible, as it would be growing even as I write!

Message-Oriented Middleware (MOM) – see *http://en.wikipedia.org/w/index.php?title=Message-oriented_middleware&oldid=340293620*

Quoting:

Message-oriented middleware (MOM) is infrastructure focused on sending and receiving messages that increases the interoperability, portability, and flexibility of an application by allowing the application to be distributed over heterogeneous platforms. It reduces the complexity of developing applications that span multiple operating systems and network protocols by insulating the application developer from the details of the various operating system and network interfaces. API's that extend across diverse platforms and networks are typically provided by MOM.

FBP is clearly an example of a MOM system!

Chap. XXVII: The FBP Explosion

See also *http://advice.cio.com/ralph_frankel/are_you_soft_in_the_middle_the_future_of_enterprise_it_rests_in_hardware_applications?commentpage=1*, which argues that the future of the IT industry rests on embedding the data path in silicon.

Publish/Subscribe (Pub/Sub for short) – *http://en.wikipedia.org/w/index.php?title=Publish/subscribe&oldid=340293990*

Quote from Wikipedia:

> Publish/subscribe (or pub/sub) is an asynchronous messaging paradigm where senders (publishers) of messages are not programmed to send their messages to specific receivers (subscribers). Rather, published messages are characterized into classes, without knowledge of what (if any) subscribers there may be. Subscribers express interest in one or more classes, and only receive messages that are of interest, without knowledge of what (if any) publishers there are. This decoupling of publishers and subscribers can allow for greater scalability and a more dynamic network topology.

The article lists advantages and disadvantages of this approach. Some of the disadvantages listed also apply to FBP systems, and need to be considered during the design process.

Grid Computing – see *http://en.wikipedia.org/w/index.php?title=Grid_computing&oldid=338970437*

Quoting:

> It is a form of distributed computing whereby a "super and virtual computer" is composed of a cluster of networked loosely coupled computers acting in concert to perform very large tasks. This technology has been applied to computationally intensive scientific, mathematical, and academic problems through volunteer computing, and it is used in commercial enterprises for such diverse applications as drug discovery, economic forecasting, seismic analysis, and back-office data processing in support of e-commerce and Web services.
>
> ...
>
> "Distributed" or "grid" computing in general is a special type of parallel computing that relies on complete computers (with onboard CPU, storage, power supply, network interface, etc.) connected to a network (private, public or the Internet) by a

conventional network interface, such as Ethernet. This is in contrast to the traditional notion of a supercomputer, which has many processors connected by a local high-speed computer bus.

Business Flows

There are a great many tools available, a number of which are listed in the Wikipedia article titled "Business Process Modeling" (BPM) – *http://en.wikipedia.org/w/index.php?title=Business_process_modeling&oldid=343275527*. Some BPM techniques are BPMN, IDEF0, and business extensions to UML. Examples of languages being introduced for BPM are BPEL and XPDL.

Obviously this has whole area has strong affinities with FBP, but at a higher level, so combining them with FBP could give us the consistent application view that Wayne Stevens talked about in his writings. I am not sure whether work has been done on combining these different levels, but it seems to me to offer interesting possibilities.

Scientific Workflows

Kepler by Bertram Ludaescher (*http://daks.ucdavis.edu/~ludaesch/Paper/kepler-lbl.ppt*) – it describes some fascinating application areas, and how they are being approached using Data Flow.

"FlowBased Solutions"

I would like to mention FlowBased Solutions as its founder Stan Williams and I worked together at IBM for a number of years. He is one of those rare people who can milk every last instruction per second out of hardware! He has been an advocate of FBP for many years, and has built some extremely fast extensions of the idea on mainframes. He is hoping to revive a patent application in this area that went "abandoned" last year (2009) – his phrase. I believe the patent application has merit, as there are some innovations in his implementation that are not at all obvious, even to someone "skilled in the art". He can be reached at *stan@flowbased.com*.

Visual Programming Languages

An enormous list is given in the Wikipedia article on Visual Programming Languages – *http://en.wikipedia.org/w/index.php?title=Visual_programming_language&oldid=338054084*. It is probably safe to say that very few of these existed 15 years ago!

Chap. XXVII: The FBP Explosion

However, here is some information about one of the earliest and most widely known of the Visual Programming Languages, LabVIEW:

LabVIEW (*http://en.wikipedia.org/w/index.php?title=LabVIEW&oldid=338785477*) (short for Laboratory Virtual Instrumentation Engineering Workbench) is a platform and development environment for a visual programming language from National Instruments. It is commonly used for data acquisition, instrument control, and industrial automation on a variety of platforms including Microsoft Windows, various flavors of UNIX, Linux, and Mac OS X.

The programming language used in LabVIEW, also referred to as G, is a dataflow programming language. Execution is determined by the structure of a graphical block diagram (the LV-source code) on which the programmer connects different function-nodes by drawing wires. These wires propagate variables and any node can execute as soon as all its input data become available. Since this might be the case for multiple nodes simultaneously, G is inherently capable of parallel execution. Multi-processing and multi-threading hardware is automatically exploited by the built-in scheduler, which multiplexes multiple OS threads over the nodes ready for execution.

For people interested in how LabVIEW looks, there is a small program that calculates a Fibonacci-sequence on *http://web.irdc.nl/wouter/2005/labview_fibonacci.png* – linked by Wouter Coene to an article on the c2 Wiki (retrieved 2010-02-12).

Fractal (*http://fractal.ow2.org/*) is a "modular, extensible and programming language agnostic component model that can be used to design, implement, deploy and reconfigure systems and applications, from operating systems to middleware platforms and to graphical user interfaces. The goal of Fractal is to reduce the development, deployment and maintenance costs of software systems in general, and of ObjectWeb projects in particular."

Here is their list of Fractal's important features:

- **recursivity** : components can be nested in *composite* components (hence the "Fractal" name).
- **reflectivity** : components have full introspection and intercession capabilities.
- **component sharing** : a given component instance can be included (or shared) by more than one component. This is useful to model shared resources such as memory manager or device drivers for instance.
- **binding components** : a single abstraction for components connections that is called *bindings* . Bindings can embed any communication semantics from synchronous method calls to remote procedure calls
- **execution model independence** : no execution model is imposed. In that, components can be run within other execution models than the classical thread-based model such as event-based models and so on.

- **open** : extra-functional services associated to a component can be customized through the notion of a control membrane [sic].

Music and Art Department

Pure Data (or Pd) (*http://en.wikipedia.org/w/index.php?title=Pure_Data&oldid=338853349*) is a graphical programming language developed by Miller Puckette in the 1990s for the creation of interactive computer music and multimedia works. Pd is very similar in scope and design to Puckette's original **Max** (*http://en.wikipedia.org/w/index.php?title=Max_(software)&oldid=338370781*) program, developed while he was at IRCAM (in Paris), and is to some degree interoperable with Max/MSP, the commercial successor to the Max language. Both Pd and Max are arguably examples of Dataflow programming languages. In such languages, functions or "objects" are linked or "patched" together in a graphical environment which models the flow of the control and audio.

In 2005, Mathieu Bouchard (*http://artengine.ca/matju*) informs me that Montréal (where I spent 8 happily bilingual years!) is now a rather big city for PureData, "maybe only next to Graz, Barcelona and Wien [Vienna]". Mathieu says he has written dataflow programs that have run at the Museum of Contemporary Arts of Montréal, Museum of Civilisation of Québec, Medienkunstlabor of Graz, Ottawa Art Gallery, Sherbrooke U Art Gallery, and High-Performance Rodeo, among others.

vvvv (*http://en.wikipedia.org/w/index.php?title=Vvvv&oldid=299772245*) (commonly pronounced 'fear fow' meaning "4 v's" in German or 'fow fear' meaning "v4" in German) is a general purpose toolkit with a special focus on real time video synthesis and programming large media environments with physical interfaces, real-time motion graphics, audio and video. **vvvv** uses a data flow approach and a visual programming interface for rapid prototyping and developing.

Lily (*http://en.wikipedia.org/w/index.php?title=Lily_(software)&oldid=338648981*) is an Open Source, browser-based visual programming language that lets users create programs graphically by drawing connections between animation, data, images, sounds, text and graphics.

Music components in JavaFBP

Here is a brief description of some components in the JavaFBP jar file which could be used as a base for writing JavaFBP symphonies!

My first prototype music component was called *PlayTune* – it accepted a stream of packets, each one containing an 2-element integer array, where the first element in the array is a frequency, and the second is a duration in milliseconds. *PlayTune* played these "note" packets, one at a time, with a 25-millisecond gap at the end of each one, by sampling a sine wave of the specified frequency, and the samples were played using classes from the `javax.sound.sampled` package.

Oddly enough, the *PlayTune* component was much simpler to write in C#FBP, as C# has a `System.beep()` method, whose parameters are `frequency` and `duration`.

To take advantage of the configurability of FBP, *PlayTune* was then split into two asynchronous components: *GenSamples*, and *SoundMixer*, and the original component deprecated. The former takes note/duration pairs and generates a stream of 1-second samples, while the latter takes these samples and feeds them to the Java `SourceDataLine`. Splitting the original *PlayTune* component in this way means that we now have a component that can accept 1-second samples created by a variety of different components.

The new *SoundMixer* component initially accepted a single stream of samples, but I realized that it could be converted to use an *array* input port, where the 1-second samples from each input port element were simply added together. This component therefore became a true mixer, where each element of the input port represents a separate "voice". With the addition of gain controls, *SoundMixer* can now be used to do real musical work.

FAUST

Thanks to John Cowan, mentioned above, for pointing this out (on the FBP Google Group). There is a description of it in French on *http://www.grame.fr/Recherche/Programmes/* – I will endeavour to translate it into English. Any mistakes I make are purely my own:

> The FAUST project (Functional Audio Stream) aims at developing a collection of techniques and tools allowing the description of algorithms for synthesis and signal processing in a high level specification language, while benefiting from efficient compilation, comparable to optimized C code. ...
>
> Generally [other systems] simulate a dataflow machine. For reasons of efficiency, that [type of] simulation treats samples not individually, but in blocks (and generally without the possibility of effectively having cycles or recursions).
>
> This is why a simple filter of the form `y(t) = a.x(t)+b.y(t-1)` very often cannot be described in these languages and must therefore be implemented in the form of an external object, using traditional programming languages.

In his post, John describes Faust as he understands it – this is his Google Group post (*http://groups.google.com/group/flow-based-programming/browse_thread/thread/f844449141d9d3e1*):

> Faust components differ from FBP components in two major ways. First, the inputs

Chap. XXVII: The FBP Explosion

and outputs of the components are numbered rather than named [shades of AMPS!], so we speak of "the first n inputs" or "the last j outputs" of a component. This does not mean that components always treat their inputs or outputs symmetrically, however: for example, the / component accepts dividends on its first input and divisors on its second input. Second, Faust programs are not written down as a *graph* of components, but using an *algebra* of components: there are five operators that construct new components out of existing ones, and you write down an algebraic formula that specifies the relationships of components. For convenience, you can give names to Faust expressions (these are inlined at compile time) and specify simple rewrite rules (macros) for abstraction (also expanded at compile time).

There are five operators in Faust, each of which accepts two operands A and B, themselves components, and produce a new component C as the result. Note that the operators are not commutative. I am sorry this is so terse: there is a short paper at <http://www.grame.fr/Ressources/pub/faust-soft-computing.pdf> and a longer tutorial covering the same ground at <http://www.grame.fr/Ressources/pub/faust_tutorial.pdf>.

The parallel operator A,B results in a component that feeds its lower-numbered inputs to A and its higher-numbered ones to B; its outputs are set up in the same way.

The serial operator A:B, the split operator A<:B, and the merge operator A:>B basically connect A's outputs to B's inputs; C's inputs are A's inputs and C's outputs are B's outputs. They differ in how additional outputs of A and inputs of B are treated. In A:B, extra inputs and outputs just become extra inputs and outputs of C. In A<:B, additional inputs of B get copies of the packets sent to the lower-numbered inputs; it's an error if the number of inputs of B is not an exact multiple of the number of outputs of A. Contrariwise, A:>B means that additional outputs of A are (fairly) merged with the first sequence of outputs, and it's an error if the number of outputs of A is not an exact multiple of the number of inputs of B.

Finally, A~B is the recursive operator, which allows for loops in the graph. The outputs of A are the outputs of C, but they are also copied, as many as possible, to the inputs of B, and B's outputs are in turn connected to the inputs of A. Any additional inputs of A become the inputs of C.

The primitive components provided Faust include _ , which passes its single input to its single output unchanged, and ! , which discards anything sent to its input. A constant is a component which emits its value on its single output forever. The usual

Chap. XXVII: The FBP Explosion

arithmetic and relational operators are raised to the domain of streams, so that + adds the values provided on its two inputs and produces a single output, and <= produces true if the value on its lower-numbered input is less than [or equal to?] the value on its higher-numbered input. These components have syntactic sugar in Faust: you can write A+B instead of (A,B):+ to parallelize A and B and pipe them into +.

In addition, there are two-way and three-way selectors for flow control, read-only and read-write table components. The GUI-based components button, checkbox, number box, and slider have a single output; how often a packet is generated (the sampling rate) is specified at compile time. Any function written in C can be used as a component in the same way as the arithmetic operators, with N inputs for its N arguments and a single output.

Long-term, it would be interesting to have a variety of Faust's algebra that deals with arbitrary FBP components, if the mismatch between named ports and numbered ports can be resolved by some suitable convention. More short-term, Faust components could be directly incorporated into a FBP framework. Because the Faust language is pure functional (unless you call an ill-behaved C function), the compiler is able to smush a whole Faust program down to single-threaded code that does the same thing as the network you actually write, but is much more efficient because there are no thread switches.

Currently, Faust can only produce C++, but I bet it would be easy to change it, given some time and effort, to generate Java and C# as well. All Faust packets are either C `ints` or C `floats`, suitable to the intended use for signal processing, and the Faust compiler does type analysis to insert conversion components as needed. This might not be so easy to extend, but few programs avoid *some* numeric processing.

Another project called ASTREE is described on the same web page, *http://www.grame.fr/Recherche/Programmes/*, that in turn uses the FAUST notation. The purpose of ASTREE is to preserve musical material using a timeless, "non-volatile" notation, independent of specific media, languages or software.

More FBP-like entries (contributed by Tom Young)

Here are some additional entries contributed by Tom Young. Space does not permit me to go into detail about these, so I have to apologize if some of them are not given the attention they deserve!

Chap. XXVII: The FBP Explosion

- DFD and VDFD – Tom Young
- SAX Filters – *http://www.saxproject.org/?selected=filters*
- Xbeans – *http://www.xbeans.org/*
- Xpipe – *http://xpipe.sourceforge.net/*
- Sisal – *http://sourceforge.net/projects/sisal/*
- Prograph – *http://en.wikipedia.org/w/index.php?title=Prograph&oldid=295129986*
- Marten – *http://www.andescotia.com/products/marten/*
- AviSynth – *http://en.wikipedia.org/w/index.php?title=AviSynth&oldid=353292202*

Tom Young can be reached at *fbp@twyoung.com*, and his Google spreadsheet (which he will be updating as time permits) is at *http://spreadsheets.google.com/pub?key=t59OKdXx3UDaXl7s-d8bjAQ&output=html*.

Thanks, Tom!

Modern programming Languages

Programming languages have evolved to include useful concurrency constructs, and these are in many cases useful to implement FBP, and for evolving FBP concepts. Some notable languages are mentioned below as they have come up repeatedly in conversations with FBP practitioners as desirable.

Erlang – see *http://ftp.sunet.se/pub/lang/erlang/*

Erlang, developed by Joe Armstrong at Ericsson, was designed to support distributed, fault-tolerant, soft-real-time, non-stop applications. The sequential subset of Erlang is a functional language, with strict evaluation, single assignment, and dynamic typing. For concurrency it follows the Actor model.

Unlike FBP, it is oriented around supporting a large number of relatively short-lived threads, and can support very large numbers of threads (a benchmark with 20 million processes was successfully performed in 2005). Erlang has been described as having "green processes", not to be confused with "green threads", and can in fact take advantage of multiple cores.

Erlang, in its present form, does not have FBP-style independent specification of connections. However, Joe Armstrong informs me that he feels that ideally we should have several layers

Chap. XXVII: The FBP Explosion

when building a system. Inside what he calls "black boxes", we would have regular programming languages. Outside the black boxes he proposes a language that describes protocols, and on top of this would be a "plumbing language" that describes the component configuration. He has specified a notation called Universal Binary Format (UBF) for the middle layer (see *http://www.sics.se/~joe/ubf/site/ubf.pdf* describing "contracts" between pairs of black boxes, and also *http://www.sics.se/~joe/ubf/site/home.html*). You will remember that Mike Beckerle came up with a typing scheme to address the same problem – it is described above in Chapter 11 (page 117).

In *http://www.jpaulmorrison.com/cgi-bin/wiki.pl?JoeArmstrongsResearchSuggestions* (retrieved 2009-12-08), Joe also suggests some interesting joint research possibilities.

In what could probably be a summing-up of this whole chapter, Joe tells me (March 2010):

> I think the world is slowly coming to the view that processes should be isolated, and should be glued together with messaging...

Obviously, I totally agree!

Axum – see *http://msdn.microsoft.com/en-us/devlabs/dd795202.aspx*

Axum (previously codenamed Maestro) is a domain-specific concurrent programming language, based on the Actor model, being developed by Microsoft. It is currently a prototype with working Microsoft Visual Studio integration. Microsoft has made a CTP (Community Technology Preview) of Axum available to the public. However, it has not been decided if and when it will be released as a supported product.

Other Microsoft concurrent programming efforts include .NET Rx, Cω (pronounced "Comega"), and possibly PowerShell and VPL (Visual Programming Language).

.NET Rx – *http://reddevnews.com/articles/2009/10/01/net-rx-framework.aspx*

Microsoft's .NET Reactive framework is based on the idea of "observable collections". Quoting from the above-mentioned web site:

> the Rx Framework consists of a pair of interfaces (IObserver/IObservable) that represent "push-based" observable collections, along with a library of extension methods that implement Microsoft's LINQ Standard Query Operators and other stream-transformation functions. ... Observable collections capture the essence of the subject/observer design pattern, [language designer Erik] Meijer said, and are especially useful for dealing with event-based and asynchronous programming.

Cω – see *http://research.microsoft.com/en-us/um/cambridge/projects/comega/doc/comega_startpage.htm*

Chap. XXVII: The FBP Explosion

About Cω Microsoft says the following:

> Cω is a strongly typed, data-oriented programming language that bridges the gap between between semi-structured hierarchical data (XML), relational data (SQL), and the .NET Common Type System (CTS). In Cω, the seemingly different worlds of XML, SQL and CTS are bridged and connected through generalization, not specialization.
>
> Besides data integration, Cω extends the C# programming language with new asynchronous concurrency abstractions, based on the join calculus. The language presents a simple and powerful model of concurrency which is applicable both to multithreaded applications running on a single machine and to the orchestration of asynchronous, event-based applications communicating over a wide area network.

Scala – see *http://www.scala-lang.org/*

Scala is a general purpose programming language designed to express common programming patterns in a concise, elegant, and type-safe way. It is fully interoperative with Java, "smoothly integrating features of object-oriented and functional languages".

Scala seems to be gaining attention because of its what Ted Neward describes as its "promise of easier coding when dealing with concurrency and writing thread-safe code" (*http://www.ibm.com/developerworks/java/library/j-scala02049.html*). In this article he refers to "several of Scala's properties that make it more amenable to writing thread-safe code such as immutable objects by default and a design preference for returning copies of objects rather than modifying their contents." In the second part he describes Scala's *Actor* concept (*http://www.ibm.com/developerworks/java/library/j-scala04109.html*). Messages are sent using the ! operator and received using `receive` – this is the same notation used by Erlang, but in most other respects these two languages are very different.

In May 2007, Philippe Monnaie, a student at the Katholieke Universiteit in Leuven in Belgium wrote, and successfully defended, a thesis on combining Scala and FBP – it can be found at *http://pmonnaie.dreamhosters.com/papers/A%20Survey%20of%20Support%20for%20Concurrency%20in%20Modern%20Programming%20Languages.pdf*.

Concurrent Haskell – *http://en.wikipedia.org/w/index.php?title=Concurrent_Haskell&oldid=335372300*

Haskell is a standardized, general-purpose purely functional programming language, with non-strict semantics and strong static typing. Concurrent Haskell extends Haskell with explicit concurrency.

The Software Transactional Memory (STM), recently added to Concurrent Haskell (2005), is described in this article, in part as follows:

> ...the STM monad [described in Wikipedia as "a kind of abstract data type used to represent computations"] ... allows us to write atomic transactions. This means that all operations inside the transaction fully complete, without any other threads modifying the variables that our transaction is using, or it fails, and the state is rolled back to where it was before the transaction was begun. In short, atomic transactions either complete fully, or it is as if they were never run at all.

This seems very similar to the concept underlying mainframe transaction processing, especially in IMS/DC, which was described in the chapter on Checkpointing (Chapter 19 – page 185).

Clojure – see *http://en.wikipedia.org/w/index.php?title=Clojure&oldid=346345858*

Quoting:

> ... is a modern dialect of the Lisp programming language. It is a general-purpose language supporting interactive development that encourages a functional programming style, and simplifies multithreaded programming. Clojure runs on the Java Virtual Machine and the Common Language Runtime.

Quite a bit of dataflow work has been done using Clojure. Justin Bozonier recently pointed me at some work done by the language's inventor, Rich Hickey, and in particular, a video of Rich's keynote speech at JVM Languages Summit 2009, discussing whether OO is truly the "end of the road", called "Are We There Yet?": *http://www.infoq.com/presentations/Are-We-There-Yet-Rich-Hickey*. A comment that particularly struck home was Rich's statement that, in OO, the time dimension is not clearly specified, so that objects may change at points in time that are not well-defined (he says it better than this). He says that data objects should be immutable, and, when modification of the data is required, should be replaced at a particular point in time by another immutable object. But, of course, data objects only changing, or being replaced, at well-defined points in time (the times when specific IP types are received by a process) are exactly what we saw in my description of the logic of an FBP batch update, described in Chapter 9 (page 90).

Go from Google, mentioned above – Vladimir Sibirov, a master student at Nizhny Novgorod State Technical University, Russia, tells me that Go "has lightweight coroutines for concurrent execution, built-in 'channel' type (very similar to ports in FBP), plenty of libraries for real world tasks and a growing [user] community", and he feels that it would be an interesting language in which to implement FBP. The Wikipedia article *http://en.wikipedia.org/w/index.php?title=Go_*

Chap. XXVII: The FBP Explosion

%28programming_language%29&oldid=413837579 states that it lacks type inheritance, generic programming, assertions, method overloading, or pointer arithmetic. The last item has up to now been key in developing non-OO FBP implementations, so it would be interesting to see what an FBP implementation using Go would look like.

Go! – a different language, by McCabe and Clark, which also sounds interesting – see *http://en.wikipedia.org/w/index.php?title=Go!_%28programming_language %29&oldid=411618374*. The authors of Go! describe it as "a multi-paradigm programming language that is oriented to the needs of programming secure, production quality, agent based applications. It is multi-threaded, strongly typed and higher order (in the functional programming sense). It has relation, function and action procedure definitions. Threads execute action procedures, calling functions and querying relations as need be. Threads in different agents communicate and coordinate using asynchronous messages. Threads within the same agent can also use shared dynamic relations acting as Linda-style tuple stores."

Hardware

nesC – see *http://nescc.sourceforge.net/*

nesC is a language from the UC Berkeley WEBS project, described as a "programming language for deeply networked systems". It is an extension to the C programming language designed to embody the structuring concepts and execution model of *TinyOS*. TinyOS is an event-driven operating system designed for sensor network nodes that have very limited resources (e.g., 8K bytes of program memory, 512 bytes of RAM).

nesC programs are built out of *components*, which are assembled ("wired") to form whole programs. Components have internal concurrency in the form of *tasks*. Threads of control may pass into a component through its interfaces. These threads are rooted either in a task or a hardware interrupt.

Graphics

The need for increasing realism in graphics requires increasing amounts of computing power, but the computations involved have been described as "embarrassingly parallel" (e.g. ray tracing), so graphics are a good candidate for the kinds of techniques we have been discussing. The March-April 2010 issue of the American Scientist (Vol. 98, No. 2), has an interesting article called "The Race for Real-time Photorealism". They report that Intel has embarked on the development of a completely new computer architecture, codenamed Larrabee, a "many-core compute engine", based on the x86 CPU architecture. It is referred to as a "general purpose GPU". In December 2009, they announced that Larrabee will be released first as a software development platform that will be used by Intel to "explore the potential of many-core applications."

Chap. XXVII: The FBP Explosion

Here is a quote from the Wikipedia article on GPUs (*http://en.wikipedia.org/w/index.php?title=Graphics_processing_unit&oldid=355416637#Stream_Processing_and_General_Purpose_GPUs_.28GPGPU.29*):

> A new concept is to use a general purpose graphics processing unit as a modified form of stream processor. This concept turns the massive floating-point computational power of a modern graphics accelerator's shader pipeline into general-purpose computing power, as opposed to being hard wired solely to do graphical operations. In certain applications requiring massive vector operations, this can yield several orders of magnitude higher performance than a conventional CPU. The two largest discrete ... GPU designers, ATI and NVIDIA, are beginning to pursue this new approach with an array of applications. Both NVIDIA and ATI have teamed with Stanford University to create a GPU-based client for the Folding@Home distributed computing project, for protein folding calculations. In certain circumstances the GPU calculates forty times faster than the conventional CPUs traditionally used by such applications.

Microprocessor Gedankenexperiment

Some years ago, a colleague and I discussed the possibility of implementing an FBP application as a network of microprocessors connected together by wires. (I don't think this has happened yet, but I include it simply because I think it *will* happen sooner or later – let's see how clear my crystal ball is!)

Each microprocessor would basically be running a single code loop which takes packets off one or more (fixed capacity) input queues in the microprocessor's memory, does some processing, and writes zero or more packets out onto the outgoing wires. When a packet arrives on a microprocessor's input wire, it triggers an interrupt, and the interrupt code stores the packet on the corresponding input queue. Such a network, we believed, would support the implementation of a wide variety of FBP applications – plus it offers the possibility of having special purpose hardware components to perform common data transforms such as merges, selects, etc., and of being able to smoothly integrate hardware and software devices.

Now, since it would be impractical to have to specify an application by plugging and unplugging wires, you would need some programmable way of selecting components, and specifying how their inputs and outputs are connected. This would seem to suggest something like FPGAs (Field-Programmable Gate Arrays) – see *http://en.wikipedia.org/w/index.php?title=Field-programmable_gate_array&oldid=344186919* – or maybe we could bring back the old plugboards!

Embedded Systems

Interesting comments in the web site of the Embedded Systems NoE (Network of Excellence),

Chap. XXVII: The FBP Explosion

"ArtistDesign" – *http://www.artist-embedded.org/artist/Brief-State-of-the-Art,1919.html*:

> In telecommunication companies, the main current interest seems to be in exploring the use of the Linux OS and its real-time extensions. QoS mechanisms, virtualization and reservation-based scheduling, multi- and many-core platforms, and data-flow based programming models are also attracting substantial interest. ...
>
> Reconfigurable hardware systems are a technique that for a long time has not been able to compete either with software-based systems or with ASIC-based solutions. However, there are signs that that is about to change, especially for applications where the gains in performance over software-based system and the faster development cycle compared to ASICs are important.
>
> The multi/many-core trend also narrows the gap between software and hardware-based implementation techniques. In both cases good models are needed for exploiting parallelism, both in the programming models and languages used and in the compilers and analysis tools. Ideally, it should be possible to execute the same application either on a FPGA with a high-level of parallelism or on a, e.g., quad-core, platform without having to change anything in the source.

"Reliable Application Development"

I did not want to leave this chapter without quoting from some of my correspondence with David Johnson, an extremely experienced programmer with over 30 years of experience in complex application development. He and I have been corresponding extensively since about 2007, and in his notes to me he describes clearly and fluently what he has learned about the programming trade. I have put the title of this section in quotes, as it is a catchphrase that we have sometimes used in connection with this correspondence. Back in 2007, I posted several sections of one of his letters on the FBP Wiki, and I am reprinting the first section and part of another section with his permission.

> I have been a software developer since 1976, and I have long been impressed with the flow-based approach to application design. My first exposure to such ideas came from Tom DeMarco's book on structured analysis in which he develops the notion of dataflow diagrams. At that time - the early 80s - I was already heavily involved in the development of distributed applications, so it was very natural to think in terms of asynchronous processes connected by various types of communications links.
>
> The surprise was that I soon found it easier, and much more reliable, to design more

traditional (i.e. single-threaded, imperative) applications by creating a simple multi-threaded scheduler as the basis for the application, and then breaking my design down into asynchronous modules that would run in some non-deterministic order under control of the scheduler. When object-oriented languages came along, this approach became even more natural since each process could be defined as a well-encapsulated class, and the scheduler was similarly a special class that did almost nothing but invoke the "run" methods of the various process objects.

This approach also made it much easier to communicate accurately and naturally with clients who otherwise would not have understood the convoluted transformations that are necessary to turn their wishes into conventional procedural code. Unfortunately, the advent of object-oriented software made the earlier "structured" approach seemingly passé, including the use of dataflow diagrams. Consequently, I often feel that I am practically the only designer who still uses such diagrams to communicate with clients...

This is all very unfortunate in my view, because the flow-based approach is not only easier for lay people like clients to understand, but it is easier for programmers also. Whenever I say that I write my own schedulers the average programmer absolutely cringes at the very idea, because they do not understand that a round-robin scheduler is often only a few lines of code. Nor do I give up much in the ability to prioritize real-time event handling, because putting the priority scheme in the scheduler is usually the wrong thing to do anyway. The processes themselves know very well if they need to run or not, and they do not have to suck their input queues dry simply because there is more than one item waiting. Rather, every process gets a chance to run on a regular basis, and anything that turns out to be a bottleneck tends to get more processor time simply because it is starving the downstream processes for work. Thus, congested nodes in the flow network get the focus they need without any special logic to handle it.

Also, because I have done a lot of work with formal communication protocols, I have a deep feeling for the power and convenience of finite state machines, so the bulk of my asynchronous processes are designed as formal state machines, which means that my designs have almost nothing in the way of built-in side-effects that can turn into pathological connections within a process. In addition, a state machine can certainly be thought of as a set of independent threads of logic that each run in some formally defined circumstance based upon the current state and the current input type. That is to say, a state machine can very well be thought of as a scheduler that selects the correct bit of code to run at any given moment.

Chap. XXVII: The FBP Explosion

Finally, if those bits of code are defined as strict functions (i.e. a mapping between domain and range sets) then one has very tight control of the entire design.

One starts by defining the formal membership rules for the sets of data handled by the system, then one can define each processing function as a strict mapping between those sets, then those functions can be assembled into state machines that implement processes, and finally the processes can be organized in a system-wide dataflow network. At every level there is a formal, objective definition of every component from the simplest data item to the system as a whole.

This means two things in particular.

First, there are a wealth of opportunities to put correctness assertions into the finished code. Inputs and outputs to individual functions can be tested to make sure they belong to the expected sets. State machines can make sure that all states encountered are properly defined, and that all inputs to the process are occurring in a permitted order (of which there may be very many), and the overall flow of data can move over links that must connect objectively defined outputs from one process to similarly defined inputs to another process. At all of these points the software can cheaply and easily detect errors, and then report very precise debugging information to the users and designers.

Second, if the system is doing something the customer says is wrong, it is relatively easy to change either the connectivity of processes, or the detailed definition of the processes themselves, because the code will have almost no implicitly defined connections internally. Changing the connectivity of processes is usually very easy, and internal details of a process are so modular that changes of only a few types are possible. Perhaps a data set definition is slightly off, perhaps a function is not quite the correct mapping between inputs and outputs, or perhaps a state machine does not have quite the correct state space, or quite the correct transitions between states. In short, all such errors tend to be very localized, and thus easy to correct without fouling up some other part of the design as a result of inadvertent messing with implicit connections between poorly encapsulated modules.

The net result for clients is that the specification process is transparent to them from the outset, and any error messages they need to take back to the designers will quickly pinpoint the exact problem. The diagnosed problems can in turn be corrected extremely quickly, and the system can go back online equally quickly, often a matter of only a few hours from first seeing the error report to getting running again.

Chap. XXVII: The FBP Explosion

In point of fact, using these methods I almost never deliver a detectable bug to customers in the first place. For years I used to give my clients a warranty that said I would fix any bug for free in the first 180 days of operation. That sounds pretty daring, but in fact I have never had such a call at all. In several cases I called the clients every couple of weeks to make sure they were not about to surprise me, but they never had a problem. In one case my work ran for two solid years on many machines with no reported errors at all.

In that last case, even my own alpha testing turned up only two bugs, both easily fixed. ...

The point of the foregoing couple of paragraphs is ... to say that these design methods work extremely well, provided only that one is reasonably disciplined about using them. You cannot take shortcuts and expect to get good results. So, while I would claim serious self-discipline, it is otherwise the methods that keep the error rate so low, and anyone can learn both discipline and the methods. Indeed, the self-discipline becomes rather easy to enforce, because it is heavily reinforced by real success. After all, who wants to be a whiny loser, when it is relatively easy to be a star in the client's view.

Unfortunately, nearly the entire industry is hopelessly stuck on the von Neumann architecture, and the relatively shallow techniques that make it moderately usable. In general I am reminded of a scene in [the movie] "Bonny and Clyde" in which they are on the run and holed up in a grungy, rural motel. Bonny asks Clyde if he would do things differently if he had known at the outset how things would turn out. Clyde misses the point of the question totally, and says, yes, he would have one state where they did no heists, so they would always have one jurisdiction where they were not wanted criminals. The software industry's addiction to the intellectual equivalent of a life of crime is almost that pathetic also. In most cases it is not an actual criminal offense to deliver buggy systems, but I've met plenty of clients who think it ought to be.

Further on, he talks about simulation (see also p. 269 above). Here is what he says:

Frankly, I have always been suspicious of the concept of rapid prototyping, partly because many key details get left out of such implementations, and partly because it gives both management and the clients a false sense of security when they see something running that looks much like what they had in mind. It often seems to provoke unrealistic expectations about how long the real implementation will take. However, that notwithstanding, I am taken with your comments about simulating a system, and I can see the possibilities for that. Two examples come to mind.

First, it is sometimes possible to use a real but lightweight component as an effective substitute for the industrial grade component that will be used in production. On one project, for example, we used the Access database in place of the MS SQL server that we intended to use in production. Access could be used by means of the same ODBC interfaces that would be used in production, so our application code did not have to be changed in order to interface to Access in stead of SQL Server; thus, we were able to realistically test our code without making a big and premature investment in the real server. When we eventually cut over to the real server we reran our suite of tests in the new environment, but as expected everything passed with flying colors. The overall point here is that Access is an effective RDBMS for simulating production, but it lacks all sorts of administrative features that would make it suitable for heavy commercial use.

Second, I am beginning to suspect that I should give more thought to some sort of interpreted simulator for distributed applications. The emphasis would be on highly graphical and canonical representations of the topology and logic of the system, but without the need to set up a real network of any proportions. Once the developers and clients had satisfied themselves that the functionality was correct in the simulation, the various parts of the system could be ported to their production platforms, which, of course, might differ considerably from one part of the system to another. This is hardly a new thought in the industry, and I myself have been thinking such things rather idly ever since I read DeMarco's book on structured analysis back in 1980. However, it is only lately that I have become convinced that the combination of flow-based analysis, state machines, and strict functions might truly be sufficient for modeling the vast majority of practical applications.

In a recent note (Feb., 2011), Dave recommended a book called "Software Abstractions: Logic, Language, and Analysis", by Daniel Jackson (ISBN 0262101149). Professor Jackson also has a web site – *http://softwareabstractions.org/* – which contains sample chapters from the book, including the entertaining, and thought-provoking, preface. He describes his book as follows:

> *Software Abstractions* introduces the key elements of the approach: a logic, which provides the building blocks of the language; a language, which adds a small amount of syntax to the logic for structuring descriptions; and an analysis, a form of constraint solving that offers both simulation (generating sample states and executions) and checking (finding counterexamples to claimed properties). The book uses Alloy as a vehicle because of its simplicity and tool support, but the book's lessons are mostly language-independent, and could also be applied in the context of

Chap. XXVII: The FBP Explosion

other modeling languages.

JavaFBP Application supporting Independent Assisted Living (IAL)

I mentioned earlier that I very seldom get feedback from actual *users* of any of the FBP implementations, so that is why I was so excited to hear from Dr. Ernesto Compatangelo of the University of Aberdeen in Scotland, *who is actually using one of them,* namely JavaFBP. Not only is his application a) interesting in its own right, b) socially conscious, but he has introduced a new pattern which he calls the "hierarchical processing model", plus he has also suggested improvements to an area of JavaFBP (and therefore C#FBP) that I probably had not paid enough attention to – namely input and output array ports. He also contributed the index at the end of this book. Thanks, Ernesto, for all your good work!

Here is his description of their application:

> [We are] aiming to develop and commercialize a system to monitor frail and vulnerable (e.g., elderly) people in their own homes, thus enabling their Independent Assisted Living (also known as Ambient Assisted Living in some European quarters).
>
> We are currently using JavaFBP as the core of a distributed infrastructure that acquires readings from a range of heterogeneous sensors (from switches to webcams), analyzes sensorial data to find out what is happening in specific areas of a home environment at any point in time, and whether this fits with the automatically learned 'normal lifestyle pattern' of the supported individual living in that environment. If a deviation wrt the expected pattern is observed, a concern notification is automatically raised by the system and reported to a remote care centre manned 24/7 for suitable action.
>
> So far, we have developed a series of FBP components and networks (each dealing with a specific kind of sensor). The FBP paradigm is particularly suitable for systems centred around sensor data acquisition, refinement, and analysis. In such systems, a cascading network of components arranged in a hierarchy of processing layers is used to gradually transform an incoming sensor data stream into a loose temporal sequence of conceptual elements such as actions, activities, or dynamically changing scenarios.
>
> The architecture underpinning this kind of systems is based on a structural pattern sometimes referred to as a "hierarchical processing model", in the sense that it is based on a hierarchy of abstractions layers, each performing part of the data processing and of the information analysis tasks. For instance, let us consider the

Chap. XXVII: The FBP Explosion

diagram shown below. Each component P1.1 ... P1.NL1 belonging to Layer 1 is responsible for processing and analyzing data from a specific sensor located in a particular area of a building; we can call this the sensor layer.

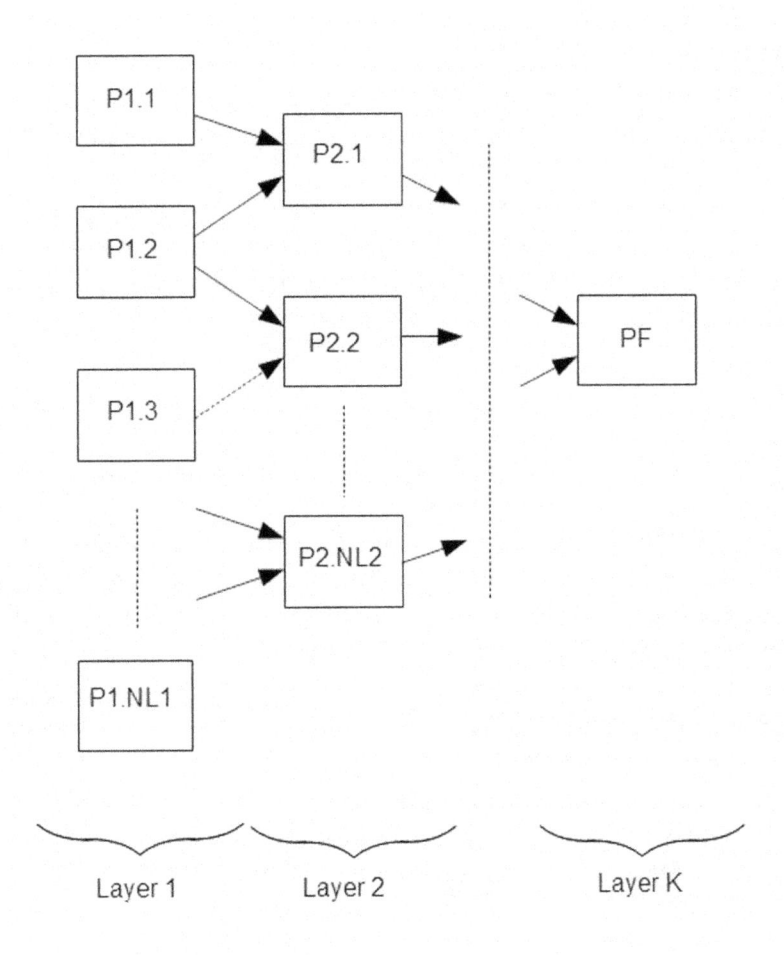

Layer 1   Layer 2   Layer K

The output of each component in Layer 1 is connected to the input of one or more components in Layer 2. Each component P2.1 ... P2.NL2 (where PNL2 ≠ PNL1) is responsible for processing and analyzing information coming from a set of diverse but related sensors. For instance, in monitoring applications, each Layer 2 component represents a specific area of a building (*e.g.*, a room) whose data analysis capabilities are based on information provided by each of the sensors located in the area. In other words, information resulting from the analysis of data acquired by each sensor positioned in a given area is used by each area processing and analyzing component

Chap. XXVII: The FBP Explosion

in Layer 2 to derive further information that refers to the area as a unit.

If P1.1 is a webcam tracking ambient movement and P1.2 is a microphone recording ambient sound, then P2.1 can jointly analyze movement and sound detected at the same time to infer that somebody has actually entered the area. In turn, a component in Layer 3 could receive analysis results from different areas to infer that a person moving from, say, Area X to Area Y to Area Z is likely to be performing an activity that involves touching base with those areas, in the given sequential order.

Component PF in the top Layer could analyze what happens in each building floor and infer whether there is any potentially out-of-normal condition, even if everything appears to be fine in each area, but the individual results do not add up to provide a "normal" overall picture.

On a more general level, he says about the "hierarchical processing model":

I am convinced that FBP can represent the right infrastructural backbone for an effective implementation of what Jeff Hawkins, in his book 'On Intelligence' [Jeff Hawkins and Sandra Blakeslee – ISBN 0805078533] has described as the hierarchical model of the human brain. In a nutshell, in FBP terms, Hawkins views the brain as a layered network where the bottom level receives its input from body sensors of various kind (vision, sound, etc). Each process (aka component activation) at this level asynchronously receives some sensorial data. Components do some simple, partial information processing, passing their result to various components in the upper layer. These get various inputs, do some 'collation' reasoning and pass their result to the upper layer, and so on. In the end the process(es) in the topmost layer make sense of all the increasingly refined and summarized partial results asynchronously derived in the lower layers, et voilà, here is reasoning and intelligence...

It is not difficult to realize that the FBP model seems to be particularly appropriate to represent the infrastructure of such a working model of the human brain and that a smart house can 'reason' in exactly the same way, with a range of different, simple sensors passing their data to a series of room-based 'partial reasoners' which, in turn, pass their intermediate results to the 'flat' ['apartment' in N. America!] (and the 'flat' layer to the building layer...).

Chap. XXVII: The FBP Explosion

To me, FBP is a clear architectural pattern on par with pipe and filter, n-tier, event-driven and data-centric architectural styles. Information flows from process to process and each process can make use of a range of specialized class instances that provide a range of OO services needed by the component instance to do whatever they need to do. So, some components will be quite massive (although functionally cohesive), while some others will be very straightforward. The analogy with electronics seems appropriate here, where integrated circuits (complex FBP components) are connected to resistors (simple FBP components). This is how we are developing our system, where components 10 lines of code long (excluding scaffolding code) are connected to other components that are several 100s (or even 1000s) of lines long.

Last but not least: the Convergence!

The following is from the FBP Wiki – written by Steve Traugott, founder/maintainer of *infrastructures.org*, in 2006, and reprinted with his permission. The bullets are in no particular order...

- Open-source schematic capture software (e.g. gEDA – see *http://www.gpleda.org/*) has gotten pretty good. It should now be possible to use existing tools to graphically create FBP applications in which FBP components are represented in the schematic the same way you'd show any other electronic components. You can then use those tools to automatically generate a SPICE netlist from the schematic, and then, with relatively simple code, convert the SPICE netlist into an FBP network description in your chosen language. Let me say that again – you can use existing tools, right now, to graphically connect FBP components in a schematic the same way you'd draw the connections between, say, integrated circuits. Those same tools will generate a SPICE netlist for you. The only piece of code missing is a small Python or Perl script to convert from SPICE to your top-level FBP application code or configuration file. You might even write your FBP application framework so that it reads the SPICE file directly...

- The appealing thing about the idea of using arbitrary EDA tools is that then people might pick their preferred tool from among many, for their preferred OS/hardware platform, with their preferred GUI features, and still get the same intermediate SPICE file out...

- Python's generators are just what the doctor ordered for writing FBP components. If you haven't seen these yet, there is an excellent tutorial (*http://www.jandecaluwe.com/Tools/MyHDL/manual/tutorial.html*) in the MyHDL

- 323 -

Chap. XXVII: The FBP Explosion

(*http://www.myhdl.org/doku.php/start*) manual. In the Python community over the last several months there has been a groundswell of interest in generators, and the co-routines, microtasks, and other things you can do with them. Most of the kinetic energy of the stackless Python effort looks like it's going to migrate over to generators as well, since generators don't require a hacked interpreter. The one thing which all of the clamor for co-routines and Stackless is missing is any sort of structure for what you do with them when you *get* them; piles of write-only code are the usual result. FBP is a great framework for dealing with this.

- Take a look at VHDL (*http://www.vhdl.org/*) and Verilog (*http://www.verilog.com/*) if you haven't already, then take a look at MyHDL.... Of special note to FBP folks, take a look at the `greetings()` example on the "Parameters, instances and hierarchy" page (*http://www.jandecaluwe.com/Tools/MyHDL/manual/intro-hier.html*) of the manual. This is a great example of a composite FBP component – and the configuration of the subnet is as plain as day.

- FPGAs are bringing chip design to the open-source world – see the "projects" page on openCores.org (*http://opencores.org/projects*). Languages fell "open" first, with C, then peripheral architecture with the PC platform, then networking with TCP/IP, then the O/S with Linux, and the CPU is next. A new breed of hobbyist is emerging; software geeks who create hardware. They code in VHDL, Verilog, SystemC (*http://www.systemc.org/home/*), or MyHDL, and create not only application-specific chips, but chips which can be reconfigured at runtime – "configurable modularity" (described on p. 7) which transcends the hardware/software interface. We know from past experience that, in this industry, this year's hobbyists are next year's professionals. The difference between hardware and software hacking is going to start getting really blurry. Who remembers when it went the other way; when Popular Electronics dried up because their readership all turned into software geeks? The pendulum is swinging back... If you really want to get FBP goosebumps, see the openCores Data Flow Processor (*http://opencores.org/project,dfp,overview*).

- Moore's law is tapping out, finally, and we're going to see more and more multi-core CPUs showing up over the next few years. This means parallel programming and loose coupling start getting more important for the average application developer; with FBP you get those for free. By the way, many of those multi-core designs are going to throw in an FPGA or two for good measure...

- The nice thing about FBP is the mobility of components. Have a slow-running component that's written in Perl, Java, or Python? Rewrite in C and move it out of the interpreter. Still too slow? Rewrite in VHDL and move it to a spare corner of your FPGA.

Chap. XXVII: The FBP Explosion

- Also converging: Games. Simulation systems. Physical modeling. Financial modeling. Lots of demand, even during the downturn. And lots of hunger for raw hardware performance. And getting *very* complex. But the complexity stays simple when you keep coupling loose.

- Bioinformatics, another source of demand. My own variation of FBP technique has for years used Lincoln Stein's "Boulder Data Interchange Format" (*http://stein.cshl.org/software/boulder/*), which he originally developed for gene sequencing.

- Web services. Or what people want from web services, but can't get without looser coupling. FBP again.

- And last but not least, SOX!!!! Sarbanes-Oxley. Workflow. Corporate accountability. Visibility of business processes and data flow, processing, and storage. You know what? The neat thing about FBP is that, when designing a workflow system, either a human or a piece of software can be an FBP process... If none of this means anything to you, then you aren't working in a U.S. public company, you don't plan a U.S. IPO, or you've been hoping it all goes away. In the wake of Enron, MCI, et al, the government oversight that used to be reserved for corporate officers and finance has now been quadrupled, extended into the I.T. organization, and applied to in-house apps and any other means of data processing and storage -- do the books right, keep controls in place, don't lose data, and *show that you're doing it*. This is being phased in slowly, over the course of a few years, so most people who are affected by it are like the frog-in-boiling-water. But the overall scale is similar to Y2K in terms of the amount of work that needs to get done. And a great deal of it is application development. And again, FBP is in the sweet spot, with its ease of auditability and rapid response to changing requirements. Right now MQ has the high ground here, and there are no clear open-source alternatives. Yet. But then again there's Python...

Chap. XXVIII: Endings and Beginnings

I did not want to call this chapter "Conclusion" as I hope it is more of a beginning than an ending. We have certainly travelled a long distance, and if you have stuck with me you are definitely to be congratulated! However, the journey in many ways is just beginning. We have come a long way, but these are only the first small steps.

As Flow-Based Programming concepts start to catch on, I believe the nature of programming will start to change. In fact, it *has* to. By now, you will have read many articles saying how we are moving into a multicore world, and how difficult it will be to program the new type of computers – one of the the most well-known being Herb Sutter's famous 2005 article, "The Free Lunch Is Over" (see *http://blogs.msdn.com/b/brianjo/archive/2004/12/28/338987.aspx*). I hope I have been able to convince you that it is not difficult at all – it's just a matter of relaxing and going with the flow!

Another symptom of the oncoming change is the number of very bright individuals who are embracing the FBP idea. One such is Justin Bozonier, who has created a "knol" about FBP – *http://knol.google.com/k/flow-based-programming*. What is a "knol", you ask? Recently, Google decided to encapsulate units of ***knowl***edge (hence the name) on a database, and encouraged people to contribute them. Justin has written a clear and entertaining summary of FBP – from a thoroughly modern point of view – enjoy! One of the quotes in Justin's knol that caught my attention is this: "When a tool can give you increased code quality *and* efficiency you know you've found something special." Read the knol!

Justin has also just started a user group on Google – the URL is *http://groups.google.com/group/flow-based-programming*.

In 1994, I predicted that this technology would have caught on massively by 2010 – well, 2010

Chap. XXVIII: Endings and Beginnings

has come and gone, and FBP *is* definitely gathering momentum, but today a surprising number of programmers are still programming in COBOL (now 50 years old, and counting)! Brad Cox points out in his "Software Industrial Revolution" material that we are still software craftsmen, making once-off items one piece at a time with very simple tools. If you want to read about how things were done before mass production, "A Book of Country Things" (Needham 1965) is worth reading. These were smart people who knew their materials, and many of their techniques were brilliant. You didn't go to the store to buy a standard part – you made whatever you needed yourself. Now, isn't it rather strange that so many programmers today would still rather build a new piece of code than (re)use one that already exists! Some of them certainly do it because they love it, and there is a role for these people to play, but modern business cannot afford to continue to have code built laboriously by hand.

In the old days, people did this because they *had* to; today, we have had to divide up the work – some people do the designs, others make them. Machines make all of us more productive. Are people less happy today? I believe only a Luddite would maintain that the old days were better. Yes, some of those old tools were works of art, but we have magical things available at our fingertips which one of those old-timers would have given his eye-teeth for. Cheaper doesn't have to mean nastier. If you believe that programmers don't reuse due to their love of their craft, I think that's wrong. Most programmers don't reuse because it's just more trouble than building new. But, you see, our experience with FBP has been completely different – in one case I mentioned earlier a programmer used an off-the-shelf component to do a function, even when she could have done the same thing by adding a single line to an adjacent PL/I component she was writing! So there are profound psychological differences between the two environments.

I believe that an important part of the change is that application developers who are trained in FBP are moving away from procedural thinking towards what we might call "spatial" thinking. Procedural thinking is quite rare in ordinary life, so it's not surprising that humans find it difficult, and that its practitioners are (viewed as) different in some ways from ordinary mortals.

If you start to look for examples of procedural thinking in real life, you discover that there are in fact very few areas where we do pure procedural thinking, but there is one which we have been doing since we lived in caves, and that is *cooking*. Some years ago at the IBM Research Center in Yorktown, Dr. Lance Miller started studying the differences between recipes and programs. He noticed that, even though recipes are basically procedural, they often have implicit parallelism which we don't notice. For instance, "add boiling water" implies that the water must have started boiling while some other step was going on, so that it would be available when needed. The term "preheated oven" is so common we probably don't even notice that it also violates sequentiality. People say and write things like this all the time without thinking – it is only if you try to execute the instructions in a rigidly serial manner (i.e. play computer) that you may run into some surprises!

The other thing he noticed was that the individual steps of the process very often start with a verb

Chap. XXVIII: Endings and Beginnings

and then add qualifiers, e.g. "boil until soft", "beat egg whites until soft peaks form", so you know very early in the sentence what kind of activity you will be doing. In programming, we usually bury the "verb" deep inside a nest of do-loops to get the same effect, e.g.

```
do while a....
  if c is true
    then
      do until b...
          compute
      enddo
  endif
enddo
```

The effect of this is that you don't know what operation you are going to do until you are deep inside a nest of do-loops or conditional statements. This would be like telling a visitor to town, "Until you come to the fountain after the church across from the train station, keep going straight". The visitor would get a pretty strange impression of your town and its inhabitants!

The other main kind of procedural behaviour in fact is just this one: following directions. Have you ever tried following someone's directions, only to find out that they forgot one item, or someone changed a street sign, and you are now facing north instead of west (if you can even figure that out). If you want to make a grown man or woman cry, ask them to assemble a child's tricycle, whose instructions have been translated into English from another language by a speaker of a third language, and which probably describe the wrong model anyway, if you could figure out what it meant. A lot like programming, isn't it? Maps are much easier because they let you visualize relationships between places synoptically, so you can handle unexpected changes, make corrections, and even figure out how to get to your destination from somewhere your informant never imagined you'd land up! On a recent trip to England, I found myself very impressed with the amount of information packed into the signs announcing "roundabouts": general shape of the roundabout, angles, destinations and relative sizes of roads entering the roundabout – and all specified visually!

This is something like the difference between conventional programming and FBP – FBP gets you away from procedural thinking and lets you think map-style.

We now have a unique opportunity, both to take advantage of the CPU power available on most programmers' desks today and to actually use this power to take advantage of natural human abilities. Just like other human abilities which we take for granted, visual processing is extremely difficult to program into a computer, and requires a lot of computer horsepower. However, many programmers today have powerful machines sitting on their desks which are basically being used

Chap. XXVIII: Endings and Beginnings

as "dumb" terminals. What we might call "visual programming" could actually start to take advantage of the relatively enormous processing power available to each programmer today. And visual programming means much more than drawing pictures to represent logic – it means developing a synergy between human and machine which takes advantage of one of the human's strong suits, not his or her weakest. A recent article by K. Kahn and V. Saraswat (1990), alluded to earlier, which I found absolutely visionary, describes an approach to a totally visual style of programming, which would not only have a visual syntax, but would also show computation using visual transformations. Software supporting this would have to be able to perform and understand topological transforms, just as humans do without effort. Interestingly, my group at IBM built a visual animation showing the creation and movement of IPs through an FBP network, and showed this at a CASE (Computer-Aided Software Engineering) conference some years ago, and this proved a very effective way of conveying some of the basic concepts of FBP. There was always a crowd around our booth! We have also speculated that visual interaction with a picture of a network would be a very natural debugging environment. I believe we now have the computer horse-power to make such approaches economically feasible – now we just have to develop the technology. The DrawFBP diagramming tool alluded to above may be viewed as a prototype of such a tool – and is constantly picking up new features as people think of neat things for it to do!

Up to now, I have concentrated on technology, and I confess to being technologically-oriented, so assume we have gotten these details out of the way. However, we also have to look at the sociological and psychological factors. What will be needed to get such a technology into use in the workplace? Well, for one thing it is going to need extensive cooperation between business and academia. As long as business and academia are two solitudes, staring at each other across a deep chasm of non-communication, we are not going to be able to make the transition to a new way of thinking. Business has gotten the impression that it has to become a bunch of mathematical geniuses to do the new programming, because the academics are broadcasting that image. So it retreats into its corner, and keeps trying to build and maintain systems using linear COBOL text. However, I don't believe that we all have to become mathematicians – nothing in this book would give a bright 16-year-old any difficulty at all.

Instead, at this point in time, business people are more willing to hire hundreds of COBOL programmers than to invest in new technologies. The problem is, if you were a CIO (maybe you are), which technology would you invest in? Well, currently it is not a very hard economic decision – it makes more sense to stay with the COBOL coders. At least you can do anything with COBOL (no, I am not refuting everything I have said in this book) – but it takes ages to do it, and the result is almost unmaintainable. Now suppose you were running a cotton plantation a couple of centuries ago, using all manual labour – not very productive, but at least output was predictable, if slow. Imagine, now, that some city slicker comes along with a cotton-picking machine, which he claims is going to improve productivity enormously. But you, the plantation-owner, figure that you are going to have more highly trained people running it, it may break

Chap. XXVIII: Endings and Beginnings

down at awkward moments, it's going to need parts from halfway across the country, and so forth. You'll do the "smart" thing, right? It wasn't until the prevailing morality started to take into account the feelings and needs of *everybody* involved *and* the technology reached a certain level of maturity that the balance tilted in favour of using technology (I wish I could say that this has happened universally, but at least it's a start). I date many of my feelings about technology to a visit I made to a match factory as a schoolboy (circa 1948) – you remember matches: those little wooden sticks with some inflammable stuff at one end – that was the nearest I've ever come to seeing humans used as robots, and I never want to see anything like it again.

I often think the attitude of business is best summed up by a cartoon I saw a few years ago – a scientist type is trying to sell a medieval king a machine-gun, and the caption says, "Don't bother me – I've got a war to fight"! Why should we change the way we do application development? Everyone's happy with the status quo, right? I don't think so. I think in fact there is a general dissatisfaction with the way things are now – it's just that nobody has shown a clear way to solve it that will benefit all the stakeholders. Since computers were invented, there has been an unending series of snake-oil salesmen, each peddling their own panacea. Why do you think each new remedy gets adopted so enthusiastically? Because there is a real need out there. So far, none of them have turned out to make the big difference that was expected, although they can usually be added to programmers' ever-expanding bag of tricks.

But, to give all groups a chance to take potshots at me, I am afraid academia is partly to blame as well. Some academics, I am afraid, are doing the modern equivalent of fiddling while Rome burns. A professor of computer science told me some years ago on a plane flight that, at his university at that time, a thesis on application development technology just wouldn't be accepted. I found this shortsightedness absolutely incredible, and he agreed. This attitude is definitely starting to change, but now another problem is starting to crop up: as I understand the thesis process, the submitters have to add something *new* to the basic concept. But how can they do this if they haven't even *tried* FBP, let alone built up a body of experience using this technology? What if engineers had to write theses on improving bridge design, without any experience with real bridges?!

I have a warning for any academics who may be reading this – there is so much stuff to read out there, that it would be quite understandable if you ignored papers like the one that appeared in the *IBM Systems Journal* back in 1978, because they aren't full of Greek letters. However, we were using these concepts to run a real live bank, and building up real experience trying to make these concepts work. This sort of experience is *priceless*, and perfectly complements the interesting theoretical work that you people are doing all over the world.

Inflexible systems not only cost money, but they contribute to users' perception of computers as inhuman, inflexible, and oppressive. How many times have you been told, "It's the computer", when confronted with some particularly asinine bit of bureaucracy? *We* know it's not the hardware's fault but too often it's the fault of some short-sighted or just over-burdened

Chap. XXVIII: Endings and Beginnings

programmer. Does the public know this? If they do, they've probably been told, "Yes, we know it's awkward, but it would cost too much to change it." Why does it cost so much? If there is only one message I want to leave you with after reading this book, it's that *the root cause of the present state of programming is the von Neumann paradigm*. It's that simple, and that difficult (you know we humans prefer things to be complex but easy, like taking a pill, but life isn't like that).

We started this book talking about how we have to relax the tight procedural nature of most of today's programming, imposed, not so much by the von Neumann machine itself, as by the mistaken belief that we still have to code according to the von Neumann model. Internally, today's computers are no longer tightly synchronous – nor are the environments that they run in. This can now be seen as a special case of a much larger issue: the key to improving productivity and maintainability in application development and to making programming accessible to a wider public is to make the world inside the computer match more closely to the world outside it. The real world is full of many entities all doing things in parallel: you do not stop breathing when I draw a breath. It is therefore not surprising that we were specifically designed to be able to function in such a world, and we get frustrated when we are forced to only do one thing at a time.

Just as our machines are starting to contain multiple processors, at a different scale we are starting to distribute our systems across different machines and/or different geographical locations around the world. Imagine a network of multiprocessor machines communicating over LANs, WANs or satellite links across the whole world, and you get a vision of a highly asynchronous, massively parallel data processing network of world-wide scope. Since this is clearly the way our business is going, why should we have to be restricted to using synchronous, non-parallel, von Neumann machines as the processing nodes?! So our applications would be networks, networking with other networks, extending eventually around the planet.

Talking about networks, a few years ago I ran across a series of books that helped me realize why the kinds of loosely connected networks we've been talking about are so attractive at a deep level. Their author is C. Alexander, who developed his idea of *patterns*, first in his seminal book "Notes on the Synthesis of Form", and then later in "The Timeless Way of Building" and "A Pattern Language". I strongly recommend them, and have added them to the Bibliography. In these he describes a set of patterns at various levels which together constitute a "language" which may be used to design spaces for living in – from houses up to cities. This language is not a linear language of sounds or text, but a way of visualizing and describing relationships within this domain. This work has inspired many people in the IT industry to hope that we could develop something similar to Alexander's work in our industry.

It has been clear for years that the disciplines of architecture in the IT industry leave much to be desired – in fact, there is a well-known saying current in the IT industry: "If builders built buildings like programmers wrote software, then the first woodpecker to come around would destroy civilization". In "Notes on the Synthesis of Form", Alexander stresses the importance of

Chap. XXVIII: Endings and Beginnings

designing maintainability into systems from the start, rather than as an afterthought: "The Mousgoum [a culture in Africa, mostly in the Cameroun – their dome-shaped houses are called tòléks] cannot afford, as we do, to regard maintenance as a nuisance that is best forgotten until it is time to call the local plumber." He explains that the Mousgoum do not use disposable scaffolding when building a house, but build it in as part of the structure, so that any part of the house that needs to be maintained is always accessible. It is interesting to note that FBP networks are also intrinsically "instrumentable": display processes can be inserted on any path to view what is going across that path, or individual processes (or groups of them) can be run independently by building "scaffolding" processes around them. It has often been observed that programming languages and methodologies are usually oriented towards the creation of the original application, rather than its long term maintainability, perhaps because psychologically getting the application working initially is thought of as an end point, rather than as the first step on a long journey! In practice, complex business applications often undergo decades of maintenance (frequently to the surprise of the original developers), done by people who cannot see the whole picture but instead are forced to work on a small piece that they do understand, praying that they have not interfered with the parts they don't!

The idea of patterns has caught on massively in the IT community in recent years, e.g. the series of "Pattern Languages of Programs" conferences now occurring regularly around the world – see *http://en.wikipedia.org/w/index.php?title=Pattern_Languages_of_Programs&oldid=329240577*. As you will probably have realized by now, FBP is nothing if not pattern-based!

Across the world-spanning network of the Internet now crawl "spiders"... Fact has caught up with fiction: John Brunner is thought to have originated the use of the word "worm" in his 1975 novel, *The Shockwave Rider*, to describe an autonomous program travelling the computer net. As everyone now knows too well, hackers have developed computer viruses, whose behaviour mirrors that of biological viruses. If you have had a system attacked by one of these critters, it may be hard for you to think kindly thoughts about what are usually perceived today as nuisances at best, and at worst something downright dangerous and destructive. However, a lot of recent work by responsible scientists has suggested that crossbreeding these two species may result in very powerful tools for making computers more user-friendly. As long ago as 1993 E. Rietman and M. Flynn described scenarios such as: worm programs assembling personalized newspapers for subscribers, using data extracted from databases all over the world; "vampire worms" taking advantage of available CPU time to do useful jobs (at night, mostly – hence the name); viruses automatically inserting hypertext buttons into text databases; viruses doing automatic database compression and expansion as time becomes available, scavenging dead data, monitoring for broken data chains, and on and on. In fact, this is now an essential part of the functioning of the Internet – except that they are usually called "spiders", not "vampire worms"! As an interesting aside, Rietman and Flynn also point out that worms could be a useful method to "*program massively parallel computers*" (their italics).

Chap. XXVIII: Endings and Beginnings

Talking about fact catching up with fiction, some recent work coming out of Xerox PARC is even more incredible. Instead of creating make-believe environments, which people can move through using the computer (Virtual Reality), how about enhancing our real-world environment with a myriad of small computing devices that we can talk to, using voice and gestures, *and that talk to each other*, perhaps about us? How about an office that automatically adjusts the temperature and humidity to suit whoever is occupying it, and plays soothing music if you want it to? How about children's building blocks that can be assembled into working computerized structures, or a pipe that you can use to point at a virtual blackboard, has a small microphone and speaker inside it, and perhaps monitors its user's health as well?! This work goes under the general name "ubiquitous computing" or "ubicomp", and it was described in Vol. 36, No. 7, of *Communications of the ACM* (Wellner et al., 1993). This enormously exciting work seems to me to be totally compatible with everything that has gone before in this book.

Speaking of intelligent building blocks, watch MIT student David Merrill's demo of "Siftables" (*http://www.ted.com/index.php/talks/david_merrill_demos_siftables_the_smart_blocks.html*). They're amazing!

A lecturer once asked us: "Where will computers be used?" and he answered: "Anywhere that it makes sense to put the word *intelligent*." For example, not just intelligent cars or planes, but intelligent offices, desks, and blackboards, intelligent bookshelves – maybe even intelligent cups and saucers.

The IBM scientist Nat Rochester once described programmers as working more closely than any other profession with what he called pure "mind-stuff". If you imagine a world-wide network of "mind stuff", then this corner of the universe is starting to see a new type of intelligence, or at least a new vehicle for intelligence. Baird Smith of IBM used to describe software as "explosive" while hardware is "implosive". While software, which is built out of mind-stuff, is becoming more and more powerful and complex, hardware is getting smaller and smaller (although more complex!) and cheaper and cheaper – as it should do, since, after all, its basic building material is sand! This is a perfect example of what Buckminster Fuller called "doing more with less".

I think we are starting to see a truly massive convergence of ideas (I quoted from Steve Traugott's comments called "The Convergence" in the previous chapter). It is unfortunate that most of the science-fiction which has been accepted by the main stream is dystopian, because most good science fiction is very optimistic and upbeat. It has always surprised me how few programmers, who live their professional lives on the cutting edge of change, actually read science fiction. Does this reflect a perception that what they do is not imaginative and exciting? Is this still another vicious cycle?

J.W. Campbell Jr., the editor of Analog, originally Astounding, was an inspiration to a generation of science-fiction readers. He taught us the value of considering new ideas objectively, avoiding the extremes either of rejecting ideas out of hand because they are new and different, or accepting

Chap. XXVIII: Endings and Beginnings

them instantly without proper evaluation. It was from his editorials that I learned the idea of "rope logic", which I believe this book embodies: the ideas described in this book are not built up on a basis of Aristotelian syllogisms, but as a multitude of small threads. While individually none of the threads may be very strong, they complement each other, resulting in a rope of logic which, in its totality, is strong enough to move pyramid blocks around (and maybe even a whole industry)! By the same token, you, my readers, may be able to snap a few of these threads, but my conviction is that the rope as a whole will remain as strong as ever. Am I deluding myself? The only possible test is the systems built using these concepts, and they are some of the sturdiest systems the companies that use them have in their collection.

While it may be true that some science fiction is naïve, some of the most exciting and forward-looking thinking going on today is described in the fiction and fact pages of today's science-fiction books and magazines. Read them and stretch your minds! If we have the will, we can make pretty good lives for ourselves. In my experience it is the pessimists (have you noticed they usually call themselves realists?) who show a certain naïveté – that of believing that things will go on just the way they are, that there will be no technological, political, commercial, social, artistic or spiritual breakthroughs. In fact, the pace of change in all areas is on an accelerating curve – if you doubt this, just look back 50 years and see how far we have come. We are only limited by our imaginations, and that's one resource that is never going to be exhausted! In fact, I believe the major obstacles to making the world a better place are not the technological challenges – there is lots of ingenuity around, just begging to be used constructively – but the entrenched interests of a small number of greedy, power-hungry people, aided and abetted by the apathy, fear, or simple ignorance, of the rest of us. Just imagine what could be done if the "developed" nations would abandon the counter-productive military approach to trying to protect the oil supply, and release all that energy and wealth to invest in a sustainable future for our planet instead! Most of us want a better world for our children and our children's children, but we have been brain-washed into believing that there is nothing we as individuals can do to make a difference, and, to ensure we keep quiet, we are being seduced by the modern equivalent of bread and circuses. We need to wake up before it's too late and realize that we *can* make a difference – if we believe we can!

Even if you feel solving the world's problems is too big a task, I see no reason why we can't at least tackle the smaller task of making programmers more productive and programming more fun – there is no law that says work has to be drudgery. In fact, when one masters a medium, and the medium fits the hand, there is a feeling of being at one with one's tools which can border on the transcendent. That's what training is about – not to turn out a generation of button-pushers, but to produce "masters". Our goal in our profession is not to be able to push a button and turn out a payroll program, but to be more like those ancient Celtic artisans who made a drinking vessel a work of art. Were they having fun? You bet they were! And so can we – so why not start right now?! And if this isn't sufficient justification by itself, wouldn't it be neat if we could have happier, more productive programmers, working for companies that are more responsive to their

Chap. XXVIII: Endings and Beginnings

clients, and saving everybody money as well (and therefore improving the quality of life for you and me). Utopian? Perhaps, but if we have a goal, we can start moving in that direction, and we can measure how much progress we have made towards getting there. If we have no goal, then we'll be just wasting energy running round in small circles.

So what's going to happen over the next couple of decades? I used to think that if you built a better mousetrap, everyone would beat a path to your door. I learned differently by personal experience – and then I read Kuhn (1970), who put it all in perspective for me. Did you know that the phlogiston theory didn't yield instantly to the oxygen theory the moment someone did the deciding experiment? Some people *never* really took to this weird "oxygen" idea!

Paradigms don't just give you new tools – they change the whole way you look at the world! If you want to learn more about paradigms, how they affect how we think and how they get adopted, Kuhn's ideas have been extended and made more accessible to today's readers by Joel Barker in a series of thought-provoking books and video tapes (e.g. Barker 1992). Necessary reading!

There will be people who say programming will never become simple, or that the man or woman in the street will never see it as enjoyable. I personally believe that computers and people will always need go-betweens, just as people from different cultures do (sometimes so do members of the same family!) – at least until the androids come along! Programmers are skilled at interpreting between people and machines and I believe there will always be a need for their services. However, by giving programmers inadequate tools, and then blaming them if they can't do the job with the tools we give them, we scare off the very people who would be best at this work. It's not too late to realize that we took a wrong tack several decades ago, and change direction.

One of the most exciting things about FBP for me is that it provides a bridge between ideas that are currently restricted to very technical papers, and businesses which think they are stuck with COBOL assembly lines for ever. We have today the potential to create a new era of productivity, based on a marketplace of reusable components. Wayne Stevens, who is responsible for a number of the ideas in this book, was very optimistic about the potential of these concepts and was tireless in promoting it within the DP community, putting his not inconsiderable reputation behind them. Where I was the *paradigm shifter*, to use Joel Barker's phrase, he was the *paradigm pioneer*. He believed, as I do, that these concepts will have a big effect on our future as an industry, and I deeply regret that he won't be around to see them become widely accepted. I have always liked the phrase, "Will those who say it can't be done please move aside and let the rest of us get on with doing it" – this was very much his attitude to life!

I and my colleagues over the years have had a glimpse of the future of the data processing industry, and I have tried to share this vision with my readers. I hope that you have enjoyed reading about it as much as I have enjoyed telling you about it!

Appendix: FBP Implementations and Diagramming Tool

The implementations described in this section are all Open Source, and are all available on the author's web site (*http://www.jpaulmorrison.com/fbp/*), as well as on SourceForge – the SourceForge SVN repository can be found at *http://flow-based-pgmg.svn.sourceforge.net/*.

THREADS

The first implementation for PCs was written in C, and was called THREADS. Its network syntax and component API are described in *http://www.jpaulmorrison.com/fbp/threads.htm*. It has interpreted and compiled versions, so applications can be developed iteratively, and then compiled to produce a single EXE file, which eliminates the network decoding phase. The compiled version control blocks are not the internal control blocks of THREADS – they are an in fact an encoding of the free-form network specification notation. This separation will allow THREADS to be extended in the future without requiring network definitions to be reprocessed.

The previous version of THREADS was actually used for production work at a major company in the US. However, as I stated above, the code was somewhat hardware- and operating system-specific, so in 2009 I started converting THREADS to use C++ and the new Windows "fibres" facility. As it is fibre-based, it cannot make use of multiple processors, but initial testing suggests that, on the other hand, it is very fast! Although the revised code has survived some of its early tests, it obviously needs a lot more testing before it becomes "industrial strength". A preliminary zip file is now (Jan. 2010) available at *http://www.jpaulmorrison.com/fbp/THREADS_32.zip*.

JavaFBP

JavaFBP is available on SourceForge (*http://sourceforge.net/projects/flow-based-pgmg*) and also

Appendix: FBP Implementations and Diagramming Tool

on the FBP web site in jar file format – the latest version is described at *http://www.jpaulmorrison.com/fbp/index.shtml#JavaFBP*. Its network syntax and component API are described in *http://www.jpaulmorrison.com/fbp/jsyntax.htm*.

The first version of JavaFBP was built by the multi-talented John Cowan, based on ideas he gleaned from the first edition of my book. I would like to thank John for supporting me, and also for guiding my first faltering steps in Java!

A sample network is shown on that web page, both in the older `connect()` method format and in the newer shorthand, based on suggestions from David Bennett. The latter is repeated here:

```
public class Xxxxxx extends Network {
 protected void define() {
   component("Read Masters",Read.class);
   component("Read Details",Read.class);
   component("Collate",Collate.class);
   component("Process Merged Stream",Proc.class);
   component("Write New Masters",Write.class);
   component("Summary & Errors",Report.class);
   connect("Read Masters.OUT", "Collate.IN[0]");
   connect("Read Details.OUT", "Collate.IN[1]");
   connect("Collate.OUT"), "Process Merged Stream.IN");
   connect("Process Merged Stream.OUTM", "Write New Masters.IN");
   connect("Process Merged Stream.OUTSE", "Summary & Errors.IN");
   initialize(new FileReader("c:\\mastfile"), "Read Masters.SOURCE");
   initialize(new FileReader("c:\\detlfile"), "Read Details.SOURCE");
   initialize(new FileWriter("c:\\newmast"),
           "Write New Masters.DESTINATION");
 }
public static void main(String[] argv) throws Exception {
       new Xxxxxx().go();
  }
 }
```

As mentioned above, the `connect()` method may also have an optional capacity value and an optional boolean value to indicate that the new (Release 2.5) IP counting facility is required. These can be specified in either order.

Appendix: FBP Implementations and Diagramming Tool

Here is a very simple example of a subnet – note the metadata.

```
@OutPort("OUT")
@InPort("IN")
public class SubnetX extends SubNet {

  @Override
  protected void define() {
    component("SUBIN", SubInSS.class);   // substream-sensitive
    component("SUBOUT", SubOutSS.class); //     do.
    component("Pass", Passthru.class);

    initialize("IN", component("SUBIN"), port("NAME"));
    connect(component("SUBIN"), port("OUT"), component("Pass"), port("IN"));
    connect(component("Pass"), port("OUT"), component("SUBOUT"), port("IN"));
    initialize("OUT", component("SUBOUT"), port("NAME"));
  }
}
```

A sample component is shown here – this is actually code for the *DeCompose* component referred to in Chapter 8 (omitting the package name and imports):

```
@ComponentDescription("Break up input packets into words")
@OutPort("OUT")
@InPort("IN")

public class DeCompose extends Component {
  InputPort inport;
  OutputPort outport;

  @Override
  protected void execute() {
    Packet p;
    while ((p = inport.receive()) != null) {
      String s = (String) p.getContent();
      boolean in_word = false;
      int word_start = 0;
      for (int i = 0; i < s.length(); i++) {
        if (!in_word && s.charAt(i) != ' ') {
          in_word = true;
          word_start = i;
        }
```

Appendix: FBP Implementations and Diagramming Tool

```java
      if (in_word && s.charAt(i) == ' ') {
        in_word = false;
        String t = s.substring(word_start, i);
        Packet q = create(t);
        outport.send(q);
      }
    }
    drop(p);
  }
}

@Override
protected void openPorts() {
  inport = openInput("IN");
  outport = openOutput("OUT");
}
}
```

C#FBP

C#FBP is available on SourceForge (*http://sourceforge.net/projects/flow-based-pgmg*) and also on the FBP web site in zip file format – get the latest version from the web page section at *http://www.jpaulmorrison.com/fbp/index.shtml#CsharpFBP*. Its network syntax and component API are described in *http://www.jpaulmorrison.com/fbp/csyntax.htm*.

The original version was converted from the then version of JavaFBP by Amanda Ge, and was later massively modified by myself, with input from David Bennett, who also suggested the shorthand connect notation supported both in JavaFBP and C#FBP.

A sample network is shown on that web page, using both formats:

```csharp
using System;
using FBPComponents;
using FBPLib;
namespace nnnnnnnnn
{
    public class Xxxxxx : Network {
    public override void Define()   {
    Component("Read Masters",typeof(Read));
    Component("Read Details",typeof(Read));
    Component("Collate",typeof(Collate));
    Component("Process Merged Stream",typeof(Proc));
```

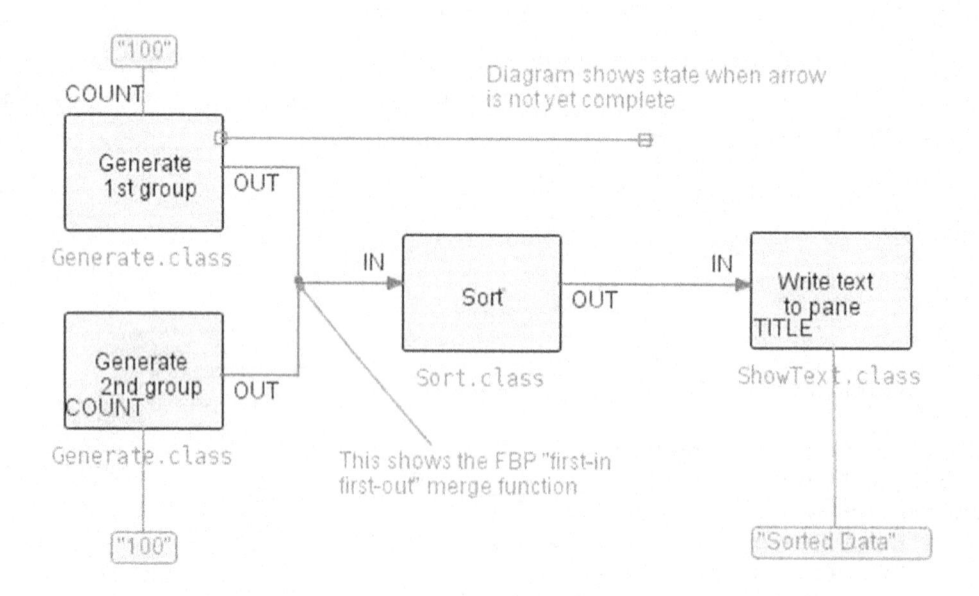

Appendix: FBP Implementations and Diagramming Tool

```
        Component("Write New Masters",typeof(Write));
        Component("Summary & Errors",typeof(Report));
        Connect("Read Masters.OUT", "Collate.IN[0]");
        Connect("Read Details.OUT", "Collate.IN[1]");
        Connect("Collate.OUT"), "Process Merged Stream.IN");
        Connect("Process Merged Stream.OUTM", "Write New Masters.IN");
        Connect("Process Merged Stream.OUTSE", "Summary & Errors.IN");
        Initialize(new FileReader("c:\\mastfile"), "Read Masters.SOURCE");
        Initialize(new FileReader("c:\\detlfile"), "Read Details.SOURCE");
        Initialize(new FileWriter("c:\\newmast"), "Write New
                Masters.DESTINATION");
    }
    internal static void Main(String[] argv) {
            new Xxxxx().Go();
        }
     }
}
```

Diagramming Tool (DrawFBP)

Several years ago, a picture-drawing tool which supports many of the concepts of FBP was written in C++ for Windows. It has now been superseded by a Java version, described at *http://www.jpaulmorrison.com/fbp/index.shtml#DrawFBP*, and is also available on SourceForge: look for the latest version. It can also be executed as a JWS application by clicking on *http://www.jpaulmorrison.com/graphicsstuff/DrawFBP.jnlp*.

Appendix: FBP Implementations and Diagramming Tool

DrawFBP does not attempt to generate diagrams from text – we have seen too many failed attempts at this – instead it allows the designer to lay out the flow as desired, after which DrawFBP captures the information from the diagram, including x-y coordinates of blocks and line bends, in an XML file, with an extension of `.drw`. The XML contains sufficient information to enable the diagram to be redrawn, but it also captures the relationships between processes and their connections, so it has enough information to generate the lists of connections used by FBP (or FBP-like) schedulers. The new version of DrawFBP can in fact generate working FBP networks, prompting the user to fill in any needed information.

DrawFBP allows files and reports, and a few other icons (e.g. users), to be added symbolically to a design, although they are not used in code generation. The above diagram shows an arrow in process of being drawn.

The latest version of DrawFBP (now available on my web site) provides a *font chooser* function, which displays all available fonts on the user's machine, showing sample text and indicating which fonts support Chinese characters. DrawFBP maintains a user profile file, which will retain, among other things, the names of the selected fonts (one for fixed format text, and one for variable).

DrawFBP supports stepwise decomposition by allowing the designer to associate either a code component, or a lower-level subnet, with a block on the diagram. Subnets are shown with a doubled outline. Double-clicking on a block will bring up the component code in a separate window in the former case, or the subnet in the latter.

A Help facility is also available, based on Java SE Desktop Technologies JavaHelp System – this function does not require access to the Internet, but is included in the DrawFBP jar file.

Here is an example of a DrawFBP diagram of *part* of a production application job, written using AMPS, that ran for about 30 years at a major Canadian bank! It should be pointed out that a number of equally complex AMPS programs are still running there – after over 35 years!

The blocks with double boundaries represent subnets. Double-clicking on these blocks brings up the designated subnet, in another panel.

You will notice a block marked MCBSIM, near the top of the diagram. MCBSIM accessed a database called the Customer Information File. The topology shown *simulates* a subroutine, but has the advantage that the topology can be "opened out", so that MCBSIM could also be used as a pure "streaming" process (depending on whether the output of MCBSIM is to be used by the component that feeds it, or a different component) – *with no change to the coding of MCBSIM.*

In the streaming mode, it is very simple to change the diagram to have as many instances of MCBSIM running in parallel as desired, just by changing the connection list, and adding a load-balancing component of some kind. This approach was described in detail in the chapter on Performance (Chapter 21 – p. 210) above.

Appendix: FBP Implementations and Diagramming Tool

Of particular interest are the boxes marked "MAXCSRT" and "INFQUEUE". These are, respectively, a stream-to-stream sort component, and a temporary storage component (subnet) that can be used to store data that is already in the required sequence. MAXCSRT was an AMPS component that drove the standard IBM disk Sort, so it had no real file size limits – although of course the number of records to be sorted affected the performance. Sort times could thus be reduced by routing already sequenced packets *around* the Sort – as shown in the diagram. By the way, all components with names starting with MAXC were "off the shelf" (precoded, pretested, application-independent).

Since a Sort of the entire input stream cannot generate any output until the entire stream has been read in, it is necessary to store Information Packets that do *not* need to be sorted until the IPs being sorted become available for further processing. A simple way to do this is to use the "Infinite Queue" subnet, described above in Chapter 15 (page 140) – in this diagram they have the descriptive text, "Hold until Sort finished", and the name of the diagram that will be brought up on a double-click (`InfiniteQueue.drw`) is shown underneath.

The symbols at the extreme left and right represent external subnet ports – in this case used as connectors to other diagrams.

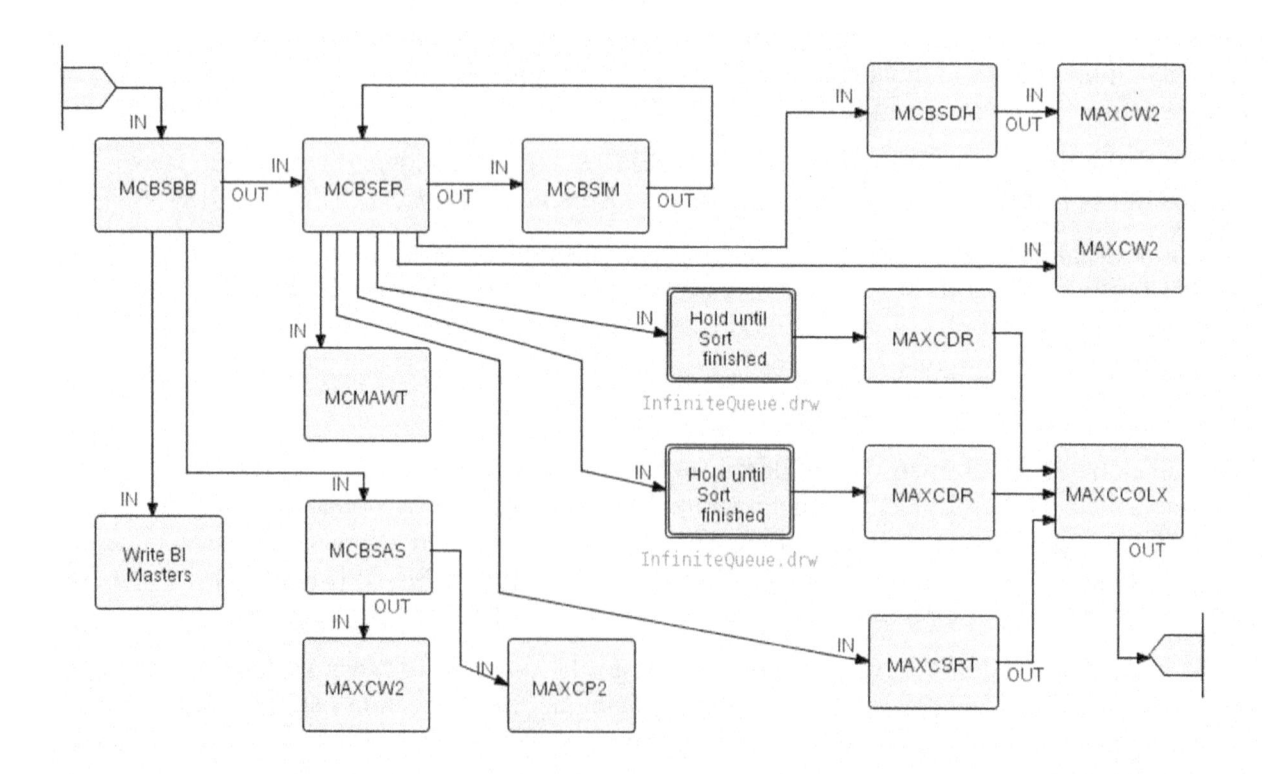

- 342 -

Glossary of Terms

4GL	4th Generation Language, typically generating HLL statements
AMPS	Advanced Modular Processing System – first version of FBP used for production work (still in use at a major Canadian company)
Applicative	describes a language which does all of its processing by means of operators applied to values
Asynchronous	independent in time, unsynchronized
Automatic ports	unnamed input or output ports used to respectively delay a process, or indicate termination of a process, without code needing to be added to the processes involved
Brackets	IPs of a special type used to demarcate groupings of IPs within IP streams
C#FBP	C# implementation of FBP concepts. For more information, see *http://www.jpaulmorrison.com/fbp/index.shtml#CsharpFBP*
Capacity	the maximum number of IPs a connection can hold at one time
Component	Reusable piece of code or reusable subnet
Composite Component	Component comprising more than one process (same as subnet)
Connection	Path between two processes, over which a data stream passes; connections have finite capacities (the maximum number of IPs they can hold at one time)
Connection Points	The point where a connection makes contact with a component
Control IP	an IP whose life-time corresponds exactly to the lifetime of a substream, which it can be said to "represent"
Coroutine	an earlier name for an FBP process
Descriptor	read-only module which can be attached to an IP describing it to generalized components
DFDM	Data Flow Development Manager, dialect of FBP – went on sale in Japan – sold several licenses
DrawFBP	FBP diagramming tool, written in Java. For more information, see *http://www.jpaulmorrison.com/fbp/index.shtml#DrawFBP*

Glossary of Terms

Elementary Component	Component which is not a composite component
FBP	Flow-Based Programming
FPE	Flow Programming Environment – term I use in this book for the product that was to follow DFDM. It was developed quite far theoretically, but never reached the marketplace
Granularity	"Grain" size of components
Higher-Level Language (HLL)	a language intermediate in level between Lower-Level Languages (e.g. Assembler) and 4th Generation Languages (4GLs)
Information Packet (IP)	an independent, structured piece of information with a well-defined lifetime (from creation to destruction)
Initial Information Packet (IIP)	data specified in the network definition, usually used as a parameter for a reusable component; it is converted into a "real" IP by means of a "receive" service call
JavaFBP	Java implementation of FBP concepts. For more information, see http://www.jpaulmorrison.com/fbp/index.shtml#JavaFBP
Looper	a component which does not exit after each IP has been handled, but "loops" back to get another one
Non-looper	a component which exits after each IP has been handled, rather than "looping" back to get another one
Port	The point where a connection makes contact with a process
Root IP	The root of a tree of IPs
Process	Asynchronously executing piece of logic – in FBP, same as "thread"
Stream	Sequence of IPs passing across a given connection
Substream-sensitivity	a characteristic of some ports of a composite component where brackets are treated as end of data
Thread	Same as "process" in FBP – often referred to as "lightweight" process
THREADS	C (or C++)-based FBP implementation. For more information, see http://www.jpaulmorrison.com/fbp/index.shtml#THREADS
Tree	In FBP, acyclic structure of linked IPs, able to be sent and received as a single unit
Synchronous	Coordinated in time (at the same time)
WYSIWYG	"What You See Is What You Get" (describes a tool where the image shown to the developer closely matches the final result in appearance)

Bibliography

W.B. Ackerman	1979	"Data Flow Languages", Proceedings National Computer Conference, pp. 1087-1095
G. Agha	1990	"Concurrent Object-Oriented Programming", Communications of the ACM, Vol. 33, No. 9, Sept. 1990
A.V. Aho and J.D. Ullman	1972	"The Theory of Parsing, Translation and Compiling", Englewood Cliffs, NJ: Prentice-Hall
C. Alexander	1964	"Notes on the Synthesis of Form", Harvard University Press, ISBN 0-674-62751-2
C. Alexander	1977	"A Pattern Language", Oxford University Press, Library of Congress Catalog Card Number 74-22874
R.G. Babb II	1984	"Parallel Processing with Large-Grain Data Flow Techniques", Computer, July 1984
J. Backus	1978	"Can Programming be Liberated from the von Neumann Style? A Functional Style and its Algebra of Programs", Communications of the ACM, Aug. 1978, Vol. 21, No. 8
R. M. Balzer	1971	"PORTS – A Method for Dynamic Interprogram Communication and Job Control", The RAND Corporation, Spring Joint Computer Conference, 1971
J.A. Barker	1992	"Future Edge: Discovering the New Paradigms of Success", William Morrow and Company, Inc., New York
G. Bell	1992	"Ultracomputers: A Teraflop before its Time", Communications of the ACM, Aug. 1992, Vol. 35, No. 8
J. Bentley	1988	"More Programming Pearls – Confessions of a Coder", AT&T Bell Laboratories
A. Black, N. Hutchison, E. Jul and H. Levy	1986	"Object Structure in the Emerald System", OOPSLA '86 Proceedings, Sept. 1986
J. Boukens and F.	1974	"CHIEF, An Extensible Programming System", Machine

Bibliography

Deckers		Oriented Higher Level Languages (W.L. van der Poel and L.A. Maarsen, eds.), North Holland Publishing Company, Amsterdam
Ed. B.V. Bowden	1963	"Faster than Thought, A Symposium on Digital Computing Machines", Sir Isaac Pitman and Sons, Ltd., London, England, 1st Edition 1953
F.P. Brooks	1975	"The Mythical Man-Month: Essays on Software Engineering", Reading, MA: Addison-Wesley
J. Brunner	1975	"The Shockwave Rider", Ballantine Books, New York
W.H. Burge	1975	"Recursive Programming Techniques", Addison-Wesley, Reading, MA
D. Cann	1992	"Retire FORTRAN: A Debate Rekindled", Communications of the ACM, Vol. 35, No. 8, Aug. 1992
N. Carriero and D. Gelernter	1989	"Linda in Context", Communications of the ACM, Vol. 32, No. 4, April 1989
M.E. Conway	1963	"Design of a separable transition-diagram compiler", Communications of the ACM, Vol. 6, No. 7, July 1963
B.J. Cox	1987	"Object Oriented Programming – An Evolutionary Approach", Addison-Wesley Publishing Company
E.W. Dijkstra	1972	"The humble programmer", Communications of the ACM, Vol. 15, No. 10, Oct. 1972
N.P. Edwards	1974	"The Effect of Certain Modular Design Principles on Testability", IBM Research Report, RC 5060 (#22344), T.J. Watson Research Center, Yorktown Heights, NY, 9/30/74
N.P. Edwards	1977	"On the Architectural Requirements of an Engineered System", IBM Research Report, RC 6688 (#28797), T.J. Watson Research Center, Yorktown Heights, NY, 8/18/77
P.R. Ewing	1988	"Bibliyna Simfoniya, 988-1988, Yuvileyne Vidannya", Prisvyachene Tisyacholittyu Khristiyanstva, GLINT Canada, Toronto
D.P. Friedman and D.S. Wise	1976	"CONS should not evaluate its arguments", Automata, Languages and Programming, Edinburgh University Press, Edinburgh
J. Gall	1978	"Systemantics: How systems work and especially how they fail",

Bibliography

		Pocket Books, Simon & Schuster
P.T. Gaughan and S. Yalamanchili	1993	"Adaptive Routing Protocols for Hypercube Interconnection Networks", Computer, 0018-9162/93/0500-0012, IEEE
D. Gelernter and N. Carriero	1992	"Coordination Languages and their Significance", Communications of the ACM, Vol. 35, No. 2, February 1992
M. Hammer, W.G. Howe, V.J. Kruskal and I. Wladawsky	1977	"A very high level programming language for data processing applications", Communications of the ACM, Vol. 20, No. 11, November 1977
J. Hendler	1986	"Enhancement for Multiple-Inheritance", SIGPLAN Notices V21, #10, October 1986
C.A.R. Hoare	1978	"Communicating Sequential Processes", Communications of the ACM, Vol. 21, No. 8, August 1978
IBM		"Messaging and Queueing Technical Reference", SC33-0850, IBM Corp.
IBM		"VM/System Product CMS Pipelines", Program No. 5785-RAC
IBM Japan	1989	"Data Flow Programming Manager (DFDM)", Product Number 5799-DJB, Form No. N: GH18-0399-0
K. Jackson and Gp. Capt. H.R. Simpson	1975	"MASCOT – A Modular Approach to Software Construction, Operation and Test", RRE Technical Note, No. 778, Royal Radar Establishment, Ministry of Defence, Malvern, Worcs., UK, 1975
M. Jackson	1975	"Principles of Program Design", Academic Press, London, New York, San Francisco
T. Capers Jones	1992	"CASE's Missing Elements", IEEE Spectrum, June 1992
K.M. Kahn and M.S. Miller	1988	"Language Design and Open Systems", The Ecology of Computation, B.A. Huberman (ed.), Elsevier Science Publishers B.V. (North-Holland)
K.M. Kahn	1989	"Objects – A Fresh Look", Proceedings of the Third European Conference on Object Oriented Programming, Cambridge University Press, July 1989
K.M. Kahn and V.A. Saraswat	1990	"Complete Visualizations of Concurrent Programs and their Executions", TH0330-1/90/0000/0007, 1990 IEEE
R.P. Kar	1989	"Data-Flow Multitasking", Dr. Dobb's Journal, Nov. 1989
R.C. Kendall	1977	"Management Perspectives on Programs, Programming and

Bibliography

		Productivity", IBM Report 1977
R. Kendall	1988	"Manufactured Programming", Computerworld Extra, June 20, 1988
W. Kim and F.H. Lochovsky	1989	"Object-Oriented Concepts, Databases, and Applications", ACM Press, Addison-Wesley
L. Krishtalka	1989	"Dinosaur Plots and other Intrigues in Natural History", Avon Books, New York
T.S. Kuhn	1970	"The Structure of Scientific Revolutions", Chicago, University of Chicago Press
K. Kuse, M. Sassa, I. Nakata	1986	"Modelling and Analysis of Concurrent Processes Connected by Streams", Journal of Information Processing, Vol. 9, No. 3
W. Lalonde, J. Pugh	1991	"Subclassing ≠ subtyping ≠ Is-a", Journal of Object-Oriented Programming, January 1991
B.M. Leavenworth	1977	"Non-Procedural Data Processing", The Computer Journal Vol. 20, No. 1, 6-9, February 1977
B. Liskov, M. Herlihy, L. Gilbert	1986	"Limitations of Synchronous Communication with Static Process Structure in Languages for Distributed Computing", Communications of the ACM, 1986, pp. 150-159
R. Milner	1993	"Elements of Interaction", Turing Award Lecture, reprinted in Communications of the ACM, Vol. 36, No. 1, Jan. 1993
J. Moad	1993	"How to Break the Distributed Logjam", Datamation, May 15, 1993
E. Morenoff and J.B. McLean	1967	"Inter-program Communications, Program String Structures and Buffer Files", Rome Air Force Base, New York, Spring Joint Computer Conference, 1967
J.P. Morrison	1971	"Data Responsive Modular, Interleaved Task Programming System", IBM Technical Disclosure Bulletin, Vol. 13, No. 8, 2425-2426, January 1971
J.P. Morrison	1978	"Data Stream Linkage Mechanism", IBM Systems Journal Vol. 17, No. 4, 1978
W. Needham	1965	"A Book of Country Things", Recorded by Barrows Mussey, The Steven Greene Press, Lexington, MA
O. Nierstrasz, S. Gibbs,	1992	"Component-Oriented Software Development", Communications

Bibliography

D. Tsichritzis		of the ACM, Vol. 35, No. 9, Sept. 1992.
D. Olson	1993	"Exploiting Chaos: Cashing in on the Realities of Software Development", van Nostrand Reinhold, New York
D.L. Parnas	1972	"On the criteria to be used in decomposing systems into modules", Communications of the ACM, Vol. 5, No. 12, Dec. 1972, pp. 1053-8
R.F. Rashid	1988	"From RIG to Accent to Mach: The Evolution of a Network Operating System", The Ecology of Computation, B.A. Huberman (ed.), Elsevier Science Publishers B.V. (North-Holland)
E. Rietman and M.F. Flynn	1993	"FAT-Eating Logic Bombs and the Vampire Worm", Analog Science Fiction and Fact, Feb. 1993
N. Shu	1985	"FORMAL, A forms oriented visual directed application development system", Computer 18, No. 8, 38-49, Aug. 1985
W.P. Stevens	1981	"Using Structured Design: How to make Programs Simple, Changeable, Flexible and Reusable", John Wiley and Sons
W.P. Stevens	1982	"How Data Flow can Improve Application Development Productivity", IBM System Journal, Vol. 21, No. 2, 1982
W.P. Stevens	1985	"Using Data Flow for Application Development", Byte, June 1985
W.P. Stevens	1991	"Software Design: Concepts and Methods", Prentice Hall International
R.E. Strom and S. Yemini	1983	"NIL: An Integrated Language and System for Distributed Computing", Proceedings of SIGPLAN '83 Symposium on Programming Language Issues in Software Systems, June 1983
R.E. Strom, D.F. Bacon, A.P. Goldberg, A. Lowry, D.M. Yellin, S.A. Yemini	1991	"Hermes: A Language for Distributed Computing", Prentice Hall
Y. Suzuki, S. Miyamoto, H. Matsumaru	1985	"Data Flow Structure for Maintainable Software in Railway Electric Substation Control Systems", CH2207-9/85/0000-0219, IEEE
T. Swan	1991	"Learning C++", SAMS, Prentice Hall

Bibliography

E.D. Tribble, et al.	1987	"Channels: A Generalization of Streams", Concurrent Prolog Vol. 1, MIT Press
D. Tsichritzis, E. Fiume, S. Gibbs and O. Nierstrasz	1987	"KNOs: KNowledge Acquisition, Dissemination and Manipulation Objects", ACM Transactions on Office Information Systems, Vol. 5, No. 4, pp. 96-112
L.G. Valiant	1990	"A Bridging Model for Parallel Computation", Communications of the ACM, Aug. 1990, Vol. 33, No. 8
J-D. Warnier	1974	"Logical Construction of Programs", 3rd edition, van Nostrand Reinhold, NY
G.M. Weinberg	1975	"An Introduction to General Systems Thinking", John Wiley and Sons, Inc., New York
B.L. Whorf	1956	"Language, Thought and Reality", Technology Press, MIT
J. Winkler	1992	"Objectivism: 'Class' Considered Harmful", Letter in Technical Correspondence, Communications of the ACM, Vol. 35, No. 8, Aug. 1992
R.J. Wirfs-Brock and R.E. Johnson	1990	"Surveying Current Research in Object-Oriented Design", Communications of the ACM, Sept. 1990, Vol. 33, No. 9
K. Yoshida and T. Chikayama	1988	"A'UM, A Stream-Based Concurrent Object-Oriented Language", Proceedings of the International Conference on Fifth Generation Computer Systems, 1988, ed. ICOT

Index

Array ports	p. 28
Automatic ports (*IN, *OUT)	p. 132, and following page
Closing ports	pp. 136, 168
Configurable modularity	p. 7
Dynamic subnets	p. 73
Explicit IP disposal	p. 26
Generalized components – no more than 4 ports	p. 45
"Hierarchical processing model"	p. 320
IIP format	p. 55
IIPs	p. 54, and following page; also p. 129
JavaFBP scalability	p. 25 See also Chap. 21, p. 220, and following page
"Long wait"	p. 159
Loopers & non-loopers	pp. 86, 95, 127 and following page
Loop-type network topology	p. 135
"Must run"	p. 134

Index

Parametrization using IIPs	p. 54, and following page; also p. 129
Port connected	p. 33
Process termination	p. 129
Productivity factor	p. 49
Report generators	p. 105
Sockets	p. 150
Stacks	p. 101; also p. 95
SubIn & SubOut processes in subnets – substream-sensitivity	p. 75
Substreams	p. 90 – impl. with stacks, p. 95; p. 97 and following page
Table look-ups	p. 67
"Tree" IPs	p. 120

(courtesy of Dr. Ernesto Compatangelo, University of Aberdeen, Scotland)